For regular and special reading teachers, here are practical strategies, materials, and activity sheets for the diagnosis and remediation of all types of reading disabilities.

COMPLETE READING DISABILITIES HANDBOOK

Ready-to-Use Techniques for Teaching Reading Disabled Students

WILMA H. MILLER

THE CENTER FOR APPLIED
RESEARCH IN EDUCATION
West Nyack, New York 10995

Library of Congress Cataloging-in-Publication Data

Miller, Wilma H.
    Complete reading disabilities handbook : ready-to-use techniques for teaching reading disabled
students / Wilma H. Miller; illustrated by Angela Maffei.
        p.   cm.
    Includes bibliographical references.
    ISBN 0-87628-249-4
    1. Reading—United States—Remedial teaching—Handbooks, manuals, etc.   2. Learning disabled children—
Education—Reading—Handbooks, manuals, etc.   3. Teaching—Aids and devices.   I. Title.
    LB1050.5.M545   1993   93-23900
    371.91′44—dc20   CIP

Printed in the United States of America

20   19   18   17   16   15   14   13   10   9   8   7

ISBN 0-87628-249-4 (S)   ISBN 0-87628-275-3 (P)

The author and publisher are grateful for the following permissions to use or adapt copyrighted material:

The story map on page 350 and the "Mind's Eye" procedure on page 362 were adapted from *Reading Comprehension: New Directions for Classroom Practice*, 2d edition, by John D. McNeil, copyright © 1987, 1984 by Scott, Foresman and Company; reprinted by permission of HarperCollins Publishers. The "K-W-L" device used in the worksheet on page 356 was adapted from Ellen Carr and Donna Ogle, "A Strategy for Comprehension and Summarization," *Journal of Reading*, 30, April 1987, pp. 626–631. The ReQuest Procedure described on page 39 was adapted from Anthony V. Manzo, "The ReQuest Procedure," *Journal of Reading*, November 1969, pp. 123–26. From Robert J. Tierney, John E. Readence, and Ernest K. Kishner, *Reading Strategies and Practices: A Compendium*, Third Edition, copyright © 1985 by Allyn and Bacon; reprinted by permission. The tables on pages 30 and 31 are from *How to Increase Reading Ability: A Guide to Developmental and Remedial Methods*, 9th Edition by Albert J. Harris and Edward R. Sipay; copyright © 1990 by Longman Publishing Group. Excerpts from *Assessing and Correcting Classroom Reading Problems* by J. Estill Alexander and Betty S. Heathington; copyright © 1988 by J. Estill Alexander and Betty S. Heathington; reprinted by permission of HarperCollins Publishers. Excerpts from Stanford E. Taylor, *Listening: What Research Says to the Teacher*, copyright 1969, National Education Association; reprinted with permission. Steps for using miscue analysis in Chapter 2 are from Susan B. Argyle, "Miscue Analysis for Classroom Use," *Reading Horizons* 29 (Winter 1989), pp. 93–102, used by permission of the Reading Center and Clinic at Western Michigan University. Material from Maude McBroom, Julia Sparrow, and Catherine Eckstein, *Scale for Determining a Child's Reader Level*, Iowa City, Iowa: Bureau of Publications, Extensions Service, University of Iowa, 1944, p. 11, used by permission of The University of Iowa. The Anticipation Guide on pages 344 and 345 is adapted from J.E. Readence, T.W. Bean, and R.S. Baldwin, *Content Area Reading: An Integrated Approach* (Dubuque, Iowa: Kendall/Hunt Publishing Company, 1981); used by permission of Kendall/Hunt Publishing Company. The Letter Q song in Chapter 5 is from *Alpha Time: Songs of the Letter People*, used by permission of New Dimensions in Education.

**THE CENTER FOR APPLIED RESEARCH
IN EDUCATION**

West Nyack, NY 10994

On the World Wide Web at http://www.phdirect.com

ABOUT THE AUTHOR

A former classroom teacher, Wilma H. Miller, Ed.D., has been teaching at the college level for more than 28 years. She completed her doctorate in reading at the University of Arizona under the direction of the late Dr. Ruth Strang, a nationally known reading authority.

Dr. Miller has contributed numerous articles to professional journals and is the author of more than sixteen other works in the field of reading education. Among the latter are *Identifying and Correcting Reading Difficulties in Children* (1972), *Diagnosis and Correction of Reading Difficulties in Secondary School Students* (1973), *Reading Diagnosis Kit* (1975, 1978, 1986), the "Corrective Reading Skills Activities File" (1977), *Reading Teacher's Complete Diagnosis & Correction Manual* (1988), and *Reading Comprehension Activities Kit* (1990), all published by The Center for Applied Research in Education.

She is also the author of an inservice aid for teachers entitled *Reading Activities Handbook* (1980), several textbooks for developmental reading, *The First R: Elementary Reading Today* (1977), and *Teaching Elementary Reading Today* (1983), published by Holt, Rinehart & Winston, Inc., and of a guide to secondary reading instruction, *Teaching Reading in the Secondary School*, published by Charles C. Thomas.

To the memory of my beloved father and mother,
William A. Miller and Ruth K. Miller,
and
Win Huppuch, Vice-President of the Education Group, C.A.R.E.,
my dear friend and professional adviser for twenty-three years

THE PRACTICAL HELP THIS BOOK OFFERS

When I ask lay people if they think the public schools are teaching reading effectively, a number usually respond that they are not completely satisfied with the job the schools are doing. Some say that more phonics should be taught and that this type of instruction would ensure good reading achievement for all children. Do you, a reading teacher, believe the schools are teaching reading skills effectively to all children? If you are a typical teacher, you would reply that we generally are doing a good job but could still do a lot better with some children. As a reading specialist with over 30 years' experience in the field, my own response is that indeed most reading teachers try their very best and are teaching reading skills effectively to most children. However, I would have to admit that there are many students in our elementary schools who do not read as well as they could.

My personal belief from visiting many classrooms and supervising teacher-trainees who tutor children with reading problems is that at least 15 percent of all students in our elementary schools have significant reading problems. In some inner-city schools the percentage may be 50 percent or higher, perhaps nearer to 100 percent. Here are some sobering statistics in relation to reading disabilities in our society at large:

- Approximately 60 million Americans are thought to read below the eighth-grade reading level.
- About 85 percent of the juveniles who pass through the court system are functionally illiterate.
- Approximately 50 percent of the inmates in U.S. prisons are thought to be functionally illiterate.

Obviously, reading ability is an extremely important factor in a person's living a successful and fulfilling life. Thus it is vitally important that reading educators effectively teach reading strategies and skills to all the students who are placed in our trust. The primary purpose of the *Complete Reading Disabilities Handbook* is to help you, the reading teacher, do this as effectively as possible.

Everyone involved in the teaching of reading should find the *Handbook* a valuable resource, including classroom reading teachers, Chapter 1 reading teachers, teachers of learning-handicapped children, reading specialists and supervisors, and K–8 administrators. It has been written in as practical a manner as possible and contains many classroom-tested reading strategies, suggestions, lists of materials, and ready-to-duplicate activity sheets to enable you to teach reading skills effectively to all of your students, whether they are learning handicapped or simply have reading problems.

Chapter 1, "What Are Reading Disabilities?" provides a brief overview of the incidence of reading difficulties in contemporary elementary schools. It identifies and explains the major causes of reading problems, including educational factors, visual and auditory defects, neurological dysfunctions, language deficits, intellectual factors, unfavorable home environments, low self-esteem, and emotional problems. The chapter also provides criteria for determining whether a student has a reading problem or rather is a slow learner already reading to the limits of his or her potential.

Chapter 2, "General Guidelines and Materials for Diagnosing Reading Disabilities," emphasizes the importance of continuous informal assessment through teacher observation with and without structured checklists. It includes a number of reproducible checklists that can be used by the reading teacher with both reading-disabled and learning-handicapped children. Checklists are provided at the emergent literacy level, the primary-grade reading level, and the intermediate-grade reading level.

This chapter also describes and illustrates other important elements of informal reading assessment, such as portfolio assessment, work samples, a modern oral reading miscue analysis, the Individual Reading Inventory, inventories in the word-identification techniques, and variations of the cloze procedure. Reproducibles include a complete Individual Reading Inventory and three variations of the cloze. You will also find various types of standardized assessment devices that can be used effectively with reading-disabled children including survey reading/achievement tests, process-oriented comprehension measures, criterion-referenced tests, visual and auditory perception tests, intelligence tests, and a number of unique tests for assessing the abilities of learning-handicapped children.

Chapter 3, "Ready-to-Use Materials for Diagnosing Disabilities in the Word-Identification Techniques," describes in specific terms with many reproducible devices how to assess disabilities in the techniques of letter naming, sight-word knowledge, phonic (graphophonic) analysis, structural (morphemic) analysis, and semantic (contextual) analysis. Included are a wealth of suggestions for assessing ability in each of these reading skills and many ready-to-use devices that can be effectively used in this assessment. This chapter will help teachers of both disabled readers and learning-handicapped children to assess reading easily and accurately.

Chapter 4, "Ready-to-Use Materials for Diagnosing Disabilities in Comprehension and Basic Study Skills," begins by briefly describing the basic characteristics of comprehension. Next, it illustrates various ways of assessing comprehension ability, including observational checklists, questioning strategies, literature-based assessment, the retell strategy, survey reading/achievement tests, and process-oriented measures of reading comprehension. The chapter provides a reproducible device of multiple acceptable responses as well as ready-to-use examples of both the cloze procedure and the maze technique. It then briefly describes the most important study skills and illustrates the following ways of assessing ability in them: observational checklists, QARs of content reading, various standardized tests, group reading inventories, and the content-oriented Individual Reading Inventory. Reproducible examples of several of these types of devices are included.

Chapter 5, "Ready-to-Use Strategies and Activities for Correcting Disabilities in the Word-Identification Techniques," contains a wealth of useful information for both reading teachers and learning disability teachers and is the most comprehensive resource in this area of which I am aware. It includes numerous strategies, lists of materials, reproducible activity sheets, and games for correcting (remediating) disabilities in letter naming (recognition), sight-word knowledge, phonic (graphophonic) analysis, structural (morphemic) analysis, and semantic (contextual) analysis at both the primary-grade and intermediate-grade reading levels.

The chapter first presents strategies and ready-to-use materials for improving visual perception ability and knowledge of the capital and lower-case letter names. These sections should be especially useful to teachers of learning-handicapped children. As you know, it is essential for a child to possess a good sight vocabulary if he or she is going to make good progress in any corrective (remedial) reading program. Therefore, many strategies, games, and reproducible activity sheets are provided for improving sight-word knowledge both in isolation and in context. The chapter also explains the innovative Reading Recovery Program in detail and shows how to best use similar strategies with disabled readers and learning-handicapped individuals in a reading improvement program.

Ability in the basic phonic elements and rules is very important to the reading success of most children and is especially crucial to the reading success of many learning-handicapped children. In order to meet these needs, Chapter 5 also provides many strategies, games, and ready-to-use materials for improving ability in auditory discrimination and phonic (graphophonic) analysis. In addition, you will find many techniques, games, and ready-to-use activity sheets for improving ability in morphemic (structural) analysis, including a comprehensive list of prefixes, suffixes, and word roots which should be of great help to reading teachers. The chapter provides ideas and reproducible activity sheets for improving ability in semantic (contextual) analysis, and closes by describing concretely how to teach spelling skills to learning-handicapped children.

Chapter 6, "Ready-to-Use Strategies and Activities for Correcting Disabilities in Comprehension and Basic Study Skills," provides detailed help for improving these skills at both the primary-grade and intermediate-grade reading levels. Since most of the strategies and materials that can be used to improve comprehension can be used equally well to improve ability in the basic study skills, no differentiation is made between them. Here is a sampling of some of the strategies that are covered in detail: wide reading with prediction of story content, the Anticipation Guide, the Directed Reading Activity (DRA), the Directed Reading-Thinking Activity (DR-TA), semantic mapping, story impressions, QARS of various types, the Concept Question Chain, reciprocal questioning, self-monitoring, visual imagery, the herringbone technique, text lookbacks, fix-up strategies, and various study skills techniques such as Survey Q3R.

Chapter 7, "Special Strategies and Delivery Systems for Teaching Reading Skills to Disabled Readers and Learning-Handicapped Students," first mentions several visual perception programs and phonic programs that can be helpful in teaching reading to learning-handicapped students. It then briefly discusses four psychological counseling programs that may be useful with learning-handicapped children: hypnosis, suggestopedia, reality therapy, and behavior modification. The chapter next describes some different delivery systems for teaching reading skills to disabled readers and learning-handicapped students: pull-out programs, resource rooms, reading clinics or labs, remedial schools, and summer reading programs. The chapter concludes by mentioning Individual Education Plans (IEPs) and the Regular Education Initiative (REI).

Four helpful appendices are included at the end of the *Handbook*. Appendix I provides a list of computer software publishers. Appendix II offers a comprehensive list of materials for use in a reading improvement program with either disabled readers or learning-handicapped students. Appendix III provides a list of test publishers, and Appendix IV offers a list of the publishers of reading materials and reading software.

You will find the following to be particularly useful features of the *Complete Reading Disabilities Handbook*:

- The spiral-bound format makes it easy to reproduce the many full-page diagnostic and corrective reading devices included.
- Provides a wealth of practical, classroom-tested strategies for improving the reading skills of *all* types of readers.
- Is equally useful in working with disabled readers and learning-handicapped children.
- Contains over 100 ready-to-duplicate devices and activities for assessing and correcting specific reading disabilities.
- Describes all of the causes of reading disabilities in simple, nontechnical language.
- Stresses how oral reading miscue analysis can be effectively used in any reading improvement program.
- Describes the contemporary Reading Recovery Program in detail and tells you in concrete terms how strategies similar to those used in Reading Recovery can be implemented in a reading improvement program.
- Includes a comprehensive list of computer software for assessing and correcting various kinds of reading problems.

- Emphasizes the effective teaching and reinforcement of letter names, an emphasis not commonly found in similar resources.
- Covers various psychological and counseling approaches that can be used with students who have emotional problems as well as reading problems.

After teaching in this field for over 30 years, I remain optimistic that we can make further progress in reading instruction. There still are far too many students who do not learn to read effectively or who do not value reading for pleasure, perhaps an even more important goal. If this handbook can help reading teachers and learning disability teachers improve the grim statistics mentioned earlier—even to a small degree—it will have served its purpose well.

Wilma H. Miller
Illinois State University

CONTENTS

CHAPTER 3: READY-TO-USE MATERIALS FOR DIAGNOSING DISABILITIES IN THE WORD-IDENTIFICATION TECHNIQUES • 122

CHAPTER 4: READY-TO-USE MATERIALS FOR DIAGNOSING DISABILITIES IN COMPREHENSION AND BASIC STUDY SKILLS • 173

CHAPTER 5: READY-TO-USE STRATEGIES AND ACTIVITIES FOR CORRECTING DISABILITIES IN THE WORD-IDENTIFICATION TECHNIQUES • 201

CHAPTER 6: READY-TO-USE STRATEGIES AND ACTIVITIES FOR CORRECTING DISABILITIES IN COMPREHENSION AND BASIC STUDY SKILLS • 339

CHAPTER 7: SPECIAL STRATEGIES AND DELIVERY SYSTEMS FOR TEACHING READING SKILLS TO DISABLED READERS AND LEARNING-HANDICAPPED STUDENTS • 379

APPENDICES • 385

What Are Reading Disabilities?

Most reading teachers are conscientious and are teaching reading skills as well as conditions permit to the children for whom they are responsible. However, we still are not completely successful with all children, and their resulting lack of reading progress can impact very negatively upon both their school success and their future personal and professional lives.

How Common Are Reading Disabilities?

We live in a technological society in which men and women travel into outer space, in which organs are successfully transplanted, and in which multitudes of data can be stored on computer disks. Why are we not able to teach all of our children to read successfully? The answer to this question is as complex as the reading process itself.

Although statistics about the incidence of reading disabilities may vary somewhat, at least 15 percent of all students in elementary schools are reading below their potential level. Others think that 10 percent to 12 percent of students in English-speaking countries have reading problems, while 50 percent to 100 percent of children in disadvantaged areas may have reading disabilities. In the United States, between 70 percent and 75 percent of the children who have reading problems are boys. Some of the reading disabilities are caused by learning disabilities, while some children simply have reading problems.

It seems appropriate here to reiterate some grim statistics about reading problems which were mentioned in the preface:

- 60 million Americans read below eighth-grade level.
- 85 percent of the juveniles processed through our court system are illiterate.
- 50 percent of the inmates in our prison system are functionally illiterate.

Thus, you can see that it is imperative to teach reading as effectively as possible to *all* students. To do so can ensure our future as a free democratic society as well as contribute to both the professional and personal lives of our citizens. We cannot afford to do less. If we could place men on the moon in 1969, we can certainly teach all children to read up to the limits of their potential.

Eddie

When I began teaching in 1958, I had a boy named Eddie in my second-grade class. Although he had had behavior problems in first grade and had already repeated first grade by the time he entered my classroom, he liked me and behaved fairly well for me. However, after two years in first grade, he was still a virtual nonreader. Because I was eager to help him learn to read, I had him come to my house every Saturday morning, where I gave him free extra help in reading—more of the same instruction at which he had already failed for two years. Although we frankly made no progress with his reading, he enjoyed his Saturday mornings with me. However, he left my second grade still a virtual nonreader. Since he had already been retained once, he was promoted to third grade where he again had bad behavior problems. When I left town three years later, he was still a nonreader and had bad behavior problems, although he always seemed to like me. I often wonder what became of Eddie. Today I could have helped him learn to read since I now know that he undoubtedly was learning-handicapped—a boy of average intelligence who needed some of the special strategies and materials such as those contained in this *Handbook* to help him learn to read successfully. The entire field of learning disabilities was unknown at that time. Yes, we have made progress in effective reading instruction in the years since I taught Eddie, but we still can make more progress.

Why Educational Reform Has Not Been More Successful in Improving Reading Instruction

In Illinois, the state in which I live and teach, the legislature passed a comprehensive educational reform package in 1985, which mandated that school districts formulate educational goals and have additional testing in all of the subject areas. This legislation is undoubtedly fairly typical of that passed in many other states and provinces in recent years, yet it does not seem to have improved reading instruction very significantly.

For one thing, the legislation often is not accompanied by financial support. Indeed, in my state financial support for all levels of education has decreased significantly recently. This educational reform instead placed even more emphasis on reading testing than there was already. At the present time, for example, third graders in Illinois may well be tested for two solid weeks every April. They are given standardized achievement tests, the Illinois Goal Assessment Program (IGAP), a process-oriented measure of reading comprehension, and basal reader tests. Such extensive testing is simply not going to solve our reading problems.

The legislators apparently assumed that such testing would assure accountability on the part of teachers, making certain that they teach the requisite skills. Instead, many teachers are being forced to "teach for the tests." They feel great pressure for their students to achieve good scores on the reading tests that they take.

Such an emphasis on test scores is misplaced. Any test score is only a representation of how well a student scored on a certain day and is subject to error in many different ways. In addition, a reading test often does a poor job of evaluating implicit (higher-level) reading skills, and it cannot measure a student's interest in reading for either information or pleasure. For these reasons, educational reform as it now exists is not going to solve the problem of many children with reading disabilities. Legislators seem to have suggested a fairly simplistic solution—more state-mandated goals and testing—to the very complex issue of effective reading instruction.

How Elementary Reading Instruction Can Be Made More Effective

Reading is a complex process, and teaching reading is likewise complex. Very briefly, however, here are some things that can be done to help ensure that reading instruction is more effective for *all* children in today's elementary schools.

• Provide preservice reading teachers with the best possible preparation, including classroom-proven effective teaching strategies, appropriate ways to individualize reading instruction, and much actual classroom teaching experience.

• Give inservice teachers access to many different effective techniques and ready-to-duplicate materials which can be used to teach reading to different kinds of students. There simply is no method or type of material that will be effective in teaching reading to all children. The more knowledge and resources a reading teacher has in his or her repertoire, the more effective a job he or she is likely to do.

• Give reading teachers access to a wealth of classroom-tested reading materials which they can use in appropriate ways with large groups of students, small groups of students, and on an individual basis. Such materials can take the form of quality children's literature of various types, basal readers, basal reader workbooks, phonic materials, ready-to-use activity sheets of various types, commercial and teacher-made games, and computer software.

• Keep class size as small as possible for effective reading instruction. Twenty students should be the maximum in the primary grades and twenty-five students should be the maximum in the intermediate grades. Unfortunately, class size generally is becoming larger, not smaller, due to budgetary constraints that cause teacher cutbacks.

• Provide more support for reading teachers. Contemporary teachers often function under more stressful conditions than teachers faced in the past. They may well have too little support from either parents or administrators. Their efforts may go unappreciated, causing them to teach reading more ineffectively than they might under optimum conditions. In addition, a number of children just do not have the discipline or supervision today that they did in the past. They therefore are more difficult both to control and motivate. In urban schools these problems obviously are especially severe.

• How can a teacher teach reading effectively when he or she must spend the majority of the school day trying to control the children? It is vital for reading teachers to have as much support as possible from both their administrators and parents. In their educational programs, administrators must be taught the strategies and materials that constitute an excellent reading program and must be impressed with the importance of supporting and valuing their teachers' efforts. There must be a concerted effort to involve parents positively with the schools, in such ways as letters of information concerning school activities, supportive telephone calls, helpful teacher-parent conferences, paid and unpaid parent helpers in the school, parent education groups, and sending sample reading strategies and materials home. Of course, these suggestions require time, money, or both and are not easy to implement.

• Encourage parents to provide a print-rich home environment and a positive reading model to help their children achieve up to the limits of their reading potential. They should also be encouraged to read to their children on a regular basis and to encourage their older children to read to them at home. Children should obtain a library card, and parents must be told how vitally important it is for them to model and encourage reading both for pleasure and for information.

• Parent education programs and other programs that involve teachers, parents, and children as *partners* in their child's reading progress are absolutely essential in an effective reading program. This, too, is difficult to implement in our contemporary society of working parents and single-parent families, a society that does not place much emphasis on the value of education. Why do you suppose that children in Japan, for example, achieve so well in school? It is mainly because education is held in such high esteem there.

- Make available unique strategies and materials which teachers can implement with learning-handicapped children to ensure the optimum amount of reading success with them. The appropriate use of these strategies and materials with my student Eddie, whom I mentioned earlier, undoubtedly would have resulted in his reading success and perhaps even in success in life for him.

- Implement early intervention programs that prevent reading disabilities. Programs like *Reading Recovery* (explained in detail in Chapter 5) and other programs are cost effective and efficient in the long run when weighed against the emotional problems that have already occurred by the time a student has had a significant reading problem for some time. A number of the strategies and materials described in the Reading Recovery Program also can be implemented in other corrective reading programs. Diagnostic-prescriptive reading instruction specifically geared toward a student's diagnosed reading difficulties would also greatly improve the effectiveness of elementary reading instruction.

- Use Regular Education Initiative (REI) to help mildly handicapped children achieve more success than they might experience in a special classroom for the handicapped, especially if they are older and would feel the stigma of being singled out for the special placement. A number of such children prefer pull-out programs for their special help. If children who are mildly handicapped or slow learning are to remain in the regular classroom, such teachers need to have access to special strategies and materials which can be used with them to effectively teach reading skills.

The *Complete Reading Disabilities Handbook* should help you implement some of the previously stated ways of improving reading instruction. It provides both preservice and inservice teachers with classroom-tested reading strategies and ready-to-use materials to diagnose (assess) and correct many different types of reading disabilities. It also provides unique strategies and materials that you can use with learning-handicapped children in both regular and special classrooms. Unfortunately, this resource cannot improve a child's home environment or the involvement that his/her parents have with the school. These tasks must be left to other means.

Major Causes of Reading Disabilities

Educational Factors

Illustration: _____

Jamie is a student in Ms. Fassino's third-grade class. He always has had great difficulty in identifying sight words and has not yet mastered all of the words on the Dolch Basic Sight Word List. He also does not seem to have an effective method of attacking an unknown word when he meets it. He usually just guesses at the unknown word without paying any attention to it except perhaps to the initial consonant. Often the substituted word does not make sense in the sentence, but Jamie does not stop to self-correct—he just attempts to read on without appearing to be concerned. He also has difficulty with comprehension, probably because he miscalls so many words due to his poor stock of sight words and his ineffective method of identifying unknown words. Ms. Fassino often becomes frustrated with Jamie because he simply cannot seem to remember the important sight words. What is especially frustrating to her is he can identify a sight word one day but will have forgotten it by the next time that he sees it. He also is fairly distractible, often has a short attention span, and is somewhat hyperactive.

Hypothesis: From examining this brief summary of Jamie and his reading problems, it is fairly obvious that one major cause of his reading difficulties probably is *educational*. Jamie may well be mildly learning handicapped and has not been provided with the appropriate reading strategies and materials to enable him to experience the reading success which should be possible for him. Perhaps he would not have the present reading disability if he had used tracing (kinesthetic) strategies with some of the especially difficult-to-retain sight words in first grade, predictable books, the language-experience approach, a well-structured, meaningful phonic approach, and activity sheets that have been especially designed for learning-handicapped students. (See Chapters 5 and 7.) Instead, Jamie was taught with the use of the basal reader approach with insufficient repetition of sight words, taught the basic phonic skills at too fast a pace for him, and taught too few of the phonic elements and generalizations in a slow, meaningful manner with concrete repetition.

NOTE: Educational factors of various types undoubtedly are the most common cause of reading disabilities in contemporary elementary schools. There are various educational factors that unfortunately can lead to reading problems. The following explores most of these factors.

What Can Happen When Reading Skills Are Taught Prematurely

One educational factor is that of presenting a formal reading program before the child is ready. *Emergent literacy* states that literacy instruction actually begins at birth and that the preschool and kindergarten programs should be a continuation of this instruction. However, children in kindergartens today are often presented with formal, structured reading programs for which they simply are not ready. Children from a privileged home environment with well-developed emergent literacy skills undoubtedly will not be harmed by such a formal program, most of which emphasize the teaching of isolated phonic elements. However, this may well not be the case for learning-handicapped children, immature children, slow-learning children, children who come from homes that did not provide a print-rich literacy environment or much prior knowledge, or children with poor auditory discrimination.

If any such children are presented with a formal reading program in kindergarten or beginning first grade before they have the requisite emergent literacy skills to profit from it, they are likely to fail almost as soon as they begin. Since a number of the reading skills are then presented in a developmental manner, such children may well fall farther and farther behind as new reading skills are presented. When a child fails to make adequate progress in reading, he or she usually develops a negative self-concept and a dislike for all reading activities, which makes it even more difficult for him or her to achieve reading success. Thus, such a child may well become disabled in reading for the rest of his or her life unless he or she receives some type of intervention either in school or at home.

However, because of the emotional difficulties that usually are the result of reading disabilities, it often becomes very difficult for such a child to make good reading progress. Thus, it is much more practical to prevent reading difficulties than it is to try to correct or remediate them. The Reading Recovery Program described in Chapter 5 is an early intervention program. In any case, an emergent literacy program always should progress forward for the child's present attainment of emergent literacy skills.

What Can Happen When a Child's Unique Reading Needs Are Not Taken into Consideration

Another fairly common education-related cause of reading disabilities is *inappropriate reading instruction*. This generally involves the use of an initial reading program that is not compatible with a child's unique needs or weaknesses. The majority of above-average and even average children probably can learn to read effectively by almost any combination of reading strategies and materials. However, this is often not true for children with unique needs, such as learning-handicapped children, children from an impoverished home environment, children with emotional problems, or children of below-average intelligence.

For the majority of children the optimum beginning reading program should consist of continuing the child's emergent literacy skills, placing emphasis upon learning letter names and letter-sound relationships in as meaningful a manner as possible, dictation using the language-experience approach, process writing, and literature-based reading instruction using predictable books, picture storybooks, and wordless books. Then the majority of the reading skills can be taught by the selective use of literature-based reading instruction, the basal reader approach, and perhaps a meaningful phonic approach if the student has the requisite auditory discrimination skills to succeed in such a program.

However, some students present unique problems that cannot be accommodated by the recommended reading strategies and materials just summarized. Most of the emergent literacy skills are beneficial for the vast majority of children. However, some children with inadequate auditory discrimination skills are taught too many phonic elements and phonic generalizations in a formal phonic program that deemphasizes comprehension. This may cause such students to focus too much on word pronunciation while paying little attention to comprehension, the heart of the reading process. On the other hand, some learning-handicapped students or perhaps slow-learning students may profit from an extensive program of phonic analysis presented in a structured manner with much concrete reinforcement.

At the beginning stages of reading, some students make the most progress with the use of *tracing strategies* or *kinesthetic approaches* that stress the sense of touch as an aid to word identification. Such tracing can take the form of a sand tray or salt tray, the use of instant pudding, shaving cream, sandpaper letters, macaroni letters, sandpaper letters, felt letters, glitter letters, or rice letters. (See Chapter 5.) Since tracing is a very time-consuming way of teaching sight words, it should be mainly used only at the beginning stages of reading instruction with children who seem to have severe difficulty in retaining important sight words. When used in this manner, it can be extremely effective for some children.

There is no one best method for presenting reading instruction to intermediate-grade students. For most of them a combination of approaches probably is the most effective. Most children of this age should have a predominantly literature-based reading program with many opportunities to read both narrative and expository materials on their instructional and independent levels. The basal reader approach may be used in a *very* selective manner, and the specialized reading skills that are required for effective reading of content materials should be taught and practiced. Chapters 5 and 6 contain a multitude of strategies and materials for use with intermediate-grade students.

Learning-handicapped students at this level need to be presented with strategies and materials that have been especially designed for them. Such strategies can take the form of a phonic program or various kinesthetic (tactile) approaches. Chapter 7 also contains a number of special techniques and materials that can be used with intermediate-grade learning-handicapped students.

In their book *Reading Difficulties: Instruction and Assessment* (New York: Random House, 1988, pp. 41–42), Barbara Taylor, Larry A. Harris, and P. David Pearson describe a teaching strategy that may be appropriate for use with a number of different reading approaches. Very briefly, it involves the following five steps:

1. Modeling
2. Guided Practice
3. Consolidation
4. Practice
5. Application

It is very important for you to be knowledgeable about the multitude of different reading strategies and materials. Only then can you present the most effective reading program for all the children in your trust.

What Results When Reading Instruction Is Not Presented at the Proper Pace

Improperly paced reading instruction is another factor that can result in reading disabilities. Sometimes reading instruction is presented at too rapid a pace without sufficient reinforcement of the important sight words and phonic elements. This undoubtedly is especially true with learning-handicapped children, children from an impoverished home environment, or slow-learning children. Such children often are not given enough meaningful reinforcement in the basic sight words and crucial phonic elements to attain mastery of them. This may well be the case in the basal reader approach and also in some phonic approaches. Therefore, the student does not attain mastery of these vital reading skills before being expected to learn additional important reading skills.

In addition, the basal reader approach and sometimes the formal phonic approach feature the use of reading achievement groups. Although the accompanying manuals emphasize that such groups should be flexible enough to encourage children to move from group to group as they progress in the reading skills, in practice the groups usually become quite rigid, and the child who is placed in the below-average group in first grade usually remains in that same group through sixth grade. Students in the below-average group often feel stigmatized and develop a negative self-concept about reading and all reading activities.

Sometimes the grade-level designation of the reading materials determines their use in a particular grade. For example, all children in a third grade are required to read a certain reader whether or not it is appropriate. This then holds back the above-average readers who may become underachievers who are not challenged and thus lose interest in reading. Perhaps even more unfortunate, this practice causes children in the below-average reading group to consistently attempt to read at the *frustration reading level*, which undoubtedly is one or more years above their actual reading level. Some children have spent their entire school career reading at the frustration reading level, causing them to dislike reading activities since they never are able to experience success with it. Fortunately, this practice does not occur as frequently in elementary schools today as it did in the past, but even now it is not uncommon in the intermediate grades where the reading range may vary from that of nonreader to the secondary school level.

What Results from the Use of Large Classes

Large classes in the elementary school, especially in the primary grades, are not conducive to optimum reading achievement. No primary-grade classroom should have more than 20 pupils, while an intermediate-grade classroom should not have more than 25 students. Unfortunately, in a time of budgetary constraints and teacher cutbacks, these optimum class sizes often are not achieved.

However, diagnostic-prescriptive individualized reading instruction should be maintained as much as possible to ensure optimum reading achievement. Such a reading program always should stress a student's strengths, while attempting to compensate for his or her weaknesses. In addition, the reading program should provide as much individual attention as possible and should teach to the child's preferred modality (channel), as may be the case with learning-handicapped children.

Why the Teacher-Pupil Relationship Is So Important

One of the most important factors that influences a child's reading success both in the classroom and in tutoring sessions is the *teacher-pupil relationship*. The significance of this relationship is indicated by the following statement from *Becoming a Nation of Readers* (Washington, D.C.: National Institute of Education, 1985, p. 85) by Richard C. Anderson, Elfrieda H. Hiebert, Judith A. Scott, and Ian A. G. Wilkinson:

> Studies indicate that about 15 percent of the variation among children in reading achievement at the end of the school year is attributable to factors that relate to the skill and effectiveness of the teacher . . . In contrast, the largest study ever done found that about 3 percent of the variation in reading achievement at the end of the first grade was attributable to the overall approach of the program.

The teacher-pupil relationship is very difficult to describe because it varies so much. Most children make the best reading progress when the teacher provides a warm, supportive, positive environment, removing great pressure from learning to read. On the other hand, a few children seem to require a much firmer teacher who will command their respect, since they need some degree of pressure to apply themselves to the difficult task of learning to read. Certainly, some children, perhaps especially in inner-city environments, have had many teachers who did not expect them to be able to perform well in school; their students have, in return, given them little in the way of reading achievement. Research has found that the self-fulfilling prophecy frequently applies in the classroom. A student often will respond only up to the limits of what his or her teachers expect.

In their book *Assessing and Correcting Classroom Reading Problems* (Glenview, Illinois: Scott, Foresman and Company, 1988, pp. 69–71), J. Estill Alexander and Betty S. Heathington have described twelve characteristics that they believe good teachers of reading should possess:.

- Effective reading teachers are teachers who read.
- Effective reading teachers have a positive sense of self-worth, especially about helping others.
- Effective reading teachers are knowledgeable.
- Effective reading teachers have a genuine affection for learners, apparent in both word and deed.
- Effective reading teachers are enthusiastic and communicate their enthusiasm to problem readers.
- Effective reading teachers accept learners as they are—their feelings, their emotional needs, and their values.
- Effective reading teachers are open and flexible, giving learners the opportunity to make suggestions regarding their own welfare.
- Effective reading teachers are warm and cooperative.
- Effective reading teachers have confidence in the learner's ability to improve his or her reading skills.
- Effective reading teachers are empathetic, not sympathetic.

- Effective reading teachers value diversity in learners.
- Effective reading teachers are structured and consistent in behavior.

In *How to Increase Reading Ability* (New York: Longman, 1990, p. 356), Albert J. Harris and Edward R. Sipay state that unsuccessful reading teachers may employ some of the following practices:

- failing to ensure readiness for learning a new skill or strategy
- instructing a child at too fast a pace
- using materials that are too difficult for a child
- giving pupils insufficient thinking time
- failing to give approval for a correct task
- expressing disapproval for a child's mistake
- asking a child to perform a task that he/she cannot do well in front of others

Characteristics an Elementary School Should Possess to Maximize the Chances of Reading Success

Research has discovered that optimum reading achievement occurs in elementary schools that possess several important characteristics. The more time spent on reading instruction, the better the reading achievement normally will be. However, this presupposes that the time spent on reading instruction is devoted to *quality* instruction such as literature-based reading instruction, meaningful reading of narrative and expository materials with predictions made before reading, and comprehension emphasized in various ways after reading instruction. It does not mean the extensive use of workbook pages, for example, just to keep the students busy and quiet.

Taylor, Harris, and Pearson (1988) state on page 40 in their book that good readers complete more contextual reading and spend more time in silent reading than in oral reading. Thus, oral reading should receive little emphasis in their program after the initial stages of reading instruction. On the other hand, they stated that lower readers demand more teacher time and task monitoring with feedback than do good readers. Because a number of teachers do not really enjoy teaching below-average readers, they may not always receive the time and attention from the teacher that they require.

Reading instruction also must be taken seriously by both the teacher and the pupils for the optimum amount of reading progress to take place. It also is very important for an elementary school to have a principal who is knowledgeable about reading instruction and who supports his or her teachers in innovative as well as in traditional practices that may lead to improved reading achievement. Obviously, there must be sufficient discipline in a classroom for reading instruction to take place. This certainly does not imply a totally quiet classroom, but rather a well-organized, professional classroom.

Other Educational Causes

There are a few other school-related causes for reading disabilities that should be mentioned. If a child has missed a great deal of school especially during the primary grades or has moved a great deal during that time, it may be difficult for him or her to make the optimum reading progress possible unless he or she is linguistically adept or has had special reading help of some type.

A Brief Summary

Educational factors of some type undoubtedly are the most common cause of reading disabilities. Fortunately, a number of these factors could be changed to result in improved reading achievement if the schools and society would work together to attempt to do so. The vast majority of children in contemporary elementary schools could learn to read at least effectively enough to function in our society, if they had well-trained teachers and well-equipped schools and a society that recognizes the worth and necessity of that learning. We really cannot afford to do less than this for our children.

Visual Defects

Illustration: _____

Jay is a boy in Ms. Coe's first-grade classroom. Although it already is February of his first-grade year, Jay still is having difficulty in learning to read. Ms. Coe has noticed that Jay still reverses a number of letters such as *g* and *q*, *b* and *d*, and *p* and *q*. In addition, he reverses simple words such as *stop* and *spot*, and *was* and *saw*. Jay often also loses his place while attempting to read, occasionally skipping an entire line of print even in simple tradebooks. In addition, he has great difficulty with workbook pages and activity sheets that have a number of items on them and seems to do better with such sheets when they are relatively simple. Since his visual acuity was evaluated at the beginning of first grade and was found to be normal, Ms. Coe suspects that Jay has a *visual perception defect*, not a vision defect, which may well be interfering with his making satisfactory progress in learning to read.

Hypothesis: From examining this very brief summary, it seems obvious that Jay undoubtedly has a *visual perception problem*. He also may be *learning handicapped*, since visual perception problems often accompany a learning disability in the early stages of reading. Special strategies and materials should have been employed with Jay in his reading instruction in preschool, kindergarten, and early first grade. Fortunately, it is not too late to provide these, although it will be more difficult for him to catch up with his peers than it would have been if this intervention had been provided earlier. Some ideas and materials for providing such intervention are provided in Chapter 5.

Note: Various kinds of visual defects are considered by reading specialists to be the most common of the physical problems that are related to reading achievement. Such defects are usually placed into two main categories—*visual perception problems* and *vision defects*.

Visual Perception Problems

Visual perception can be defined as the selection and organization of the various sensory data people meet in their environment. There seems to be a relation between visual perception ability and reading achievement, especially if the perception of both letter names and sight words is stressed in the initial reading problem. Research has shown that visual perception tasks that stress letter identification (discrimination) and sight-word identification (discrimination) influence primary-grade reading achievement much more than does the discrimination of geometric forms. Therefore, you should use geometric forms and patterns of some type *only* with the child who is very weak in visual perception ability along with other visual perception activities such as those suggested in

Chapter 5. Visual perception difficulties are somewhat common among learning-handicapped children and slow-learning children.

Common Vision Defects

Research has found that vision difficulties contribute to reading disabilities about 50 percent of the time to some degree. Some children with inadequate vision can become average or even good readers because they are able to compensate for their vision defect. However, all children should have regular vision testing and appropriate corrective measures. No child should have to face the task of reading with inadequate vision.

A first-grade child must have adequate near-point vision to be able to see the printed words on the page. Sometimes the eye muscles are not finely enough developed to allow children to have adequate near-point vision when they enter first grade. Although these muscles normally develop later, reading problems can result in first grade if children are asked to do an excessive amount of book reading before they are visually ready to do it. For such children, the extensive use of the language-experience approach with its large charts and Big Books may be especially helpful.

Myopia (Nearsightedness). The most common visual defect in elementary-school children is *myopia,* or *nearsightedness.* This is a refractive error that causes students to hold the book close to their eyes to be able to read the print without its blurring. It also causes children difficulty in seeing the words written on the chalkboard unless they are seated near the front of the classroom. A myopic child always should be fitted with corrective contact lenses or eyeglasses because such a vision defect causes headaches, blurred vision while reading, and difficulty in reading as effectively as possible without great effort.

Hyperopia (Farsightedness). Although found less frequently among children than adults, the other fairly common vision defect is *hyperopia,* or *farsightedness.* This also is a refractive error which probably influences reading problems more than any other vision defect. Farsighted children have some difficulty with near-point vision such as is required in reading since they must move the material away from their faces to be able to read it.

Lack of Binocular Coordination. Another vision defect which occasionally causes reading problems is a child's lack of fusion of the two eyes. When a reader looks at a printed page, he or she sees two images, and the eyes must be able to fuse or join the two images into one image if he or she is to be able to see the printed words clearly. This lack of *binocular coordination* or *fusion* usually occurs in young children and may be corrected by the child's doing the eye exercises recommended by an ophthalmologist or an optometrist. Binocular fusion can be tested by using one of the devices described later in this section.

Astigmatism. *Astigmatism* is also a refractive error and usually exists with either myopia or with hyperopia. This vision defect causes the print to be blurred and therefore results in eye fatigue. Astigmatism also often results in headaches which make it difficult to concentrate on reading.

Anseikonia. A fairly uncommon vision defect is called *anseikonia.* This is a condition in which the eyes have a different size or shape in the image of an object in each eye. When there is no difference in the refractive error of the two eyes, the difference in image size is due to a different physical size of the eyeball. A student with this vision defect would have difficulty fusing and thus have difficulty in learning to read.

Some Ways to Test Visual Acuity

The old *Snellen Chart* is not adequate for judging vision for reading instruction since it tests a child's sight at far-point instead of at near-point as is required in reading. Neither does it evaluate the fusion ability of a child. The vast majority of elementary schools today do vision testing using one of the following types of instruments:

Keystone Complete School Vision Screening Program
Mast/Keystone
2212 East 12th Street
Davenport, IA 52803

Ortho-Rater
Bausch & Lomb Optical Company
Rochester, New York 14602

School Vision Tester
Bausch & Lomb Optical Company
Rochester, NY 14602

Titmus II Vision Tester—Pediatric Model—Preschool and Primary
Titmus
Ophthalmic Products Division
P.O. Box 191
Petersburg, VA 23804

You also may gain some clues to possible vision problems by using the A-B-C's of vision: (a) the *appearance* of the eyes—redness, watering of the eyes, or frequent styes; (b) the *behavior* of the child—signs of nervousness, how far the book is held away from the eyes, and the posture of the body; and (c) the *complaints* of the child—frequent headaches, seeing double, blurring of the printed material, and nausea.

Joan M. Harwell has included a very useful "Educator's Checklist of Clues to Visual Problems" in her book *Complete Learning Disabilities Handbook* (West Nyack, New York: The Center for Applied Research in Education, 1989, pp. 207–208) that helps you observe vision defects and visual perception deficits in the following areas:

- appearance of the eyes
- complaints when using the eyes at work
- behavioral signs of visual problems such as eye movement abilities, eye teaming abilities, eye-hand coordination abilities, visual form perception, and refractive status

Auditory Defects

Illustration: _____

Rita is a second-grade girl in Ms. Bellott's classroom who has had great difficulty in learning to read. Even in the second grade she only reads at about the primer level. Her first-grade class was taught reading skills with the formal phonic program *Alpha One*, and she also was taught beginning reading skills in kindergarten using *Alpha Time*, a phonic readiness program. She never has been able to differentiate effectively between the various phonic elements, especially the short vowel sounds. This was extremely frustrating both to Rita and her teacher since the various phonic elements were presented in many different ways such as letter people, teacher-constructed and commercial games, and activity sheets. Rita has learned some environmental words by sight. The language-experience approach, Big Books, and predictable books were not used with her.

Hypothesis: Rita undoubtedly had poor auditory discrimination in kindergarten but nonetheless was required to try to learn letter-sound relationships through the formal phonic program mandated for use in her kindergarten. It is very likely that her teacher used the program in the prescribed way, not modifying it for Rita in a way that might have assured her some degree of success. She should have had reading instruction in both kindergarten and first grade in ways in which she could have experienced success—by using the language-experience approach, Big Books, predictable books, literature-based reading instruction, extensive use of sight-word teaching, and perhaps a limited use of tactile strategies.

Common Auditory Defects That May Contribute to Reading Disabilities

Auditory defects undoubtedly are less often related to reading disabilities than are visual defects, unless the child is required to learn to read by a formal phonic program when he or she has inadequate auditory discrimination. K. A. Kavale reported a direct, though low, correlation between auditory processing and reading success in an article "The Relationship Between Auditory Perceptual Skills and Reading Ability: A Meta-Analysis" (*Journal of Learning Disabilities*, November 14, 1981, 539–546).

Auditory defects can be divided into two major categories: *auditory acuity defects* and *auditory discrimination defects. Auditory acuity* is the ability to hear sounds found in the environment and defects may be related to reading disabilities if there is a high-frequency loss. It is said that about 5 percent of elementary-school children have a significant hearing loss.

Auditory discrimination normally is defined as the ability to differentiate between the likeness and differences in the sounds that are found in oral language. A child with good auditory acuity can have inadequate auditory discrimination. In fact, this is fairly common among disabled readers, especially in kindergarten and the early primary grades.

In his book *Listening: What Research Says to the Teacher* (Washington, D.C.: National Education Association, 1969), Stanford E. Taylor has described three different levels of listening. He states that the lowest level is *hearing*, which refers to the sound waves being received and modified by the ear. Since hearing is a physical phenomenon, it cannot be taught. *Listening* is the level at which a person becomes aware of sound sequences. At this middle level a person is able to identify and recognize the sound sequences as known words if the words are in their listening vocabulary. *Auding* is the highest level and involves giving meaning to the sounds and assimilating and integrating the oral message. At this level a person is able to perform all the high-level comprehension skills that are usually associated with reading.

Another subskill in this area is *auditory memory* or *auditory span*. It is listening to and then remembering a series of sounds, digits, or words. It is considered to be one element of intelligence and thus is found on the Wechsler Intelligence Scale for Children (WISC-R), an individual intelligence test.

Auditory discrimination and *auditory blending* (the ability to blend a series of sounds into a recognizable word) can well be related to reading progress especially in a reading program that places great emphasis on learning phonic elements and generalizations. As stated earlier, a child with good auditory acuity still may have auditory discrimination difficulties, but a child obviously cannot have good auditory discrimination ability with inadequate auditory acuity. When a child's acuity is low, his or her reading achievement also may well be low.

A child with poor auditory discrimination should not be taught initial reading skills with a formal phonic approach or even with a basal reader approach that contains considerable phonic elements. A few children are not auditorily mature enough to be taught many phonic elements and rules until they are eight years old. The child with inadequate auditory discrimination should be taught reading using the language-experience approach, Big Books and predictable books, literature-based (whole language) instruction, or a tactile or kinesthetic approach. Sight words should be greatly emphasized with such a child.

A few learning-handicapped children have a weak auditory channel and do not profit from a formal phonic approach, but this may be less common than those children who have a weak visual channel. A few learning-handicapped children are weak in both the visual and auditory channels and need to be primarily taught by a tactile approach, especially at the beginning.

It is interesting to note that even totally hearing-impaired children can learn to read effectively if the proper methods and materials are used. Such approaches often are some variation of the language-experience approach, the basal reader approach, and literature-based reading instruction.

All children in the elementary school must be given auditory screening tests on a regular basis to determine if they have hearing problems. Here is a partial list of audiometers and their manufacturers:

Auditory Instrument Division
7375 Bush Lake Road
Minneapolis, MN 55435

Auditory Instrument Division
Zenith Radio Corporation
6501 West Grand Avenue
Chicago, IL 60635

Beltone Electronics Corporation
Hearing Tests Instruments Division
4201 West Victoria Street
Chicago, IL 60646

Precision Acoustics Corporation
55 West 42nd Street
Chicago, IL 60635

Royal Industries
Audiotone Division
P.O. Box 2905
Phoenix, AZ 85036

The Wepman Auditory Discrimination Test may be of some use in identifying children in kindergarten and first grade and learning-handicapped children who are especially weak in auditory discrimination ability. However, it should be used only as one tentative indicator of auditory discrimination ability along with teacher observation and perhaps other standardized tests. It should not be used with children who do not speak standard English, as they may not be able to differentiate between all of the sounds on this test. Here is the publisher of this device:

Wepman Auditory Discrimination Test

Language Research Associates, Inc.
P.O. Drawer 2085
Palm Springs, CA 92262

In *Reading Difficulties: Their Diagnosis and Correction* (Englewood Cliffs, New Jersey: Prentice Hall, 1989, pp. 53–54), Guy L. Bond, Miles A. Tinker, Barbara B. Wasson, and John B. Wasson present the following behavioral characteristics of *hearing impairment* that you may want to watch for:

- Inattention during listening activities
- Frequent misunderstanding of oral directions or requests for repetition of statements
- Turning one ear toward the speaker or thrusting head forward when listening
- Intent gazing at the speaker's face or strained posture while listening
- Monotone speech, poor pronunciation, or indistinct articulation
- Complaints of earache or hearing difficulty
- Insistence on closeness to sound sources
- Frequent colds, discharging ears, or difficult breathing

Learning Disabilities

Illustration: _____

Jeff is a student in Mr. Bernstein's fourth-grade class who reads at about the second-grade instructional reading level. Even though he can accurately pronounce words at about the third-grade level, he has great difficulty retelling the material or responding to higher-level (implicit) comprehension questions. It is very frustrating for Mr. Bernstein since Jeff sometimes can recognize a word instantly but cannot do so a short time later. He is a boy of above-average intelligence, has adequate visual and auditory acuity, and comes from a stable, middle-class environment. He has never been successful either with reading or spelling, although he is capable in math. Jeff also is somewhat distractible but not excessively so. He has been tested for a learning disability, but since the tests indicated no real evidence of a learning disability, Jeff was placed in Mr. Bernstein's class with no additional help from a learning disabilities teacher.

Hypothesis: From examination of this very brief summary it appears that Jeff is mildly learning-handicapped. Sometimes a learning handicap that is this mild is not easy to ascertain. Jeff should have been presented with reading instruction much earlier using some of the strategies and materials that have been specially designed for learning-handicapped children. A few of these are the following: perhaps a formal phonic approach using tracing strategies as an aid to word identification, other tracing strategies such as a salt tray or a sand tray for especially difficult-to-remember sight words, the language-experience approach, predictable books, or literature-based reading instruction (see Chapters 5 and 7).

At this time, Mr. Bernstein needs to request additional testing for Jeff to see if he can then enlist the help of the learning disabilities teacher in planning a program for him. Meanwhile, it is essential that Jeff be able to practice reading at his independent and low instructional reading levels to develop fluency and so that he can effectively retell the material. He may need to learn some simple strategies for improving both his prediction and comprehension abilities. He may also profit from the use of medication such as Ritalin®, Dexedrine®, or Cylert®. It is very important that Jeff's reading disability be improved as soon as possible so that he has the best chance of achieving success in school. Much of the material presented in the intermediate grades and above is dependent upon his possession of adequate reading ability with good comprehension.

Learning disabilities are sometimes called *minimal brain dysfunction*, but the latter term is not precise. Learning disabilities are said by some specialists to be a central nervous system dysfunction. Others say that they are the result of brain degeneration. Learning disabilities can also be defined as significant difficulty in the acquisition of listening, reading, spelling, writing, or arithmetic skills.

Sometimes a learning disability is called *dyslexia*, which can be defined as severe reading disability. This term may be used more commonly today than it was in the past. Unfortunately, the term *dyslexia* may also be used with students who simply have a significant, specific reading disability but do not really have a learning disability. A number of specialists in the area believe that educators should use any label for a child very cautiously since the label may cause the child considerable harm.

The estimates as to how many people have learning disabilities varies from as low as 2 percent to over 20 percent. According to Harris and Sipay (1989, page 159), the number ranges from 2 percent to about 4 percent. There also is a continuum of learning disabilities that ranges from mildly handicapped to severely handicapped. A number of specialists in this area prefer the term *learning handicapped* over *learning disabled* since handicap indicates a condition that one should give recognition to, make adjustments for, and allow a person to achieve in spite of (Harwell, 1989, p.3). Since I agree with this, the term *learning handicapped* will be used in this *Handbook*.

Although neurologists have not entirely determined what is involved in minimal brain dysfunction, they have isolated a few basic characteristics. They generally agree that minimal brain dysfunction is not brain damage in the traditional sense but rather is brain functioning that is not completely normal in some way. A learning-handicapped child can be weak in the visual channel (modality), the auditory channel (modality), or in both visual and auditory channels (modalities). Although possible, it is fairly uncommon for a child to be weak in the tactile (kinesthetic) channel.

There are a number of tests that are used by school psychologists to determine whether a child has a learning handicap. Although most of these tests are quite useful, some of them are not completely valid or reliable, and the results from such a test always should be interpreted cautiously. Here are a few tests that are often used in determining a learning handicap:

- Wechsler Intelligence Scale for Children, Revised (WISC-R)
- Wechsler Adult Intelligence Scale, Revised (WAIS-R)
- Tests for handedness, dominance, and knowledge of left and right, such as the Harris Tests of Lateral Dominance
- Bender Visual-Motor Gestalt Test
- Developmental Test of Visual Perception
- Illinois Test of Psycholinguistic Ability (ITPA)

You can get a complete description of these tests from the school psychologist in your school building or school district.

There are a few other factors that you should understand about learning disabilities. It is common for learning disabilities to run in a family, especially among the boys. It is not unusual for a father who is learning handicapped to have one or more sons with the same condition. The incidence of learning disabilities increase under the following conditions:

- children who experienced postbirth traumas
- children who had neonatal seizures
- children who had chronic ear infections
- children who had head traumas
- children whose mothers experienced difficult pregnancies
- children whose mothers had difficult labors
- children whose mothers ingested alcohol or drugs during pregnancies
- children whose mothers were younger than 16 or older than 40 at the time of the birth

It also is interesting to note that between 60 percent and 80 percent of the students who are classified as learning handicapped have significant reading disabilities.

On pages 6–10 of her book, Harwell (1989) has an excellent checklist you can use in making an assessment of a learning handicapped child. It assesses behavior in the following ten categories with some overlap between the categories:

- visual perceptual deficits
- visual perceptual/visual motor deficits
- auditory perceptual deficits
- spatial relationships and body awareness deficits
- conceptual deficits
- memory deficits
- motor output deficits
- attention deficit disorders
- failure syndrome
- serious emotional overlay

Although it is not possible to mention all of the items contained in this checklist in this *Handbook*, here are several of the items I have most commonly observed in learning handicapped children that you may want to look for. The actual diagnosis of a learning disability must, of course, be made by a team of specialists in an elementary school.

- ☐ reversals of letters or words (This is fairly common among children in kindergarten and first grade and should not be thought of as particularly relevant until second grade.)
- ☐ cannot copy accurately
- ☐ often loses place or skips lines while reading
- ☐ reading improves with larger print or fewer distractions on the page
- ☐ cannot color within the lines
- ☐ illegible handwriting
- ☐ letters collide and no space between word boundaries
- ☐ mirror writing (hold the paper up to the mirror and you are able to read it)
- ☐ messy papers

- ☐ difficulty with auditory discrimination
- ☐ cannot follow directions
- ☐ accident prone
- ☐ cannot make closure on an activity
- ☐ may do better with word identification in isolation than in sentence context
- ☐ has difficulty responding to implicit (higher-level) comprehension questions
- ☐ cannot think in an orderly, logical manner
- ☐ cannot remember a sight word even a short time after he or she seems able to identify it automatically
- ☐ has a limited sight vocabulary
- ☐ cannot remember what was just seen or heard
- ☐ makes the same error again and again: perseveration
- ☐ has difficulty with cutting, pasting, coloring, and writing activities
- ☐ cannot sit or stand still
- ☐ often falls out of his or her chair
- ☐ cannot finish assignments on time
- ☐ visually or auditorily distractible
- ☐ short attention span
- ☐ daydreams or looks out of the window
- ☐ rarely completes school work
- ☐ disorganized: loses items
- ☐ class clown, acting out behavior
- ☐ immature behavior: seems to be immature or babyish for his or her age
- ☐ lashing out or destructive behavior
- ☐ withdrawn
- ☐ anxious, tense, or fearful

Denny

While writing this *Handbook*, I recalled a second-grade boy named Denny who I had during my early elementary teaching career. His mother and I became good friends during the school year in which I taught her son. I now am aware as I read this list of behaviors that Denny had the classic profile of a learning-handicapped child. However, in 1959 no one had ever heard of learning disabilities so his handicap went undiagnosed and uncorrected. Indeed, in retrospect, I did everything wrong with him, and he made no reading progress at all in my class.

By 1975, when Public Law 94-142 (which requires that whenever possible, handicapped students be placed in regular classrooms) was passed, learning disabilities were understood fairly well. Today Denny's learning handicap could have been diagnosed before he entered second grade, and he could have been provided with the special strategies and materials that might have enabled him to make good reading progress. Imagine how that could have changed his life for the better. Perhaps medication such as Ritalin®, Dexedrine®, or Cylert® might also have been helpful with Denny.

Language Deficits

Illustration: ────────────────────────────────────

Rose is an African-American child from the inner city of a large urban area. She is now in fourth grade and is reading at about the third-grade level. Although she can understand standard dialect and uses it occasionally, she still prefers to speak using elements of African-American dialect in many situations including school. Do you believe that her use of this dialect has contributed to her difficulties in reading?

Hypothesis: If her teacher accepted Rose's language and emphasized reading for meaning instead of concentrating on word-perfect oral reading, it is doubtful that her lower-than-grade-level reading achievement is primarily due to her use of African-American dialect. On the other hand, if her first- and second-grade teachers emphasized word-perfect oral reading, Rose's dialect certainly may have contributed to her reading difficulties. Another contributing factor might be a lowered self-esteem if the African-American dialect were criticized. Some people believe that the differences between African-American dialect and standard dialect are becoming greater, not less, than they were in the past. However, it is the responsibility of the school to model standard English and attempt to teach it at least as an alternative language to African-American dialect, without negating the child's own language or heritage.

Common Language Deficits or Differences That May Contribute to Reading Disabilities

In some instances oral language and dialect differences can be a contributing cause of reading disabilities. A child normally cannot learn to read effectively unless he or she has a good command of oral language. This is one reason that non-English speaking children usually learn oral English before trying to learn to read in English. The child who has a poor command of oral English usually will have difficulty in learning to read. However, it is important to remember that a child might have reading problems even if he or she speaks English well. The lack of standard English oral language may compound, not cause, the reading disability.

However, language deficits and differences certainly may be a contributing factor to reading disabilities for a number of children. Some examples of these are as follows: the non-English-speaking child, a child who speaks a nonstandard dialect, a mentally handicapped child. Normally the true bilingual child does not have significant problems because he or she is fluent in spoken English as well as the native language. Phonic analysis may be especially difficult for children with language deficits or differences as the sounds are not heard as they are in English.

In summary, it may be somewhat difficult for speakers of a nonstandard dialect to learn to read if their oral language does not match the language found in their reading materials. However, by the time a child enters kindergarten, he or she usually has a good understanding of standard oral English, primarily because of the influence of television. In any case, it may be advantageous for such a child to use the language-experience approach so that his or her reading materials can match the oral language.

Dialects or *accents* from different areas may also have some relation to reading disabilities, especially if phonic elements are strongly emphasized in the reading program. For example, most formal phonic approaches and the phonic elements contained in basal readers are based on standard English, which is considered the "prestige" dialect in the United States. If a child does not use this dialect, some of the phonic elements may be very difficult for him or her to differentiate. For example, my father came from western Pennsylvania, where the word *creek* was pronounced as if it were spelled *crick*. How could he possibly mark the first *e* in this word long when he did not hear it that way? This regional dialect or accent difference may cause the most difficulty for children from the South or the Northeast areas of the United States where the accent diverges the most from the standard dialect.

Speech defects such as improper articulation, lisping, or stuttering may be related to reading problems. However, speech defects are probably not a very common cause of reading disabilities. If a child cannot articulate the sounds in exactly the way in which his or her teacher does, that child may have some difficulty with phonic analysis.

If a child stutters or stammers, he or she will certainly dislike reading orally. Children who stutter may also develop low self-esteem, which may make it more difficult for them to learn to read effectively.

Gender Differences

In the United States a child's sex has been related to reading disabilities. As you undoubtedly are aware, many more boys than girls in this country have reading problems. From 60 percent to 90 percent of the students referred for special reading help in Chapter I reading programs or in reading clinics are boys. The same can be said for boys in France and Japan. However, in Germany, boys normally do better in reading than do girls. In Canada, girls are the better readers, while in England, boys are the better readers. On Israeli kibbutzes, boys and girls are about equal in reading achievement.

There may be a number of cultural reasons why boys in the United States and Canada do not achieve as well in reading as do girls. For example, primary-grade boys often are less mature than girls of the same age and thus not as proficient in emergent literacy skills. Girls generally do surpass boys in verbal ability, while boys usually have better developed mathematical skills. However, since the 1970s boys have gained in verbal ability, and still maintain their superiority in mathematical skills. Often boys are thought by their teachers to be more energetic, vigorous, and difficult to control. There also may be more language interaction with girls than with boys, both in the home and in school. In addition, boys may look upon reading as feminine and thus not particularly desirable.

In the United States girls did better at ages of 9, 13, and 17 on each of the five NEAP assessments than did boys.

In summary, gender differences in reading achievement may be an example of a self-fulfilling prophecy, in which teachers in the United States and Canada seem to expect girls to learn to read more effectively than they do boys. However, as mentioned earlier, learning disabilities that may result in reading disabilities are much more common in boys than they are in girls. The entire area needs additional research before definitive conclusions can be drawn about the relationship between gender and reading achievement.

Health Problems

General health may be related to reading progress in several ways. For example, if a child is *malnourished* or *chronically fatigued*, it obviously will be more difficult for him or her to learn to read effectively than it would be under optimum conditions. Often a child cannot concentrate in school because of poor nutrition in the home. Such a child may lack drive and energy. Malnutrition in the home can be combated by school breakfast, milk, and lunch programs. A number of children watch television much later on school nights than they should. Although parents should try to limit late-night television viewing, this often is not done, since television is a convenient babysitter for tired, overworked parents. As everyone knows, there are far too many children in contemporary society who are living below the poverty level and in less-than-ideal circumstances.

A number of *illnesses* such as frequent colds, asthma, tonsillitis, diabetes, allergies, headaches, and upset stomach can result in frequent school absences that in turn may lead to reading problems because of missed instruction. This may be especially crucial in first and second grades. Since reading normally is taught in a fairly developmental manner, missed instruction at any stage can result in reading disabilities.

There are a few genetic factors that may be related to reading disabilities. For example, a number of poor readers have poor coordination and appear awkward while walking or running. As another example, Sadie Decker and Bruce G. Bender evaluated the reading abilities of both fraternal and identical twins and found that where reading difficulties occurred in one fraternal twin, only 50 percent to 65 percent of the time did the difficulties occur in the other fraternal twin. On the other hand, when the disability occurred in identical twins, 80 percent to 90 percent of the time the disability occurred in both twins. (See their article, "Converging Evidence for Multiple Genetic Forms of Reading Disability" in *Brain and Language*, 33, March 1988, pages 197–215.)

An *endocrine* or *glandular malfunction* may occasionally contribute to reading problems. This probably is the case with less than 10 percent of the reading disabilities. You might see a child with *hypothyroidism*, meaning that the thyroid gland does not function as well as it should. This can result in his or her behaving in a sluggish, tired manner that makes it difficult for him or her to profit from reading instruction. On the other hand, *hyperthyroidism* occurs when the thyroid gland functions too much. Children with hyperthyroidism are overactive and thus may have difficulty in concentrating on reading instruction. Malfunctions of the thyroid gland often can be corrected by proper medication.

To summarize, physical problems may well have some relationship to reading disabilities. However, often they are more likely to be a contributing factor to reading difficulties than they are to be the sole cause.

Intellectual Causes

Illustration: _____

Marty is a student in Ms. Jefferson's second-grade class. As a result of teacher observation and basal reader tests, he apparently reads on about the middle first-grade level. He can identify some sight words and understands the most relevant phonic analysis skills which have been presented to him. Marty can answer literal (explicit) comprehension questions fairly well but has great difficulty making predictions about story content, retelling a story, and answering interpretive (implicit) comprehension questions. He does not enjoy reading for pleasure. Although he generally is well behaved, Marty daydreams more than he should in school, especially when he finds his tasks difficult. Although he is quite well coordinated, he seems a little slower than most other second-graders in his actions and in learning. Do you believe that he probably has a reading disability?

Hypothesis: Although it is difficult to be certain from this brief summary, it appears that Marty probably is a child with below-average intellectual ability who may be performing at or perhaps even above his potential level. To be certain of this diagnosis, the school psychologist would have to give Marty an individual intelligence test such as the Wechsler Intelligence Scale for Children, Revised or the Stanford-Binet Intelligence Scale, Revised. Some children with below-average intelligence are labeled as disabled readers when they really are not.

How Intellectual Level Can Contribute to Reading Disabilities

While some members of the public think that most children with reading disabilities have below-average intelligence, the fact is that most children with reading disabilities have either average or above-average intelligence. Success in early reading more often is a product of prior experiences rather than intelligence. The child who has been exposed to a print-rich environment prior to school entrance—such as being read to regularly, being exposed to letter names, simple letter-sound relationships, and environmental print—is likely to do much better in reading than the child who has not.

Intelligence is a combination of innate potential and environmental conditions. This indicates that an optimum home environment certainly can increase a child's intellectual level to some extent. Beginning in the later primary grades, intellectual ability becomes very important to reading success. Certainly from that time on children with high IQ scores are generally among the best readers in a class. However, every reading teacher has known a number of *bright underachievers*. Since reading requires a degree of abstract intelligence, a child with below-average intellectual ability often may have difficulty with interpretive (implicit) comprehension.

It is important for any child with a reading disability to be given a valid *individual intelligence test* by a qualified professional such as the school psychologist. The best such test is the Wechsler Intelligence Scale for Children, Revised. This test has two major components: *verbal*, which is based on spoken or written language, and *performance*, which is based on spatial or numerical relationships. However, some psychologists prefer the Stanford-Binet Intelligence Scale, Revised or the Kauffman Assessment Battery for Children (K-ABC). Since any group intelligence test often evaluates reading ability as well as intelligence, the disabled reader's true intellectual ability is often underestimated on such a test.

Preferred Learning Modality

Sometimes *cognitive style* (the child's preferred *modality* or *method of learning*) is related to his or her reading achievement. Some children seem to learn word identification most effectively by a visual (sight) method and others from an auditory (phonic) approach, while a few children seem to have the most success with a tactile (touch) or kinesthetic approach. Cognitive style is one indication of mental ability. While a child of average or above-average intellectual ability usually can learn to read effectively with either a visual, an auditory, or a combination approach, a learning-handicapped child has great difficulty with word identification and may profit from an emphasis on one or another approach to the virtual exclusion of the others, especially at the beginning stages of reading.

In her book on page 41, Harwell (1989) has included a useful checklist that can help you determine a child's preferred learning modality so that you can provide the optimum method or combination of methods for teaching reading. Very briefly, Harwell has included the following major headings in this checklist. A few of the most important items in each portion of this checklist for you to consider are:

- The Visual Learner
  —learns by seeing
  —readily recognizes words by sight
  —relies on initial consonants or word form for identification
  —has good visual imagery
  —has good handwriting
- The Auditory Learner
  —enjoys talking and listening
  —relies on and is competent in phonic analysis
  —tries to solve problems in a verbal manner

- The Kinesthetic (Tactile) Learner
  —learns most effectively by doing
  —is not competent in spelling
  —has great difficulty in word identification either by sight or by phonic analysis
  —has inadequate oral language
  —does not enjoy reading activities
  —does not seem to use either the visual or the auditory channel effectively

Mental Impairment: How Educable and Trainable Mentally Handicapped Children Should Be Taught Reading

Most mentally impaired children have an intelligence quotient that averages around *80*. They often may have great difficulty in a formal beginning reading program upon entering first grade. Instead, such children need informal reading instruction emphasizing the language-experience approach, the teaching of letter names and letter-sound relationships in a slow, deliberate manner with frequent concrete repetition; the teaching of sight words with the same concrete, repetitive instruction perhaps involving tracing strategies; and the use of predictable books, picture storybooks, and wordless books. Each reading skill must be presented and reinforced until the child attains complete mastery of it. Children may have the most difficulty with implicit (interpretive) comprehension because of their sometimes limited degree of abstract intelligence. Such children often respond well to extrinsic motivation such as stickers, graphs of progress, or tokens. They normally can learn to read well enough to attain success in our contemporary society with a well-planned and carefully executed reading program.

Trainable mentally impaired (TMI) students also can attain such a degree of reading success with early intervention and a reading program that builds upon their unique strengths. I am very fond of a sixteen-year-old girl with Down's syndrome who has had intervention of every type since she was about two years old. At the age of sixteen she reads on about the latter third-grade or beginning fourth-grade level with good literal (explicit) comprehension and less good, but fair, interpretive (implicit) comprehension. Her potential reading level probably will be at about the fourth-grade level or a little above. I also have seen the language-experience approach used very effectively with high-school-aged TMI students. Their pictures and self-written stories were typical of children in about the second grade.

Prior Knowledge and Self-Monitoring

It is very important that a child have good prior knowledge and schema if he or she is to be able to comprehend reading material effectively. The child must bring *prior knowledge* to bear on the printed material to be able to comprehend since effective reading is a combination of prior knowledge (nonvisual information) and the printed material (visual information). The more prior knowledge a child has, the less he or she needs to depend upon the printed material. This is why a history major, for example, normally can read a history textbook more rapidly and efficiently than a person who has little background or interest in history. A child's prior knowledge is stored and organized in his or her brain in what is *schema* (the plural is *schemata*). Well-developed schema on a topic greatly improves a child's comprehension. Culturally different children may not possess the prior knowledge and schema required for effective comprehension in the typical reading materials that are found in schools.

It also is important for a child to monitor or evaluate his/her own reading to determine if effective comprehension is taking place. This self-monitoring is called *metacognition*, which simply means "thinking about thinking." Good readers normally are very effective in metacognition, while disabled readers are not. Such children must be taught and given the opportunity to monitor their own reading so that they know whether they are reading effectively and what to do if they are not. They need to be taught *fix-up strategies* such as those described in Chapter 6 of this book.

The Home Environment and Reading

Illustration: _____

Amanda is a first-grade child in Ms. Welles's class. Although she is a beautiful child with big brown eyes and brown braids who first appears well adjusted and happy, unfortunately this is not the case. Amanda was sexually abused (raped) by her own father when she was three, and he cannot contact her, although he is not in prison. She lives alone in a mobile home with her mother. Amanda has had virtually no success in learning letter names, letter-sound relationships, or sight words or even in reading predictable books.

Although Amanda has had counseling since she was raped, she still evidences much maladjustment about the incident. For example, one day she asked me (the college supervisor of her reading tutor) why I always hugged her so tight. Indeed, I had never touched her at all, although I did like her very much and felt that she also liked me. One day she blurted out in her first-grade class: "My father raped me when I was three!"

Hypothesis: It is obvious that Amanda's extremely difficult home environment had resulted in emotional maladjustment that undoubtedly has hindered her success in learning to read. Although we tried countless interesting strategies and materials with her in the emergent literacy tutoring, we had very little success. We tried tracing strategies, the language-experience approach, simple teacher-constructed reading games, reading storybooks aloud to her, wordless books, picture storybooks, predictable books, prediction activities, and extrinsic rewards—all with very, very little success. It was truly heartbreaking to know Amanda and what had happened in her life already.

Elements of the Home Environment That May Contribute to Reading Disabilities

As stated earlier, far too many children in today's society live in homes that are less than ideal in terms of being stable, happy, print-rich homes that motivate effective reading achievement. We have tutored a number of kindergarten children, for example, who had never heard a book read to them prior to school entrance or had the opportunity to explore books or manipulative materials of any type. We have tutored children who have come to school unkempt, malnourished, tired, and disinterested. Sadly, we also have tutored children both in kindergarten and elementary school who were sexually abused as early as the age of two. As everyone knows, single-parent families are common today, as are children with divorced parents. We have tutored many children from both types of homes. It may be fairly difficult for one parent to fulfill both parental roles although it certainly is possible.

Many research studies have been done over the years on the relation of the home environment to reading achievement. All of them have discovered that if there are few reading materials and models of adult reading behavior in the home, the result will be children who are "at risk" of reading disabilities. They also have found that children from higher socio-economic homes tend to be better readers than children from lower socio-economic homes. In addition, the studies have found that family values can greatly influence reading achievement. If disadvantaged families place a high value on education, their children are more likely to do well in school. On the other hand, some parents place too much pressure on their children to succeed, which may cause reading problems. A parent who is overprotective also may cause a child to have reading difficulties. Certainly death and divorce in a family can have a negative impact on a child's reading achievement. As stated earlier in this chapter, it is extremely important to involve parents in their children's education to aid in reading success.

Children from less-than-ideal home environments are found in the inner-city of large urban areas, in rural areas, on Native American reservations, and in virtually every other part of the United States and Canada. Indeed, there are many children from middle-class and upper-class homes who do not have an ideal home environment.

In any case, a number of children enter school with little of the prior knowledge about literacy that other children may possess. Unless they are given compensatory help either before school entrance or upon school entrance, they usually will experience little reading success and will fall farther and farther behind as they progress through the elementary school. Very often in inner-city schools and in schools of other types such as on Native American reservations (for example, the school in northern Wisconsin on the Lac du Flambeau Chippewa Reservation), teachers may expect little in the way of reading achievement. This lack of expectation results in the self-fulfilling prophecy that was mentioned earlier.

Poverty can further influence reading achievement because a poor child may be malnourished, may not obtain adequate testing, may have uncorrected physical problems such as vision, hearing, or dental problems, and perhaps most important, may have inadequate role models in reading. Imagine the potential difference in emergent literacy attainment between such a child and the child who has been read to on a daily basis since infancy, comes from a print-rich home environment, and has gone on many family outings. On the average, which child do you think will achieve more reading success in school?

What are the simple answers to the complex problems of children who come from less-than-optimum home environments? I certainly do not have such answers—I wish that someone did. It is surprising to me that not all such children have significant reading problems. Indeed, some of them make excellent reading progress with the help of well-educated, dedicated reading teachers who are determined to teach them to read up to the limits of their potential. Our society certainly needs to seriously consider how we can afford to waste so many children because of an inadequate education and circumstances which are beyond their control. However, since the children of poverty have no voice or power, their needs are often not taken seriously.

Social-Emotional Causes and Self-Esteem

Illustration: _____

Rod is a student in Mr. Tucker's fifth-grade class. According to a standardized achievement test given near the end of fourth grade, he is reading at about the middle third-grade level. Although he knows a number of sight words, he does not seem to have an effective method of word attack and does not use context clues effectively or monitor his own reading. In spite of miscalling a number of words while he is reading orally and probably also while reading silently, he has fairly good literal (explicit) comprehension but has considerably more difficulty with interpretive (implicit) comprehension. However, Rod exhibits many symptoms of unsatisfactory emotional adjustment. For example, he acts out, is aggressive and hostile, and is a class clown. His acceptable behavior in school probably influences reading achievement since he often refuses to sit down and complete his work in an acceptable manner. Do you think that his emotional maladjustment has caused his reading disability?

Hypothesis: Although it is impossible to draw definite conclusions without knowing much more about when Rod's difficulties began, the most typical scenario is that he entered school at least fairly well adjusted but began to exhibit emotional problems as a result of his reading disabilities. This may be the case with most disabled readers.

Elements of Emotional Adjustment That May Influence Reading Achievement

Since reading is a very complex process, a number of different factors can impact upon a child's success. One of the more important factors is *emotional adjustment*. The beginning stages of emergent literacy require that a child possess a number of different personality characteristics. Success in emergent literacy usually requires that the child be curious, emotionally mature, responsible, independent, and able to follow simple directions. If a child does not possess one or even several of these characteristics, it does not necessarily follow that he/she will develop reading disabilities. However, normally a child should possess many of these personal characteristics to achieve reading success.

Most children enter school expecting to learn to read effectively if they indeed do not already know how to read and write as a result of the emergent literacy experiences to which they have been exposed at home. In addition, most students enter school with a sufficient degree of emotional adjustment to be able to learn to read and write up to the limits of their potential if they have effective, appropriate reading instruction and a good teacher-pupil relationship. Therefore, emotional maladjustment alone is not a very common cause of reading disability. However, it certainly can be a significant contributing factor as it was in the example of Amanda mentioned earlier in this chapter. However, a child often can become emotionally maladjusted if he/she does not learn to read as well as he/she should. Emotional maladjustment then occurs because learning to read is a very important developmental task for the vast majority of children. Those who do not learn to read effectively have failed this important developmental task and often develop emotional maladjustment and a low self-image.

Therefore, emotional maladjustment and reading disabilities often form a *reciprocal relationship* in which reading difficulties lead to slight emotional maladjustment. This maladjustment may lead to more severe reading disabilities, which in turn lead to a more severe emotional maladjustment.

In most cases, the emotional adjustment of a child improves greatly as his/her reading skills improve in an excellent diagnostic-prescriptive reading program with a good teacher-pupil relationship. Sometimes psychological or guidance counseling in conjunction with reading instruction will result in the optimum amount of reading improvement.

However, there are a few children who resist learning to read in school for various reasons. For example, they may make a conscious refusal to learn to read to punish their parents or as a result of too much parental pressure. Some children may want to remain so dependent on their parents that they may resist the "grown-up" task of learning to read. Then, too, a few children may be too distractible, hyperactive, or inattentive to make good reading progress.

In any case, disabled readers can display many different kinds of behaviors in school. Occasionally they can appear passive, withdrawn, and disinterested. However, some—like Rod in the example given earlier—are aggressive, hostile, and destructive. From my experience the latter type of behavior is the more common. As stated earlier, all types of emotional maladjustment usually improve with good reading instruction and good teacher-pupil rapport.

A Child's Self-Esteem Can Contribute to Reading Disabilities

There often may be significant relationships between a child's self-concept and his/her reading success. Students with a negative self-concept may have difficulty profiting from reading instruction up to the limits of their potential. However, a child's self-concept will improve along with his/her reading skills if the child is provided with excellent reading instruction. Negative self-esteem more often is a product of the child's reading disabilities rather than the cause. When you believe a child can make reading improvement, the child usually will make reading improvement—another example of the self-fulfilling prophecy.

Interests and Attitudes

A child's interest in reading and his/her attitudes toward reading activities can greatly influence success in reading. A child who is truly interested in a book's topic may well be able to read it even if it is on his/her frustration reading level. On the other hand, a child's lack of interest in a book certainly can result in a virtual refusal to attempt to read it. That is why it often is helpful for you to give some type of "interest inventory" so that the child's interest can be capitalized upon in selecting reading materials. Unfortunately, it often is difficult to find any type of reading materials that will really interest a truly reluctant reader.

A child's attitude toward reading and his/her motivation to read either for pleasure or information can also influence his/her degree of success in reading. For example, if a child comes from a home in which reading is not valued or he/she sees no relevance to what must be read, it may be difficult to motivate him/her to read. This is why it is so important to try to provide a child with materials that he/she considers to be relevant and meaningful. A significant lack of motivation perhaps can result in reading disabilities in extreme incidences.

The Relationships Among Reading Disability, Handwriting, and Arithmetic _____

It is interesting to briefly explore the relationships between reading problems, handwriting competence, and arithmetic ability. According to Harris and Sipay (1990, pages 356–358), there is a correlation of .05 to .08 between reading ability and spelling ability. This indicates that a good reader is likely to be a good speller. However, a child also can be a good reader and a poor speller (about 2 percent of the population), or a poor reader and a poor speller. Good readers are less likely to misspell phonetically regular words than phonetically irregular words. However, the misspellings of a number of disabled readers appear to be unrecognizable, but may be only phonetically inaccurate.

Poor handwriting occurs fairly often among disabled readers. Poor handwriting may be an expression of dislike for all types of reading activities, but also may be a sign of poor hand-eye coordination. Disabled readers often are below average in arithmetic also, although often not as far below average as in reading and spelling. It is not unusual for a learning handicapped child to have fairly good mathematical skills while having very poor reading and spelling skills.

The Significance of the Multiple Causation Theory of Reading Disabilities _____

Rarely is there a single cause of reading disabilities. Often there are a constellation of causes operating together that result in a child's reading difficulties. Reading is a complex process requiring visual and auditory perception abilities, word identification ability, comprehension ability, adequate prior knowledge and schema, and effective metacognition (monitoring of reading comprehension). Therefore, it is logical that there often are several causes for a case of reading disability.

As one example, a child may not have good emergent literacy skills before being exposed to a formal beginning reader program. Therefore, he/she may not experience success in beginning reading, and a poor self-image and emotional maladjustment may result causing further difficulties in reading. This also can happen when a child does not learn to read effectively because of inappropriate reading instruction. For example, a visual defect such as uncorrected myopia may cause reading problems that, in turn, can lead to emotional maladjustment. Therefore, you can see that it is often difficult to determine a single cause for a child's reading problems.

It is important for you to attempt to determine the causes of a disabled reader's reading difficulties. However, it is necessary for you to treat the symptoms of the reading disabilities while you try to discover the causes for the problems. You can formulate tentative hypotheses or guesses as to why the child has the disability, which later can be confirmed or disconfirmed. In addition, disabled readers can give invaluable help themselves in determining why they have the reading disability. Although certainly this is true with intermediate-grade students, it also is possible with primary-grade children.

Some of the Criteria for Determining Reading Disability _____

When selecting children for inclusion in a remedial or corrective reading program, it is important to determine whether a student is *underachieving* (perhaps reading at grade level but less than his/her intellectual ability would allow), a *disabled reader* (reading below his/her potential level and grade level), or a *slow learner* (reading as well as could be expected in the light of his/her intellectual potential).

Normally you must consider the child's chronological age, intelligence or mental age, present reading ability, and possibly listening comprehension ability in determining whether or not he/she is reading up to the limits of his/her potential. Although it may not always be necessary to attempt to be precise in determining potential for reading improvement, at times it is important to determine this with as much precision as possible so that children can be admitted to special reading programs in the light of their true reading needs and potential for reading improvement.

In any case, you undoubtedly will find the entire issue of determining potential for reading improvement very complex and possibly time consuming. As an example, Harris and Sipay (1990) devote nineteen pages (162–180) of their book to this topic, with much of the material being quite complicated.

Carol Winkley has suggested a very simple way to determine reading expectancy. In "Building Staff Competence in Identifying Underachievers" (*The Underachiever in Reading*, H. A. Robinson, ed., Supplementary Educational Monograph No. 92, University of Chicago Press, 1962, pp. 155–162), she recommends using stanine scores (1–9) from reading and intelligence tests. The score from the intelligence test must be at least two stanines higher than that of the reading test in order to indicate that the child has a reading disability. This simple means may be acceptable for the teacher's own use but probably is not precise enough for selecting students for inclusion in special reading programs.

The Bond and Tinker readinq expectancy formula has often been used in the past (1989, pages 41–42). It is said to function fairly accurately with students who are of average intelligence, but sets too-high expectations for slow-learning students and too-low expectations for bright children. In any case, here is the Bond and Tinker formula:

$$\text{Reading Expectancy } (RE) = \frac{YRI \times IQ}{100}$$

In this formula, *YRI* means years of reading information, *IQ* is intelligence quotient, and 100 is a constant. For example, an eight-year-old student whose IQ is 90 and who had received reading instruction for two years, by the end of second grade would have an RE of 2.8.

$$2.8 = \frac{2 \times 90}{100} + 1$$

Harris and Sipay (1990) explain in their book what appears to be a very useful procedure for identifying reading disabilities. It uses the concepts of reading expectancy age, reading expectancy quotient, and reading quotient. In this formula *reading expectancy age* is an estimate of the reading age and, therefore, the level of reading achievement that a student should be able to attain. This formula gives priority to the importance of intelligence but also considers other age-related characteristics. Here is the formula:

$$\text{Reading Expectancy Age (R Exp A)} = \frac{2\text{MA} + \text{CA}}{3}$$

A reading expectancy quotient expresses how a pupil's actual level of reading compares with his/her expected reading level. It uses the reading age (add the grade equivalent score on a reading test and 5.2—for example, 3.2 + 5.2 = 8.4) and the reading expectancy age. The number *5.2* is used because there normally is a regular difference of 5.2 years between chronological age and grade equivalent, since the typical child in American public schools enters first grade at 6.2 and is promoted regularly. In any case, here is this formula:

$$\text{Reading Expectancy Quotient (R Exp Q)} = \frac{\text{RA}}{\text{R Exp A} \times 100}$$

Reading expectancy quotients that range between 90 and 110 are considered to be normal while those below 90 are considered to be examples of reading disability or underachievement—the farther below 90, the greater the disability or underachievement. If the R Exp Q is above 110 it indicates reading above expectancy. To help determine both reading expectancy age and reading expectancy quotient, two tables from the Harris and Sipay book are given here. The "Reading Expectancy Age Table" shows selected combinations of chronological age and intelligence quotients. You must interpolate as needed. The "Reading Expectancy Quotients Table" uses reading age and reading expectancy to determine the quotients, and those printed in bold type fall within the normal range.

Reading Expectancy Ages for Selected Combinations of Chronological Age and Intelligence Quotient

IQ	CHRONOLOGICAL AGE												
	7.2	7.7	8.2	8.7	9.2	9.7	10.2	10.7	11.2	11.7	12.2	12.7	13.2
140	9.1	9.6	10.3	10.9	11.6	12.1	12.9	13.4	14.1	14.7	15.4	15.9	16.7
135	8.8	9.4	10.1	10.6	11.3	11.8	12.5	13.1	13.8	14.3	15.0	15.5	16.2
130	8.6	9.1	9.8	10.3	11.0	11.5	12.2	12.7	13.4	13.9	14.6	15.1	15.8
125	8.4	8.8	9.5	10.0	10.7	11.2	11.9	12.3	13.0	13.5	14.2	14.7	15.4
120	8.1	8.6	9.3	9.7	10.4	10.9	11.5	12.0	12.7	13.1	13.8	14.3	14.9
115	7.9	8.3	9.0	9.4	10.1	10.5	11.2	11.7	12.3	12.7	13.4	13.8	14.5
110	7.6	8.1	8.7	9.2	9.8	10.2	10.9	11.3	11.9	12.4	13.0	13.4	14.0
105	7.4	7.9	8.4	8.9	9.5	9.9	10.5	11.0	11.5	12.0	12.6	13.0	13.6
100	7.2	7.7	8.2	8.7	9.2	9.7	10.2	10.7	11.2	11.7	12.2	12.7	13.2
95	6.9	7.4	7.9	8.3	8.9	9.3	9.7	10.4	10.8	11.3	11.8	12.2	12.7
90	6.7	7.1	7.6	8.0	8.6	8.9	9.5	9.9	10.4	10.8	11.4	11.7	12.3
85	6.4	6.8	7.4	7.7	8.2	8.6	9.1	9.5	10.0	10.4	10.9	11.3	11.8
80	6.2	6.6	7.1	7.4	7.9	8.3	8.8	9.2	9.7	10.0	10.5	10.9	11.4
75	6.0	6.3	6.8	7.2	7.6	8.0	8.5	8.8	9.3	9.7	10.1	10.5	11.0
70	5.7	6.1	6.5	6.9	7.3	7.7	8.1	8.5	8.9	9.3	9.7	10.1	10.5
65	5.5	5.9	6.3	6.6	7.0	7.3	7.8	8.1	8.6	8.9	9.3	9.6	10.1
60	5.3	5.6	6.0	6.3	6.7	7.0	7.5	7.8	8.2	8.5	8.9	9.2	9.8

Note: Any expectancy age in the table can be changed into an expectancy grade equivalent by subtracting 5.2 years.

From *How to Increase Reading Ability: A Guide to Developmental and Remedial Methods* by Albert J. Harris and Edward R. Sipay. Copyright © 1990 by Longman Publishing Group. Used with permission.

Reading Expectancy Quotients for Selected Combinations of Reading Expectancy Age and Reading Age

	READING EXPECTANCY AGE											
Reading Age	6.7	7.2	7.7	8.2	8.7	9.2	9.7	10.2	10.7	11.2	11.7	12.2
6.2	92	86	80	75	71	67	63	60	57	55	52	50
6.7	100	93	87	81	77	72	69	65	62	59	57	54
7.2	107	100	93	87	82	78	74	70	67	64	61	59
7.7	114	106	100	93	88	83	79	75	71	68	65	63
8.2	122	113	106	100	94	89	84	80	76	73	70	67
8.7	129	120	112	106	100	94	90	85	81	78	74	71
9.2	137	128	119	112	106	100	95	90	86	82	79	75
9.7	145	135	126	118	111	105	100	95	91	87	83	80
10.2	152	142	132	124	117	111	105	100	95	91	87	84
10.7	160	149	139	130	123	116	110	105	100	96	91	88
11.2	167	156	145	137	129	122	115	110	105	100	96	92
11.7	175	163	152	143	134	127	121	115	109	104	100	96
12.2	182	169	158	149	140	133	128	120	114	109	104	100

From *How to Increase Reading Ability: A Guide to Developmental and Remedial Methods* by Albert J. Harris and Edward R. Sipay. Copyright © 1990 by Longman Publishing Group. Used with permission.

2

General Guidelines and Materials for Diagnosing Reading Disabilities

Many people who are not in the field of education believe that the standardized tests given each school year are an accurate way of determining a student's reading progress. They believe that these test scores provide definitive information about a student's reading achievement and, therefore, enable the teacher to place that child into a particular reading group or class. As any experienced reading teacher knows, a standardized test score may be in error in a number of different ways and *never should be thought of as an infallible indicator of a student's true reading ability or status.* Instead, these teachers understand that diagnosis or assessment of reading progress should be a continuous, daily process which occurs in classrooms and points the way toward more effective diagnostic-prescriptive reading instruction. Indeed, if such assessments would take place regularly in elementary and special classrooms, many cases of reading disability could be prevented or at least minimized. Diagnosis should take the form of both informal and standardized devices.

The Differences Between Reading Assessment and Reading Diagnosis

At the beginning, it undoubtedly is important to define the terms *assessment* and *diagnosis* as they normally are used by reading specialists today. *Assessment* can be defined as gathering information to meet the particular reading needs of a child. *Diagnosis or testing* can be defined as one particular method for obtaining information about a child. It seems obvious that assessment is considerably more informal than diagnosis or testing when the terms are defined this way.

Assessment should always be considered an essential part of instruction and therefore should occur continuously. Often, it is more useful in determining a child's reading strengths and weaknesses than standardized diagnosis especially if it is done by an experienced reading teacher. Assessment is usually recommended by contemporary reading specialists more frequently than diagnosis. Informal, process-oriented assessment of reading competencies *may be* more commonly used in the future than standardized tests if administrators, school-board members, and parents will accept it. However, a number of people place too much faith in standardized test scores, which correspondingly discourages the use of informal teacher assessment.

Such informal assessment should be done on an individual or small-group basis. It should be the basis for subsequent diagnostic-prescriptive teaching of reading for an individual child or a small group of children.

On the other hand, testing or diagnosis generally requires the use of some type of standardized device which is given to a group of children or to an individual child: standardized survey reading/achievement tests, basal reader tests, individual or group diagnostic reading tests, process-oriented measures of reading comprehension, or criterion-referenced tests. The standardized testing of reading has been stressed in the past and continues to receive emphasis primarily because of the accountability movement in education. As stated earlier, assessment may receive more well-deserved emphasis in the future if the accountability movement will allow for this.

An Emergent Literacy Behavioral Checklist

This is a checklist that kindergarten and first grade teachers can use in assessing a child's competence in the most important emergent literacy skills. It should be equally useful with both "average" and learning-handicapped children. You can duplicate and use it in its present form or modify it, if necessary, to suit your particular needs.

EMERGENT LITERACY BEHAVIORAL CHECKLIST
(For Children of All Abilities, Including Learning-Handicapped Children)

Name_____ Grade_____ Teacher_____ Date_____

A. Understanding the Terms Used in Reading (Concepts about Print)

1. Is able to locate the title of a book ☐
2. Is able to locate the author of a book ☐
3. Is able to locate the front of a book ☐
4. Understands the concept of a *letter* ☐
5. Understands the concept of a *word* ☐
6. Understands what a *period* and a *comma* are ☐

B. Visual Discrimination and Perception

1. Understands *left-to-right progression* ☐
2. Is able to discriminate between letters such as *a* and *e* ☐
3. Is able to discriminate between letters such as *g* and *q* (reversals) ☐
4. Is able to discriminate between letters such as *m* and *w* (inversions) ☐
5. Is able to discriminate between such non-look-alike words as *run* and *jump* ☐
6. Is able to discriminate between such look-alike words as *stop* and *spot* ☐
7. Is able to complete a jigsaw puzzle of about fifteen pieces ☐
8. Is able to recognize word boundaries (white spaces between words) ☐
9. Is able to keep his/her eyes on the line ☐
10. Is able to draw an acceptable person with a pencil ☐

C. Auditory Discrimination

1. Is able to rhyme words ☐
2. Is able to discriminate between the various consonant sounds ☐
3. Is able to discriminate between the different long vowel sounds ☐
4. Is able to discriminate between the different short vowel sounds ☐

D. Letter-Name Knowledge

1. Is able to identify most or all of the lower-case letter names in isolation ☐
2. Is able to identify most or all of the lower-case letter names in context ☐
3. Is able to identify most or all of the upper-case letter names in isolation ☐
4. Is able to identify most or all of the upper-case letter names in context ☐
5. Is able to give the sounds of most or all of the consonants ☐

6. Is able to give the sounds of most or all of the long vowels (*a, e, i, o, u*) ☐

7. Is able to give the sounds of most or all of the short vowels (*a, e, i, o, u*) ☐

E. Knowledge of Environmental Print (Common Sight Words)

1. Is able to recognize by sight about five to seven words that are commonly found in the daily environment (STOP, McDonalds, Crest®, Wal-Mart, K-Mart, Cheerios®, Alpha-Bits®, etc.) ☐

2. Is able to recognize his/her own first name ☐

3. Is able to recognize by sight a word the day after it was presented ☐

F. Writing Activities

1. Uses scribbling or letter strings (random letters) to indicate that he/she understands the purpose of writing ☐

2. Is able to use inventive spelling on appropriate occasions which require it (writing stories, writing letters or notes, writing cards, etc.) ☐

3. Is able to print his/her own first name correctly ☐

4. Is able to copy sight words correctly that he/she can recognize ☐

G. Word Understanding and Listening Comprehension

1. Is able to select the correct meaning for words such as *nest, monster, insect,* or *dinosaur* ☐

2. Is able to understand such terms as *over, under, top,* and *bottom* ☐

3. Is able to pick out a word that does *not* go with a group of four words (classify or categorize as chair, table, *computer*, sofa) ☐

4. Is able to answer questions at various levels (explicit—factual and implicit—interpretive and critical) after listening to a picture storybook or a tradebook ☐

5. Is able to retell a picture storybook or a tradebook after listening to it being read ☐

H. Conceptual Ability

1. Has a fairly good imagination (average to that of his/her peers) ☐

2. Seems to be as "creative" as the other members of his/her group ☐

I. Oral Language Usage

1. Is able to speak in complete sentences ☐

2. Is able to speak in compound or complex sentences ☐

3. Uses interesting, precise vocabulary ☐

4. Seems to enjoy participating in such activities as sharing time, conversation, role-playing, and dramatic play ☐

J. Laterality

1. Is able to differentiate between his/her right and left hands ☐
2. Is able to differentiate between his/her right and left feet ☐

K. Motor Coordination

1. Is able to walk forward and backward on a balance beam ☐
2. Is able to catch a large ball with ease ☐
3. Seems generally well coordinated when playing games ☐
4. Is able to run, jump, skip, and gallop fairly well ☐
5. Is able to use manipulative materials such as scissors, paste (glue), crayons, markers, and paint brushes fairly effectively ☐
6. Does not demonstrate perseveration (giving the same response again and again even if incorrect) ☐
7. Has scribbling or handwriting that appears about average with his/her peers ☐
8. Is able to draw a fairly accurate circle, square, rectangle, and diamond (however, the diamond is very difficult for most children at this level) ☐

L. Memory Ability

1. Is able to remember what was just seen ☐
2. Is able to remember what was just heard ☐
3. Is able to remember a letter name, letter sound, or sight word one or several days after it was presented ☐
4. Is able to remember the primary (basic) colors ☐

M. Social-Emotional Adjustment

1. Appears to be appropriately independent, self-reliant, and mature for his/her age ☐
2. Appears to have a positive self-image ☐
3. Is able to follow simple directions ☐
4. Is able to concentrate on something that interests him/her for at least 10 to 15 minutes ☐
5. Is able to work and play well with other children ☐
6. Is able to sit still as well as most of the other children in the group ☐
7. Has adequate frustration toleration ☐
8. Does not appear excessively fidgety or distractible ☐
9. Appears fairly well organized ☐

A Primary-Grade Checklist for Observing Reading Competencies and Weaknesses

Here is a ready-to-duplicate checklist you can use to aid observation of a child's reading strengths and weaknesses in the various reading skills, including word identification skills, comprehension skills, beginning study skills, and oral and silent reading fluency. Equally useful with both "average" and learning-handicapped children, you can reproduce this checklist in its present form or modify it in any way necessary to suit your particular students.

An Intermediate-Grade Checklist for Observing Reading Competencies and Weaknesses

Here is a ready-to-use checklist for you to use as an aid in the observation of intermediate-grade children's reading strengths and weaknesses in the various reading skills, including word-identification techniques, comprehension skills, study skills, oral reading fluency, and silent reading ability. This checklist is equally applicable to both "average" and learning-handicapped children.

You can duplicate this checklist in its present form or modify it to suit your particular situation.

PRIMARY-GRADE CHECKLIST FOR TEACHER OBSERVATION OF A CHILD'S READING SKILLS
(For Children of All Abilities Including Learning-Handicapped Children)

Name_____ Grade_____ Teacher_____ Date_____

I. Word Identification Techniques

A. Sight Word Recognition

1. Is able to recognize most or all of the words on any basic sight-word list such as the *Dolch Basic Sight Word List, Fry's Instant Words,* or *Hillerich's 240 Starter Words* ☐

2. Seems to be able to remember a sight word the day after or several days after it was presented ☐

3. While reading orally or silently seems to recognize most of the words encountered on an automatic basis ☐

4. Is able to effectively learn hard-to-retain sight words by using some type of tracing strategy such as felt letters, sandpaper letters, a sand tray, a salt tray, or by the use of instant pudding or shaving cream ☐

B. Phonic (Graphophonic) Analysis

1. Is able to provide the sounds of all the consonants and is able to provide a word that begins with each of them ☐

2. Is able to provide a word that begins with each of the common consonant sounds ☐

3. Is able to recognize and provide a word containing the common consonant digraphs such as *voiced th, voiceless th, sh, ch, ph,* and *wh* ☐

4. Is able to recognize all of the common phonograms such as *−ack, −all, −ick, −ell, −ill, −in, −en,* etc. ☐

5. Is able to provide the long vowel sounds for *a, e, i, o, u* ☐

6. Is able to provide the short vowel sounds for *a, e, i, o, u* ☐

7. Understands the use of r-controlled vowels ☐

8. Is able to give a word beginning with the soft and hard sounds of *c* ☐

9. Is able to give a word beginning with the soft and hard sounds of *g* ☐

10. Understands the function of the final *e* marker ☐

11. Understands that *k* is silent in *kn,* that *w* is silent in *wr,* and that *g* is silent in *gn* ☐

12. Is able to give a word containing a diphthong such as *oi, oy, ou,* and *ow* ☐

© 1993 by The Center for Applied Research in Education

13. Understands and is able to apply these phonic generalizations:

   a. When there are two vowels found side by side, the long sound of the first vowel is usually heard, while the second one is usually not heard ☐

   b. When a vowel is found in the middle of a one-syllable word that ends with a consonant, the vowel is usually short ☐

   c. When the same two consonants are found side by side, only one consonant is heard ☐

   d. When the only vowel letter is found at the end of the word, the letter usually stands for the long sound ☐

   e. When a word contains two vowels, one of which is *final e*, the first vowel is long and the *final e* is silent ☐

14. Is able to blend a series of sounds into a recognizable word (skill in auditory blending—especially important to success in a program that stresses synthetic phonic analysis) ☐

15. Is able to filter out extraneous noise—is fairly competent in the auditory channel (modality) ☐

C. Structural (Morphemic) Analysis

1. Is able to add the common suffixes such as *–s, –es, –ed, –ing, –ly, –y, –ful, –er, –en, –ness* and *–less* ☐

2. Understands the basic function of prefixes and can add such prefixes as *un–, in–, re–,* and *dis–* to base words ☐

3. Is able to recognize some less common contractions by sight such as *we'll, you'll, I've, shouldn't, couldn't, wouldn't, o'clock, they've, they'll,* and *they're* ☐

4. Is able to understand the use of the possessive such as *my sister's dress* ☐

5. Is able to divide words of two or three syllables correctly ☐

6. Is able to understand and apply the principle of the *final silent e* while adding a suffix to the base word ☐

7. Is able to understand and apply the principle of *doubling the final consonant* in a short word with one vowel before adding the suffix ☐

8. Is able to understand and can apply the principle of changing *y* to *i* before adding the suffix *–es* ☐

9. Usually uses structural analysis skills before applying phonic analysis skills in decoding an unknown word when applicable ☐

D. Contextual (Semantic) Analysis

1. Usually substitutes words for unknown words that make sense in sentence context and that are grammatically correct while reading aloud ☐

2. Usually can pronounce words correctly in context that might not be pronounced accurately in isolated word lists ☐

3. Is able to complete about 80 percent or more of the deleted words with the correct word or synonym from a traditional cloze exercise at the second-grade or third-grade reading level ☐

4. Is able to complete a contextual analysis exercise correctly at the second-grade or third-grade reading level in a written form such as the following:

   The girl who lived in the woods saw a _____

   > money
   > porcupine
   > pretty

   walking down the road one day. ☐

5. Understands the use of figurative language at a rudimentary level (personification and figures of speech) ☐

II. Comprehension Skills

A. *Explicit (Literal or Factual) Comprehension*

1. Is able to answer explicit (literal, recall, or factual) comprehension questions from material at about the second-grade or third-grade reading level that the child has read for himself/herself ☐

2. Is able to retell a story written at about the second-grade or third-grade reading level in approximately the correct sequence ☐

3. Is able to orally state the main idea of a story or a picture storybook ☐

4. Does better with explicit comprehension than with implicit comprehension ☐

5. Is able to carry out written directions of about three to five steps in about the correct order ☐

6. Is able to locate the significant details in a story or picture storybook ☐

7. Is able to locate the directly stated main idea in a paragraph at the second-grade or third-grade reading level if it is placed in the topic sentence of that paragraph ☐

B. *Implicit (Interpretive) Comprehension*

1. Is able to answer implicit (interpretive) comprehension questions at about the second-grade or third-grade reading level (questions that call for interpreting, inferring, drawing conclusions and generalizations, predicting outcomes, and summarizing) ☐

2. Is able to predict story content effectively before reading a story and then confirm or disconfirm the predictions during and after reading ☐

3. Is able to orally or in writing summarize a story or a picture storybook in one or two sentences ☐

4. Is able to understand and apply very simple cause-effect relationships ☐

5. Is able to understand and orally state an author's purpose for writing a story ☐

6. Is equally competent in implicit comprehension and explicit comprehension ☐

C. Critical (Implicit) Comprehension

1. Is able to answer questions that call for critical or evaluative responses from material at about the second-grade or third-grade reading level ☐

2. Is able to distinguish between real and make-believe (fact or fantasy) with some degree of competence ☐

3. Is able to understand and recognize the feelings, actions, and motives of story characters with some degree of competence ☐

D. Creative (Script or Schema-Implicit) Comprehension

1. Is able to relate what he/she reads or has read to himself/herself in some way that contributes to his/her improvement ☐

2. Is able to follow up reading in a problem-solving manner such as by cooking or baking activities, art activities, construction activities, dramatic play, creative dramatics, rhythm activities, or creative writing of prose or poetry ☐

III. Study Skills

1. Is able to use a table of contents at the second-grade or third-grade reading level ☐

2. Is able to use the page numbers in a book to locate the required page ☐

3. Is able to understand and interpret pictures and simple maps ☐

4. Is able to use these elements of a simplified dictionary: guide words, entry words, and definitions; at this reading level, these reading skills should be mastered at a fairly simple level ☐

IV. Oral Reading

1. Seems to enjoy reading orally ☐
2. Uses good expression while reading orally ☐
3. Is able to stay on the correct line while reading orally ☐
4. Does not reread a line or skip a line while reading orally ☐
5. Is able to read in phrases or groups of words fairly well instead of reading in a word-by-word manner ☐
6. Observes punctuation marks such as periods and commas while reading orally ☐
7. Does not usually lose his/her place while reading orally ☐
8. Comprehends fairly well what he/she has read orally ☐
9. Appears to have no significant speech disorders while reading orally ☐

V. Silent Reading

1. Seems to enjoy reading as evidenced by reactions during the reading of a story or a picture storybook ☐
2. Uses word identification skills well to decode unknown words while reading silently ☐
3. Comprehends material that is read silently ☐
4. Uses correct posture and book position while reading silently ☐
5. Reads somewhat more rapidly silently than orally ☐
6. Usually avoids lip movements, subvocalization, finger pointing, and head movements while reading silently ☐

INTERMEDIATE-GRADE CHECKLIST FOR TEACHER OBSERVATION OF A CHILD'S READING SKILLS
(For Children of All Abilities Including Learning-Handicapped Children)

Name_____ Grade_____ Teacher_____ Date_____

I. Word Identification Techniques

A. *Sight Word Recognition*

1. Is able to recognize all of the words on any basic sight-word list ☐

2. Is able to recognize all of the words on Harris-Jacobsen Core List (a sight-word list encompassing the sixth-grade reading level) or on any other comprehensive sight-word list ☐

3. Seems to be able to remember a sight word the day after or several days after it was presented ☐

4. While reading orally or silently seems to be able to recognize most of the words encountered on an automatic basis ☐

5. Seems to be able to recognize the majority of the words in content textbooks, such as social studies and science, on an automatic basis ☐

6. If necessary, primarily for learning-handicapped or disabled readers: Is able to effectively learn hard-to-retain sight words by some type of tracing strategy such as the Fernald Tracing Method ☐

B. *Phonic (Graphophonic) Analysis*

1. Is able to effectively use all of the consonant elements that were presented and reinforced in the primary grades to decode unknown words ☐

2. Is able to use all of the vowel elements that were presented and reinforced in the primary grades to decode unknown words ☐

3. Is able to blend a series of sounds into a recognizable word (skill in auditory blending) ☐

4. Seems to be competent in the use of the auditory channel (modality) ☐

5. Is able to determine when it is appropriate to use phonic analysis as the most effective word-identification technique ☐

6. Understands and can effectively apply the major phonic analysis generalizations that were presented in the primary grades ☐

7. Seems to be equally competent in using phonic analysis in decoding unknown words both in narrative and in content reading ☐

C. Structural (Morphemic) Analysis

1. Is able to add all of the suffixes to base words that were presented in the primary grades ☐

2. Is able to add suffixes such as these to base words: *–less, –ible, –able, –ment,* and *–ish* ☐

3. Is able to add all of the prefixes to base words that were presented in the primary grades ☐

4. Is able to add prefixes such as these to base words: *sub–, under–, semi–, dis–, ante–,* and *anti–* ☐

5. Is able to correctly divide multisyllabic words into syllables ☐

6. Is able to use primary, secondary, and tertiary accents (stresses) ☐

7. Is able to understand and use the principles of adding suffixes with a spelling change that were presented in the primary grades ☐

8. Is able to understand and use the important structural analysis generalizations that were presented in the primary grades ☐

9. Is able to understand and can use these important accent generalizations:

   a. In inflected or derived forms of words, the primary accent normally falls on or within the root word ☐

   b. The primary accent usually occurs on one of the first two syllables in words of one or more syllables ☐

10. Can use the meaning of prefixes, suffixes, or word roots to determine the approximate meaning of unknown vocabulary found in content area reading ☐

11. Usually uses structural analysis before using phonic analysis in decoding unknown words ☐

D. Contextual (Semantic) Analysis and Vocabulary Knowledge

1. Usually substitutes words for unknown words that are semantically and syntactically correct while reading orally or silently ☐

2. Usually is able to pronounce words correctly in context that might not be pronounced correctly in isolation ☐

3. Is able to complete about 70 percent to 80 percent of the omitted words correctly or with a synonym from a cloze exercise constructed on the fourth-, fifth-, or sixth-grade reading level ☐

4. Understands such figurative language as *idioms, similes,* and *metaphors* ☐

5. Understands the use of *synonyms, antonyms,* and *homonyms* ☐

6. Understands the use of *homophones, homographs,* and *onomatopoeic* words ☐

II. Comprehension Skills

A. *Explicit (Literal or Factual) Comprehension*

1. Is able to answer explicit (literal, recall, or factual) comprehension questions about narrative or content material at the intermediate-grade reading level that the child has read for himself/herself ☐

2. Is able to retell a story written at about the fourth-, fifth-, or sixth-grade reading level ☐

3. Is able to locate the directly stated main idea and/or topic sentence in a paragraph ☐

4. Is able to state orally the main idea of a basal reader story, a content textbook selection, or a tradebook ☐

5. Is able to state the main idea of a basal reader story, a content textbook selection, or a tradebook in written form ☐

6. Is able to effectively read and carry out directions at the appropriate reading level ☐

7. Is able to locate irrelevant or unimportant details in content material ☐

8. Understands the meaning of specialized vocabulary terms in the content areas of social studies, science, and mathematics ☐

B. *Implicit (Interpretive) Comprehension*

1. Is able to answer implicit (interpretive) comprehension questions (questions that call for interpreting, inferring, drawing conclusions and generalizations, predicting outcomes, and summarizing) about narrative or content material at the intermediate-grade reading level that he/she has read for himself/herself ☐

2. Is able to locate the implied main idea in a paragraph ☐

3. Is able to apply cause-effect and/or comparison-contrast relationships ☐

4. Is able to summarize narrative or content material in several sentences or in a written paragraph ☐

5. Is able to determine an author's purpose for writing a narrative or content selection ☐

6. Is able to test in writing the hypotheses about a selection that were made before reading it ☐

7. Does equally well with implicit comprehension and explicit comprehension ☐

C. *Implicit (Critical) Comprehension*

1. Is able to answer questions that call for critical or evaluative responses from narrative or content material at the intermediate-grade reading level that he/she has read for himself/herself ☐

2. Is able to distinguish between fact and opinion ☐

3. Is able to compare material from several different sources such as a tradebook and a content textbook ☐

4. Is able to determine an author's biases in a writing selection of any kind ☐

5. Is able to recognize the common propaganda techniques, such as testimonials and the bandwagon effect ☐

6. Is able to evaluate the actions of individuals or groups ☐

7. Is able to critically read parts of the newspaper such as the editorials, letters to the editor, and advertisements ☐

8. Is able to estimate the answer to a verbal problem in arithmetic ☐

9. Does equally well with the elements of implicit comprehension and explicit comprehension ☐

D. Creative (Script or Schema-Implicit) Comprehension

1. Is able to effectively relate what was read to his/her own life in some way that contributes to his/her welfare ☐

2. Is able to follow up his/her reading in a problem-solving way such as by creative writing of prose or poetry, storytelling, art activities, construction activities, rhythm activities, dramatic activities, and pantomiming ☐

3. Does equally well with these elements of implicit comprehension as with explicit comprehension ☐

III. Study Skills

1. Is able to use all the elements of a dictionary at the appropriate reading level to locate the pronunciation or meaning of unknown words which are met in narrative or content reading (alphabetical sequence, guide words, diacritical marking, and most important, choosing the correct definition for use in the actual reading situation) ☐

2. Is able to use a thesaurus effectively ☐

3. Is able to use such textbook aids as the table of contents, index, glossary, appendices, subheadings, and footnotes ☐

4. Is able to interpret various kinds of maps, charts, diagrams, pictures, tables, and schedules ☐

5. Is able to use appropriate reference books in the content areas of social studies and science ☐

6. Is able to use the library card catalog at least to some extent ☐

7. Is able to use such parts of an encyclopedia as the key words, volume numbers, guide words, entry words, and cross-references ☐

8. Is able to outline a content textbook chapter using main headings and subordinate headings ☐

9. Is able to take acceptable notes from a content textbook at the appropriate reading level ☐

10. Is a *flexible reader* (able to adjust reading rate to satisfy his/her purpose for reading and the difficulty of the reading material) ☐

11. Is able to *skim* the reading material to gain an overall impression ☐

12. Is able to *scan* the reading material to locate a specific fact, name, or date ☐

IV. Oral Reading

1. Seems to enjoy reading aloud before an audience ☐
2. Does not seem to be tense while reading aloud ☐
3. Uses good expression while reading aloud ☐
4. Observes punctuation marks while reading aloud ☐
5. Reads aloud in thought units or groups of words ☐
6. Is able to comprehend what he/she has read aloud ☐
7. Usually avoids inhibiting factors such as head movement and fingerpointing while reading aloud ☐

V. Silent Reading

1. Seems to enjoy reading silently as evidenced from reactions while reading silently ☐

2. Uses all of the word-identification techniques (sight-word recognition, phonic analysis, structural analysis, and contextual analysis) independently to decode unknown words met in narrative and content reading ☐

3. Seems to effectively comprehend material that is read silently ☐

4. Adjusts reading rate to the reading material (demonstrates reading flexibility) ☐

5. Reads silently about twice as rapidly as orally ☐

6. Is able to select appropriate reading material for recreational reading ☐

7. Chooses to read for pleasure as a recreational activity at least fairly often ☐

8. Demonstrates correct posture and book position while reading silently ☐

9. Avoids inhibiting factors while reading silently such as lip movements, subvocalization, head movement, and fingerpointing ☐

10. Appears to be a more competent silent reader than oral reader ☐

Additional Ways of Assessing (Diagnosing) Reading Disabilities _____

As stated earlier, for many reasons informal assessment or diagnosis of reading strengths and weaknesses is more practical and useful than standardized assessment. However, since it appears less "scientific" and precise to some administrators and to a number of parents and school board members, it is not as commonly used as it should be. However, some of the techniques described and illustrated in this part of the chapter may make the use of informal assessment devices more useful for many classroom reading teachers and learning disability teachers.

Portfolio Assessments and Work Samples

It is extremely important to keep examples of a child's work over a time period for a number of reasons: (1) these work samples show the child in a concrete manner the type and quantity of his/her reading improvement; and (2) such work samples can be extremely useful during parent-teacher conferences to illustrate a child's specific progress or lack of mastery in certain reading skill areas.

It is extremely important for all disabled readers, and especially for learning-handicapped students, to see their progress in a concrete, meaningful manner. Therefore, portfolio assessment and work samples are usually quite effective for this type of child.

Examples of the child's work can be included in what is called *portfolio assessment*. Briefly, this means that the child's work is placed into a labeled folder or notebook and then kept and added to over a time period. Although portfolio assessment may contain a number of different types of child's work, here are some examples of the work which could be included:

- An observational checklist that the teacher has completed for a child (see the previous section). This checklist can be used in total or in part later on to illustrate the child's mastery of some of the reading skills in which competence had not been attained at the earlier observation.
- Tape-recorded oral reading protocols (explained in detail in the next section).
- Tape-recorded oral reading protocols that are analyzed by *miscue analysis* (illustrated later in this section). This analysis may show the child's reading strengths in a concrete manner.
- Graphs of progress that show concretely a child's progress in a specific area of reading attainment such as the following:

  —mastery of a word on a sight-word list such as the *Dolch Basic Sight Word List*

  —mastery of a certain sequence of phonic principles

  —completion of a certain level of basal reader, basal reader workbook, or phonic workbook

  —completion of a certain number of books or pages of books read

This "graph of progress" was constructed for a third-grade severely disabled reader who knew virtually no sight words at third-grade entrance.

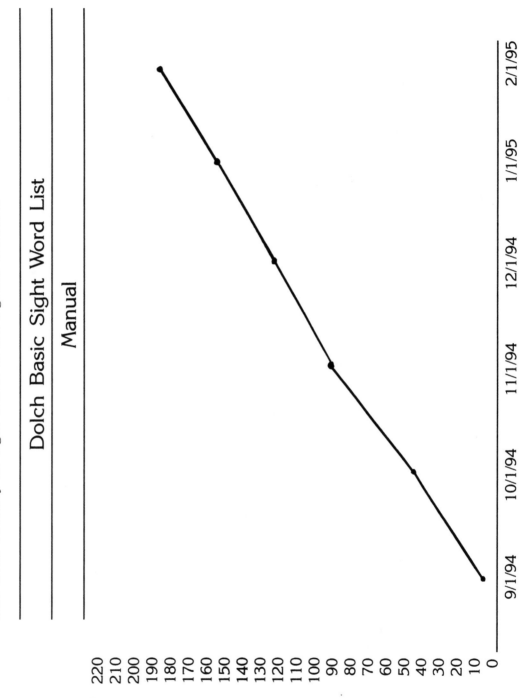

Dolch Basic Sight Word List

Manual

Tape-Recorded Oral Reading Protocols

Tape-recorded oral reading protocols can be extremely useful in both corrective and remedial reading programs. Their most common purpose is to simply show a child and his/her parents reading progress over time in a very concrete, meaningful way. They are also very easy to implement, for example:

• Have the child read a passage orally while you record it on cassette tape. A primary-grade child can easily learn to tape record his/her own reading, which then saves the teacher time. After a time period, have the child record the same oral passage again and have him/her compare the two performances. Tape-recorded oral reading protocols can be used on a regular basis throughout the school year to provide students with a concrete record of their actual reading progress during that time.

• As an alternative, the child can read aloud along with a commercial or teacher-prepared tape and then replay it, noting his/her errors using some very simple coding system he/she has learned. Later, the child can read the same material again noting if he/she has made fewer errors.

We have often used tape-recorded oral reading protocols very successfully in tutoring sessions of various kinds. However, we have found that teacher-prepared tapes are normally more effective than are commercial tapes since the child usually reads more slowly than the commercial reader. The teacher-prepared tapes provide the child with greater feelings of success.

Oral Reading Miscue Analysis

The concept of oral reading miscue analysis is mainly credited to the work of Kenneth and Yetta Goodman of the University of Arizona, and to some of their associates.

Miscue analysis is based upon the study of psycholinguistics. Stated simply, this theory maintains that deviations from the printed text are not truly *errors* but instead are *miscues*. They normally are classified into some variation of the following:

• *graphophonic (graphonic or graphic) miscues*—those deviations in which there is a graphic change in the deviation (the substitution of *talk* for *take*)

• *semantic miscues*—those deviations in which there is a meaning change in the deviation (the substitution of *house* for *horse*)

• *syntactic miscues*—those deviations in which there is a substitution in the grammatical structure of the sentence (turning a question into a statement)

Miscue analysis also maintains that some deviations from print are more important than others. Those miscues are considered to be the most significant if they interfere with comprehension or change the meaning of the material greatly. On the other hand, some deviations do not alter the meaning of the material very much. I call the former type of miscues *major oral reading miscues* and the latter *minor oral reading miscues* (explained in detail in the next section of this chapter).

The work of Yetta Goodman, Dorothy Watson and Carolyn Burke and others is presented in *Reading Miscue Inventory: Alternative Procedures* (Katonah, NY: Richard C. Owen, 1987). Although it is possible for the reading teacher or special education teacher to use this inventory, I have found it time-consuming and therefore not particularly well suited for the busy reading teacher.

One useful, fairly simple system for coding oral reading miscues which you might consider using was developed by Susan B. Argyle and is described in her article "Miscue

Analysis for Classroom Use" (*Reading Horizons*, 29, Winter 1989, pp. 93–102). Very simply, it attempts to determine if the miscue caused a meaning change, a graphic change, or was a self-correction. If the student's miscues resulted in few meaning changes, they undoubtedly are not very significant since they probably would not interfere with comprehension. If the student made a number of miscues that resulted in graphic changes, he/she possibly may need additional instruction or reinforcement in phonic analysis or structural analysis depending upon their frequency or whether they interfered significantly with comprehension. If the student made a number of self-corrections, he/she probably does not have a very significant reading problem as compared with the student who does not recognize his/her miscues and therefore does not attempt to correct them.

In general, Argyle recommends the following steps for using class miscue analysis:

1. Choose reading material that is unfamiliar to your students. This may be part of a basal reader story or a passage from a content textbook. Usually even adept readers make some miscues with totally unfamiliar material.
2. Copy the reading selection.
3. If you want to administer this material individually, tell the students that it is not a test, in order to reduce their anxiety.
4. Have the student read the passage orally without any preparation. Tape recording helps you to code all of the miscues but may not be completely practical in a noisy setting. It is possible to code the errors while the student reads, but it is fairly difficult.
5. Place the miscues on a summary sheet so that they can be analyzed.

Here is a very brief example of how Argyle's coding system may work:

Omission	a (gravel) road
Addition	a ʌ new gravel road
Pause	a /gravel/ road
Substitution	a gravel ride ~~road~~
Repetition	a gravel road (underlined)
Reversal	a gravel road (circled with reversal marks)
Correction	a gravel road (underlined)
Word Supplied by Teacher	a gravel road (T marked)

Illustration of the Oral Reading Coding System

An oral reading passage entitled "The Friendly Deer" was written on the second-grade reading level and taken from my book, *Reading Teacher's Complete Diagnosis and Correction Manual* (West Nyack, NY: The Center for Applied Research in Education, 1988, page 78). It was given to Aimee, a second-grade child who had evidenced reading difficulties. The passage was tape recorded, and Aimee's teacher coded her miscues using the system just described. The coded copy of this reading passage is now included.

THE FRIENDLY DEER

(Second-Grade Reading Level)

My father and I were ~~driving~~ *diving* down a (gravel) road in the North Woods. Suddenly we saw a ~~large deer~~ *big deck* standing by the side of the ^*old* road about a ~~block~~ *black* away. He was looking at us.

My father drove very (slowly) /closer to the deer. After awhile, our car was ^*standing* right beside the deer. We stopped ~~driving~~ *diving*, and the deer never moved. He looked at us with his (big) brown eyes, and we looked //~~back~~ *black* at him. After a little while, he put his ~~tail~~ *tall* down and started to w*T*ag it just like a dog. His ~~tail~~ *tall* was brown on top and white //underneath and not very long. He wagged it (several) times and seemed so friendly. Then the deer made (several) /noises that ^*really* sounded like he was talking to us. It was like a //snorting sound. He seemed to really like us.

After a little while, the deer walked (slowly) *very* into the woods still snorting. I wonder who he ~~thought~~ *though* we were. He wasn't afraid of us (at) (all) and he really seemed to like us. Both my father and I hope we can see him // (again) ~~someday~~ *somewhere*.

SUMMARY SHEET OF ORAL READING MISCUES

Student's Name _____ Date _____

	TEXT	MISCUE	MEANING CHANGE	GRAPHIC B	M	E	SELF-CORR.
1.	driving	diving	yes	—	✔	✔	
2.	gravel	—	partial	—	—	—	
3.	Suddenly	—	partial	—	—	—	
4.	large	big	partial	—	—	—	
5.	deer	deck	yes	✔	—	—	
6.	—	old	partial	—	—	—	
7.	block	black	yes	✔	—	✔	
8.	slowly	—	yes	—	—	—	
9.	—	standing	partial	—	—	—	
10.	driving	diving	yes	—	✔	✔	
11.	big	—	partial	—	—	—	
12.	back	black	yes	—	✔	✔	
13.	tail	tall	yes	✔	—	✔	
14.	wag	—	yes	—	—	—	
15.	tail	tall	yes	✔	—	✔	
16.	underneath	—	yes	—	—	—	
17.	wagged	—	yes	—	—	—	
18.	several	—	yes	—	—	—	
19.	several	—	yes	—	—	—	
20.	really	—	yes	—	—	—	
21.	snorting	—	partial	—	—	—	
22.	—	very	yes	—	—	—	
23.	slowly	—	partial	—	—	—	
24.	thought	though	yes	—	—	—	*
25.	at	—	partial	—	—	—	
26.	all	—	partial	—	—	—	
27.	again	—	partial	—	—	—	1
28.	someday	somewhere	yes	✔	—	—	
				5/	3/	6/	

Total 100%/ 18%/ 11%/ 21%/ 4%

Aimee's teacher then transferred her miscues to a brief summary sheet she had constructed. This summary sheet contains a list of all of Aimee's oral reading miscues. For each miscue the correct word is written first. Then as close a representation as possible of the child's response is written in each instance. If the miscue resulted in a complete meaning change, the word *yes* is written, while if only a partial meaning change occurred, the word *partial* is written. Next, each miscue is analyzed in terms of a graphic change in either the *beginning, the middle,* or *the end of the word.* In either instance a — is normally written for a miscue in that part of the word, while a ✔ is written for a correct response in that part of the word. If the child self-corrects a miscue, the self-correction also is noted.

After coding Aimee's responses on the summary sheet, her teacher attempted to analyze some of her reading strengths and weaknesses mainly in terms of patterns of behavior which can be seen. (A similar type of analysis is done in the early intervention Reading Recovery program which is described in detail in Chapter 5.) The reading teacher will find that it takes considerable time to become adept in the interpretation of oral reading miscues and to develop in-depth understanding of the reading process.

You will notice that Aimee made seventeen errors that interfered with comprehension and eleven miscues that only partially interfered with comprehension.

The percentages of graphophonic (phonic) similarities that Aimee made were also coded by her teacher. You will notice that Aimee made a total of 28 oral reading miscues on this passage out of a total of 194 words. This indicates that she mispronounced about *14* percent of the words and pronounced about *86* percent of them correctly. This percentage is below the 90 to 95 percent level that ordinarily comprises the *instructional reading level.* Therefore, this passage probably is on Aimee's *frustration reading level.*

From the number of miscues that interfered fairly significantly with comprehension, Aimee's teacher inferred that she has some difficulty with reading comprehension. However, because Aimee did make a number of miscues that resulted in only partial meaning changes, her comprehension was not believed to be as inadequate as if she had made all or nearly all meaning changes which were complete.

Aimee's teacher then tried to notice if Aimee appeared to be more competent in identifying the *beginnings, middles,* or *endings* of the miscued words. Aimee's teacher noticed that she had the most difficulty with word middles, the next most difficulty with word beginnings, and the least difficulty with word endings. It is fairly typical for a child to have the most difficulty with word middles because they typically contain the vowel sounds which are the most difficult for almost all children to discriminate and to identify. Although a child is usually the most competent in identifying word beginnings, this was not the case with Aimee. However, she was nearly as good at identifying word beginnings as she was word endings. Aimee's teacher also noted that she made only one self-correction, also indicative of a child with significant oral reading miscues who does not *monitor* his/her reading comprehension to see if reading makes sense.

Since the slash marks in the coding of Aimee's reading behavior indicate pauses in her oral reading, it appears that although she does not really have oral reading fluency, there are not as many pauses as are typical of students who truly read in a word-by-word manner.

In summary, here are some of Aimee's reading strengths:

- a fair knowledge of word endings and beginnings
- fair oral reading fluency

Here are some of her reading weaknesses:

- comprehension
- making meaning changes that have semantic acceptability (make sense in sentence context)

- ability to identify word middles
- the use of self-corrections or monitoring her own reading

Aimee's program of reading improvement should contain a number of different elements to ensure her optimum reading progress. She certainly must be given reading materials that are on her own instructional or independent reading level. Additional analysis should be done to determine this level with some degree of accuracy. One way of doing this is with the use of the "Individual Reading Inventory" (described and illustrated in detail in the next section of this chapter). She must also receive extensive instruction and reinforcement in the importance of using context clues to determine the meaning of unknown words and of monitoring her own reading carefully by making self-corrections when appropriate. In addition, she needs instruction and reinforcement in the various elements of reading comprehension and metacognition (monitoring her own reading to ensure that she is understanding). Strategies and materials for improving both comprehension ability and metacognition at Aimee's reading level are found in Chapter 6 of this *Handbook*.

Aimee should probably also have some instruction and/or reinforcement in the use of phonic analysis, especially in relation to word middles (long and short vowel sounds). Strategies and materials for this purpose are found in Chapter 5 of this *Handbook*.

In summary, the preceding is just one way in which a variation of oral reading miscue analysis can be used to determine a student's reading strengths and weaknesses. You will notice that although it is fairly simple to implement and modify, since it is an informal device, it does require considerable experience and knowledge of the reading process to administer. This technique, therefore, would have to be used judiciously by an inexperienced teacher of reading.

The Individual Reading Inventory

The Individual Reading Inventory (IRI) can also be called an informal reading inventory. It is an informal device designed to determine a student's approximate *independent, high instructional, instructional, low instructional,* and *frustration reading levels*. The inventory can also be used to determine a child's specific reading skills, competencies, and weaknesses. Although it can be given to all students in an elementary classroom, it normally is only given to disabled readers or learning-handicapped students due to the time involved in its individual administration and scoring. Most often, it is given near the beginning of tutoring sessions by Chapter I reading teachers and by teachers in a reading clinic for disabled readers with whom they are going to work. However, it can certainly be a useful assessment device for learning-handicapped students.

Although the Individual Reading Inventory is not accepted as a useful diagnostic device by all contemporary reading specialists, it can be fairly useful in determining a child's *tentative reading levels* and reading competencies and weaknesses. However, the results of an IRI always should be thought of as only a very tentative indicator of a child's independent, instructional, frustration, and capacity levels.

The IRI as it is used today probably originated with Emmett A. Betts and his doctoral student, Patsy A. Kilgallon. Kilgallon established criteria for accuracy in word identification and comprehension which she then tested on forty-one students ("A Study of Relationships Among Certain Pupil Adjustments in Language Situations," doctoral dissertation, Pennsylvania State College, 1942). In their version of the IRI, the students read each passage silently and then orally, a different procedure than normally used when giving the IRI today. Betts then determined the independent, instructional, and frustration reading levels and also the listening comprehension level in his textbook *Foundations of Reading Instruction* (New York: American Book Company, 1946, pp. 438–485).

NOTE: I use somewhat different criteria in this book as a result of my experience with hundreds of children over the past twenty-nine years.

In any case, the IRI varies somewhat in format according to the different reading specialists who give it. The version presented here can be used by any elementary reading teacher, Chapter I reading teacher, or reading teacher in a reading clinic:

1. *Establish rapport with the child.* It is necessary to establish rapport with the child before giving an IRI, especially if you do not know the student well. Ask the child questions about his/her interests, hobbies, view of reading ability, and strengths and weaknesses in reading. Ask the child questions about family only if this is pertinent to the assessment and can be done tactfully and sensitively.

2. *Give a sight-word test.* Give the child a sight word test such as *Fry's Instant Words*, the *Dolch Basic Sight Word List*, the *Kucerra-Francis Corpus (Dale Johnson Sight Word List)*, or *Hillerich's 240 Starter Words*. (A copy of *Fry's Instant Words* is found later in this section.) This type of test usually should be given only to children who are severely or moderately disabled readers and who have evidenced a clear weakness in sight word recognition by teacher observation.

3. *Give the graded word lists.* The graded word lists of the IRI are lists of words that begin at the preprimer or primer level and end at the twelfth-grade reading level. There normally are about twenty to twenty-five words on each graded list. The child is to read each word aloud and continue until he/she reaches the obvious frustration level. The major purpose of giving the sight word lists is to determine how well a child can pronounce words in isolation in comparison to pronouncing them in context and to determine at about which level to begin having him/her read the oral reading paragraphs.

   Note: A learning-handicapped child may often be able to pronounce words in isolation more effectively than in (sentence) context.

4. *Give the graded oral reading paragraphs.* The graded oral reading paragraphs are a series of passages that begin at the preprimer or primer level and often continue through the twelfth-grade reading level. Some of the passages can be used for a silent reading measure or for a listening comprehension test. Often there are two or more forms of the graded paragraphs so they can be used for pretesting and post-testing to evaluate both silent reading ability and oral reading ability. Obviously, all students do not read all the paragraphs either silently or orally. Students usually read aloud a paragraph that is about two or more grade levels below their estimated instructional reading level. This estimation can be made from the word lists mentioned earlier or from teacher observation of previous classroom reading performance (if feasible). In a later part of this section are detailed directions on how to evaluate the graded oral reading paragraphs of an IRI. A sample set of graded word lists and graded oral reading paragraphs are also included in this section.

5. *Give inventories in the word-identification techniques.* The last part of an IRI *may* be giving an informal inventory in the word-identification techniques of phonic analysis, structural analysis, and contextual analysis.

Since this description of the IRI has been very brief, you may want more detail on how to construct your own IRI or how to use commercial IRIs. You may consult the following source:

Wilma H. Miller, *Reading Diagnosis Kit, Third Edition* (West Nyack, New York: The Center for Applied Research in Education, 1986, pp. 190–192)

List of Commercial Individual Reading Inventories

Here is a fairly comprehensive listing of the commercially-available IRIs:

Analytical Reading Inventory. (Woods and Moe, 1989). Each of three forms consists of seventeen graded twenty-word lists (primer–grade 6) and ten graded passages (primer–grade 9). It contains six comprehension questions at primer and first-reader levels; eight comprehension questions at the other levels. The following question types are provided: literal, terminology, cause-effect, interpretive, and drawing conclusions. Two expository subtests consisting of graded social studies and science passages (nine each, grades 1–9) are also included. Designed for grades 1–9. Merrill Publishing Company.

Basic Reading Inventory. (Johns, 1991). Each of three forms consists of ten graded twenty-word lists (preprimer–grade 8) and ten graded passages (preprimer–grade 8). Words on the lists are first shown quickly and unknown words are presented again untimed. It contains four comprehension questions at the preprimer level and ten questions at the other levels, which are: one main idea, five literal, two interpretive, one vocabulary, and one critical. Designed for grades 1–8. Kendall/Hunt Publishing Company.

Classroom Reading Inventory. (Silvaroli, 1990). Each form has eight graded twenty-word lists and eight to ten graded passages (preprimer–grade 8 or grades 1–8). Each passage is followed by five comprehension questions that are literal, interpretive, or vocabulary. There is an optional spelling test. Forms A and B are for grades 1–6; Form C is for junior high school; and Form D is for senior high school and the adult level. Designed for grades 1–adult level. William C. Brown Publishing Company.

Ekwall/Shanker Reading Inventory. (Ekwall and Shanker, 1993). This consists of four forms, each of which contains eleven graded word lists, (primer–grade 9) and eleven graded passages (preprimer–grade 9). (There is no primer level.) There are five comprehension questions at the preprimer level and ten at the other reading levels. They consist of the following: literal, interpretive, and vocabulary. This inventory also contains a Quick Survey Word List and the El Paso Phonics Survey. Designed for grades 1–9. Allyn and Bacon.

Burns/Roe Informal Reading Inventory. (Burns and Roe, 1993). This contains two graded word lists (preprimer–grade 12) and four sets of graded passages (preprimer–grade 12). There are eight questions at the preprimer–second reader level; ten questions at the others (with six types on each passage: main idea, detail, sequence, cause-effect, interpretive, and vocabulary). The silent reading measures and the listening comprehension tests are optional. Designed for grades 1–12. Houghton Mifflin, and Nelson (Canada).

New Sucher-Allred Reading Placement Inventory. (1986). This consists of two forms, each of which contains twelve word lists and twelve oral reading selections. There are five comprehension questions per passage (literal, interpretive, cause-effect, and main idea). Designed for grades 1–9. McGraw-Hill.

Basic Directions for Giving and Evaluating the Graded Word Lists and Graded Oral Reading Paragraphs of an IRI

It is essential for you to tape record the entire administration of any IRI, since it is difficult to mark the miscues as the child reads. In addition, it often makes a student nervous when he/she notices you marking miscues of various kinds. Therefore, all of the marking should be done at a later time when the tape is played. It also may be necessary to replay the tape several times to locate all of the miscues.

When using the graded word lists on any IRI, it is normal to have a child begin pronouncing the words aloud on a word list that is at least two reading levels below the estimated instructional reading level. Have the student continue pronouncing the words on the graded word lists until he/she reaches the point where he/she is able to pronounce fewer than about 80 percent to 90 percent of the words on a list correctly. Later, when you evaluate the performance on the graded word lists, a + can be written by each word pronounced correctly, while a − or 0 can be written by each word pronounced incorrectly. The child's mispronunciation of a word can also be written on the teacher's copy of the word lists. The percentages contained on the word list of any IRI can be used to determine the child's ability to pronounce the word lists in terms of his/her independent, instructional, or frustration reading levels.

Then you normally have the child begin reading the graded passages. In some instances, one set of passages can be used to assess performance in oral reading, while a corresponding form can be used to assess performance in silent reading so that a comparison can be made between a child's oral and silent reading abilities. Sometimes there is quite a difference in this ability. This certainly may be the case with a learning handicapped student.

In any case, have the child begin reading the paragraph that corresponds to the level at which 80 percent or 90 percent of the listed words are recognized. It is very important to have the child begin reading aloud at a low enough level so that he/she will experience success at the beginning and not become discouraged. The child should continue reading succeeding paragraphs aloud until the frustration reading level is reached, indicated by signs of frustration and nervousness. This point is clearly evident even to an inexperienced reading teacher. After the child has completed reading each paragraph, ask the comprehension questions which accompany that paragraph. If you wish, you also can read aloud the next difficult paragraph and ask the comprehension questions that accompany it in order to establish the *potential* or *capacity level*. This is the reading level which a child theoretically may be able to reach under optimum conditions.

At a later time, you can mark the child's oral reading miscues by playing back the tape recording. You can mark the child's oral reading miscues by a variety of systems. Here is the one I use, but any system with which you are familiar is equally useful:

• **Omission**—Circle the entire word or letter sound.

$$\text{(elephant)}$$

• **Additions**—Insert with a caret.

$$\overset{\bullet}{\text{nice}} \atop \wedge$$

• **Substitutions/Mispronunciations**—Draw a line through the word and write in the substituted word.

- **Reversals**—Use the transposition symbol.

quickly and

- **Repetitions**—Use a wavy line to indicate a repetition of more than two words.

a black umbrella

- **Words Aided**—If a child says nothing after about five seconds, provide the word and cross it out.

why

Since the two major purposes for giving the graded oral reading paragraphs of an IRI are to determine a child's approximate reading level and to determine the pattern of miscues made, you then must evaluate the child's performance on the paragraphs. Since this is too complicated to explain here, you are encouraged to examine a source such as the following if you need more help in understanding it:

Wilma H. Miller, *Reading Diagnosis Kit, Third Edition* (West Nyack, New York: The Center for Applied Research in Education, 1986, Chapters 3 and 8.)

Here are the next steps to take in evaluating the IRI contained in this *Handbook*. You should consult the manual of any other IRI you may want to give to locate the corresponding material:

1. Count as a *major oral reading miscue* and deduct *one point* for any error that interferes with comprehension. Some examples may be *red* for *rain*, *stop* for *spot*, *horse* for *home*, *talk* for *take*, or *one* for *once*.

2. Count as a *minor oral reading miscue* and deduct *one-half point* for any deviation from the printed text that does *not* seem to interfere significantly with comprehension. Some examples are *old* for *elderly*, *fast* for *quickly*, *little* for *tiny*, *white* for *ivory*, and *large* for *huge*.

3. Count an *addition* as half an oral reading miscue if it does not change the meaning of the material significantly. Usually an addition is a minor oral reading miscue since it does not interfere very significantly with comprehension.

4. Do *not* count a *self-correction* as an error if it occurs within a short period of time such as five seconds. A self-correction usually indicates that the student is *monitoring* his/her own reading and attempting to read for meaning.

5. Count a *repetition* as half an oral reading miscue if it occurs on two or more words. A repetition of a single word may indicate that the student is trying to monitor his/her own reading or correcting the error.

6. Do not count more than *one oral reading miscue* on the same word in any one

paragraph. For example, if the child mispronounces the same word more than once while reading a graded passage, count it as an error only once.

7. Do not count an oral reading miscue on any *proper noun* which is found in any graded passage.

8. Deduct *one point* for any word that a student cannot pronounce after about five seconds *if that word interferes with comprehension*. Deduct *one-half point* for any word that a student cannot pronounce after about five seconds *if that word does not seem to interfere with comprehension*.

9. Do not count oral reading miscues that seem to exemplify a child's *cultural and regional dialect*. To consider this point, you must be quite familiar with the basic characteristics of the child's speech patterns, as in the African-American dialect or the Hispanic dialect.

When you have marked all of the miscues from a series of graded passages, you can use the information just presented to determine the child's approximate independent, instructional, and frustration reading levels. However, you should consult the manual of the IRI you are using for this information since the percentages for the different reading levels vary somewhat.

The characteristics of the three major reading levels used in the IRI included in this *Handbook* are:

- *Independent reading level*—The point at which a child is about 99 percent accurate in word identification and has about 95 percent or better comprehension.

- *Instructional reading level*—The point at which a student is about 90 percent accurate in word identification and has about 75 percent or better comprehension.

- *Frustration reading level*—The point at which a student is less than about 90 percent accurate in word identification and has less than about 50 percent accuracy in comprehension.

From using graded oral reading paragraphs with hundreds of children over a period of many years, adding several other reading levels to the three basic levels can be helpful in placing children in reading materials. You also can use the following three subcategories of reading levels:

- *Low independent reading level*
- *High instructional reading level*
- *Low instructional reading level*

This *Handbook* uses these three subcategories of reading levels in addition to the three basic ones. Since the IRI necessarily is an informal assessment device, you must use your own judgment in arriving at these reading levels, and you must take into account a child's word-identification and comprehension skills together. I usually weigh the child's performance on comprehension more highly than I weigh his/her performance on word identification, since comprehension is obviously more important. As you know, comprehension is the capstone of the reading process. Using the three additional appropriate reading levels is justified since the graded oral reading paragraphs are informal devices and should never be thought of as infallible indicators of a child's accurate reading levels.

It may be useful at this point to indicate how the preceding information can be applied to determine a child's reading level in an actual situation. (Taken from Wilma H. Miller's *Reading Teacher's Complete Diagnosis & Correction Manual*. West Nyack, New York: The Center for Applied Research in Education, 1988, page 80.)

SEEING REDHORSES

(third-grade reading level)

Have you ~~ever~~ **every** seen a redhorse? A redhorse is (not) any kind of horse, but ~~rather~~ **instead** it is a (medium-sized) fish.

As Ashley and Tommy <u>and their parents</u> were driving along a **old** road in the woods in (northern) Wisconsin, they saw an old man ~~standing~~ **staying** on a small (wooden) bridge. He <u>was looking</u> down into the creek that went under the bridge. Tommy's father stopped the car, and Tommy jumped out. <u>He asked the old man what he</u> was looking at. The man showed him a ~~huge~~ **big** ~~school~~ of fish that was swimming down the creek. Tommy asked the **old** man what kind of fish they were, and the man said that they were called redhorses. Then the rest <u>of the family</u> got out of the car to look at the fish.

The creek had <u>hundreds and hundreds</u> of redhorses swimming in it. There were so many that some were swimming (almost) on top of each other. A redhorse is a fish about a foot or more long with a (red-colored) head and a **big** grey body. Since they swim near the ~~bottom~~ of a creek or river, they are called "~~bottom-feeding~~ fish."

After awhile, Ashley, Tommy, <u>and their parents</u> left. However, they drove by the creek (again) an hour later. The redhorses were still swimming down the creek. ~~Most~~ **Many** people ~~that~~ **which** the children talked to later said that redhorses are not very good to eat. Many of ~~these~~ **the** people had never seen such a big school of them (either) No one seemed to know how they got their funny name.

The child made the following seven major miscues, each of which resulted in a deduction of one point. These miscues included substitutions, omissions, and words aided. The substitutions and omissions were considered major oral reading miscues since the meaning of the material was altered significantly. The omission of the word *red-colored* was considered a major miscue since that word was considered significant to the overall meaning of the passage. Here is a list of the major miscues in this passage:

every	red-colored
not	bottom
staying	bottom-feeding
school	

In addition, the child made the following twenty minor miscues, each of which resulted in a deduction of one-half point. These miscues included substitutions, omissions, repetitions, and additions. The substitutions and omissions were considered to be minor oral reading miscues since the meaning of the material was not changed significantly. The additions also were thought of as minor miscues since they did not alter the meaning of the material significantly. As stated earlier in this section, a repetition of two or more words results in a deduction of one-half point.

Here is a list of the minor oral reading miscues in this passage:

rather	of the family
medium-sized	hundreds and hundreds
and their parents	almost
old	big
northern	and their parents
wooden	again
He was looking	most
He asked the old man	that
huge	these
old	either

The child made a total of seventeen miscues (seven points and ten points). Subtract 17 from 259 (the number of words in this passage) to determine how many words the student pronounced correctly—**242.** Divide 259 (words in this passage) into 242 (total words that the student pronounced correctly) to obtain the percentage of correct words. This results in approximately 93 percent accuracy in word identification, which is the high instructional reading level. The student would have had to attain about 233 words correctly pronounced to reach the low instructional reading level.

Remember to use your judgment in determining the low independent, high instructional, and low instructional reading levels and to weigh the comprehension score somewhat higher than the word identification score for the reasons explained earlier.

Samples of Word Lists and
Graded Oral Reading Paragraphs

Included here are sample word lists and graded oral reading paragraphs from the primer through the twelfth-grade reading level. Two sets of these materials should be duplicated from this book. One set of word lists should be duplicated for the student to pronounce, and another set should be duplicated on which to record the scores. One set of graded oral reading paragraphs at the appropriate reading level should be duplicated without the comprehension questions and the formula for scoring. This is the set from which the student reads aloud. The other set contains the comprehension questions and the formula for scoring and is the set which you evaluate. The child's set (both the word lists and the graded passages) can be laminated for durability, and it should not show the reading level.

Two additional sets of graded word lists and oral reading passages can be found in the following source:

Wilma H. Miller, *Reading Diagnosis Kit, Third Edition* (West Nyack, New York: The Center for Applied Research in Education, 1986, Chapter 8)

One set of word lists and graded passages can be found in the following source:

Wilma H. Miller, *Reading Teacher's Complete Diagnosis & Correction Manual* (West Nyack, New York: The Center for Applied Research in Education, 1988, pages 69–95)

These additional word lists and passages can be used for pretesting and post-testing or for different kinds of administration such as oral-silent-oral, silent-oral, oral-silent, and silent-oral-silent.

It is very difficult to discriminate between Level Nine through Level Twelve. Therefore, the reading levels determined from these four word lists and two sets of reading passages should always be considered very tentative.

GRADED WORD LISTS

Preprimer

1. said
2. big
3. help
4. come
5. can
6. have
7. but
8. are
9. three
10. back
11. look
12. green
13. you
14. make
15. then
16. house
17. not
18. play
19. you
20. will
21. black
22. to
23. and
24. see
25. book

90%—22 or 23 correct

Primer

1. was
2. could
3. children
4. know
5. what
6. saw
7. around
8. mother
9. now
10. old
11. fly
12. very
13. have
14. into
15. yellow
16. tree
17. what
18. about
19. went
20. cake
21. all
22. way
23. hold
24. your
25. over

90%—22 or 23 correct

First Reader

1. please
2. flower
3. snowman
4. brown
5. children
6. father
7. drop
8. birthday
9. men
10. kind
11. story
12. cry
13. tell
14. street
15. buy
16. why
17. rabbit
18. ball
19. walk
20. paint
21. behind
22. give
23. her
24. again
25. laugh

90%—22 or 23 correct

Second Reader	*Third Reader*	*Fourth Reader*
1. beautiful	1. magic	1. predict
2. everyone	2. beginning	2. knowledge
3. should	3. thankful	3. canoe
4. write	4. crawl	4. vicious
5. sorry	5. museum	5. decorate
6. people	6. reason	6. windshield
7. instead	7. bush	7. parachute
8. breakfast	8. planet	8. official
9. cupcake	9. discover	9. dignity
10. eyes	10. enough	10. island
11. love	11. precious	11. dozen
12. reach	12. fright	12. exercise
13. people	13. honor	13. bound
14. save	14. several	14. machine
15. strong	15. unusual	15. experience
16. carry	16. hour	16. motion
17. first	17. escape	17. coward
18. together	18. wiggle	18. servants
19. friend	19. soup	19. legend
20. present*	20. enemy	20. force
21. write	21. either	21. nephew
22. hurt	22. remember	22. barrel
23. fall	23. matter	23. weather
24. until	24. inventor	24. ghost
25. does	25. diamond	25. weight

90%—22 or 23 correct   **90%—22 or 23 correct**   **90%—22 or 23 correct**

---

*Either pronunciation should be considered correct.
 pres'ent
 present'

Level Five	Level Six	Level Seven
1. territory	1. microphone	1. humidity
2. plateau	2. privacy	2. monarch
3. muscle	3. particle	3. terrain
4. telegram	4. reluctant	4. algebra
5. grease	5. applause	5. alliance
6. pierce	6. demon	6. neutral
7. orchard	7. liberty	7. boulevard
8. pouch	8. pounce	8. geological
9. parallel	9. wreath	9. horizontal
10. argument	10. moisture	10. perpetual
11. dissolve	11. sensitive	11. exception
12. manager	12. insurance	12. sculpture
13. considerable	13. contract*	13. warden
14. salmon	14. midstream	14. exaggerate
15. scientist	15. antibiotic	15. collapse
16. briskly	16. burro	16. progressive
17. kindle	17. helicopter	17. famine
18. region	18. hearth	18. merchandise
19. typical	19. transfusion	19. shrine
20. octave	20. envelope	20. ambitious
21. vinegar	21. request	21. thresh
22. amount	22. contrary	22. notable
23. intestines	23. sausage	23. uranium
24. prevent	24. surf	24. segment
25. yarn	25. hustle	25. domestic

90%—22 or 23 correct   **90%—22 or 23 correct**   **90%—22 or 23 correct**

© 1993 by The Center for Applied Research in Education

---

*Either pronunciation should be considered correct.
con'tract
contract'

Level Eight

1. miscellaneous
2. jaunt
3. quota
4. competent
5. juvenile
6. sequence
7. belligerent
8. recruit
9. intrigue
10. tremor
11. discipline
12. prescription
13. arrogant
14. custody
15. embankment
16. yacht
17. authentic
18. browse
19. rehearsal
20. currency
21. universal
22. substantial
23. masquerade
24. politician
25. extension

90%—22 or 23 correct

Level Nine

1. memorable
2. ecstasy
3. consecutive
4. aggressive
5. priority
6. indispensable
7. legitimate
8. aquatic
9. originate
10. obsolete
11. countenance
12. malicious
13. quadruple
14. regime
15. heathen
16. avalanche
17. adversary
18. gist
19. physique
20. spouse
21. agitate
22. enviable
23. judicial
24. harmonize
25. insignia

90%—22 or 23 correct

Level Ten

1. vigilant
2. pilgrimage
3. opaque
4. qualm
5. heirloom
6. eccentric
7. superlative
8. disreputable
9. crypt
10. callous
11. rhapsody
12. exuberant
13. conveyance
14. atrocious
15. artisan
16. infidel
17. fallacy
18. oratory
19. phenomenal
20. devastate
21. eloquent
22. callous
23. spasm
24. bereaved
25. fictitious

90%—22 or 23 correct

Level Eleven

1. labyrinth
2. exhilarated
3. virtuoso
4. philanthropy
5. vehement
6. oscillate
7. epitaph
8. celestial
9. nutritious
10. physiology
11. memoir
12. awry
13. gauntlet
14. financier
15. hypothesis
16. whimsical
17. confidentially
18. amethyst
19. gullible
20. kinetic
21. assimilate
22. claimant
23. knoll
24. bohemian
25. malign

90%—22 or 23 correct

Level Twelve

1. harangue
2. gregarious
3. ignominious
4. colloquial
5. blasphemy
6. utilitarian
7. echelon
8. desultory
9. facsimile
10. tertiary
11. zealot
12. rhetoric
13. digression
14. gauche
15. charlatan
16. epoch
17. digression
18. obtuse
19. symmetry
20. prolific
21. pedagogy
22. bourgeois
23. atrophy
24. inveigle
25. pique

90%—22 or 23 correct

ORAL READING PASSAGE

Name_____ Grade_____ Teacher_____ Date_____

A TAN DOG (Preprimer)*

Pat has a tan dog.

The dog's name is Jill.

Pat and Jill take two walks a day.

Jill has a blue ball.

She likes to run after her ball.

She likes to jump too.

She likes to eat her dog food.

Pat has a lot of fun with Jill.

Jill has fun too.

© 1993 by The Center for Applied Research in Education

---

*The readability level of this passage was computed by the Spache Readability Formula.

A TAN DOG

1. What is the dog's name? (L-E)*

    Jill

2. What color is Jill's ball? (L-E)

    blue

3. Who do you think usually throws the ball for Jill? (I-I)

    Pat

    any other member of Pat's family

    any one of Pat's friends

4. Why do you think that Pat and Jill go for walks every day? (I-I)

    Jill needs to go to the bathroom

    Jill likes to walk

    Pat likes to walk with Jill

    Jill likes to be outside

5. What do you think are some of the ways in which Pat has fun with Jill? (I-I)

    throwing the ball for her

    walking with her

    playing with her

Number of words in this selection _____54_____

Number of word-identification miscues _____

Word-Identification Miscues

    Independent reading level _____0_____
    Low independent reading level approx. _____1_____
    High instructional reading level approx. _____2–4_____
    Instructional reading level approx. _____5_____
    Low instructional reading level approx. _____6_____
    Frustration reading level _____7+_____

Number of comprehension errors _____

Comprehension Errors

    Independent reading level _____0_____

    Instructional reading level _____1_____

    Frustration reading level _____2+_____

---

*In each of the oral reading passages in this *Handbook*, L-E represents Literal—Explicit and I-I represents Interpretive—Implicit.

ORAL READING PASSAGE

Name_____ Grade_____ Teacher_____ Date_____

THE BABY DEER (Primer)*

I saw a baby deer last summer. It was brown with white spots all over it. The baby deer had pretty big brown eyes. It had a shiny black nose too.

I saw the baby deer run after its mother. One time it almost fell down on the road. Then the baby deer's mother ran into the woods. The baby deer ran into the woods after her. I saw the mother deer waiting in the woods for her baby. Then I saw the baby deer run to its mother in the woods.

© 1993 by The Center for Applied Research in Education

---

*The readability level of this passage was computed by the Spache Readability Formula.

THE BABY DEER

1. What color were the baby deer's eyes? (L-E)

    brown

2. Who was the baby deer following? (L-E)

    its mother

    the mother deer

3. Why do you think the baby deer almost fell down? (I-I)

    its legs were long and thin

    it couldn't run as fast as its mother could

4. Why do you think the mother deer was waiting for her baby in the woods? (I-I)

    so that the baby deer wouldn't get lost

    a mother deer always tries to take care of her baby

    she knew that her baby couldn't run as fast as she could

5. Why do you think the mother deer waited in the woods for her baby instead of waiting on the road? (I-I)

    it was safer to wait in the woods

    a car couldn't hit either one of them in the woods

    a deer feels safer in the woods than it does on a road

Number of words in this selection _____92_____

Number of word-identification miscues _____

Word-Identification Miscues

Independent reading level _____0–1_____
Low independent reading level approx. _____2–3_____
High instructional reading level approx. _____4–6_____
Instructional reading level approx. _____7–9_____
Low instructional reading level approx. _____10–11_____
Frustration reading level approx. _____12+_____

Number of comprehension errors _____

Comprehension Errors

Independent reading level _____0_____

Instructional reading level _____1_____

Frustration reading level _____2+_____

ORAL READING PASSAGE

Name_____ Grade_____ Teacher_____ Date_____

THE BIG, BIG TURTLE (1)*

One day last summer Joey saw a big, big turtle. Joey lives with his mother and father and little sister. They all live in a house in the big woods.

One morning Joey was going to take his dog out. He saw a big, big turtle in the garage. Joey and his dog almost stepped on the turtle.

Joey and his mother tried all day to get the turtle out of the garage. They didn't want it to die. They tried to give it meat to eat. They held the meat so that the turtle would go out. They tried to push the turtle with a rake. At last the turtle went out of the garage. He went down to the lake. There he was safe.

© 1993 by The Center for Applied Research in Education

---

*The readability level of this passage was computed by the Spache Readability Formula.

THE BIG, BIG TURTLE

1. What did Joey find in the garage? (L-E)

   a turtle

   a big, big turtle

2. What did Joey and his mother try to give the turtle to eat? (L-E)

   meat

3. Why do you think the turtle might die if it stayed in the garage? (I-I)

   it would starve to death

   it wouldn't have any food to eat

   it wouldn't have any water to drink

4. Why do you think Joey and his mother had to be careful when they tried to push the turtle out with the rake? (I-I)

   so that they wouldn't hurt it

5. Why do you think the turtle went back to the lake when it left the garage? (I-I)

   it would be safe there

   it was used to living by the lake

Number of words in this selection _____126_____

Number of word-identification miscues _____

Word-Identification Miscues

Independent reading level _____0–1_____
Low independent reading level approx. _____2–3_____
High instructional reading level approx. _____4–6_____
Instructional reading level approx. _____7–11_____
Low instructional reading level approx. _____12–13_____
Frustration reading level _____14+_____

Number of comprehension errors _____

Comprehension Errors

Independent reading level _____0_____

Instructional reading level _____1_____

Frustration reading level _____2+_____

ORAL READING PASSAGE

Name_____ Grade_____ Teacher_____ Date_____

MOST ANIMALS DON'T WANT TROUBLE (2)*

Did you know that most wild animals try to
avoid trouble if they can? Jenny didn't learn
that until she spent the summer in the North
Woods with her grandfather and grandmother.

Jenny first found that out about wild
animals when she was walking on a road in the
woods one day. She saw a porcupine way down
the road coming toward her. Jenny could tell
that the porcupine didn't seem to see her. As
she and the porcupine came closer and closer,
Jenny really wondered what it would do.
Finally, as they met on the road, the porcupine
saw her. As soon as it saw her, the porcupine
turned and walked into the woods as quickly as

© 1993 by The Center for Applied Research in Education

*The readability level of this passage was computed by the Spache Readability Formula.

it could. Even though the porcupine had sharp

quills, it didn't want trouble.

Another time Jenny met a large black bear

when she was walking on the road. The bear

looked at Jenny for awhile. Then it walked

across the road into the woods. It also didn't

want trouble.

MOST ANIMALS DON'T WANT TROUBLE

1. Who did Jenny spend the summer with? (L-E)

   her grandfather and grandmother

2. What animal has sharp quills? (L-E)

   a porcupine

3. Why do you think most wild animals try to avoid trouble if they can? (I-I)

   they don't like to fight unless they have to

   they only fight if they don't have any other choice

4. How do you think a porcupine can use its quills to protect itself if it has to? (I-I)

   it can stick them into another animal if that animal gets too close

   once an animal has had quills in it from a porcupine, it never bothers a porcupine again

5. Why do you think that the bear looked at Jenny for a while? (I-I)

   it may have never seen a person before

   it was curious about who Jenny might be

Number of words in this selection _____167_____

Number of word-identification miscues _____

Word-Identification Miscues

   Independent reading level _____0–2_____
   Low independent reading level approx. _____3–4_____
   High instructional reading level approx. _____5–8_____
   Instructional reading level approx. _____9–15_____
   Low instructional reading level approx. _____16–17_____
   Frustration reading level _____18+_____

Number of comprehension errors _____

Comprehension Errors

   Independent reading level _____0_____
   Instructional reading level _____1_____
   Frustration reading level _____2+_____

© 1993 by The Center for Applied Research in Education

ORAL READING PASSAGE

Name_____ Grade_____ Teacher_____ Date_____

BILL COSBY (3)*

Bill Cosby is a very good example for all children that they can be anything that they want to be.

When Bill was a child, he was very poor. Although he was very bright, he did not do well in school. Instead of studying, he usually told jokes to the other children. However, he always promised his mother that he would get an education someday. He kept that promise after he had become famous.

After having been in the Navy and in college for awhile, he began working as a comic in clubs. After a little while, he began acting on television in a show with a white man. People liked this show, and Bill Cosby made a lot of money. He was the first black man who was equal to a white man on television.

After making some other television shows and commercials, Bill Cosby began acting in a show called the *Cosby Show*. In it Bill Cosby played a doctor, and his wife was a lawyer. Their family had five children. This show became very popular, and both black and white children liked it very much. Bill Cosby tried hard to act like a real father in this show.

In real life Bill Cosby is married and has five children. For most of the time when his children were growing up, the family lived on a farm in the East.

All of his life Bill Cosby has tried hard to show that people are mostly alike no matter what color skin they have.

© 1993 by The Center for Applied Research in Education

*The readability level of this passage was computed by the Spache Readability Formula.

BILL COSBY

1. What did Bill Cosby often do in school instead of studying? (L-E)

   tell jokes

2. How many children does Bill Cosby have in real life? (L-E)

   five

3. Why do you think Bill Cosby told jokes in school instead of studying? (I-I)

   he didn't like to study

   he wanted the other children in his class to like him

   he wanted attention from the other children and from his teacher

4. Why was it important to Bill Cosby to play a black man on television who was equal to a white man? (I-I)

   black people are as good as white people

   black people and white people are the same except for the color of their skin

5. Why did both black children and white children like the *Cosby Show*? (I-I)

   it showed what a real family can be like

   it showed a father and mother that most children would like to have

Number of words in this selection _____255_____

Number of word-identification miscues _____

Word-Identification Miscues

Independent reading level _____0–3_____
Low independent reading level approx. _____4–7_____
High instructional reading level approx. _____8–12_____
Instructional reading level approx. _____13–21_____
Low instructional reading level approx._____22–25_____
Frustration reading level _____26+_____

Number of comprehension errors _____

Comprehension Errors

Independent reading level _____0_____
Instructional reading level _____1_____
Frustration reading level _____2+_____

ORAL READING PASSAGE

CANADA GEESE (4)*

Canada geese are among the most fascinating and amazing of any of the birds in the world. Most of us have seen large flocks of Canada geese flying in a V outline high in the sky in the spring and fall.

Scientists have studied the migration of Canada geese for many years. Although they still do not really understand how Canada geese know exactly where to fly, they are beginning to figure out something about it. Scientists now believe that each Canada goose is born imprinted with a route which follows the stars. This can be called a "star map" which shows each Canada goose exactly where to fly.

Canada geese always fly in a V outline. The leader of the outline becomes very tired from breaking the air waves. That is why a flock of geese changes its leader many times on each migration north or south. The rest of a flock flies in the V outline to take advantage of the updrafts made by the wings of the bird in front of it. These updrafts make it easier for each Canada goose to fly.

A Canada goose has a shining black head and neck with an oval patch of white. It has a pale gray chest and a gray-brown body and wings. It also has a white belly and black tail feathers. The average goose weighs about ten pounds. Canada geese use their legs as a landing gear when they come down from flying much as an airplane uses landing gears when landing in an airport.

All baby Canada geese are born in the summer in Canada when it is safe for them. However, they each mate for life in the winter somewhere in the south.

© 1993 by The Center for Applied Research in Education

---

*The readability level of this passage was computed by the Dale-Chall Readability Formula.

CANADA GEESE

1. What kind of outline do Canada geese fly in? (L-E)

   V outline

2. What part of a Canada goose's body serves as landing gear? (L-E)

   its legs

3. How could a scientist try to prove that Canada geese are born with a "star map"? (I-I)

   try to let a flock of young geese fly south without an experienced leader

   put geese in a planetarium where there are make-believe stars

4. What parts of a leader goose's body may become the most tired? (I-I)

   its wings

   its neck

5. Why do you think that Canada is a fairly safe place for baby Canada geese to be born in? (I-I)

   it is not likely hunters are there

   there may not be many enemy animals

   there are not many people there

Number of words in this selection _____288_____

Number of word-identification miscues _____

Word-Identification Miscues

    Independent reading level _____0–3_____
    Low independent reading level approx. _____4–7_____
    High instructional reading level approx. _____8–12_____
    Instructional reading level approx. _____13–25_____
    Low instructional reading level approx. _____26–29_____
    Frustration reading level _____30+_____

Number of comprehension errors _____

Comprehension Errors

    Independent reading level _____0_____
    Instructional reading level _____1_____
    Frustration reading level _____2+_____

ORAL READING PASSAGE

THE OCTOPUS (5)*

The octopus is a fascinating although in some ways a frightening creature of the sea. As one example, an octopus shoots water from the tube that protrudes from the loose bag of skin covering its body. This helps it to move quickly through the sea.

An octopus has eight webbed arms. Each arm is about two feet long and contains double rows of powerful suction discs. These discs are helpful to an octopus in capturing its food. One of the most unique features of an octopus is its ability to grow back an arm which has been pulled off by an enemy such as an eel. There is no bleeding when the arm is torn off since an octopus can contract its blood vessels. It takes a young octopus about six weeks to grow a new arm.

When an octopus finds a lobster for its meal, it floats down over the lobster like a parachute and envelopes it. Then the octopus bites its victim with the black beak that is hidden in the circle of its arms. An octopus paralyzes its victim with the venom contained in its bite.

Another interesting fact about an octopus is its ability to change colors depending upon the emotions that it is feeling. It has a transparent outer layer of skin that can be red, brown, or very pale depending upon whether the octopus is happy, excited, or frightened.

A female octopus usually lays about 50,000 eggs, each one the size of a grain of rice. Each tiny egg is attached to a thread. The octopus then glues each cluster of eggs to the ceiling of a cave which she has chosen. The eggs hang there like tiny bunches of grapes. Of the baby octopuses that are hatched about a month later, only about two or three live long enough to become adults.

*The readability level of this passage was computed by the Dale-Chall Readability Formula.

© 1993 by The Center for Applied Research in Education

THE OCTOPUS

1. How many arms does an octopus have? (L-E)

   eight

2. What type of food are octopus eggs like? (L-E)

   grains of rice

3. What might happen to an octopus if it could not contract its blood vessels when it has an arm torn off? (I-I)

   it would bleed to death

   it couldn't stop the bleeding

4. Why do you think it is helpful to an octopus to have its beak well hidden? (I-I)

   its victim can't see the beak until it is bitten by it

   its victim doesn't know what to protect itself from

5. What dangers do you think a baby octopus faces? (I-I)

   fish could eat it

   crabs could eat it

   shrimp could eat it

   shore birds could eat it

Number of words in this selection _____310_____

Number of word-identification miscues _____

Word-Identification Miscues

Independent reading level _____0–3_____
Low independent reading level approx. _____4–8_____
High instructional reading level approx. _____9–13_____
Instructional reading level approx. _____14–28_____
Low instructional reading level approx. _____29–31_____
Frustration reading level _____32+_____

Number of comprehension errors _____

Comprehension Errors

Independent reading level _____0_____
Instructional reading level _____1_____
Frustration reading level _____2+_____

© 1993 by The Center for Applied Research in Education

ORAL READING PASSAGE

Name_____ Grade_____ Teacher_____ Date_____

THE NAVAHO NATIVE AMERICANS (6)*

The Navaho tribe of Native Americans undoubtedly is among the most well known and influential of any of the tribes that are found in the United States. The Navaho people live on a huge reservation in the southwestern area of the country which encompasses parts of northeastern Arizona, northwestern New Mexico, and a small portion of Utah.

The Navahos are especially well known for their silver and wool crafts. The Navaho silversmiths, who are usually men, can shape silver so that it shimmers like the brilliance of the desert sun where these people live. Often turquoise gem stones are combined with silver in pieces of jewelry such as necklaces, bracelets, earrings, and pendants. The Navaho silversmiths also design and execute belts, belt buckles, and superb serving trays. The Navaho weavers, who typically are women, work on looms to create brilliantly colored blankets and rugs. The geometric patterns seem to represent the mesas, cliffs, and canyons which characterize Navaho country. Navaho men learned how to use silver from Mexican silversmiths, while Navaho women probably learned weaving from their Pueblo Native American neighbors in the late 1600s.

Most Americans who are not Native American are astonished to learn that the Navahos played a unique and important role in helping the United States attain its victory in World War II. Many people were surprised that so many Navahos chose to enlist when their people had been so mistreated by the federal government for so many years. However, an impressive number of Navahos thought of themselves as being both Navaho and American and wished to serve their country. The Navaho

© 1993 by The Center for Applied Research in Education

*The readability level of this passage was computed by the Dale-Chall Readability Formula.

language served as the basis for a unique code in the Pacific theater of war. The Navaho Codetalkers, a group of about two hundred Navahos, contributed a remarkable chapter to their people's proud history. It is unfortunate that this contribution is not well known today.

THE NAVAHO NATIVE AMERICANS

1. In what area of the United States do the Navaho people live? (L-E)

   southwestern

   southwest

2. In which war did the Navahos play a significant part? (L-E)

   World War II

3. Why do you think the Navahos often use turquoise gemstones in their silver jewelry? (I-I)

   it may be easy for them to get it

   it may be mined in the Southwest

4. Why was the Navaho language probably well suited to be used as a secret code? (I-I)

   the Japanese had never heard of it

   it was not known by our enemies in the war

   it may have been a hard language to understand

5. Why do you think so few Americans know about the Navaho Codetalkers? (I-I)

   Native American culture has not been studied very much in our schools

   World War II happened a long time ago

Number of words in this selection _____313_____

Number of word-identification miscues _____

Word-Identification Miscues

   Independent reading level _____0–3_____
   Low independent reading level approx. _____4–8_____
   High instructional reading level approx. _____9–13_____
   Instructional reading level approx. _____14–28_____
   Low instructional reading level approx. _____29–31_____
   Frustration reading level _____32+_____

Number of comprehension errors _____

Comprehension Errors

   Independent reading level _____0_____
   Instructional reading level _____1_____
   Frustration reading level _____2+_____

© 1993 by The Center for Applied Research in Education

ORAL READING PASSAGE

Name_____ Grade_____ Teacher_____ Date_____

LORRAINE HANSBERRY—BLACK PLAYWRIGHT (7)*

It is indeed unfortunate that most young people never have heard of the famous black woman playwright Lorraine Hansberry. Had she not suffered a tragic premature death from cancer in 1965 at the age of only thirty-four she might well still be writing memorable plays such as the one for which she still should be remembered.

Lorraine spent her childhood on the south side of Chicago with her father, mother, a sister Mamie, and two brothers Carl and Perry. During her childhood the family attempted to live in an integrated neighborhood but were unsuccessful because of the restrictive ordinances typical of that time. These laws stated that a black family could not move into a segregated neighborhood. Although Lorraine's father challenged the law, he did not win the case until it was tried years later before the United States Supreme Court.

As she was growing up, Lorraine became increasingly aware of the destructive racial prejudice against her people. She determined that she must make a contribution to the true liberation of her people, and she believed that perhaps her writing might be the way. To help her achieve her goal, she studied at the New School for Social Research in New York and also wrote for the black newspaper *Freedom*.

In 1953 Lorraine married a student at New York University who was active in the Progressive Movement named Bob Nemiroff. After her marriage, Lorraine's writing took up much of her time as she worked on novels, several plays, and an opera at the same time. One day she decided to write a genuine, contemporary play describing the lives of a black family living on the south side of Chicago. Although Lorraine's family had been wealthier than that, she had known many black families who lived in ghettos and had struggled to make a better life for themselves. Thus,

*The readability level of this passage was computed by the Dale-Chall Readability Formula.

Lorraine's idea became the very famous play *A Raisin in the Sun*, which depicts the different ways family members would spend some money if it were available.

Lorraine Hansberry's play *A Raisin in the Sun* was named Broadway's best play of 1959. Lorraine was the first black person and the youngest American playwright ever to receive this award. After she became famous, she continued to work for the Civil Rights Movement. After her death in 1965, Bob Nemiroff, her former husband, whom she had divorced in 1964, read the papers which she had left him in her will. He organized her work into a play called *To Be Young, Gifted, and Black*, a play which still is performed on college campuses.

LORRAINE HANSBERRY—BLACK PLAYWRIGHT

1. What illness caused Lorraine's death in 1965? (L-E)

   cancer

2. What is the title of the play that was named Broadway's best play of 1959? (L-E)

   A Raisin in the Sun

3. Why do you think restrictive ordinances were unfair? (I-I)

   a family should be able to live wherever it wants to and can afford to

   a person should not be discriminated against because of his/her race

4. Why do you think it was a good experience for Lorraine to work on the newspaper *Freedom* when she was young? (I-I)

   it helped her learn to write

   it helped her understand more about the problems that black people face

   it helped her meet some new people

5. Why do you think it might be helpful for a white person to see the play *A Raisin in the Sun*? (I-I)

   it would show him/her how difficult life can be

   it might help him/her understand black people better

   it can show him/her what life in the ghetto can be like

Number of words in this selection _____437_____

Number of word-identification miscues _____

Word-Identification Miscues

Independent reading level _____0–5_____
Low independent reading level approx. _____6–11_____
High instructional reading level approx. _____12–20_____
Instructional reading level approx. _____21–37_____
Low instructional reading level approx. _____38–44_____
Frustration reading level _____45+_____

Number of comprehension errors _____

Comprehension Errors

Independent reading level _____0_____
Instructional reading level _____1_____
Frustration reading level _____2+_____

ORAL READING PASSAGE

Name_____ Grade_____ Teacher_____ Date_____

AUSTRALIAN BIRDS THAT USE A THERMOMETER (8)*

The mallee bird of Australia is a superb example of the high degree of instinct that can be found in a wild creature. This unique species of bird is one of the birds known as "mound builders." Its remarkable characteristics only have been understood for about thirty-five years. This species of bird has mainly been studied by an Australian scientist named H. J. Frith.

The mallee bird is about as large as an average turkey. For its nest it builds a huge mound of sand and vegetable rubbish. Each mallee bird devotes eleven out of twelve months of each year to taking care of its nest, an inordinate amount of its entire life span.

In May the male birds dig a large pit in the sand, scraping the earth out with backward thrusts of their large, powerful feet and legs. In June, with the onset of the Australian winter, they fill the pit with vegetable rubbish scratched together from a wide area. The winter rains come then, causing the vegetable rubbish to ferment and heat up. In August the birds mix sand with the decaying vegetable rubbish in a smaller pit at the center of the mound in what will be the actual incubation chamber for the eggs.

The egg laying begins in September by the time the mixture of sand and vegetation in the smaller pit has reached a level of 92° F (33.5°C). Then the compost, the mixture of sand and leaves at the center, is opened up by the mallee bird and if he is satisfied that the temperature is satisfactory, the hen lays an egg in the hole after she has tested the temperature also. The female bird lays eggs one on top of another at intervals of two days through seventeen days for about four months.

The birds test the temperature of the mound daily and are careful to keep it at an even level. If the mound shows signs of becoming overheated, the mallee bird opens it to allow excess heat to escape. If the mound is too cool, it is opened up so that the sun's rays can heat it. The mallee bird apparently is guided by its tongue and the inside of its mouth, which together act as a living thermometer when it picks up a beakful of the materials in the mound.

_____

*The readability level of this passage was computed by the Dale-Chall Readability Formula.

© 1993 by The Center for Applied Research in Education

AUSTRALIAN BIRDS THAT USE A THERMOMETER

1. What is the name of the bird described in this passage? (L-E)

   mallee bird

2. At what temperature must the mound be kept? (L-E)

   92°F or 35.5°C

3. How does a mallee bird know that it must keep its mound at a precise temperature so that its eggs will hatch? (I-I)

   it was born with that instinct

   it is part of the bird's nature

4. Why do you think the mallee bird has strong legs? (I-I)

   it has to dig a large pit in the sand for its nest

   it is a hard job to dig a pit in the sand

5. Why do you think the temperature in the mound must be tested every day? (I-I)

   if it became too hot or too cold the eggs would not hatch

   the eggs require a certain temperature in order to hatch

Number of words in this selection _____390_____

Number of word-identification miscues _____

Word-Identification Miscues

   Independent reading level _____0–4_____
   Low independent reading level approx. _____5–10_____
   High instructional reading level approx. _____11–18_____
   Instructional reading level approx. _____19–33_____
   Low instructional reading level approx. _____34–39_____
   Frustration reading level _____40+_____

Number of comprehension errors _____

Comprehension Errors

   Independent reading level _____0_____
   Instructional reading level _____1_____
   Frustration reading level _____2+_____

ORAL READING PASSAGE

Name_____ Grade_____ Teacher_____ Date_____

TALES OF SEARCHING FOR HIDDEN TREASURE (9)*

History abounds with unique tales of the different means fortune hunters have employed in their search for hidden treasure such as gold, silver, and jewels of all descriptions. Their efforts ranged from very primitive many years ago to the contemporary scientific means which are commonly used today.

For hundreds of years the divining rod was the primary tool used to presumably locate buried treasure. The branch of a divining rod was always cut from a special tree that commonly was a hazel, a willow, or a holly. However, only an individual who supposedly was endowed with a "special gift" was able to induce the divining rod to twist and turn toward earth containing gold, or even more often, the often precious commodity of water.

One of the most interesting of the tales related to searching for treasure concerns Captain Thomas Dickinson and his giant derrick. In 1830 the British frigate *Thetis* was sailing east with 800,000 dollars in gold and silver coins when it lost its bearings and crashed into the huge wall of stone named Cape Frio. Later, Captain Dickinson installed a derrick in the cave in which the *Thetis* sank. This derrick was half the length of an entire football field and consisted of twenty-two pieces of wood held together with dowels, iron bolts, hoops, and wrappings of four-inch rope. Dickinson then hung a diving bell from the end of the derrick like a weight on the end of a fishing pole. His men used chains and cables to lower and raise the derrick and to move it from side to side so that they could place the bell where they wanted it and then lift it out. The diving bell enabled a diver to rest while breathing fresh air. Although the bell was open at the bottom to allow a diver to enter and leave, the air inside kept the water out. After fourteen months of intense effort, most of the treasure from the *Thetis* was recovered.

Three sophisticated inventions from World War II are now used in the recovery of treasure. One is *scuba* which stands for *s*elf-*c*ontained *u*nderwater *b*reathing *a*pparatus. *Sonar* is used by contemporary treasure hunters to locate sunken ships. As they tow a sonar device behind a search boat, it fires electrical impulses into the water which bounce off whatever they hit and send back echoes that are picked up by a recorder. *Metal detectors* or *magnetometers* now are used by treasure hunters to find metal objects as deep as twenty feet underground.

*The readability level of this passage was computed by the Dale-Chall Readability Formula.

TALES OF SEARCHING FOR HIDDEN TREASURE

1. What was the most common device used to attempt to locate both gold and water many years ago? (L-E)

   the divining rod

2. From what did Dickinson and his men hang a diving bell? (L-E)

   a derrick

3. Why do you think the divining rod was not always successful in helping a person locate gold? (I-I)

   there is no scientific evidence to prove that it really worked

4. Why was the diving bell necessary if a man were to be successful in finding the sunken treasure on the *Thetis*? (I-I)

   a person could not breathe underwater without it

   a person would die otherwise while trying to locate the sunken treasure

5. What kinds of treasure can be located by the use of metal detectors? (I-I)

   gold or silver jewelry

   metal ores

   coins

Number of words in this selection _____419_____

Number of word-identification miscues _____

Word-Identification Miscues

Independent reading level _____0–4_____
Low independent reading level approx. _____5–10_____
High instructional reading level approx. _____11–19_____
Instructional reading level approx. _____20–37_____
Low instructional reading level approx. _____38–42_____
Frustration reading level _____43+_____

Number of comprehension errors _____

Comprehension Errors

Independent reading level _____0_____
Instructional reading level _____1_____
Frustration reading level _____2+_____

ORAL READING PASSAGE

Name_____ Grade_____ Teacher_____ Date_____

THE DOG WHELK (10-12)* †

The dog whelk is a carnivorous snail that lives on the seashore along with countless other seashore creatures such as barnacles, mussels, starfish, sea urchins, and periwinkles. Marine zoologists have studied all of these sea animals extensively and as a result of their meticulous research, we now are cognizant of the characteristics which dog whelks possess.

Since the dog whelk is a carnivorous snail, its diet mainly consists of mussels or barnacles but not seaweed of any variety. The dog whelk moves quietly along, gobbling up the animals underneath it, such as the barnacle which it apparently kills or sedates with a substance called *purpurin* that it has secreted, a purple dye which drugs its victim. Then the dog whelk extends its *proboscis*, a trunk-like extension of its head which protrudes through the mouth opening, and uses its *radula*, or coiled tongue, to eat the barnacle.

Although a dog whelk has considerably more difficulty eating a mussel than a barnacle because the mussel shell is larger and tougher, it has the ability to do so. The dog whelk climbs onto the shell and bores a very neat round hole through the mussel's shell with its radula. After the task is accomplished, this carnivorous snail simply devours the mussel.

Carnivorous snails were not the first living thing to inhabit the seashore because plants, which are self-sufficient, appeared there earlier. While plants are self-sufficient, animals always have depended upon plants since they either eat plants themselves or eat other animals that have eaten plants.

Under the spiral shell with its siphon groove, one can observe the soft portion of the dog whelk. There is the muscular foot which supports the shell and moves it along with a series of contractions. There is the stumpy head with its odd-looking tentacles that can be pulled into the head if the dog whelk senses danger. In times of danger, a long, strong muscle, the *columnella*, which stretches back into the smallest section of the spiral, pulls the snail into its shell and closes it mostly in by shutting the *operculum* which is made of a horny material.

---

*The readability level of this passage was computed by the Dale-Chall Readability Formula.
†It was decided that it was too difficult to differentiate between passages at the tenth-grade reading level, eleventh-grade reading level, and twelfth-grade reading level. Therefore, one passage was written that should be fairly appropriate for all three of these levels.

© 1993 by The Center for Applied Research in Education

THE DOG WHELK

1. What type of snail is the dog whelk? (L-E)

   carnivorous

   meat- or flesh-eating

2. What is the dog whelk's *radula*? (L-E)

   tongue

   coiled tongue

3. Why do you think it is useful for the dog whelk to sedate a barnacle before attempting to eat it? (I-I)

   it then has no defenses

   the barnacle's muscles then provide no resistance

4. Why do you think it is helpful for a dog whelk to climb onto a mussel before attempting to drill a hole into it? (I-I)

   it would be easier when the mussel is directly under it

   **the radula probably has more power when the mussel is directly
     under it**

5. Why do you think it is important for the dog whelk's foot to be muscular? (I-I)

   the single foot must be very strong to support the shell and move it along

   there is only one foot to hold up the shell and move it along

Number of words in this selection _____454_____

Number of word-identification miscues _____

Word-Identification Miscues

   Independent reading level _____0–5_____
   Low independent reading level approx. _____6–11_____
   High instructional reading level approx. _____12–20_____
   Instructional reading level approx. _____21–36_____
   Low instructional reading level approx. _____37–41_____
   Frustration reading level _____42+_____

Number of comprehension errors _____

Comprehension Errors

   Independent reading level _____0_____
   Instructional reading level _____1_____
   Frustration reading level _____2+_____

© 1993 by The Center for Applied Research in Education

Variations of the Cloze Procedure _____

The cloze procedure was developed in 1953 by Wilson L. Taylor ("Cloze Procedure: A New Tool for Measuring Readability," *Journalism Quarterly*, 30, Fall 1953, pages 415–433) and is based on the psychological theory of *closure* which presumes that a person wants to finish any incomplete pattern. The cloze procedure is based upon the *prediction* aspects of reading, which indicate that a reader wants to predict the unknown words he/she may encounter in a passage. The cloze procedure, therefore, makes use of both semantic (word meaning) and syntactic (sentence structure) clues to help a reader deduce the unknown words he/she may meet in reading.

The cloze procedure has a number of different variations, each of which can be valuable in improving a child's ability in both comprehension and contextual analysis. In addition, one variation of the cloze procedure can be used as a useful alternative for determining a child's independent, instructional, and frustration reading levels.

In either case, you can construct a variation of the cloze procedure from a basal reader story, supplementary reading materials, a tradebook, or a content textbook. To construct a cloze procedure, choose a passage of about 250 words at what is believed to be the child's approximate instructional reading level. Then type the first and last sentences of the passage with no deletions on a word processor, ditto master, or stencil. Every *n*th word is deleted throughout the rest of the passage unless the selected word is a proper noun or an unduly difficult word. I recommend that every tenth word be omitted at the primary-grade reading level, every eighth word at the intermediate-grade reading level, and every fifth word at the upper-intermediate-grade reading levels and above. Although many reading specialists recommend omitting every fifth word for all children, my experience has indicated that this is simply too difficult for young children, especially with the traditional cloze procedure.

When the traditional cloze procedure is used to determine a child's approximate reading levels, you must count as correct only those completed blanks that are the same as the original passage, although incorrect spelling is not marked as incorrect.

Useful Variations of the Cloze Procedure

There are a number of variations of the traditional cloze procedure that reading teachers have used effectively in improving ability in both comprehension and contextual analysis. However, any variation of the cloze procedure must be preceded by many *cloze readiness activities* if the child is to be successful with later actual cloze activities.

My teacher-trainees have used many variations of the traditional cloze procedure to improve the competency of the children whom they have tutored in both contextual analysis and in comprehension. I recommend an easy version of cloze for the primary grades, in which all the omitted words are written in random order in columns at the bottom of the sheet containing the passage.

Another simple version for use in the primary grades has each of the deletions with two or three options being placed under it. This version is similar to an inventory in contextual analysis as explained in Chapter 3 of this *Handbook*. One other fairly easy version of cloze for use in the primary grades combines graphophonic (phonic) clues along with semantic (meaning) clues. In this variation the beginning letter or the first two letters (consonant blend or consonant digraph) are placed at the beginning of the omission. One other fairly easy version has random deletions with the deleted word quite easy to deduce.

One version often used at about the third- or fourth-grade reading level combines word length clues and semantic (meaning) clues. Each omitted word is replaced by a typewritten space as long as the omitted word. For example, here is how the word *monkey* would look if it were deleted from this kind of cloze procedure: _ _ _ _ _ _

NOTE: In all of the other versions of cloze, the length of each blank space should be about *fifteen typewritten spaces long.*

There are other useful variations of the cloze procedure. A number of these variations are most useful with students who are reading at about the intermediate-grade reading level or above. Some examples of these are the random omissions of nouns, verbs, adjectives, or adverbs. In each case, also, any noun, verb, adjective, or adverb that makes sense in that blank should be considered correct.

Some other contemporary variations of cloze include deleting entire sentences in a random manner, deleting more than one word at a time, deleting an entire phrase (such as a prepositional phrase), or deleting the unimportant words in a passage. You can construct a number of your own variations of the cloze procedure which are equally useful as the versions described here.

How to Score the Variations of the Cloze Procedure

As was stated earlier, the most common version of the cloze procedure is the *traditional version*, although I doubt it is the most useful one. In any case, after you have constructed the traditional cloze procedure, deleting every fifth word from the passage (with the exception of the first and last sentences), students should be encouraged to complete each blank space with the exact omitted word. The procedure is not timed.

In evaluating *only the traditional cloze procedure*, you must first count the number of blanks in the passage. This should usually be about fifty blanks. Then count the number of blanks that were completed with the exact omitted word. Then divide the total number of blanks into the number of blanks completed with the exact omitted words to obtain a percentage. For example, if a traditional cloze procedure contained fifty blanks and the student completed twenty of the blanks with the exact omitted word (even if spelled incorrectly), divide 50 into 20 to get a percentage (the student got 40 percent of the blanks correct). Then the following percentages can be used to get a rough estimate of the child's reading levels:

- 60 percent or more of the blanks completed with the exact omitted word—independent reading level
- 40 percent to 60 percent of the blanks completed with the exact omitted word—instructional reading level
- less than 40 percent of the blanks completed with the exact omitted word—frustration reading level

Remember that these percentages can be used only when every fifth word is deleted from a passage.

Other reading specialists use slightly different percentages for determining a child's approximate reading levels. Since none of the percentages have been sufficiently verified by objective research to be entirely accurate, the reading levels determined from the traditional cloze procedure should always be used only as an additional check on the reading levels determined from an IRI.

Although research has not established an exact level at which a child can be judged competent in the use of contextual analysis or comprehension by the use of any of the variations of the cloze procedure, you undoubtedly can use an 80-percent competency level as the approximate instructional reading level. For example, over a period of more than fifteen years hundreds of my students used the 80-percent competency level as the instructional reading level in most of the variations of the cloze procedure. As a result, I have found it to be quite accurate in comparison with the instructional reading level determined both from an Individual Reading Inventory and the traditional cloze procedure.

Samples of Cloze Exercises at the Third-Grade, Fourth-Grade, and Fifth-Grade Reading Levels*

Here is a sample cloze exercise at the third-grade reading level that combines graphophonic (phonic) clues and semantic (meaning) clues; a sample cloze procedure at the fourth-grade reading level using random deletions; and a sample traditional cloze exercise at the fifth-grade level. You may duplicate any of these cloze procedures in their present form and use them in your reading improvement program with either competent or disabled readers or with learning-handicapped children. You can also use them as models in constructing your own cloze exercises. (The answers are given at the end of the chapter.)

---

*The ready-to-duplicate cloze procedures contained in this chapter can be used for either assessment or teaching in semantic (contextual) analysis and comprehension. They could equally well have been included in Chapter 6.

CLOZE PROCEDURE COMBINING SEMANTIC (CONTEXTUAL) ANALYSIS AND GRAPHOPHONIC (PHONIC) ANALYSIS

(Third-Grade Reading Level)

Name_____ Grade_____ Teacher_____ Date_____

Read this story about Walt Disney to yourself. The first letter or the first two letters of each omitted word have been put in the blank space as a clue. Write each <u>entire</u> omitted word in the space. When you are done, read the story again to be sure it makes sense.

WALT DISNEY

Almost every child today has heard the name "Disney."

However, not very many children know much about Walt

Disney, a v_____ interesting man.

Walt Disney spent much of his childhood i_____

Missouri where he learned to love animals. When he

w_____ a boy, he liked to draw cartoons, especially of

th_____ animals he had seen. When he grew up, Walt

dr_____ cartoons to earn a living for awhile.

However, he quickly b_____ interested in making

his cartoons move in films. This pr_____ is called

"animation," which means that artists draw cartoons,

c_____ them out, photograph them, and then move a

part of th_____ bodies a tiny bit and photograph

them again.

Walt devoted m_____ of his life to improving the

animation of cartoons f_____ films. He was the crea-

tor of the cartoon character Mickey Mouse a_____ of

such famous animated films as <u>Snow White and</u>

99

th_____ Seven Dwarfs and Cinderella. During this

time of his l_____, Walt earned and lost much money

since some of h_____ films were very successful and

some were not.

However, Walt i_____ just as famous for creating two

very popular amusement p_____—Disneyland in

California and Walt Disney World in Florida. Millions

o_____ children and adults have visited these very

famous parks a_____ have enjoyed them very much.

Walt Disney had b_____ a heavy smoker for much of

his life. He developed lung cancer i_____ 1966 at the

age of sixty-five and died. However, his cartoon characters,

animated films, and amusement parks still give people much

happiness and fun.

CLOZE PROCEDURE USING WORD LENGTH AS A CLUE

(Fourth-Grade Reading Level)

Name_____ Grade_____ Teacher_____ Date_____

Read to yourself this story about the gray kangaroo that lives in eastern Australia. Write a word in each blank that makes sense and contains the right number of letters. When you have finished the story, read it again to be sure it is correct.

THE GRAY KANGAROO

The gray kangaroo of eastern Australia certainly is one

of the most fascinating wild animals in the whole world. One

of the most interesting facts about ____ ____ ____ ____ kan-

garoos is how the babies are born. ____ ____ ____ baby kan-

garoo is called a <u>joey</u> and ____ ____ born only thirty days

after its father ____ ____ ____ mother mate. The tiny <u>joey</u> is

less ____ ____ ____ ____ one inch long and weighs much less

____ ____ ____ ____ an ounce. Only the strongest babies ever

____ ____ ____ ____ long enough to reach the safety and

____ ____ ____ ____ of the mother's pouch. Although a <u>joey</u>

____ ____ ____ ____ ____ leaves the pouch for a short time

____ ____ ____ ____ it is about eight months old, it

____ ____ ____ ____ stay in its mother's pouch part of

____ ____ ____ time until it is about 300 days

____ ____ ____. A <u>joey</u> will not be fully grown

____ ____ ____ ____ ____ it is about 18 months old.

Gray ____ ____ ____ ____ ____ ____ ____ ____ ____ are

fairly large animals. The males are

____ ____ ____ ____ ____ ____ <u>bucks</u> and may stand more than seven ____ ____ ____ ____ tall and weigh up to 120

pounds. ____ ____ ____ females are called <u>does</u> and are usu-

ally ____ ____ ____ ____ ____ four feet tall. All of them have

____ ____ ____ ____ ____ ____ ____-brown fur, while the tips

of their ____ ____ ____ ____ ____ and the fingers of their

hands are ____ ____ ____ ____ ____. They also have large

dark eyes fringed with

____ ____ ____ ____ ____ ____ ____ ____ ____. They all must

groom themselves regularly with ____ ____ ____ ____ ____

tongue, teeth, and claws since they get ____ ____ ____ ____

ticks and fleas.

Although gray kangaroos may ____ ____ ____ ____ to be

as old as twenty-three, most ____ ____ ____ ____ ____ live

that long because of disease, other

____ ____ ____ ____ ____ ____ ____, and drought. The <u>does</u>

can have babies ____ ____ ____ ____ ____ they are about

sixteen years old. If you are not able to see a gray kangaroo

in Australia, you probably can see one in a zoo.

TRADITIONAL CLOZE PROCEDURE

(Fifth-Grade Reading Level)

Name_____ Grade_____ Teacher_____ Date_____

Silently read this passage about Princess Diana's childhood. Write a word in each blank that makes sense. When you have completed the passage, reread it to be sure it is correct.

PRINCESS DIANA'S CHILDHOOD

Almost everyone has read countless stories about Princess Diana of England. However, not very many _____ are familiar with the _____ story of her childhood.

_____ neither one of them _____ it, Diana and Charles _____ first met while she _____ only a baby and _____ was a teenager. Diana _____ born in 1961 at Park House, _____ of the two country _____ owned by the queen, _____ the royal family spent _____ winter and summer holidays. Park House _____ elegant, containing ten bedrooms _____ servants' quarters and garages. Diana _____ two older sisters and _____ younger brother, and she _____ particularly close to him. _____ Diana was surrounded by _____ during her childhood, she _____ felt comfortable with them _____ though she was from _____ aristocratic, not royal, family.

Diana's _____ family life very unfortunately _____ when she was only _____, after her mother chose _____ divorce her father and

© 1993 by The Center for Applied Research in Education

_____ another man. However, she _____ made the adjustment quite _____ and tried hard to _____ her younger brother who _____ not. A short time _____ Diana was sent to _____ expensive boarding school where _____ too tried hard to _____, although she had not _____ to go. Even at _____ age, she showed a _____ combination of self-confidence and _____ and learned how to _____ her own way without _____ too aggressive.

As a _____, Diana attended another exclusive _____ school. Although she never _____ or drank there, she _____ have a great weakness _____ candy. Diana was not _____ good student and had _____ difficulty with mathematics and French. _____ Diana was not highly _____ to do well in _____, she did not pass _____ of her required examinations _____ she was sixteen. It _____ about this time when Diana _____ Charles for the first _____ as an adult. Although Charles had been dating her older sister, apparently it was Diana who captured his interest.

Some Standardized Ways of Assessing (Diagnosing) Reading Disabilities

This part of the chapter briefly explains the more common and useful ways of assessing (diagnosing) reading disabilities. However, it is important at the beginning to provide the following statement about the role of standardized assessment in any reading improvement program, either for disabled readers or learning-handicapped students:

• Any standardized device is only a very tentative indicator of those qualities it is attempting to assess. It must never be thought of as an infallible measure of those qualities. A child's performance on any device can be influenced by countless number of factors, including but not limited to: his/her interest in taking the test, his/her rapport with the examiner, his/her health the day of the testing, and the personal environment of the testing setting.

• A child should never be placed into a group, classroom, or program as the result of a standardized device. The device always should be used along with teacher observation.

• Administrators should realize that teachers often are a much better source of diagnostic information than are standardized devices. I would normally place much more faith in an experienced teacher's assessment of a student's strengths and weaknesses than I would in any type of standardized device.

• Results from a standardized device should never be the sole means used to evaluate a teacher's performance.

Standardized Survey Reading or Achievement Tests

Almost all children with whom you will be working have been given a number of standardized survey reading tests during their school careers. Although such a test can be given alone, most often it is given as part of an achievement test battery that also includes tests in other curricular areas such as language usage, social studies, science, and arithmetic. Sometimes the survey reading test (most often, word meaning and comprehension) can be purchased separately from the rest of the achievement test battery.

A standardized survey reading test or the reading subtests of an achievement test battery try to evaluate a child's general or overall reading ability in the word identification skills (normally only at the primary-grade reading level), word meaning (vocabulary), sentence or paragraph comprehension, and sometimes study skills in such content areas as science and social studies. Usually students who score one year or more below grade level in the primary grades and two years or more below grade level in the intermediate grades should be given an Individual Reading Inventory or some type of diagnostic reading test to try to determine their specific reading skill strengths and weaknesses.

A standardized survey reading test is a group-administered, norm-referenced test (you can compare the results achieved by your group of children with the results achieved by a similar group of students in the standardization sample). Usually these are students of the same grade level, sex, socio-economic group, and geographic location. Norms can be reported in *grade equivalent scores*, *percentile ranks*, *stanines*, or *standard scores*.

• Although they are not valid and are not recommended by the International Reading Association, *grade equivalents* are still probably the most commonly used means to report a child's scores. Grade equivalent scores often *overestimate* a student's actual instructional reading level. The grade equivalent score is the grade level for which a raw score is the median score.

• A *percentile rank* indicates how a student compares in performance with other students of his/her age or grade.

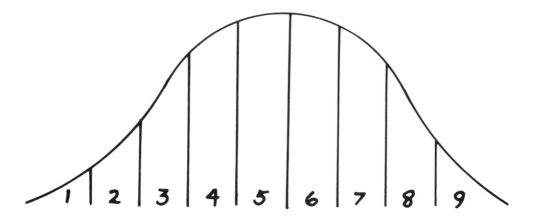

• *Stanines* are normalized standard scores that range from a low of 1 through a high of 9, with 5 being the average performance.

• A *standard score* is a normalized score that allows you to compare a child's performance on a number of different tests. It is the only type of score that can be averaged from test to test.

Any standardized test should be reliable and valid to be useful. *Reliability* refers to the degree to which a test provides consistent results, while *validity* indicates the degree of truthfulness or accuracy with which a test measures what it is supposed to measure.

A standardized survey reading test or the reading subtests of an achievement test have these main advantages:

• They serve as a useful screening device to determine which students need additional individual testing.
• They normally are easy to administer and to score. Often this type of test takes from about 45 minutes to 1½ hours to give, and the scoring can be entirely done by computer.
• They are usually reliable and valid.
• They reflect the reading programs of most elementary schools.
• They are formulated by test experts and experts in the field of reading.
• They can be given by a virtually untrained examiner.

However, all of these tests have the following significant limitations:

• They are not free of cultural bias and often discriminate against children from minority groups or children who speak nonstandard English.
• They often are not passage dependent. The child may be able to answer the comprehension questions without reading the material.
• They use only short reading passages to evaluate reading comprehension. This is unlike the reading skills required in actual school reading.
• They have considerable difficulty in evaluating a child's ability in implicit (higher-level) comprehension, since only one answer is possible for any question.
• They may well overestimate the child's actual instructional reading level due to the guessing factor and to the difficulty of obtaining a true estimate of a child's grade equivalent at the upper and lower ends of the scale.

These limitations indicate forcefully why a child's score on a standardized survey reading test or the reading subtests of an achievement test should *always* be thought of as only a tentative indicator of his/her actual instructional reading level.

A Partial List of Tests

Here is a very brief description of a few useful standardized survey reading or achievement tests. Keep in mind that these are only a few of the better tests; this is not a comprehensive list.

California Achievement Tests; Reading (1987). This test is available in two forms and is designed for use in grades K–12. Levels 11 (grades K.6–2.2), 12 (1.6–3.2), and 13 (2.6–4.2) contain subtests on phonic analysis, vocabulary, and comprehension. Level 13 also contains a structural analysis subtest. Levels 14–16 (grades 3.7–7.2) and 17–20 (6.6–12) have vocabulary and comprehension subtests.

California Test Bureau
Del Monte Research Park
Monterey, CA 93940

Gates-MacGinitie Reading Tests (1989). This test is available in either one or two forms and is designed for use in grades K–12. The PRE Test level is available in Form K (grades K.7–1.2) and contains four subtests that evaluate elements of emergent literacy. Level R is available in Form K (grades 1.0–1.9) and contains three parts that evaluate elements of phonic analysis, sight words, and context. Level 1 is available in Form K (grades 1.4–1.9) and evaluates vocabulary and comprehension. Level 2 is available in Forms K and L (grade 2) and evaluates vocabulary and comprehension; Level 3 is available in Forms K and L (grade 3) and evaluates vocabulary and comprehension; Level 4 is available in Forms K and L (grade 4) and evaluates vocabulary and comprehension; Level 5/6 is available in Forms K and L (grades 5 and 6) and evaluates vocabulary and comprehension; Level 7/9 is available in Forms K and L (grades 7–9) and evaluates vocabulary and comprehension; and Level 10/12 is available in Forms K and L (grades 10–12) and evaluates vocabulary and comprehension.

The Riverside Publishing Company
8420 Bryn Mawr Avenue
Chicago, IL 60601

Iowa Silent Reading Tests (1973). These tests measure the ability to apply reading strategies to different types of tasks. The Reading Efficiency Index shows the relative effectiveness of reading rate and comprehension. Level 1 (grades 6–9) and Level 2 (grades 9–14) contain subtests of vocabulary, comprehension, and directed reading (work-study skills including locational skills, skimming, scanning, and reading efficiency).

Psychological Corporation
555 Academic Court
San Antonio, TX 78204

Iowa Test of Basic Skills (1986). Levels 5 (K–1.5), 6 (K.8–1.9), 7 (1.7–2.6), and 8 (2.5–3.5) measure listening, word analysis, and vocabulary. Levels 6–8 also evaluate reading comprehension. Levels 9–14 (grades 3, 4, 5, 6, 7, and 8–9) have vocabulary, comprehension, and reference strategies subtests. It also lists behavioral objectives to which the test items were written.

Riverside Publishing Company
P.O. Box 1970
Iowa City, IA 52244

Metropolitan Achievement Test: Reading (1986). This test evaluates reading ability in comprehension and is available in two forms, designed for K–12 students at different levels.

Psychological Corporation
555 Academic Court
San Antonio, TX 78204

SRA Achievement Tests: Reading (1978). Levels B (grades 1–2) and C (2–3) subtests in letters and sounds, listening comprehension, vocabulary, and reading comprehension. Level B also evaluates auditory comprehension. Levels D (grades 3–4), E (4–6), F (6–8), G (8–10), and H (9–12) evaluate vocabulary and comprehension. Two forms designed for Grades 1–12.

SRA
155 North Wacker Drive
Chicago, IL 60606

Stanford Achievement Test: Reading (1987). Includes Primary 1 (grades 1.5–2.9), Primary 2 (2.5–3.9), Primary 3 (3.5–4.9), Intermediate 1 (4.5–5.9), Intermediate 2 (5.5–7.9), and Advanced (7.0–9.9). At various levels this test evaluates word-study skills, word reading, literal and inferential comprehension, vocabulary, and listening comprehension. Two forms designed for grades 1–9.

Psychological Corporation
555 Academic Court
San Antonio, TX 78204

Standardized Process-Oriented Measures of Reading Comprehension

The newest standardized testing thrust in comprehension seems to be some variation of a process-oriented measure of reading comprehension. This type of device is found in a number of state-mandated tests and in some basal reader tests.

These new types of standardized reading tests attempt to reflect contemporary research in reading comprehension. This research has discovered that reading is an active process that always involves the combination of prior knowledge, the printed material, and the child's reading strategies. Thus, reading involves combining the reader, the text, and the context of the reading material.

- *Reader elements* include such factors as prior knowledge, attitudes toward reading and the topic, ability to read the material, and knowledge of the appropriate strategies to use to improve comprehension.
- *Text elements* include such factors as the genre or type of material, how the author has structured the information, the difficulty of the material, and the organization of the text.
- *Context* includes such elements as the reader's purpose for reading, the setting where the reading takes place, and how the reader has to demonstrate his/her comprehension of the material.

The standardized process-oriented measures of reading comprehension normally employ an entire passage for the child to read. This passage often contains the actual pictures, tables, maps, or diagrams found in the reading material, which can be either narrative or expository material. This passage may be copied from an appropriate basal reader or content textbook at an appropriate reading level. The rationale behind this concept is that a longer passage is more like the actual reading a child does at school and at home.

Often prior to reading the passage the child completes a *topic familiarity (prior knowledge) section* that contains a brief summary of the selection followed by a number of questions of some type to assess the child's prior knowledge. The test next usually contains the complete narrative or expository passage. As stated earlier, often the entire passage is reprinted in the test booklet from the original basal reader story or content textbook.

The test may contain a number of *constructing meaning* questions. These questions differ from those found on the typical survey reading or achievement test in that they may have more than one possible correct answer. Both textually explicit (literal) and textually implicit (interpretive or critical) questions are used as well as application questions of some type.

The child's understanding and use of reading strategies also are usually contained in this type of standardized test. Such strategies may take the form of text lookbacks (looking back in the passage to locate the correct answer), rereading, reading only the first line in each paragraph, skimming, scanning, using contextual analysis, or using a dictionary.

Very briefly, here are a few advantages of process-oriented measures of comprehension:

- This type of test uses an entire narrative or expository passage with all of its inherent features, instead of using a short passage to evaluate reading comprehension. This more nearly duplicates actual reading situations.

- They teach the child that it is possible for an objective question to have more than one correct answer.

- They stress the effective use of the various word identification skills in the context of sentences and paragraphs. This is consistent with the whole language philosophy.

- They emphasize the importance of activating (using) prior knowledge before reading material. This greatly enhances comprehension ability.

- They demonstrate to the child that there are different purposes for reading different types of material.

Here are a few of the main limitations of the use of this type of test:

- It can be frustrating for the child to answer the comprehension questions when there is more than one correct answer if he/she has not had extensive practice with this concept prior to actually taking the test. Otherwise, the child often just marks the first correct answer that he/she sees and does not even read the remaining alternatives.

- Since each child's prior knowledge is different, it is difficult to score the topic familiarity (prior knowledge) section objectively.

- It is fairly difficult to evaluate a child's understanding and use of the appropriate reading strategies in this type of test.

- Teachers may feel threatened when this type of test is used to evaluate the performance of their children or—even worse—their own performance. Many of the teachers in Illinois I have spoken to who give the test dislike it.

In summary, a process-oriented measure of comprehension may have some value if it is used to help teachers emphasize the most important reading skills and strategies. It may be harmful if it is considered infallible and used to evaluate a teacher's performance.

Criterion-Referenced Tests

Although *criterion-referenced tests* may not be as widely used in reading improvement programs as they were in the past, it may be helpful for you to have some knowledge of them. They also are called *mastery tests* and deal with one or more of the reading subskills and specify the point at which the child may have mastered that subskill. They are not norm-referenced, but they may be used to evaluate a child's strengths and weaknesses in all of the word identification, comprehension, and study skills. The major purpose of their use is to help the teacher individualize reading instruction more effectively.

Here are the major advantages of these tests:

- They may help the reading teacher be sure that a child has truly mastered important reading skills.
- The child need not learn nor practice a reading skill that he/she already knows.

Here are the major limitations of these tests:

- They fragment the reading process. This is not in keeping with the whole language philosophy.
- The 80-percent criterion level is an arbitrary and often inaccurate cutoff point.
- It is difficult for such a test to evaluate ability in higher-level (implicit) comprehension skills.

Standardized Diagnostic Reading Tests

A *standardized diagnostic reading test* is an individually-administered or group-administered test that attempts to determine a child's specific strengths and weaknesses in the various word identification and comprehension skills. It often also tries to ascertain a child's approximate independent, instructional, and frustration reading levels. Such a test is usually used with a child who has not performed well on a standardized survey reading or achievement test. Such a student normally is reading one or more years below grade level in the primary grades and two or more years below grade level in the intermediate grades.

A diagnostic reading test can evaluate word-identification ability in such subskills as knowledge of letter names; sight-word knowledge; understanding of various phonic elements such as consonants, consonant blends, vowels, word families, and auditory blending; understanding of various structural elements such as prefixes, suffixes, base or root words, and syllabication; and contextual analysis. In addition, a diagnostic reading test can also assess competency in vocabulary knowledge, explicit and implicit comprehension, and rate of reading.

Since diagnostic reading tests have been prepared by test experts, they typically are both reliable and valid. They also have been field tested and revised as a result of this testing. Most of them contain tables of norms such as percentile ranks and stanines with which to compare your students' results.

If you give a disabled reader or a learning-handicapped child an Individual Reading Inventory, you normally would *not* give him/her an individual diagnostic reading test, although you might wish to administer a group diagnostic reading test. An individual diagnostic reading test and an IRI evaluate about the same reading skills in approximately the same manner. You normally choose to give a diagnostic reading test when you want to give a child a valid and reliable device.

Although most IRIs are not valid and reliable since they have not been constructed in the same manner as a standardized test, they still can be useful in the determination of a child's reading strengths and weaknesses.

Nevertheless, I prefer to give a child an IRI instead of a diagnostic reading test, but acknowledge that other reading teachers prefer to give an individual or group diagnostic reading test.

Normally you can give a group diagnostic reading test to a mildly or perhaps moderately disabled reader to whom you do not wish to take the time to give an individual device. Since a group diagnostic reading test can be given to a group of students at the same time, it does not require the administration time of either an individual diagnostic reading test or an IRI. However, you can also give a group diagnostic reading test on an individual basis if the student is only mildly disabled.

Most individual and group diagnostic reading tests evaluate a student's reading competencies and weaknesses quite effectively through about the eighth-grade instructional reading level. Therefore, they can be used with secondary school students who are functioning at the eighth-grade level or below.

A standardized individually administered or group-administered diagnostic reading test has these main advantages:

- Since it is standardized, it is more valid and reliable than the typical Individual Reading Inventory.
- It effectively ascertains a student's specific reading skill strengths and weaknesses and establishes his/her correct instructional reading level. Therefore, a child's corrective or remedial reading program can be appropriately prescribed.

However, each of these tests has the following limitations of which you should be aware:

- The individually administered diagnostic reading test normally takes considerable time to learn how to give, to actually administer, and to score. However, a group diagnostic reading test usually does not contain this limitation.
- They are not free of cultural bias and often discriminate against children from minority groups or children who speak a nonstandard English dialect.
- The group diagnostic reading tests are not particularly valid in assessing a student's ability in phonic analysis. For example, most group tests in phonic analysis require sound-symbol association, while reading requires symbol-sound association, a much more difficult task since there are so many different sounds to choose from, especially in the case of vowel phonemes.
- Nonsense words (pseudowords) often are used to evaluate competency in word identification, because the words on such a test must be unknown to the student if he/she is to demonstrate ability to apply phonic analysis or structural analysis effectively. Although nonsense words can be useful in testing word-identification skills, a number of students do not respond well to a subtest containing many such words since they have no association (referent) for the child.

A Partial List of Tests

Here is a brief description of a few useful standardized individual or group diagnostic reading tests. They should be thought of only as representative of some of the tests in this category:

Diagnostic Reading Scales (1981). This is an individual norm-referenced and criterion-referenced test. It contains three word lists (40 to 50 words each); two sets of eleven graded passages (preprimer–seventh reader), with seven or eight comprehension questions, each mainly at the literal (explicit) level; and twenty supplementary decoding tests (mainly phonic analysis). The word-recognition criterion for oral reading is norm-referenced, while the comprehension criterion for oral and silent reading and listening comprehension is criterion-referenced. The instructional level is based on oral reading, while the independent level is based on silent reading. It is designed for grades 1–7.

California Test Bureau
Del Monte Research Park
Monterey, CA 93940

Durrell Analysis of Reading Difficulty (1980). This individual test contains five primary- and three intermediate-level paragraphs each followed by mainly literal (explicit) questions. The instructional level (oral reading) is primarily based on reading time with comprehension given some consideration. There are five different primary and intermediate-level paragraphs for silent reading. The independent level for silent reading is based upon reading time and retelling of the material. There are six passages available for assessing listening comprehension. The criterion for listening comprehension is no more than two incorrect answers out of seven or eight for about a 75-percent level. Word recognition/word analysis consists of four fifty-word lists. The words are flashed first and then unknown words are shown untimed. The listening/vocabulary test consists of five fifteen-word lists, and the student indicates in which of three categories the word belongs. The sounds-in-isolation test measures symbol-sound associations. The spelling test consists of two twenty-word lists and fifteen words dictated on the phonic-spelling-of-words test. The test also includes tests devoted to visual memory for words and identifying sounds in words. In addition, the test evaluates prereading phonic abilities.

Psychological Corporation
555 Academic Court
San Antonio, TX 78204

Gates-McKillop-Horowitz Reading Diagnostic Tests (1981). This battery contains fifteen individually-administered tests. The oral reading test has seven paragraphs. The score is based *solely* on the number of word recognition errors. The reading sentences test contains four sentences that are read orally, and the score is based on word recognition. The flash and untimed tests are based on the same four ten-word lists. The word attack portion of the test assesses syllabication, recognition, and blending of common word parts; decoding nonsense words (pseudowords), making symbol-sound associations for single consonants, and naming upper- and lower-case letters. The recognition of visual form of sounds evaluates sound-symbol association of single vowels. The auditory tests evaluate blending and discrimination. Spelling and writing skills are evaluated by a written expression test. The battery is designed for students functioning at grades 1–6 reading levels.

Teachers College Press
1234 Amsterdam Avenue
New York, NY 10027

Stanford Diagnostic Reading Test (1984). This test battery consists of four levels: Red (grades 1.5–4.5), Green (3.5–6.5), Brown (5.5–8.5), and Blue (7.5–13.0). The skill areas and grades at which each is measured are: auditory discrimination, grades 1.5–6.5; phonic analysis, grades 1.5–8.5; auditory vocabulary (meanings of spoken words), grades 1.5–8.5; literal (explicit) and interpretive (implicit) reading comprehension, all grades; structural analysis, grades 3.5–13.0; reading rate, grades 5.5–13.0; word parts (knowledge of affixes and base words), vocabulary, and skimming and scanning, grades 7.5–13. Each level is available in two forms, and the four levels cover grades 1–13.

Psychological Corporation
555 Academic Court
San Antonio, TX 78204

Woodcock Reading Mastery Test, Revised (1987). This is an individual test. Form G has six subtests: visual-auditory learning; letter identification, word-identification; word attack (decoding nonsense words); and word comprehension (modified cloze test of sentence comprehension). Form H contains only the last four of the previously mentioned subtests. The test is available in two forms.

American Guidance Service
Publishers Building
Circle Pines, MN 55014

Visual and Auditory Perception Tests

As stated in detail in Chapter 1, a learning-handicapped child may well have difficulty either with visual perception or auditory perception ability. Therefore, it may be helpful for a child—especially in the primary grades—to be given a visual perception or auditory perception test if he/she evidences a weakness in either or both of these channels.

A Partial List of Visual Perception Tests

Here is a brief description of some of the most common visual perception tests:

Bender Visual-Motor Gestalt Test (1963). This individual test measures perceptual-motor integration whereby the child copies nine abstract designs which remain in view. The child's reproductions are scored on the basis of departures from the models.

American Guidance Service
Publishers Building
Circle Pines, MN 55014

or

Psychological Corporation
555 Academic Court
San Antonio, TX 78204

Frostig Developmental Test of Visual Perception (1966). This test consists of five subtests: eye-motor coordination (drawing continuous lines between increasingly narrow boundaries); figure-ground (picking out and outlining geometric forms of differing sizes, shadings, textures, and positions); constancy of shape (discriminating among geometric forms of differing sizes, shadings, textures, and positions); position in space (distinguishing between figures in the same or reversed or rotated positions); and spatial relations (joining dots to reproduce forms and patterns shown). It is designed for ages 7 and 8.

Consulting Psychologists Press
577 College Avenue
Palo Alto, CA 94306

Benton Revised Visual Retention Test (1974). This individual test is designed to assess visual perception, visual memory, and visual-motor integration. Ten designs, one at a time, are shown briefly, and the child tries to draw each one. It also gives IQ equivalent scores.

Psychological Corporation
555 Academic Court
San Antonio, TX 78204

Developmental Test of Visual-Motor Integration (1989). This is an individual test that measures ability to integrate visual perception and motor behavior. The child copies up to twenty-four geometric forms of increasing difficulty. It is designed for ages 3 to 18.

Modern Curriculum Press
13900 Prospect Road
Cleveland, OH 44136

Psycho-educational Inventory of Basic Learning Abilities (1968). This evaluates fifty-three basic learning abilities in six areas: gross motor development, sensory-motor integration, perceptual-motor skills, language development, conceptual skills, and social skills. It is designed for children aged 5–12.

Fearon/Janus/Quercus
500 Harbor Boulevard
Belmont, CA 94002

Auditory Memory Span Test (1975). This individual test requires the ability to retain and recall sets of single-syllable words spoken by the examiner. The sets range from two to six words. The test is available in two forms.

Language Research Associates
P.O. Drawer 2085
Palm Springs, CA 92262

or

Stoelting Company
1350 South Kostner Avenue
Chicago, IL 60623

Lindamood Auditory Conceptualization Test (1971). This is an individual test consisting of four parts: precheck (understanding needed to take the test); identifying the number of sounds heard and determining whether they are the same or different; indicating the sequence and determining the number of sounds in a syllable; and changes in the sound pattern when sounds are added, deleted, or changed. The understanding of the task is indicated by manipulating colored blocks. It is available for preschool through adult.

DLM Teaching Resources
One DLM Park
Allen, TX 75002

Purdue Perceptual-Motor Survey (1966). This is an individual test with a series of eleven tasks measuring balance and posture, body image, perceptual-motor skills, ocular control, and form perception. It is designed for ages 6 to 10.

Psychological Corporation
555 Academic Court
San Antonio, TX 78204

A Partial List of Auditory Discrimination Tests

Here is a brief description of two common auditory discrimination tests:

Goldman-Fristoe-Woodcock Test of Auditory Discrimination (1976). This test measures speech sound discrimination and is designed for ages four and up.

American Guidance Service
Publishers Building
Circle Pines, MN 55014

Wepman Auditory Discrimination Test, Revised (1987). This test contains forty pairs of words the child is to discriminate between when pronounced by the examiner. The teacher asks the child whether each word pair is the same or different. It cannot be used with children or teachers who do not speak the standard dialect.

Language Research Associates
P.O. Drawer 2085
Palm Springs, CA 92262

Some Individual and Group Intelligence Tests and Their Place in a Reading Improvement Program

Intelligence tests are used in any reading improvement program both with those children who are learning handicapped and with those who are not. An individual intelligence test is more valid than a group intelligence test since any group intelligence test tends to measure some degree of reading ability as well as intellectual ability. Thus, disabled readers of any type do not score well on the group intelligence test, and teachers sometimes believe that these readers do not have the intellectual potential which they actually possess.

However, even an individual intelligence test is only an estimate of a child's actual intellectual ability, since the results can be influenced by so many factors. The intelligence test results can be influenced by test anxiety, the child's physical health that day, the child's lack of prior knowledge (especially for minority group children), and the rapport between the examiner and the child, for example.

Most individual intelligence tests must be given by a school psychologist, a psychiatrist, or perhaps a guidance counselor. Most often, the individual intelligence test is given by the school psychologist in the district. Each student who is classified as "learning handicapped" is given a test of this type. You can learn to give such a test yourself if you enroll in a post-graduate-level course on testing.

Many reading specialists and psychologists think the *Wechsler Intelligence Scale for Children, Revised (WISC-R)* (Psychological Corporation, 555 Academic Court, San Antonio,

Texas 78204) is the most valid individual intelligence test for use in any reading improvement program with average and learning-handicapped students. It is designed for children from ages 5 to 15, while a parallel individual intelligence test—the *Wechsler Adult Intelligence Scale, Revised (WAIS-R)*—is designed for students older than 15. It is available from the same publisher.

The WISC-R yields a *verbal intelligence quotient*, a *performance intelligence quotient*, and a *full-scale intelligence quotient*. Since the verbal score is usually considered the most highly related to reading success, a number of disabled readers score somewhat more highly in the performance area. On the whole, disabled readers do not score well in the arithmetic, information, digit span, and coding subtests. They often do better on the subtests for comprehension, picture completion, block design, picture arrangement, and object assembly. Their performance often is mixed on the similarities and vocabulary subtests.

On the WISC-R (1974), the six subtests on the Verbal Scale are the following:

- *Information*: This subtest consists of thirty questions to evaluate a child's general range of knowledge and background. It may be influenced to some extent by cultural background.

- *Comprehension*: This subtest contains seventeen questions believed to be a test of "common sense" that evaluates a child's ability to use past information and to evaluate past experiences.

- *Arithmetic*: This subtest consists of eighteen questions that evaluate the child's ability to solve arithmetical problems. All questions must be answered orally.

- *Similarities*: This subtest of seventeen questions measures the child's ability to use logical reasoning processes to notice similarities.

- *Vocabulary*: This subtest contains thirty-two words that measure the child's knowledge of the meaning of words. This subtest is often one of the most effective predictors of reading achievement.

- *Digit Span*: This is a measure of a child's ability to remember a series of digits forward and backward.

In the WISC-R the Performance Scale consists of the following six subtests:

- *Picture Completion*: This subtest consists of a series of twenty-one pictures, each of which contains a missing part. The child must indicate the missing part either verbally or by pointing to the answer.

- *Picture Arrangement*: This subtest consists of twelve different series of pictures. Each series is placed in front of the child in mixed order. Then the child must arrange the pictures in order.

- *Block Design*: The child is given blocks with different designs on them. The child must arrange the blocks so that they match a pictured design shown by the examiner.

- *Object Assembly*: This subtest consists of four form boards the child is required to complete. Each is timed.

- *Coding (Digit Symbol)*: The child is required to make associations between various symbols. This subtest provides some information about the child's speed and accuracy of learning.

- *Mazes*: This subtest is not used often unless one of the other subtests is spoiled in the administration of the test. It consists of a series of eight pictured mazes the children have to find their way through.

In the past the *Stanford-Binet Intelligence Scale, Revised* (1986) was more commonly used in reading improvement programs than it is today. It contains fifteen subtests in four areas: verbal reasoning (vocabulary, comprehension, absurdities); abstract/visual reasoning (pattern analysis, matrices, paper folding and cutting, copying); quantitative comprehension (quantitative, number series, equation building); and STM (memory for sentences, digits, and objects). This test yields scores for each subject, for each of the four general areas, and a complete score. The scores correspond to IQs that are now called "Standard Age Scores." It is designed for ages 2 to adult.

Riverside Publishing Company
8420 Bryn Mawr Avenue
Chicago, IL 60631

The *Peabody Picture Vocabulary Test, Revised (PPVT-R)* is an individual intelligence test that is sometimes used in a reading improvement program. It is not normally given to a learning-handicapped child in the screening process in place of another individual intelligence test. However, this test can be given by a reading teacher. It consists of a number of pictures that are shown to the child. The child points to the picture that best illustrates the word spoken by the examiner. It is available in two forms and is normally given to children from ages 2½ to 4.

American Guidance Service
Publishers Building
Circle Pines, MN 55014

Other Tests

Here is a brief description of a few other useful individual intelligence tests:

Goodenough-Harris Drawing Test (1963). This is a nonverbal test of mental ability. The child's drawings of human figures are compared to twelve ranked drawings and scored for presence of up to seventy-three characteristics. There are separate norms for boys and girls. It is used with children ages 3 to 15.

Psychological Corporation
555 Academic Court
San Antonio, TX 78204

Kuhlman-Anderson Test (1982). This evaluates academic potential and consists of eight subtests, four verbal and four nonverbal in levels K (kindergarten), A (grade 1), B (2), CD (3–4), D (4–5), EF (5–7), G (7–9), H (9–12)

Scholastic Testing Service
450 Meyer Road
P.O. Box 1056
Bensenville, IL 60606

Otis-Lennon School Ability Test (1987). This evaluates abstract thinking and reasoning ability in levels Primary 1 (grade 1), Primary II (2–3), Elementary (4–5), Intermediate (6–8), and Advanced (9–12). There are two forms.

Psychological Corporation
555 Academic Court
San Antonio, TX 78204

Slosson Intelligence Test (1981). This is an individual brief measure of intelligence. Many of the items are similar to those on the Stanford-Binet. It is designed for ages 2–18.

Stoelting Publishing Company
1350 S. Kostner Avenue
Chicago, IL 60623

Several Unique Tests for Assessing Abilities of Learning-Handicapped Children

The following tests may be useful in assessing the abilities of learning-handicapped children. Many of the tests mentioned earlier in this chapter and in Chapter 1 are also useful with this kind of child.

Houston Test for Language Development (1978). This test evaluates vocabulary, comprehension, word attack, and listening as well as nonverbal communication. It has two forms and is designed for infancy through 6 years of age.

Stoelting Publishing Company
1350 S. Kostner Avenue
Chicago, IL 60623

Harris Tests of Lateral Dominance (1958). This is an individual test to evaluate knowledge of left and right; hand preferences; simultaneous writing with both hands; speed and coordination in writing, tapping, and dealing cards; monocular and binocular tests of eye dominance; and foot dominance.

Psychological Corporation
555 Academic Court
San Antonio, TX 78204

Diagnostic Test of Arithmetic Strategies (1984). This test evaluates ability to perform addition, subtraction, multiplication, and division. The analysis of performance allows for identification of faulty computational strategies and probable strengths. It is designed for grades K through 6.

Pro-Ed
5341 Industrial Oaks Boulevard
Austin, TX 78735

Illinois Test of Psycholinguistic Abilities, Revised (ITPA-R) (1969). This individual test evaluates abilities in three dimensions: channels of communication, psycholinguistic processes, and levels of organization. It contains twelve subtests: auditory reception, visual reception, auditory association, verbal expression, manual expression, grammatic closure, visual closure, and sound blending. It is designed for ages 2–10.

Slosson Educational Publications
P.O. Box 280
East Aurora, NY 14052

Test for Auditory Comprehension of Language, Revised (1985). This is an individual test of listening comprehension covering word classes and relations, morphemes, and elaborated sentence constructions. It is designed for ages 3–7.

DLM Teaching Resources
One DLM Park
Allen, TX 75002

Test of Language Development–2 (1988). This is an individual test. The primary edition (ages 4–8) has seven subtests that measure various components of receptive and expressive language (word meaning and use, grammar, articulation, auditory discrimination). The intermediate edition (ages 8–12) has six subtests that measure word meaning and use, as well as three aspects of syntactic and semantic knowledge.

Pro-Ed
5341 Industrial Oaks Boulevard
Austin, TX 78735

Kerby Learning Modality Test (1980). This individual brief screening test is designed to measure visual, auditory, and motor activity strengths and weaknesses. It has eight subtests: visual and auditory discrimination, visual and auditory closure, visual and auditory memory, and visual and auditory motor coordination.

Western Psychological Service
Box 775
Beverly Hills, CA 90213

Learning Style Identification Scale (1981). This test identifies five learning styles based on the child's internal sources of information (feelings, beliefs, attitudes) and external sources of information (other people, events, social institutions). It is designed for grades 1–8.

Educators Publishing Service
75 Moulten Street
Cambridge, MA 02238

Halstead-Reitan Neuropsychological Test Battery (1979). This individual test consists of three batteries: *Reitan-Indiana Neuropsychological Test Battery for Children* (ages 5 to 8), thirteen tests assessing a broad range of neurological functions; *Halstead Neuropsychological Test Battery for Children* (ages 9 to 14), eleven tests; *Halstead Neurological Test Battery for Adults* (ages 15 and up).

Neuropsychological Laboratory
The University of Arizona
Tucson, AZ 85721

Luria-Nebraska Neuropsychological Battery (1980). This individual test assesses a broad range of neuropsychological functions. It consists of 269 discrete, scored items in fourteen scales: motor, rhythm, tactile, visual, receptive and expressive language, writing, reading, arithmetic, memory, intellectual, pathognomonic, and left and right hemisphere. It requires a trained examiner and is available in two forms. It is designed for ages 15 and up.

Western Psychological Service
Box 775
Beverly Hills, CA 90213

Luria-Nebraska Neuropsychological Battery: Children's Revision (1987). This individual test assesses a broad range of neuropsychological functions similar to those listed in the preceding test. It includes screening and diagnosing general and specific cognitive deficits. It is not useful with children who have low verbal ability. It requires a trained examiner and is designed for ages 5 through 12.

Western Psychological Service
Box 775
Beverly Hills, CA 90213

Neurological Dysfunctions of Children (1979). This individual screening device is for deciding whether to refer a child for a neurological examination. It is a series of eighteen yes-no items. The first sixteen items require the child to perform simple tasks such as walking along a straight line, touching a finger to his/her nose, and following a moving object with his/her eyes. It is designed for ages 3 through 10.

American Guidance Service
Publishers Building
Circle Pines, MN 55014

Quick Neurological Screening Test (1978). This individual brief screening test assesses fifteen areas of neurological integration. It samples motor development, control of large and small muscles, motor planning and sequencing, sense of rate and rhythm, spatial organization, visual and auditory perception, balance and cerebellar-vestibular function, and attention. It is designed for ages 5 through adult.

Slosson Educational Publications
P.O. Box 280
East Aurora, NY 14052

or

Psychological Corporation
555 Academic Court
San Antonio, TX 78204

ANSWERS TO "WALT DISNEY"

very	cut	his
in	their	is
was	much	parks
the	for	of
drew	and	and
became	the	been
process	life	in

Note: In this variation of the cloze procedure, every tenth word was omitted. However, there is a slight variation from this pattern of deletions due to the difficulty of completing a word in that position.

ANSWERS TO "THE GRAY KANGAROO"

gray	will	tails
The	the	black
is	old	eyelashes
and	until	their
than	kangaroos	both
than	called	live
live	feet	do not
food	The	animals
first	about	until
when	grayish	

Note: Every eighth word was omitted from this passage except when the deletion would have caused undue difficulty.

ANSWERS TO "PRINCESS DIANA'S CHILDHOOD"

people	had	well	boarding
accurate	one	help	smoked
Although	was	did	did
remembers	Because	later	for
probably	royalty	an	a
was	always	she	great
he	even	adjust	Since
was	an	wanted	motivated
one	stable	this	school
estates	ended	unique	all
where	six	shyness	when
both	to	get	was
[was] is	marry	appearing	met
and	apparently	teenager	time

Note: Every fifth word was deleted from this traditional cloze procedure unless it was a proper noun. If you wish to use the formula contained earlier in this section, only the exact omitted word can be scored as correct. However, if you do not wish to use this formula, a synonym of the omitted word can be counted as correct.

3

Ready-to-Use Materials for Diagnosing Disabilities in the Word-Identification Techniques

Do you believe that most disabled readers and learning handicapped students in the primary and lower intermediate grades are competent in the various word-identification techniques? If you answered "no" to this question, you are absolutely correct. Disabled readers at this level typically have great difficulty with sight-word recognition or phonic (graphophonic) analysis. On the other hand, both disabled readers and learning handicapped students at the intermediate-grade level seem to have the most difficulty with comprehension, especially higher-type comprehension.

What Constitutes Letter-Name Knowledge?

Letter-name knowledge has been found by research to be very predictive of primary-grade reading achievement. Although a child probably could learn to read without knowledge of the letter names, it is essential for all children to learn the letter names fairly near the beginning of reading instruction.

Letter-name knowledge consists of two separate elements, *letter recognition* and *letter identification*. The latter is the more difficult of the two since it's usually easier for a child to select a letter from several options than it is for him/her to name that same letter. Since it is easier, letter recognition is sometimes taught before letter identification. In tutoring kindergarten children who have difficulty with emergent literacy, my teacher-trainees often stress letter matching first, then letter recognition, and finally letter identification. However, letter identification normally is the final goal.

Research has not found an order for teaching the letter names. My teacher-trainees normally teach the letters in the child's own first name first. Although many children enter kindergarten printing their name in all capital letters, we try to teach it the proper way: Betsy. After the child has learned to recognize and identify the letters in his/her first name, we often teach the more useful letters next. You can choose to teach the easier letters instead.

It is important for children to learn the difference between a *letter* and a *word*; a number of entering kindergarten children are not aware of the difference. It is also important for the child to learn to use the proper term. For example, the letter *w* can be called either a *capital letter* or an *upper-case letter*. The terms *big* and *little* should not be used because the letter *h* might well be thought of as "big" by a child

At the emergent literacy stage, it is important to determine which capital and lower-case letter names a child knows. We normally do this at the beginning of kindergarten tutoring with the children who are recommended for special help by their teachers. After we have made the assessment (see the next section for details), we attempt to teach the child the letter names he/she needs to know. This is often a very difficult task for the children whom we work with since a number of these children later will be classified as learning handicapped. It can take as long as ten half-hour tutoring sessions for the child to learn up to three letter names. (All of the strategies we use to teach the letter names are found in Chapter 5 of this *Handbook*.) The various tracing strategies normally have been the most effective in teaching letter names.

Assessing Letter-Name Knowledge in Isolation

Letter-name knowledge can be assessed both in isolation and in context. Although the whole-language philosophy prefers that letter-name knowledge be assessed and taught in word and sentence context, the letter names must be taught and practiced in isolation some of the time, especially with children who have a very difficult time with them and with learning handicapped children.

When possible, letter-name knowledge is best evaluated in isolation by using *individual letter cards*. Simply print each capital and lower-case letter name on a separate small card (about 2 or 3 inches square) with a marking pen.

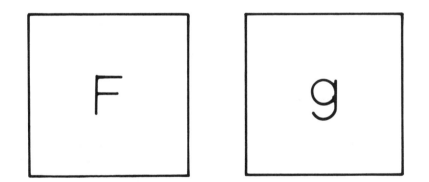

Then present the capital and lower-case letter names in random order and have the child identify each one of them. If you wish to stress the lower-case letter names first, do not assess the child's ability in the capital letter names until later.

We usually use some type of word puzzle to see if a child can match each capital letter name to its lower-case counterpart. To construct a series of puzzles, cut oaktag or posterboard into pieces about 5 or 6 inches long and 2 or 3 inches wide. Then print each capital letter and its matching lower-case letter on the piece of oaktag with a marking pen, and cut each puzzle apart using different types of cut. Here are some examples.

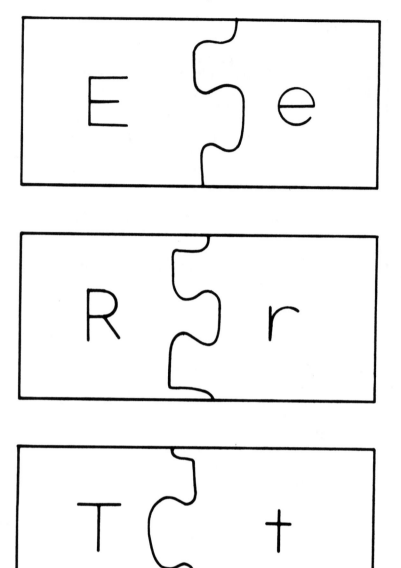

Place all of the puzzle parts into a large brown envelope. Then have the child try to put each puzzle together by matching each capital letter with its lower-case counterpart. Have the child pronounce each capital and lower-case letter name as the puzzle is assembled and state whether it is a capital or lower-case letter.

Although the preceding activities are valuable in stressing letter identification, each activity must be done individually and they are very time-consuming for a teacher to do. Therefore, you may want to assess a child's ability in letter recognition instead, although it probably is not quite as valid. If this seems more feasible, an assessment sheet for this purpose can be used.

Assessment Sheets for Evaluating Letter-Name Recognition

Here are assessment sheets you can use to help determine a child's ability in letter recognition. You can duplicate and use the sheets in their present form or modify them in any way you wish.

TEACHER'S COPY
ASSESSING LETTER RECOGNITION IN ISOLATION
(Emergent Literacy Level)

Upper-Case Letter Recognition in Isolation

1. Put your finger on the line that begins with the apple.
   In that line put an X on the capital E.

   F E L R D

2. Put your finger on the line that begins with the flower.
   In that line put an X on the capital M.

   N A H M W

3. Put your finger on the line that begins with the spoon.
   In that line put an X on the capital A.

   A K P V Y

4. Put your finger on the line that begins with the tree.
   In that line put an X on the capital B.

   R B D P Q

5. Put your finger on the line that begins with the house.
   In that line put an X on the capital C.

   C E S G O

6. Put your finger on the line that begins with the car.
   In that line put an X on the capital S.

   G O C S Z

7. Put your finger on the line that begins with the man.
   In that line put an X on the capital I.

   I J T E H

8. Put your finger on the line that begins with the cat.
   In that line put an X on the capital K.

   Y K R P Z

9. Put your finger on the line that begins with the ball.
   In that line put an X on the capital D.

   G S R P D

10. Put your finger on the line that begins with the fork.
    In that line put an X on the capital O.

    C O Q D U

Name_____ Date_____

UPPER-CASE LETTER RECOGNITION IN ISOLATION

F	E	L	R	D
N	A	H	M	W
A	K	P	V	Y
R	B	D	P	Q
C	E	S	G	O
G	O	C	S	Z
I	J	T	E	H
Y	K	R	P	Z
G	S	R	P	D
G	O	Q	D	U

Lower-Case Letter Recognition in Isolation

1. Put your finger on the line that begins with the woman.
   In that line put an X on the lower-case c.

   s i o c e

2. Put your finger on the line that begins with the knife.
   In that line put an X on the lower-case t.

   t l f k z

3. Put your finger on the line that begins with the dog.
   In that line put an X on the lower-case m.

   h m n w c

4. Put your finger on the line that begins with the kite.
   In that line put an X on the lower-case w.

   v m w x y

5. Put your finger on the line that begins with the sun.
   In that line put an X on the lower-case b.

   b h d a g

6. Put your finger on the line that begins with the umbrella.
   In that line put an X on the lower-case g.

   q p g y j

7. Put your finger on the line that begins with the snowman.
   In that line put an X on the lower-case k.

   k y l i f

8. Put your finger on the line that begins with the tree.
   In that line put an X on the lower-case r.

   r t v e f

9. Put your finger on the line that begins with the snake.
   In that line put an X on the lower-case i.

   l j i n h

10. Put your finger on the line that begins with the fish.
    In that line put an X on the lower-case p.

    q p b d a

CHILD'S COPY
ASSESSING LETTER RECOGNITION IN ISOLATION

Name_____ Date_____

LOWER-CASE LETTER RECOGNITION IN ISOLATION

s   i   o   c   e

t   l   f   k   z

h   m   n   w   c

v   m   w   x   y

b   h   d   a   g

q   p   g   y   j

k   y   l   i   f

r   t   v   e   f

l   j   i   n   h

q   p   b   d   a

Assessing Letter-Name Knowledge in Context _____

As stated earlier, letter-name knowledge can be assessed and taught in context as well as in isolation. According to the proponents of the whole language philosophy, letter-name knowledge is best assessed and presented in the context of words and sentences.

Proponents of whole language correctly believe that letter-name knowledge is most meaningful to children when letter names are found in their own dictated or written language-experience stories, in predictable books, or in easy-to-read tradebooks. For example, the letter *f* undoubtedly has more meaning to a child when he/she finds it in the words in his/her own language-experience story or locates all of the words with a *f* in them from a predictable book that has just been read and enjoyed. (Chapter 5 presents a number of meaningful ways in which letter-name knowledge can be presented and reinforced in context.)

Assessment Sheet for Recognizing Upper-Case and Lower-Case Letter Names in Context

Here is a ready-to-duplicate sheet to help assess a child's ability to recognize the upper-case and lower-case letter names in context. You can duplicate and use this activity sheet in its present form or modify it in any way you wish.

TEACHER'S COPY
ASSESSING LETTER RECOGNITION IN CONTEXT
(Emergent Literacy Level)

1. Put your finger on the line that begins with the giraffe.

   Circle all of the capital and lower-case g's that you can find in the sentence on that line.

   Go get a glass of milk for me.

2. Put your finger on the line that begins with the mouse.

   Circle all of the capital and lower-case a's that you can find in the sentence on that line.

   Ann and Amy are nice girls.

3. Put your finger on the line that begins with the star.

   Circle all of the capital and lower-case j's that you can find in the sentence on that line.

   Joe and Jack can jump just fine.

4. Put your finger on the line that begins with the book.

   Circle all of the capital and lower-case r's that you can find in the sentence on that line.

   I hope Ray runs right home.

5. Put your finger on the line that begins with the bird.

   Circle all of the capital and lower-case m's that you can find in the sentence on that line.

   My mother makes nice meals.

6. Put your finger on the line that begins with the glass.

   Circle all of the capital and lower-case b's that you can find in the sentence on that line.

   That boy has a big black dog named Buddy.

7. Put your finger on the line that begins with the pig.

   Circle all of the capital and lower-case p's that you can find in the sentence on that line.

   Patty put a big rag in the pail.

© 1993 by The Center for Applied Research in Education

8. Put your finger on the line that begins with the moon.

   Circle all of the capital and lower-case <u>f</u>'s that you can find in the sentence on that line.

   Fred's father is a good farmer.

9. Put your finger on the line that begins with the turkey.

   Circle all of the capital and lower-case <u>t</u>'s that you can find in the sentence on that line.

   Take that new toy to your room.

10. Put your finger on the line that begins with the television.

   Circle all of the capital and lower-case <u>w</u>'s that you can find in the sentence on that line.

   Who wants to get a white kitten?

Name_____ Date_____

Go get a glass of milk for me.

Ann and Amy are nice girls.

Joe and Jack can jump just fine.

I hope Ray runs right home.

My mother makes nice meals.

That boy has a big black dog named Buddy.

Patty put a big rag in the pail.

Fred's father is a good farmer.

Take that new toy to your room.

Who wants to get a white kitten?

Sight-Word Knowledge

It is extremely important for all children in elementary school to be competent in *sight-word knowledge*. Sight-word knowledge consists of two different elements: *sight-word recognition* and *sight-word identification*. The latter is the more difficult of the two since a child must be able to identify a word, not merely recognize it, in actual reading.

However, sight-word recognition—the less relevant skill—is more commonly assessed and practiced in elementary reading instruction. Although sight word recognition may be an acceptable skill to assess and practice, it certainly is more useful to provide diagnosis and instruction in sight-word identification.

Sight words can be described in a number of different ways. They are those words that a reader recognizes immediately upon seeing. A reader does not have to stop and analyze sight words by using word-identification techniques such as phonic (graphophonic) analysis or structural (morphemic) analysis. However, sight words also can be described as those words that do not have a regular sound-symbol relationship. Therefore, such words cannot be analyzed effectively but are most effectively recognized as a total unit or word. Some examples of sight words are *have, of, father, said, dog, though, through,* and *off.*

Environmental print is a concept now recognized as very important in emergent literacy. These are words commonly found in the environment of preschool and kindergarten children. They are part of the child's environment, and he/she learns to recognize and identify them mainly by noticing them and asking an adult or older sibling what that word is. Some common examples of environmental print are: *STOP, McDonald's, Wal-Mart, Target, Cheerios®, Crest®, Hardees,* and *Campbell's.*

Although more detail about sight-word knowledge is provided in Chapter 5, the most useful sight words are found in one of the common sight word lists, the *Dolch Basic Sight Word List*, which was formulated by the late Edward Dolch of the University of Illinois in 1941. Although you may think the list must be dated, this is really not the case because the words contained in it are comparable to those contained in the newer word lists. This list of 220 service words is said to make up about 70 percent of the words found in most first-grade readers and about 65 percent of the words contained in most second-grade and third-grade readers. As with all sight-word lists, the majority of words contained in the Dolch List are *structure* or *function words*, which means they have no referent. For example, the word *of* does not represent anything as does the word *dog*, which is not a structure or function word. Structure or function words are harder for most children to learn or identify than *content words*, which have a concrete referent. Some examples of structure or function words are *the, though,* and *would*; some examples of content words are *elephant* and *run.*

You can obtain a copy of the Dolch List for a nominal cost from the following address:

Garrard Publishing Company
1607 North Market Street
Champaign, IL 61820

The following table can be used to determine a child's approximate instructional reading level as established by the performance on the Dolch Basic Sight Word List. I have found these percentages *applicable* to the other sight-word lists also. (The percentages are from Maude McBroom, Julia Sparrow, and Catherine Eckstein, *Scale for Determining a Child's Reader Level*. Iowa City, Iowa: Bureau of Publications, Extension Service, University of Iowa, 1944, p. 11.

Words Recognized	Reading Level
0–75	Preprimer
76–120	Primer
121–170	First Reader
171–210	Second Reader
More than 210	Third Reader or above

Edward Fry, Professor Emeritus of Rutgers University, also has compiled a new version of his Instant Words, which he first compiled in 1957. The first 100 words make up half of all written materials, and the 300 words make up 85 percent of all written materials. A copy of *Fry's Instant Words* is included in Chapter 5 of this book and can be reproduced. There are several other useful sight-word lists; however, you should find the preceding two undoubtedly the most useful.

Assessing Sight-Word Knowledge in Isolation

Sight-word knowledge can be assessed both in isolation and in context. Although the whole language philosophy prefers that sight-word knowledge be assessed and taught in sentence and story context, some of the sight words should be taught and practiced in isolation especially with children who have a very difficult time remembering them and with learning-handicapped children who often have extreme difficulty remembering them.

At the emergent literacy level, you may wish to evaluate a child's knowledge of environmental print. As stated earlier, these are words a child is likely to meet in his/her environment. Knowledge of environmental print often is related to success in emergent literacy.

Activity Sheets for Assessing Knowledge of Environmental Print in Isolation and in Context

Here are two devices for assessing a child's knowledge of environmental print in isolation and in context. You can duplicate them in their present form or modify them in any way you wish.

1. Put your finger on the line that begins with the flower.
   In that line put an X on the word that says Wal-Mart.

Walkman   **Wal-Mart**   **Walker**

2. Put your finger on the line that begins with the cat.
   In that line put an X on the word that says STOP.

STOP   **SPOT**   **TOP**

3. Put your finger on the line that begins with the apple.
   In that line put an X on the word that says McDonald's.

Donald   **McDonald's**   **McCoy**

4. Put your finger on the line that begins with the pencil.
   In that line put an X on the word that says Crest.

Creep   **Rest**   **Crest**

5. Put your finger on the line that begins with the light bulb.
   In that line put an X on the word that says Soup.

Soup   **Sip**   **Sup**

6. Put your finger on the line that begins with the tree.
   In that line put an X on the word that says Mother.

Mother   **Map**   **Milk**

7. Put your finger on the line that begins with the star.
   In that line put an X on the word that says Hardee's.

Hard   **Hardee's**   **Help**

8. Put your finger on the line that begins with the cup.
   In that line put an X on the word that says School.

Skip   **Should**   **School**

9. Put your finger on the line that begins with the book.
   In that line put an X on the word that says Corn.

Corn   **Could**   **Can**

10. Put your finger on the line that begins with the lion.
    In that line put an X on the word that says Street.

String   **Street**   **Treat**

CHILD'S COPY
ASSESSING ENVIRONMENTAL PRINT IN ISOLATION
(Emergent Literacy Level)

Name_____ Date_____

Walkman   Wal-Mart   Walker

STOP   SPOT   TOP

Donald   McDonald's   McCoy

Creep   Rest   Crest

Soup   Sip   Sup

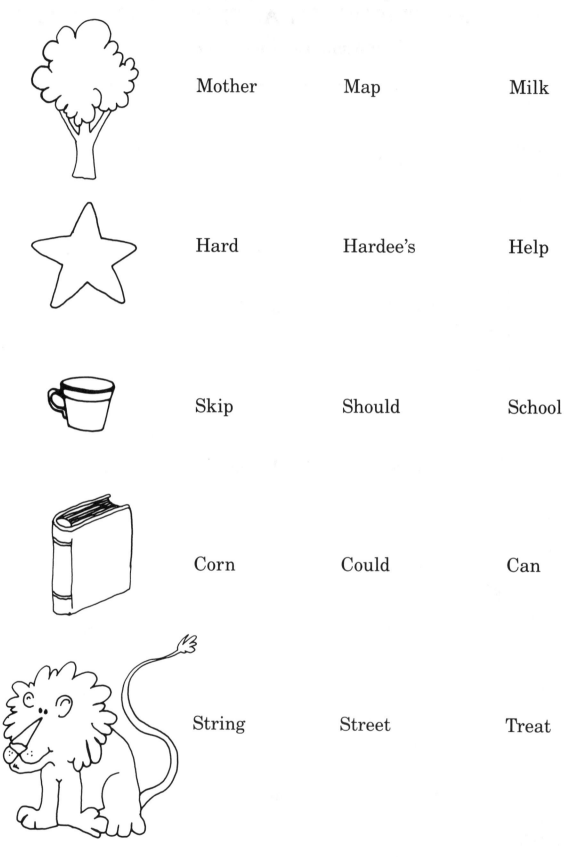

Mother	Map	Milk
Hard	Hardee's	Help
Skip	Should	School
Corn	Could	Can
String	Street	Treat

TEACHER'S COPY
ASSESSING ENVIRONMENTAL PRINT IN CONTEXT

(Emergent Literacy Level)

© 1993 by The Center for Applied Research in Education

1. Put your finger on the line that begins with the man.
   In the sentence on that line put an X on the word Wal-Mart.

   We like to go to Wal-Mart.

2. Put your finger on the line that begins with the elephant.
   In the sentence on that line put an X on the word STOP.

   A STOP sign is red and white.

3. Put your finger on the line that begins with the tree.
   In the sentence on that line put an X on the word McDonald's.

   It is fun to go to McDonald's.

4. Put your finger on the line that begins with the girl.
   In the sentence on that line put an X on the word Crest.

   I like to use Crest toothpaste.

5. Put your finger on the line that begins with the house.
   In the sentence on that line put an X on the word soup.

   I like to eat soup for lunch.

6. Put your finger on the line that begins with the ball.
   In the sentence on that line put an X on the word mother.

   I love my mother very much.

7. Put your finger on the line that begins with the sun.
   In the sentence on that line put an X on the word Hardee's.

   We like to go to Hardee's to eat.

8. Put your finger on the line that begins with the moon.
   In the sentence on that line put an X on the word school.

   I like to go to school.

9. Put your finger on the line that begins with the drum.
   In the sentence on that line put an X on the word corn.

   I don't like to eat corn.

10. Put your finger on the line that begins with the snowman.
    In the sentence on that line put an X on the word street.

    We live on a very nice street.

CHILD'S COPY
ASSESSING ENVIRONMENTAL PRINT IN CONTEXT
(Emergent Literacy Level)

Name_____ Date_____

We like to go to Wal-Mart.

A STOP sign is red and white.

It is fun to go to McDonald's.

I like to use Crest toothpaste.

I like to eat soup for lunch.

I love my mother very much.

We like to go to Hardee's to eat.

I like to go to school.

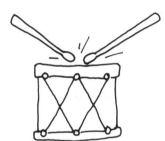

I don't like to eat corn.

We live on a very nice street.

Using a Sight-Word List to Assess Words in Isolation

Sight-word knowledge can be assessed in isolation by placing a random sampling of words from a sight-word list such as the *Dolch* list or *Fry's Instant Words* either on individual word cards or by printing or typing them in short lists.

It is important to place each selected sight word on an individual word card for children who are reading at the beginning primary-grade level. These are often children in first grade, disabled readers who are functioning at about that reading level, or learning-handicapped children. Many students with learning disabilities have difficulty pronouncing sight words on a list. Such a child may well become frustrated just from seeing all of the words on such a list, and subsequently may not make much of an effort to pronounce the words.

To construct such word cards, randomly select about twenty words from the level of the sight-word list you wish to use. Then print each word on a separate small card (about 2 or 3 inches square) with a marking pen. Then present the word cards in random order and have the child identify each one of them.

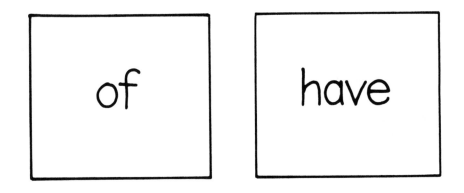

You also can evaluate a child's sight-word knowledge in a group setting by using an assessment device designed for this purpose. However, you should understand that such a device evaluates ability in sight-word recognition instead of sight-word identification. As you remember from the discussion earlier in this chapter, sight-word identification, not sight-word recognition, is required in reading. Even though such a device saves considerable time and may therefore be more practical, it is not quite as accurate as an individually administered device. Therefore, a group-administered device may be more beneficial for less disabled readers.

Activity Sheets for Assessing Sight-Word Recognition in Isolation

Here are devices for assessing a child's sight-word recognition in isolation on the first-, second-, and third-grade levels. You can duplicate them in their present form or modify them to suit your particular needs.

These are the words you should pronounce from each sheet:

First-Grade Level	Second-Grade Level	Third-Grade Level
1. you	1. want	1. start
2. two	2. very	2. second
3. their	3. small	3. river
4. have	4. found	4. family
5. long	5. give	5. example
6. into	6. spell	6. earth
7. part	7. know	7. music
8. did	8. right	8. while
9. people	9. old	9. enough
10. who	10. kind	10. talk
11. on	11. animal	11. plant
12. call	12. still	12. below
13. than	13. and	13. between
14. first	14. great	14. paper
15. but	15. say	15. young
	16. change	16. food
	17. place	17. walk
	18. line	18. carry
	19. try	19. without
	20. little	20. face

ASSESSING SIGHT-WORD RECOGNITION
IN ISOLATION
(First-Grade Level)

Name_____ Grade_____ Teacher_____ Date_____

In each line <u>circle</u> the <u>word</u> that your teacher pronounces.

1. you   was   be   this

2. with   which   two   look

3. if   their   at   make

4. more   have   from   find

5. her   would   down   long

6. may   made   into   some

7. part   water   first   down

8. see   go   did   get

9. so   these   people   no

10. who   long   down   oil

11. way   boy   on   find

12. him   call   now   down

13. over   than   could   as

14. did   day   first   will

15. use   an   but   or

ASSESSING SIGHT-WORD RECOGNITION IN ISOLATION

(Second-Grade Level)

Name_____ Grade_____ Teacher_____ Date_____

In each line circle the word that your teacher pronounces.

1. new	want	show	only
2. most	very	point	page
3. small	three	letter	mother
4. home	different	found	answer
5. man	sentence	give	work
6. air	spell	change	put
7. small	year	live	know
8. right	before	does	another
9. any	old	large	because
10. good	just	kind	picture
11. need	play	away	animal
12. still	should	world	high
13. study	land	through	tell
14. our	just	where	great
15. after	say	think	back
16. change	again	much	help
17. me	place	our	most
18. sound	hand	well	line
19. big	set	try	thing
20. little	too	even	such

ASSESSING SIGHT-WORD RECOGNITION
IN ISOLATION
(Third-Grade Level)

Name_____ Grade_____ Teacher_____ Date_____

In each line <u>circle</u> the <u>word</u> that your teacher pronounces.

1. near	don't	start	thought
2. second	sometimes	mountain	head
3. group	four	river	almost
4. family	real	above	soon
5. begin	example	once	book
6. carry	never	close	earth
7. music	body	color	grow
8. example	eye	while	few
9. watch	enough	face	idea
10. talk	mile	children	until
11. miss	might	plant	country
12. below	between	add	left
13. next	hard	between	hard
14. river	sea	mile	paper
15. young	open	list	every
16. own	food	along	keep
17. seem	night	white	walk
18. hear	stop	carry	began
19. took	once	without	miss
20. idea	eat	face	color

© 1993 by The Center for Applied Research in Education

Assessing Sight-Word Knowledge in Context _____

As stated earlier, sight-word knowledge can be assessed in context as well as in isolation. Assessment of sight-word knowledge in the context of sentences and paragraphs is in keeping with whole-language philosophy. However, it may not be particularly useful with learning handicapped children; their assessment can be more effectively done in isolation.

Proponents of the whole-language approach correctly state that sight-word knowledge is most meaningful to children when the sight words are found in their own dictated or written language-experience stories, in predictable books and in other easy-to-read tradebooks. For example, the sight word *laugh* probably is easiest for most children to remember when it is found in a dictated or written experience story. The sight word *what* is very easily remembered when the book *Brown Bear, Brown Bear, What Do You See?* is read by a child. (Chapter 5 presents a number of interesting, meaningful ways in which sight words can be presented and reinforced in sentence and story context.)

Activity Sheets for Assessing Sight-Word Recognition in Context

Here are devices you can use to assess a child's sight-word recognition in context. You can duplicate them in their present form or modify them any way you wish.

SPECIAL NOTE: The same sight words are used at the first-grade, second-grade and third-grade levels in the devices to assess sight-word recognition in isolation and in context. Thus, the teacher can make a direct comparison between a child's ability in sight-word recognition in isolation and context.

Although this is not always the case, a learning-handicapped child sometimes does better in sight-word recognition in isolation than in context. On the other hand, some disabled readers sometimes do better in sight-word recognition in context than in isolation.

These are the words you should pronounce from each sheet:

First-Grade Level	*Second-Grade Level*	*Third-Grade Level*
1. you	1. want	1. start
2. two	2. very	2. second
3. their	3. small	3. river
4. have	4. found	4. family
5. long	5. give	5. example
6. into	6. spell	6. Earth
7. part	7. know	7. music
8. did	8. right	8. while
9. people	9. old	9. enough
10. who	10. kind	10. talk
11. on	11. animal	11. plant
12. call	12. still	12. below
13. than	13. world	13. between
14. first	14. great	14. paper
15. but	15. say	15. young
	16. change	16. food
	17. place	17. walk
	18. line	18. carry
	19. try	19. without
	20. little	20. face

ASSESSING SIGHT-WORD RECOGNITION
IN CONTEXT

(First-Grade Level)

Name_____ Grade_____ Teacher_____ Date_____

In each sentence <u>circle the one word</u> that your teacher pronounces.

1. Are you a happy boy?

2. Jay saw two dogs and two cats.

3. I saw their mother.

4. I have a black cat.

5. That is a long nail.

6. Billy ran into his house.

7. I ate part of an apple.

8. Did you see that girl?

9. Sam saw three people at school.

10. Who is that new boy?

11. My cat is on the table.

12. Can you call my friend for me?

13. I am bigger than Fred.

14. My first name is Sara.

15. I can't go, but I am happy that you can.

© 1993 by The Center for Applied Research in Education

ASSESSING SIGHT-WORD RECOGNITION IN CONTEXT

(Second-Grade Level)

Name_____ Grade_____ Teacher_____ Date_____

In each sentence <u>circle the one word</u> that your teacher pronounces.

1. Do you want to get a skateboard for your birthday?
2. My grandfather is a very old man.
3. That is a very small piece of cake.
4. Jim found a dime on the way to school.
5. Will you give me a game for my birthday?
6. I don't know how to spell the word <u>giraffe</u>.
7. Do you know how old Kay is?
8. My mother wants me to come right home after school.
9. I am seven years old.
10. My grandmother is a very kind woman.
11. A cat is the animal that I like the best.
12. Tony still is my best friend.
13. I don't know much about the world.
14. I think that candy is great.
15. I don't think you should say that about Sue.
16. My little sister should change her clothes.
17. The place my mother likes best is home.
18. Draw a line under the word <u>yellow</u>.
19. Can you try to be quieter?
20. Jack has a little brother.

ASSESSING SIGHT-WORD RECOGNITION IN CONTEXT

(Third-Grade Level)

Name_____ Grade_____ Teacher_____ Date_____

In each sentence <u>circle the one word</u> that your teacher pronounces.

1. Yesterday morning my father's car wouldn't start.

2. Dave's little brother is in second grade at our school.

3. My father can swim all the way across the river.

4. My best friend has a very nice family.

5. Jeff's father is a very good example of a nice man.

6. Everyone should take better care of our Earth.

7. Mike doesn't like to take music lessons very much.

8. Can you wait for me while I finish my book?

9. Bert doesn't have enough money to buy a new bicycle.

10. Maria doesn't want to talk to me any more.

11. A plant never grows well for my mother.

12. It was five degrees below zero yesterday morning.

13. We live between two very good neighbors.

14. Please pick that paper up right now.

15. His father is a young man.

16. My favorite food certainly is pizza.

17. I like to walk to school unless it's too cold.

18. Can you carry these groceries home for me?

19. I don't like to eat a hamburger without catsup.

20. That little boy's face is very dirty.

© 1993 by The Center for Applied Research in Education

Phonic (Graphophonic) Analysis

It is possible for a child to be a competent reader with limited phonic analysis ability. Nevertheless, *phonic (graphophonic)* analysis certainly is an extremely important skill for most children to learn. It is essential for all children to master at least the most rudimentory phonic elements such as consonants, long and short vowels, consonant blends, consonant blends, consonant digraphs, diphthongs, and phonograms (word families). Phonic analysis is often considered an important skill for learning-handicapped children to master, unless the child is very weak in the auditory channel (auditory discrimination or auditory memory).

Although more detail about phonic analysis is provided in Chapter 5, it can be defined as using phoneme-grapheme (sound-symbol) relationships to decode unknown words. To be an effective technique, the unknown word should be in the child's *speaking vocabulary* so that he/she will recognize it as an actual word after it is analyzed by the use of phonic elements. Phonic analysis is often more useful when combined with contextual analysis. As an example, notice how the addition of an initial consonant in the following sentence helps you to determine the omitted word:

Sally would like to get a d_____ for her birthday.

> bracelet
> doll
> kitten

Therefore, it is very important to assess a child's specific strengths and weaknesses in the various elements of phonic (graphophonic) analysis with as much precision as possible so that you know which important phonic elements and rules the child must learn and practice.

Assessing Phonic (Graphophonic) Analysis in Isolation

A child's ability in phonic (graphophonic) analysis can be assessed either in isolation or in *sentence* or *story context*. Although the majority of the proponents of the whole-language philosophy believe assessment and instruction should be made in context, it may be more useful for the assessment to be made in isolation, especially for severely disabled readers and learning-handicapped children. Such children often have extreme difficulty in discriminating between some of the phonic elements, especially those of the *short vowel sounds*. Discriminating between short *e* and short *i* are extremely difficult for such children.

There are several devices you can use to effectively assess a child's ability in phonic (graphophonic) analysis. They are: observational checklists, individually-administered inventories in phonic (graphophonic) analysis, and group-administered inventories in phonic (graphophonic) analysis. (Chapter 2 of this *Handbook* contained several observational checklists you can use to assess a child's ability in the various word-identification and comprehension techniques.) However, this chapter does include an individually administered and a group-administered inventory in phonic analysis.

Individually Administered Inventory in Phonic (Graphophonic) Analysis

The individually-administered inventory in phonic (graphophonic) analysis is at the second-grade reading level. It normally is more accurate to give a moderately or severely disabled reader or a learning-handicapped child an individually administered inventory in phonic analysis since this type of device evaluates phonic analysis skills the same way they are used in reading. For example, such an inventory evaluates symbol-sound relationships similar to what is required in actual reading. On the other hand, a group-administered phonic analysis inventory assesses ability in sound-symbol relationships, an easier task but one that is not required in actual reading situations. However, a group-administered inventory in phonic analysis does save you time and, therefore, may be acceptable for mildly disabled readers.

You can duplicate and use this inventory in its present form if it seems relevant or modify it any way you want. You also can use it as a model for constructing your own phonic analysis inventory.

Note to the Teacher and Answer Key

You may not want to include the directions for each section of the following inventory on the child's copy. If they are contained on the child's copy, you may want to read each direction aloud or have the child read it aloud.

The hard and soft sounds of *c* as in the words *cup* and *city* and the hard and soft sounds of *g* as in the words *gum* and *gem* both should be considered correct.

Both the voiced *th* as in the word *them* and the voiceless *th* as in the word *thin* should be considered correct.

pōte	hĕt	drĭck	kner
fōat	jōld	stŭt	scrŭt
lēat	zāke	vŭt	glăt
māpĕt	dūble	vādȳ	nŭtter

INDIVIDUALLY ADMINISTERED ORAL PHONIC (GRAPHOPHONIC) ANALYSIS INVENTORY

(Second-Grade Level)

Name_____ Grade_____ Teacher_____ Date_____

1. Pronounce a word beginning with each <u>consonant sound</u> or pronounce the <u>consonant sound</u> in isolation.

d	c	f	t	m	s
j	p	r	w	b	g

2. Pronounce a word beginning with each <u>consonant blend</u> or pronounce the <u>consonant blend</u> in isolation.

scr	fl	st	gr	sn	dr
bl	str	sm	tw	fr	cl

3. Pronounce a word beginning with each <u>consonant digraph</u> or pronounce the <u>consonant digraph</u> in isolation.

sh	th	ch	ph	wh

4. Pronounce each group of letters as they would be pronounced in a <u>word</u>.

gn	wr	kn	ck

5. Pronounce each <u>diphthong</u> in isolation or give a word containing that <u>diphthong</u>.

oi	ow	oy	ou

6. Pronounce each <u>nonsense word (pseudoword)</u> using the correct phonic rule.

pote	het	drick	kner
foat	jold	stut	scrut
leat	zake	vut	glat

7. Pronounce each <u>nonsense word (pseudoword)</u> by blending the two syllables together.

map et	du ble	va dy	nut ter

billow	cascade	codfish	drone
katydid	knapsack	shadow	stride
district	clench	droll	distill

Group-Administered Inventory in Phonic (Graphophonic) Analysis

This is a group-administered inventory in phonic (graphophonic) analysis at about the fourth-grade reading level. As stated earlier, although a group-administered inventory in phonic analysis saves time, it normally is not as accurate in diagnosing competencies and weaknesses in phonic analysis as an individually administered one. Therefore, you should use it with only moderately disabled readers at that level.

You can duplicate and use this inventory in its present form or modify it any way you want. In addition, you can use it as a model for constructing your own phonic analysis inventory

The answers are given at the end of this chapter.

GROUP-ADMINISTERED PHONIC (GRAPHOPHONIC) ANALYSIS INVENTORY

(Fourth-Grade Level)

Name_____ Grade_____ Teacher_____ Date_____

1. Mark the vowels <u>long or short</u> in each of these words and then pronounce each word.

billow	cascade	codfish	drone
katydid	knapsack	shadow	stride
district	clench	droll	distill

2. Underline the <u>vowel</u> in each word that is <u>r-controlled</u> and then pronounce each word.

clergy	contractor	circle	harness
lurch	person	surface	tower

3. Underline the <u>vowel</u> in each word that represents the <u>schwa sound</u> and then pronounce each word.

vagrant	absolute	bantam	barracks
caravan	cobra	concentrate	dismal

4. Underline the <u>consonant blend</u> in each word and then pronounce each word.

scramble	straight	platinum	prickle
flamingo	criticism	clipper	glimpse

5. Underline the <u>consonant digraph</u> in each word and then pronounce each word.

anguish	photograph	whiff	shadow
thunderclap	charcoal	treacherous	triumph

6. Underline the <u>diphthong</u> in each word and then pronounce each word.

avoid	boyhood	outrageous	prowl
exploit	coward	pay	slouch

7. Underline the <u>vowel digraph</u> in each word and then pronounce each word.

receipt	dread	reasonable	measure
creature	breath	weather	belief

8. Underline the <u>words</u> that contain the <u>soft c or g sounds</u> and then pronounce each word.

constitution	custom	combine	gardenia
celebrate	cinder	gemstone	canoe

9. Underline the <u>words</u> that contain the <u>hard c or g sounds</u> and then pronounce each word.

        cove   comedian   genuine   course

        gallant   gingerly   guide   canyon

10. Put a / (slash mark) through each <u>silent letter</u> in these <u>words</u> and then pronounce each word.

        design   knot   iodine   knowledge

        wreckage   gnat   stride   gnome

11. Mark each <u>vowel</u> in these <u>nonsense words (pseudowords)</u> either <u>long, short, or silent.</u>

        blate   chune   shap   scry

        cheach   bladdy   script   nute

        fleach   gleet   tugle   vome

12. Each of these words is spelled <u>phonetically.</u> Write each word using the correct <u>spelling on the line below that word.</u>

ə bun′dens   dred

_____   _____

bus′əl   här′nis

_____   _____

par′ə līz   mut′ər

_____   _____

ri pent′   rəz′ e dənt

_____   _____

tär′nish   ser′fis

_____   _____

yon′dər   hej

_____   _____

© 1993 by The Center for Applied Research in Education

How Oral Reading Miscue Analysis Emphasizing
Phonic (Graphophonic) Analysis Is Used in Assessment _____

As you may remember from the detailed discussion found in Chapter 2 of this *Handbook*, *oral reading miscue analysis* is very helpful in assessing a child's competency in various aspects of reading performance. One of those aspects was a graphic change that is part of phonic analysis ability.

Susan B. Argyle's system for coding oral reading miscues was described and illustrated in detail in that chapter. For example, if a student made a number of miscues that resulted in *graphic changes*, he/she probably may need some instruction in either phonic analysis or structural analysis depending upon their frequency or whether or not they interfered significantly with comprehension.

If you refer back to the *Summary Sheet of Oral Reading Miscues* on page 53, you can determine from this analysis whether the child made the graphic change in the beginning, middle, or end of a word. Thus, you will know whether you should probably stress initial consonants, initial consonant blends, initial consonant digraphs, medial vowels, medial vowel digraphs, r-controlled vowels, final consonants, or final consonant blends. This simple oral miscue analysis, therefore, should provide you with a wealth of information about a student's abilities in phonic analysis without expending a great deal of time and effort.

How Ability in Phonic (Graphophonic)
Analysis Is Assessed in Context _____

As previously stated, phonic (graphophonic) analysis can be assessed in context as well as in isolation. Assessment of phonic analysis ability in the context of words, sentences, and paragraphs is in keeping with the contemporary whole-language philosophy. However, such assessment in context may not be very useful with learning-handicapped children. In many cases their diagnosis (assessment) can be more effectively made in isolation.

Proponents of the whole-language approach correctly state that phonic analysis probably is more meaningful to most children when the words to be analyzed phonetically are found in actual reading materials, such as dictated or written language-experience stories, predictable books, or other easy-to-read tradebooks. For example, the sound of the consonant *b* probably is the most meaningful to a child when it is used in an entire word such as the word *big*.

Here is an example of how to assess a kindergarten child's knowledge of phonic analysis during demonstrations of the language-experience approach using dictated stories. After a child or several children dictate a language-experience story, ask the child or children to circle and pronounce all of the words that begin with a certain consonant such as *f*, *m*, *s*, or *t*. Next you might ask them to circle and pronounce any word that rhymes with a target word, such as *run*. Predictable books and other easy tradebooks could be used for the assessment of ability in phonic analysis in about the same way.

Ability in phonic analysis can also be assessed in context using various types of activity sheets. In the next section of this chapter, you will find a ready-to-duplicate activity sheet that can be used for this purpose. The variation of the cloze procedure that combines phonic analysis and context can also be used for assessing competency in phonic analysis. (As you remember, Chapter 2 contained a ready-to-use example of the version of the cloze procedure about Walt Disney; therefore, one is not included here.) *Computer software* can be used effectively to assess, teach, and reinforce various elements of phonic analysis. Appendix I of this *Handbook* contains a list of computer software sources.

A number of the diagnostic tests listed and described in Chapter 2 can also be very helpful in assessing a child's specific strengths and weaknesses in the various elements of phonic analysis. You are encouraged to refer back to that chapter for information on the content of these standardized devices.

Device for Assessing Ability in Phonic (Graphophonic) Analysis in Context

Here is a ready-to-duplicate activity sheet for assessing ability in phonic analysis. You can duplicate and use this sheet in its present form or modify it any way you wish. You also can use it as a model for your own device of this type.

The answers are given at the end of this chapter.

GROUP-ADMINISTERED
PHONIC (GRAPHOPHONIC) ANALYSIS
ASSESSMENT DEVICE IN SENTENCE CONTEXT
(Approximately Third-Grade Level)

Name_____ Grade_____ Teacher_____ Date_____

Read each sentence to yourself and do what it tells you to do.

1. Circle the word in this sentence that contains a <u>long vowel sound</u>:

   Mark wants to get a game for Christmas.

2. Circle a word in this sentence that contains a <u>short vowel sound</u>:

   The month of July is very hot.

3. Circle the word in this sentence that contains an <u>r-controlled vowel sound</u>:

   Paul's new shirt has black and white stripes.

4. Circle the word in this sentence that contains a <u>consonant blend</u>:

   Josie really liked to see the large snake at the zoo.

5. Circle the word in this sentence that contains a <u>consonant digraph</u>:

   I saw a very thin man at the park yesterday.

6. Circle the word in this sentence that contains a <u>vowel digraph</u>:

   Patti hopes that it will not rain today.

7. Circle the word in this sentence that contains a <u>final-e marker</u>:

   Pam's mother bought a big cake for her eighth birthday party.

8. Circle the word in this sentence that contains a <u>schwa sound</u>:

   My pencil just broke, and I can't do my homework.

9. Circle the word in this sentence that contains a <u>hard c sound</u>:

   Joan is not able to have a cat since she lives in an apartment in the city.

10. Circle the word in this sentence that contains a <u>soft c sound</u>:

    When it gets cold outside, mice may try to come into the house.

11. Circle the word in this sentence that contains a <u>hard g sound</u>:

    A goat may not always be a gentle animal.

12. Circle the word in this sentence that contains a <u>soft g sound</u>:

    Sally wants to give Betsy a gemstone for her birthday.

13. Circle the word in this sentence that contains a <u>silent letter</u>:

    I hurt my knee very badly yesterday.

14. Circle the word in this sentence that contains a <u>silent letter</u>:

    Sally is going to write to her grandmother today.

15. Circle the word in this sentence that contains a <u>silent letter</u>:

    No animal is truly dumb.

Structural (Morphemic) Analysis

Structural analysis or *morphemic analysis* can be defined as using word structure or word parts to determine the pronunciation and meaning of unknown words encountered during reading. This word-identification technique is especially helpful in improving vocabulary using meanings of prefixes, suffixes, and word roots.

Although structural analysis is discussed in more detail in Chapter 5, very briefly it is composed of a number of different subskills. One important subskill is the attaching of a prefix or suffix (affix) to a base or root word to form a derivative. This technique of word identification also deals with *inflections*, changes in a word that are made for grammatical reasons. For example, an inflection occurs when the singular form of the word *boy* is made into the plural form by adding the suffix *s*.

Structural analysis also deals with the term *morpheme* which is the smallest unit of meaning in a language. Some other subskills of structural analysis are the understanding and use of syllabication, compound words, stress, and word origins.

With the emphasis on whole language, structural analysis often should be taught and practiced in the context of meaningful reading. However, structural analysis skills should occasionally be presented and reinforced in isolation and in phrase context. Yet for many children, structural analysis may be more useful than phonic analysis since it deals with larger, more meaningful units of language. However, it continues to be important for phonic elements to be emphasized with many learning-handicapped children.

In general, structural analysis is often the most useful when used in conjunction with contextual analysis or phonic analysis. For example, if a child is to attack a polysyllabic word structurally, he/she must be able to decode each of the syllables by the use of phonic analysis and then blend the syllables together into what should be a recognizable word (a word in the child's speaking vocabulary). After the word has been analyzed both structurally and phonetically, the child must determine whether it makes sense in sentence context.

Chapter 5 of this *Handbook* presents lists of the meanings of the most common and useful prefixes, suffixes, and word roots. In addition, that chapter presents many classroom-tested strategies and materials for teaching and practicing the various elements of structural analysis both with average and learning-handicapped students.

How Ability in Structural (Morphemic) Analysis Is Assessed in Isolation

There are several ways in which ability in structural analysis can be assessed in isolation. One is by using teacher observation with the aid of a structured checklist. Several observational checklists which contained parts devoted to the observation of structural analysis ability are given in Chapter 2 of this *Handbook*.

Individually administered or group-administered inventories also can be used to ascertain ability in elements of word structure. Normally it is not necessary to administer an individual inventory in structural analysis as is the case with an inventory in phonic analysis. Most often a group inventory will be sufficient to give you sufficient insight into a child's competencies and weaknesses in structural analysis.

Any such inventory in structural analysis can attempt to determine a child's ability in such subskills of word structure as: prefixes, suffixes, base or root words, contractions, compound words, syllabication, and accent (stress). As an aid for constructing your own structural analysis inventory, you can consult the appropriate pages of the manuals or workbooks of a basal reader series or other commercial materials. After evaluating the structural analysis inventory, you should try to present and/or reinforce the specific subskills of word structure in which the student has been determined to lack competence.

Group-Administered Inventory for Assessing Competency in Structural Analysis in Isolation

Here is a group-administered inventory in structural analysis at the intermediate-grade reading level. You can duplicate and use the inventory in its present form or modify it to suit your needs. You can also use it as a model in constructing your own variation of this type of inventory if you wish.

The answers are given at the end of this chapter.

NOTE: *Oral reading miscue analysis* can also be helpful in assessing a child's competency in structural analysis. Although it may not be quite as useful in structural analysis as it is in phonic analysis, it still may be used for this purpose if you want. You should see Chapter 2 of this *Handbook* for a discussion of how to make this analysis.

GROUP-ADMINISTERED STRUCTURAL (MORPHEMIC) ANALYSIS INVENTORY IN ISOLATION

(Intermediate-Grade Level)

Name_____ Grade_____ Teacher_____ Date_____

1. Underline the base or root word in each word.

precisely	scratchy	absolutely	annoyed
prepaid	untangle	replace	calculating
savagely	befell	submerge	encircle

2. Underline the prefix in each word.

disappear	prepay	unusual	antifreeze
export	postdate	microwave	unearth
misspell	inconvenient	defrost	enlarge

3. Underline the suffix in each word.

affectionate	worthless	childhood	painter
cautiously	faithful	mosquitoes	swallowed
manageable	velvety	drifting	gloomily

4. Write the plural of each noun on the line.

ox _____   volcano _____

speech _____   canoe _____

tomato _____   valley _____

donkey _____   princess _____

country _____   goose _____

5. Divide these compound words by placing a / between each word.

hummingbird	headquarters	sandbank	whiplash
ferryboat	locksmith	sunshine	whirlwind
forefinger	overboard	bowstring	blueberry
lumberjack	steamboat	huckleberry	bumblebee

6. Divide these words into <u>syllables</u> by placing a / between each syllable.

advantage	commotion	encourage	capable
ferry	enormous	topple	helicopter
skeleton	vanish	pioneer	yonder
stampede	rudder	wilderness	occasion

7. Mark the <u>accented (stressed) syllable</u> for each word in this way: be/long′.

adopt	extend	legend	octopus
plantation	preserve	propose	relate
scholarship	sober	torrent	elastic
moderate	computer	admit	borrow

Assessing Ability in Structural (Morphemic) Analysis in Context _____

As stated earlier, *structural (morphemic) analysis* ability can be assessed in context as well as in isolation. As you are aware, assessment of structural analysis ability in the context of sentences and paragraphs is in keeping with the current whole-language philosophy. However, such assessment in context may not be particularly useful with learning-handicapped children. In some cases, such diagnosis probably can be made more effectively in isolation.

Proponents of the whole-language approach accurately state that structural analysis undoubtedly is the most relevant to many children when the words to be analyzed structurally are found in actual reading materials of various types such as basal readers, tradebooks, or content textbooks. For example, the analysis of the word *microscope* probably is more meaningful when it takes place during an actual science reading assignment than from a list of words.

You can use a dictated language-experience story to assess the structural analysis ability of kindergarten children. To do so, after a child or several children dictate the story, ask the child or children to circle *s*, *ed*, or *ing*, making sure that the letters indeed were suffixes in the way in which they were used in the story.

Variations of the cloze procedure with different syntactic elements such as deleted nouns, adjectives, and verbs can be used to ascertain a child's understanding of the various syntactic elements. Ability in structural analysis in context also can be assessed by different types of activity sheets. In the next part of this chapter, you will find a ready-to-use activity sheet you can use for this purpose. Computer software also can be used to assess, teach, and practice various elements of structural analysis. Appendix I of this *Handbook* contains a list of computer software manufacturers and distributors.

Several of the diagnostic tests listed and described in Chapter 2 can also be useful in assessing a child's specific strengths and weaknesses in the different elements of word structure. You can refer to Chapter 2 for information on the content of these tests.

Device for Assessing Ability in Structural (Morphemic) Analysis in Context

Here is a ready-to-use device for assessing ability in structural analysis. You can duplicate and use this device in its present form or modify it any way you want. In addition, you can use it as a model for making your own activity sheet.

The answers for this activity sheet are given at the end of this chapter.

GROUP-ADMINISTERED STRUCTURAL (MORPHEMIC) ANALYSIS INVENTORY IN CONTEXT

(Intermediate-Grade Level)

Name_____ Grade_____ Teacher_____ Date_____

1. Underline each word in this sentence that is <u>a base or root word.</u>

Crabs exemplify creatures possessing flattened shells.

2. Underline each word in this sentence that contains a <u>prefix.</u>

The submarine rapidly moved through the ocean,
apparently incapable of being destroyed.

3. Underline each word in this sentence that contains a <u>suffix.</u>

The ponies on the island smelled the storm and plunged against
their stalls trying to escape.

4. Underline each word in this sentence that is a <u>plural.</u>

On ranches, roping horses and cutting horses
are the most prized horses and are usually saved for special occasions.

5. Underline each <u>compound word</u> in this sentence.

My father has a grindstone in his basement workshop where
he likes to spend some time.

6. Underline each <u>one-syllable word</u> in this sentence.

Figure skating has always been one of my favorite winter sports.

7. Underline each <u>two-syllable word</u> in this sentence.

A baby beaver is a cunning little fellow
in soft brown fur with an innocent, round face.

8. Underline each <u>three-syllable word</u> in this sentence.

Many animals that spend a great deal of time in the water
have developed unusual ears so that they are protected from the water.

9. Underline each <u>four-syllable word</u> in this sentence.

Apparently a dog is usually a highly affectionate, loyal animal.

10. Underline each <u>five-syllable word</u> in this sentence.

It is absolutely essential for each student
to master the multiplication facts if this is possible.

Semantic (Contextual) Analysis _____

Semantic (contextual) analysis is a word-identification technique in which the reader determines the meaning and, less often, the pronunciation of the unknown words in the reading material by examining the context in which they are found. The context may be a sentence, adjacent sentences, paragraph, or perhaps an entire passage. Semantic analysis also involves the use of syntactic or word-order clues.

Semantic analysis is the most useful technique of word identification in most cases, unless the reading material is too difficult. It also reflects the whole-language philosophy effectively since semantic analysis stresses reading as a global, language-based process that emphasizes comprehension of what is being read.

Although semantic analysis is a useful technique of word identification when it is used alone, it may become even more useful when it is combined with phonic analysis, as the following example illustrates:

> Shirli wore a r_____ dress to the birthday party.
> blue
> red
> pink

Semantic analysis can be stressed as early as the emergent literacy stage. It is also important that children be encouraged to supply words that make sense while reading both orally and silently even if the words that they provide are not the same as those found in the reading material. Children need to be encouraged to become risk-takers in their reading as long as the supplied words make sense in context.

Assessing Ability in Semantic (Contextual) Analysis _____

There are a number of ways you can assess a student's ability in the use of semantic analysis. One of the easiest and most effective is simply to observe the student's reading to see if the supplied words make sense in context and to determine if he/she comprehends adequately. A child normally has to be adept in semantic analysis to be able to comprehend effectively. Such teacher observation possibly can be made more effective by using a structured checklist, such as the one given in Chapter 2 of this *Handbook*.

Oral reading miscue analysis also can be a very effective means of determining a child's ability in the use of context. As you remember from Chapter 2, Susan Argyle's coding system for oral reading miscues emphasized whether the miscue significantly changed the meaning of the material. As you remember, this coding system also emphasizes whether the child made a complete or partial meaning change. If you have questions about this type of analysis, you are encouraged to refer to Chapter 2.

It is obvious that one of the most effective ways of assessing a child's competency in semantic analysis is simply to observe his/her oral and silent reading in an informal manner. You can note whether the child makes meaningful substitutions in oral reading. If he/she usually makes meaningful substitutions while reading orally, it is obvious that he/she makes good use of semantic analysis. On the other hand, if the child substitutes words that normally do not make sense in sentence context, he/she probably does not have a good command of semantic analysis.

A child's comprehension ability also can be used to determine to some extent his/her ability in semantic analysis. If a child has effective comprehension skills of material that has been read either silently or orally, he/she undoubtedly makes good use of context clues. On the other hand, the child who does not comprehend well often does not monitor his/her comprehension and is not very concerned whether the reading material makes sense.

You also can make a comparison between a child's ability to identify words in isolation and in context as a measure of his/her competency in semantic analysis. Often a learning-handicapped child is able to identify words in isolation more effectively than in context. On the other hand, most children are able to identify words in context better than they can identify words in isolation since they can make use of context while attempting to identify the unknown words. As explained earlier in the chapter, this is also the case in letter recognition and in identifying environmental print.

In addition to the assessment device given in the next section, the cloze procedure can be used to assess competency in semantic analysis as explained and illustrated in detail in Chapter 2 of this *Handbook*. That chapter also contained three ready-to-duplicate examples of the cloze procedure that you can use as models for constructing other variations of this device. You are encouraged to refer to Chapter 2 for the discussion and examples of the cloze procedure.

Criterion-referenced tests, too, can be used to assess strengths in semantic analysis. This type of test was discussed in detail in Chapter 2, and, again, you are encouraged to refer to that chapter for detail about this kind of test.

Individually Administered Assessment Device for Determining a Child's Competency in Identifying Words in Isolation and in Context

Here is an assessment device to help you determine an intermediate-grade child's ability to identify identical words in isolation and in context. You can duplicate and use this assessment device in its present form or modify it in any way you wish. You also can use it as a model for your own related type of assessment device.

INDIVIDUALLY ADMINISTERED DEVICE FOR ASSESSING COMPETENCY IN IDENTIFYING WORDS IN ISOLATION AND IN CONTEXT

(Approximately Fifth-Grade Level)

Name_____ Grade_____ Teacher_____ Date_____

© 1993 by The Center for Applied Research in Education

Identifying Words in Isolation

Pronounce each of these words out loud.

1. compass
2. indicate
3. ferry
4. prey
5. clench
6. petunia
7. release
8. prowl
9. solution
10. skeleton
11. phantom
12. aisle
13. glacier
14. oxygen
15. international
16. prairie
17. knowledge
18. delicate
19. adopt
20. capable
21. enormous
22. coax
23. jog
24. perch
25. urgent

Identifying Words in Context

Read each of these sentences aloud trying to pronounce each of the underlined words correctly.

1. A compass can be very useful in the forest in case a person becomes lost.
2. My teacher did not indicate whether I did well on the arithmetic test that I took last week.
3. A ferry is a boat that carries people, animals, or goods back and forth, from one landing place to another.
4. Mice and birds often are prey of cats.
5. I should try not to clench my teeth when I become really angry.
6. A petunia is a very small, beautiful flower.
7. Unfortunately, I was not able to release the rabbit from its cruel trap.
8. A fox must prowl around to search for food.
9. Before you try to solve an arithmetic problem, you should try to estimate the solution.
10. A few children like to portray a skeleton for Halloween.

11. A <u>phantom</u> is a dim or shadowy appearance that may frighten a person.

12. The bride and her father walked down the <u>aisle</u> before the wedding.

13. I will be able to see a huge <u>glacier</u> when I travel to Alaska next summer.

14. A person needs to breathe <u>oxygen</u> in order to survive.

15. The word <u>international</u> can be defined as having to do with more than one country.

16. The <u>prairie</u> in our country had tall grass and few trees.

17. Although Maria's parents speak Spanish very well, she has no <u>knowledge</u> of it at all.

18. Pink is a pretty, <u>delicate</u> color.

19. Sandy would very much like to <u>adopt</u> a golden retriever puppy.

20. I think my mother is a <u>capable</u>, efficient person.

21. A whale is an <u>enormous</u> sea mammal.

22. Jay could not <u>coax</u> his father into taking him along on a trip to Walt Disney World.

23. Since I hurt my knee, I cannot <u>jog</u> anymore.

24. An owl will never fall off its <u>perch</u> in a tree.

25. My father received an <u>urgent</u> telegram from my older sister in the Marines.

Answers to "Group-Administered Phonic Analysis Inventory"

1. bĭllōw   căscădé   cŏdfĭsh   drōné
   kātȳdĭd   knăpsăck   shădōẃ   strīdé
   dĭstrĭct   clĕnch   drŏll   dĭstĭll

2. cl<u>er</u>gy   contract<u>or</u>   ci<u>r</u>cle   harness
   l<u>ur</u>ch   p<u>er</u>son   s<u>ur</u>face   tow<u>er</u>

3. vagr<u>a</u>nt   ab<u>s</u>olute   bant<u>a</u>m   barr<u>a</u>cks
   car<u>a</u>van   cob<u>ra</u>   conc<u>e</u>ntrate   dism<u>a</u>l

4. <u>scr</u>amble   <u>str</u>aight   <u>pl</u>atinum   <u>pr</u>ickle
   <u>fl</u>amingo   <u>cr</u>iticism   <u>cl</u>ipper   <u>gl</u>impse

5. angui<u>sh</u>   <u>ph</u>otogra<u>ph</u>   <u>wh</u>iff   <u>sh</u>adow
   <u>th</u>underclap   <u>ch</u>arcoal   trea<u>ch</u>erous   triump<u>h</u>

6. av<u>oi</u>d   b<u>oy</u>hood   <u>ou</u>trageous   pr<u>ow</u>l
   expl<u>oi</u>t   c<u>ow</u>ard   p<u>ay</u>   sl<u>ou</u>ch

7. rec<u>ei</u>pt   dr<u>ea</u>d   r<u>ea</u>sonable   m<u>ea</u>sure
   cr<u>ea</u>ture   br<u>ea</u>th   w<u>ea</u>ther   bel<u>ie</u>f

8. constitution   custom   combine   gardenia
   <u>celebrate</u>   <u>cinder</u>   <u>gemstone</u>   canoe

9. <u>cove</u>   <u>comedian</u>   genuine   <u>course</u>
   <u>gallant</u>   gingerly   guide   <u>canyon</u>

10. desi/g/n   /k/now   iodiné   /k/nowledgé
    /w/reckage   /g/nat   stridé   /g/nomé

11. blāté   chūné   shăp   scrȳ
    chēach   blăddy   scrīght   nūté
    flēach   glēét   tūglé   vōmé

12. abundance   dread   bustle   harness
    paralyze   mutter   repent   resident
    tarnish   surface   yonder   hedge

Answers to "Group-Administered Phonic (Graphophonic) Analysis Assessment Device in Sentence Context"

1. game
2. hot
3. shirt
4. snake
5. thin
6. rain
7. cake
8. pencil
9. cat
10. mice
11. goat
12. gemstone
13. knee
14. write
15. dumb

Answers to "Group-Administered Structural (Morphemic) Analysis Inventory in Isolation"

1. precise   scratch   absolute   annoy
   paid   tangle   place   calculate
   savage   fell   merge   circle

2. dis   pre   un   anti
   ex   post   micro   un
   mis   in   de   en

3. ate   less   hood   er
   ly   ful   es   ed
   able   y   ing   ly

4. oxen
    speeches
    tomatoes
    donkeys
    countries

    volcanoes
    canoes
    valleys
    princesses
    geese

5. humming/bird
    ferry/boat
    fore/finger
    lumber/jack

    head/quarters
    lock/smith
    over/board
    steamboat

    sand/bank
    sun/shine
    bow/string
    huckle/berry

    whip/lash
    whirl/wind
    blue/berry
    bumble/bee

6. ad/van/tage
    fer/ry
    skel/e/ton
    stam/pede

    com/mo/tion
    enor/mous
    van/ish
    rud/der

    en/cour/age
    top/ple
    pi/o/neer
    wil/der/ness

    ca/pa/ble
    he/li/cop/ter
    yon/der
    oc/ca/sion

7. adopt'
    plan/ta'/tion
    schol'/ar/ship
    mod'/er/ate

    ex/tend'
    pre/serve'
    so'/ber
    com/put'/er

    leg'/end
    pro/pose'
    tor'/rent
    ad/mit'

    oc'/to/pus
    re/late'
    elas'/tic
    bor'/row

ANSWERS TO "GROUP-ADMINISTERED STRUCTURAL (MORPHEMIC) ANALYSIS
INVENTORY IN CONTEXT"

1. exemplify
2. submarine
    incapable
3. ponies
    smelled
    plunged
    stalls
    trying
4. ranches
    horses
    horses
    horses
    occasions
5. grindstone
    workshop

6. has
    been
    one
    of
    my
    sports
7. baby
    beaver
    cunning
    little
    fellow
8. animals
    developed
    protected
9. Apparently
    affectionate
10. multiplication

Ready-to-Use Materials for Diagnosing Disabilities in Comprehension and Basic Study Skills

Many years ago I tutored a junior high school student at The University of Arizona Reading Clinic who could pronounce every word in her content textbooks correctly but could not even understand the lower-level, much less the higher-level, concepts presented in those textbooks. She certainly was not reading in any real sense. Obviously, it is essential to assess a student's competencies and weaknesses in the various elements of comprehension in order to help the child. This chapter is designed to help you do this as well as to make such an assessment in basic study skills.

What Is Reading Comprehension?

Although reading comprehension is a very complex process, it can be defined in simple terms such as *constructing and reconstructing meaning from the printed material*. It is an interactive process that requires the use of prior knowledge (previous experiences) which the reader combines with the information on the printed page. In most instances, prior knowledge is more important than the printed material. The more prior knowledge a reader possesses, the less printed material needs to be used.

Contemporary comprehension also emphasizes the use of prediction strategies and the setting of purposes for reading. In addition, it stresses metacognition (self-monitoring of the reading material). These aspects of comprehension are described and illustrated in detail in Chapter 6.

Comprehension often is thought of as a global, language-based process that can be divided into two major areas: vocabulary knowledge (word meaning) and the understanding of what is read. However, a number of reading specialists still find it useful to think of the following elements (levels) of reading comprehension:

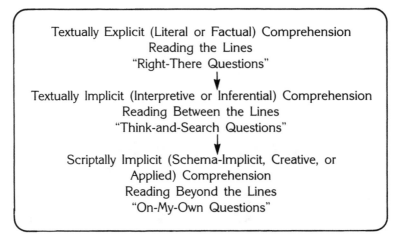

How Observational Checklists Are Used in Assessing Comprehension

One of the simplest, most effective means of assessing competency in the various elements of comprehension is by teacher observation. As explained in Chapter 2, such teacher observation can occur on an individual basis, group basis, or in a whole-class setting. Teacher observation is easy to implement since it can occur along with teacher instruction.

Teacher observation often can be enhanced by the use of a structured checklist that gives you direction in what behaviors to look for when making the observations. The primary-grade and intermediate-grade checklists included in Chapter 2 contain sections devoted to assessing comprehension at both of these reading levels. Therefore, an observational checklist is not included in this chapter, and you are encouraged to refer to the checklists in Chapter 2. You can duplicate the checklists and use them in their entirety or use just the portions devoted to the assessment of comprehension abilities.

Some Types of Questioning Strategies

Questions posed before, during, or after reading are the single most effective means of assessing comprehension ability. In addition, they are one of the easiest assessment strategies to implement since they often can be used along with teacher instruction in comprehension.

Questions can be used *before reading instruction* for a variety of purposes. They can be used to assess and activate prior knowledge, to help a student formulate purposes for reading, and to make predictions about story content. Questions posed before reading are often crucial in determining a student's success in reading the material.

Questions used *during reading* can determine how effectively a student is comprehending the material. You can determine whether the material is appropriate and motivating for the student. Predictions made by the child at varying intervals throughout the reading can add to the student's comprehension of the remainder of the material.

Questions *after reading* have been the most common means of assessing comprehension ability in the past, and they still remain useful. You can formulate questions of various types (explained later) to evaluate a student's competency in various aspects of reading comprehension. The kind of questions asked after comprehension should help you determine the kinds of strategies the student used during the actual reading.

It may be useful at this time to think about what really constitutes a question. Most people undoubtedly believe that the *wh-type interrogative sentences* are questions: *Who,*

What, Which, When, Where, Why, and *How*. Linguists often add *yes-no questions* and *tag questions*, such as "My father can drive very well, don't you think?" They also add *intonation questions*, such as "Ellie went to church?" and *cleft questions*, such as "Where was it that Ellie went?" (a question in which the latter part contains the actual question).

You should also think about some kinds of instructional directions that do not meet the grammatical test of being described as true questions. Such questions can be called *pseudoquestions*. Pseudoquestions can be thought of as "questions in disguise." Pseudoquestions often may be used on essay examinations and may use such words as *name, discuss, describe, enumerate, list*, or *provide a reason*. You can understand the characteristics of pseudoquestions by examining the following true question and the pseudoquestion:

> What were some of the causes of Operation Desert Storm?
> Describe some of the causes of Operation Desert Storm.

It is clear that both can be called questions, although the second one does not meet the grammatical test for a true question.

Examples of Questioning Strategies for Before and During Reading

NOTE: A number of the questioning strategies described in this chapter for assessment can also be used for the *teaching or improvement of comprehension* explained in Chapter 6 of this *Handbook*.

Prereading questioning is not usually used as often or extensively as postreading questioning for the assessment of competency in reading comprehension. However, prereading questioning can be crucial to both the assessment and improvement of reading comprehension. Prereading questions can be used to activate prior knowledge and to set purposes for reading a selection.

The child's prior knowledge must be activated (used) in order for him/her to read a selection effectively. Assessment of ability in prior knowledge enables you to know what material must be presented *before reading* to ensure the maximum amount of reading success for each child.

The following anecdote from P. David Pearson and Dale D. Johnson's *Teaching Reading Comprehension* (New York: Holt, Rinehart and Winston, 1978, p. 192) illustrates why it is important to help a child activate his/her prior knowledge:

> Recall what Charlie Brown does whenever he gets a new book. Before he even looks at the book, he counts the pages—625 pages: "I'll never learn all that!" He is defeated before he starts, before he has had a chance to realize that he does not have to learn *all* that. It is not *all* new. He already knows something about it. He has not given himself the chance to learn what he already knows about what he is supposed to know.

Both you and the child should try to activate a student's prior knowledge. You can do this in a number of different ways. For example, you can attempt to relate what the child is going to read to what he or she already knows by asking questions such as these from a basal reader story based on the book *Sarah, Plain and Tall* (Patricia Maclachlan):

- Have you ever read the library book *Sarah, Plain and Tall*? If you have read it, what did you think about that book?

- Did you see the Hallmark Hall of Fame Presentation of *Sarah, Plain and Tall* that starred Glenn Close as Sarah? If you did see it, perhaps you can contrast this book with that television presentation when you read it.

- Have you read other books that were set in pioneer times? What were their names and what did you like about these books?

You can also activate prior knowledge by using semantic mapping (webbing), described and illustrated in detail in Chapter 6, a film, a filmstrip, a computer simulation, pictures, a demonstration, an experiment, a television program, or many other devices. Any such activity should help a student either support or reject his/her prior knowledge about the upcoming reading selection. A number of other ways and examples of activating prior knowledge are also found in Chapter 6 of this *Handbook*.

Questions of various types presented prior to reading a selection can significantly influence the quality of a student's subsequent reading of the material. Without these questions, a number of students read any material in a meaningless manner with no purpose except reaching the end of the material. These questions can be either teacher-formulated or student-formulated. As much as possible, the prereading questions should be meaningful, important, and high-level.

Any teacher-generated question should be a model for student-developed questions for reading and learning. In addition, a purpose-setting question should address a central theme and should encourage students to think. After having some exposure to teacher-generated questions, students should be able to formulate their own questions for reading to answer. This obviously should be the ultimate goal in prereading questions.

Here are some examples of teacher-formulated questions:

- In what ways are domestic cats similar to such wild cats as tigers, leopards, panthers, and cougars?
- Compare and contrast Billy's and Marsha's feelings about camping in a tent.
- What are Mike's feelings about his parents being divorced, and how does he finally learn to deal with those feelings?
- Based upon what happens in the story, how does Amy feel about her grandfather coming to live with her family?
- What do you think may be the difficulties of trying to live in space for a long period of time?

Here are some examples of teacher prompts that may help students formulate their own questions to attempt to read to answer:

- Based upon the title of the story, find out what the story may be about.
- Read the introduction to the material and then attempt to predict the content of the material.
- Given a set of related words, predict the topic of the selection and the most important areas to be covered.
- Considering the setting and characters in the material, try to predict the major events in the story.

It is very important that students learn to return to either the teacher-generated or student-generated questions after reading the material and discuss their findings so that the purpose-setting questions remain a relevant and meaningful activity that students can understand since it improves their comprehension.

The *ReQuest Procedure* or *reciprocal questioning* is also a useful technique for assessing comprehension ability using questioning strategies during reading. Explained and illustrated in detail in Chapter 6, this procedure simply involves having both the reading teacher and the student ask each other various types of questions during the reading selection. These questions should clearly indicate to you the child's ability in both answering and formulating questions about the reading material.

Examples of Questioning Strategies for After Reading

There are several different questioning strategies that can be used after reading a selection to assess reading comprehension. One of the oldest techniques for evaluating reading comprehension is called the *retelling* or *tellback strategy*. Interestingly enough, it is considered very effective by proponents of the whole-language and of the Reading Recovery Program.

Retelling was first used in the 1920s as the only way of assessing comprehension on the first standardized reading tests. However, it fell into disuse for many years because of the difficulty of accurately evaluating children's answers on such tests. Instead, standardized tests favored the multiple-choice format to assess comprehension ability.

To use this very simple, effective technique, have the child read a passage on the instructional or independent reading level and ask: "What was this story about?" or "Can you tell me all that you remember about this material?" The child's responses can be tallied if you wish to take the time to list all of the major points in the material and then keep a record of which important points the child mentioned in the retelling. However, normally this is not necessary since you usually judge how well a child understood the material simply by listening to the retelling and viewing it as a whole.

Using questions as an assessment technique perhaps can be improved by reading these very important points written by Ronald T. Hyman. Most reading teachers consider them to be very valuable in improving their own questioning skills both for assessing and improving comprehension.

1. Let all students know that they will be called on.

2. In addition to letting all students know that they will be called on, ask students not to call out answers. Rather, make sure that a specific student is called on to answer each question.

3. Do not call on volunteers more than 10 percent to 15 percent of the time. If the reading teacher calls only on the volunteering students, he or she does not get a true picture of the number of students who do not know the answers to various questions which are asked.

4. Call on volunteers mainly for those types of questions that ask the student to give his or her own opinion.

5. Be sure that the questions are passage dependent; that is, that the child cannot answer the question unless the material has been read. Questions that are not passage dependent can mainly be answered from the child's own prior knowledge.

6. Try to ask concise questions. For example, instead of asking "Why did the United States fight in Operation Desert Storm?" a more valuable question might be "What were some of the main reasons the United States felt it was necessary to participate in Operation Desert Storm?"

7. The reading teacher should give children enough time to answer a question. Some research studies have found that many teachers give children less than five seconds in which to respond to a question. The teacher should allow a child five to ten seconds in which to respond to a question. This gives him/her thinking time. However, this is not done by most teachers at all levels of education because they don't wish to embarrass a student who may not know the answer and because many other students in the reading group or class are usually waving their hands and want to blurt out the answer. Although it is often exceedingly difficult to do, it is important for reading teachers to give students time to gather and organize their thoughts before trying to answer a question.

8. All children should be urged to answer at least some of the questions rather than allowing them to say "I don't know." Otherwise, some children may persist in simply saying "I don't know" in answer to most questions.*

Using Survey Reading or Achievement Tests to Assess Comprehension Skills

Standardized survey reading or achievement tests were explained and illustrated in detail in Chapter 2 of this *Handbook*. They were described as group-administered, norm-referenced devices that attempt to evaluate a student's overall ability in word identification skills, word meaning, and sentence or paragraph comprehension.

Therefore, it is obvious that such a test can be used to make a rough estimate of a student's competencies and weaknesses in general comprehension skills. However, you should remember that although such a test is simple to give and to score, it gives a limited indication of a child's comprehension skills and should be supplemented by other means.

Using Process-Oriented Devices to Assess Comprehension Ability

Standardized process-oriented measures of reading comprehension are among the newest types of devices for the evaluation of reading comprehension. These contemporary standardized reading tests try to reflect the latest research in reading comprehension. Such research has found that reading is an active process that involves the use of a combination of different reading skills, including knowledge about how to read and the reader's existing prior knowledge of the material to be read. Thus, reading always should involve the combination of the reader, the text, and the context of the reading material:

- The reader element includes such aspects as prior knowledge, attitudes about reading and about the topic, ability to read the text, and knowledge of strategies to enhance comprehension of the material.
- The text element includes such elements as the genre, how the author has organized the information, the difficulty of the text, and the structure of the material.
- Some common contexts involved in reading are the reader's purpose, the setting where the reading takes place, and how the reader has to show his/her comprehension of the material.

Process-oriented measures of comprehension differ from traditional standardized survey reading/achievement tests in a number of important ways.

1. Before reading the material, the student must complete a *topic familiarity (prior knowledge)* inventory of some type to make an assessment of his/her prior knowledge.
2. Then the student reads an *entire passage* instead of reading only a number of short passages as has been the traditional procedure.

---

*("Questioning for Improved Reading," *Educational Leadership*, vol. 39, January 1982, pp. 307–309) Reprinted with permission of the Association for Supervision and Curriculum Development. Copyright 1982 by the Association for Supervision and Curriculum Development. All rights reserved.

3. The *constructing meaning assessment* contained in this type of device typically has questions that require more than one answer. For example, some of the comprehension questions contain one answer, some have two answers, while others have three answers that are correct. Even though the child knows that a question can have more than one correct answer, he/she does not know how many correct answers any question will have.

Thus, you can see that such process-oriented measures of comprehension attempt to stress implicit (interpretive, critical, or creative) comprehension rather than only explicit (literal) comprehension which has typically been the case with survey reading/achievement tests. In addition, the long passages used in this type of test can be either narrative or expository and may contain maps, graphs, tables, charts, and diagrams as well as text.

Example of a Process-Oriented Measure of Reading Comprehension

Here is a ready-to-duplicate example of a process-oriented measure of comprehension at the intermediate-grade reading level. If it seems applicable, you can duplicate and use it in its present form. However, more important, it should serve as a model for you in constructing your own version.

The answers are given at the end of this chapter.

NOTE: Any answer that a student can defend should be considered correct for all three sections of this process-oriented measure of comprehension.

PROCESS-ORIENTED MEASURE OF READING COMPREHENSION
(Intermediate-Grade Level)

Name_____ Grade_____ Teacher_____ Date_____

BEAVERS—A MARVEL OF NATURE

Topic Familiarity

This story is about some of the characteristics of beavers and how they live their lives. Think about what might be in a story like this and what kinds of things that you might learn. There may be 1, 2, or 3 correct answers for each question. Circle the word Yes or No in front of each possible answer to the question.

1. Which of these topics is likely to be in this story?

   Yes   No   chisel-like front teeth
   Yes   No   flat tail
   Yes   No   feathers
   Yes   No   seashore
   Yes   No   fur

2. What human occupations do you think beavers have been compared to?

   Yes   No   lumberjacks
   Yes   No   farmers
   Yes   No   builders
   Yes   No   pilots
   Yes   No   ranchers

3. Which of these animals do you think are most closely related to beavers?

   Yes   No   rats
   Yes   No   skunks
   Yes   No   squirrels
   Yes   No   seals
   Yes   No   deer

Now read this passage about beavers to yourself.

© 1993 by The Center for Applied Research in Education

BEAVERS—A MARVEL OF NATURE

Since I spend the summers near a lake in northern Wisconsin, I have seen beavers, beaver dams, and beaver lodges many times. I also have seen countless trees that were systematically cut down by beavers. Some beavers that built a dam in a marsh about two blocks from my house once flooded a gravel road so that my neighbors and I could not go to town for almost an entire day. However, until I recently read a book about the fascinating lives of beavers, I did not completely realize how unique these creatures are.

Since beavers usually work under cover of darkness, few people realize the remarkable physical characteristics that beavers possess that make it possible for them to be nature's leading lumberjacks and builders.

Although most people do not realize it, beavers are actually very large rodents and are related to other such rodents as mice, rats, squirrels, chipmunks, and muskrats. Although beavers are descended from a huge prehistoric rodent that stood about eight feet tall and weighed about 700 pounds, a beaver usually is about four feet long and weighs about 50 pounds. However, an exceptionally large beaver can weigh up to 100 pounds. The beaver is classified as a rodent primarily because of its teeth. It has four unusually large chestnut-colored chisel-like front teeth that are separated from the ordinary rear teeth they use for chewing food by a wide gap. The teeth in the beaver's lower jaw may be two or more inches long, while those in the upper jaw are usually at least one inch long. The two front upper teeth are used to get a firm grip, while the two front lower teeth are used for the actual gnawing. Together, a beaver's teeth can cut down a tree as thick as your thigh in about fifteen minutes.

In addition, a beaver's lips are so flexible that it can draw them together to close the gap between the gnawing teeth and the chewing teeth. Therefore, the beaver is in no danger of swallowing a mouthful of splinters, nor does it run the risk of swallowing so much water that it may drown when gnawing on wood underwater. Amazingly, a beaver can gnaw throughout its entire life, which is about ten or twelve years long, because rodents are the only animals whose teeth never stop growing. In addition, using them only sharpens the beaver's cutting teeth. When they are in use, the upper teeth constantly grind against the two lower teeth, which sharpens them so that they are like knives. All rodents also have very short tongues which makes it possible for them to avoid biting their tongue while gnawing.

181

The beaver's eyelids, too, are unique and well suited to its life in the water. For example, a beaver's eyelids are so transparent that it can close them underwater to protect its eyes but still let the beaver see clearly. Interestingly, on land these same "windowpane" eyelids are tough enough to serve as safety goggles to shield the beaver's eyes from flying splinters when it is cutting or gnawing. Furthermore, a beaver's ears always fold shut at the moment it submerges to keep its ear passages free of water. Its nostrils also are equipped with valve-like flaps of skin that close when it dives so that water cannot get into the beaver's lungs.

One characteristic that a beaver does not have in common with other rodents is its unique tail. The tail is covered with leathery scales and dotted with a few coarse hairs. It serves several very important and unique purposes. A beaver's tail serves as the signaling device both when a tree that it has cut is almost ready to come down and also when it detects an approaching enemy. In both cases the beaver slaps its tail with such force that a noise like a pistol shot will ring through the woods for a half-mile or more to warn all nearby beavers that danger threatens. In swimming, a beaver uses its broad tail as a rudder. Perhaps most interesting of all, its tail also serves as a comfortable "stool" on which the beaver can sit upright while gnawing down trees.

In addition to its many other unique characteristics, a beaver's entire breathing apparatus is a true miracle of nature. For example, a beaver has oversized lungs that allow it to stay underwater for as long as fifteen minutes. In addition, the beaver's body can absorb great amounts of carbon dioxide without being poisoned, as humans would be. When the beaver surfaces, its lungs can be filled three-quarters full of fresh air, while a human can renew only one-fourth of his/her lung contents. The beaver's heartbeat also automatically slows down so that it can stay submerged for long stretches, thus reducing the amount of oxygen it needs.

A beaver's forepaws are also unique and valuable. The five toes on each paw have long, strong claws that are ideal for digging, and the toes can pick up, carry, and manipulate almost any object that can be grasped. In fact, the forefeet almost seem to be like the hands of a human. For its size, a beaver has very large hind feet that measure up to seven inches across when the webbed toes are fully spread. Their great width gives the beaver a powerful swimming kick and also enables its hind feet to support the beaver in soft mud much as snowshoes keep a person from sinking in deep snow. In addition, the toenails on the first two toes of each hind

© 1993 by The Center for Applied Research in Education

foot are split in half with narrow gaps between the halves like the gaps between the teeth of a comb. These serve as the beaver's fur-combing nails. Amazingly, the split nails on the second toe of each foot can be opened and closed like a tiny pair of pliers so that the beaver can pull out splinters if any ever get wedged between its teeth while gnawing.

Among the countless other interesting physical characteristics possessed by a beaver is its fur. Beaver fur consists of a thick mat of soft underfur about three-quarters of an inch long, and a protective outer layer of heavy coarse hairs about two-and-a-half inches in length. A beaver grooms its fur by combing it with its paws to coat the fur with a waterproof oil that is secreted by two large oil glands located under the tail. When a beaver's underfur is thoroughly waterproofed, a beaver never gets really wet to the skin. Since a beaver spends considerable time under icy water, many people have compared a beaver's oiled underfur to a suit of warm underwear or to a scuba diver's wet suit.

When you consider all of the truly remarkable physical characteristics possessed by beavers, you can understand why they have been called one of nature's most interesting creatures. However, nature seems to have overlooked one important fact in designing the physical characteristics of beavers—the fact that a beaver often must walk on land. Although a beaver's short powerful legs are well adapted for swimming and for constructing dams, lodges, and canals, they are not well suited to walking and running. Therefore, on land a beaver is as slow and awkward as it is swift in the water. Even a human, who is one of nature's slower creatures, can run a beaver down in about two or three hundred feet. This is the main reason why the beaver builds dams, lodges, and canals—so that it is well protected in the water where it is best adapted to live safely.

© 1993 by The Center for Applied Research in Education

Constructing Meaning Questions

There may be one, two, or three correct answers for each question. Circle the word Yes or No in front of each correct answer to the question.

1. What other animals are beavers most closely related to?

   Yes No   chipmunks
   Yes No   deer
   Yes No   muskrats
   Yes No   mice
   Yes No   skunks

2. Why do you think it is important for a beaver's lips to protect it from swallowing splinters?

   Yes No   splinters might harm a beaver's digestive system
   Yes No   a beaver probably cannot digest wood splinters well
   Yes No   a beaver does not like the taste of wood
   Yes No   a splinter does not taste very good to a beaver
   Yes No   a beaver only enjoys eating the flesh of other animals

3. Why do you think it is important for beavers to have a short tongue?

   Yes No   so that they will not injure their tongue while chewing
   Yes No   a short tongue is more attractive than a long tongue
   Yes No   a short tongue may attract a beaver of the opposite sex
   Yes No   a short tongue is more practical for swallowing than a long tongue is
   Yes No   a beaver's tongue must be red, not pink, in color

4. Why do you think it is important for beavers to have transparent eyelids to use while swimming?

   Yes No   water could injure a beaver's eyes if the eyelids did not cover them
   Yes No   beavers could not see while swimming otherwise
   Yes No   beavers need eyelids to be attractive-looking animals
   Yes No   an opaque eyelid like a human's would not enable a beaver to see while swimming
   Yes No   most rodents do not have eyelids

© 1993 by The Center for Applied Research in Education

5. What are some of the uses for a beaver's tail?

    Yes No   it serves as a warning device for other beavers when it is slapped down

    Yes No   it acts as a rudder for a beaver while swimming

    Yes No   it serves as a stool while a beaver is gnawing down trees

    Yes No   it is very attractive to a beaver's overall appearance

    Yes No   it enables a beaver to run more quickly

6. Why do you think a beaver's heartbeat slows down automatically when it is submerged in water?

    Yes No   it reduces the amount of oxygen that a beaver needs to breathe

    Yes No   it slows down the rate at which a beaver's oxygen is burned

    Yes No   it pushes a beaver's blood through its arteries and veins faster

    Yes No   it enables a beaver to swim faster

    Yes No   it enables a beaver to stay under water a shorter time than it would otherwise

7. Why do you think a beaver's front feet are often compared to the hands of a human?

    Yes No   they can pick up small objects

    Yes No   they can carry small objects

    Yes No   they can be folded like a person's hands

    Yes No   they can manipulate small objects

    Yes No   a beaver can walk and run on them

8. What are some of the uses of a beaver's split rear toenails?

    Yes No   they help a beaver remove splinters from between its teeth

    Yes No   they are used to help a beaver groom its fur

    Yes No   they help a beaver run more quickly

    Yes No   they help a beaver swim more rapidly

    Yes No   they add to a beaver's overall beautiful appearance

Reading Strategies

1. Pretend you will take a test on this passage in two minutes. This means you don't have the time to reread the whole passage, but you want to make sure you know how all of the parts of the passage fit together. Which of these would help

you understand how all the parts of the passage fit together? Circle the word Yes or No in front of each correct answer.

Yes No   rereading the parts of the passage you are not sure about

Yes No   asking yourself what the main idea of the passage is

Yes No   looking quickly through the paragraphs

Yes No   looking up the meaning of the word rodent

Yes No   rereading that part of the passage that described a beaver's transparent eyelids

2. Pretend you are talking with your classmates about this passage. One of them asks you what point the author was trying to make. Which of these would help you tell your classmates your opinion about what point the author was trying to make? Circle the word Yes or No in front of each correct answer.

Yes No   It is about how nature has enabled beavers to adapt to their environment.

Yes No   It is about how destructive beavers can be to the trees that grow near where they live.

Yes No   It is about how a beaver cannot run quickly on land because of its short, powerful legs.

Yes No   It is about how beavers are like all other rodents.

Yes No   It is about how beaver fur should not be used for coats or hats because of its importance to the environment.

Using Criterion-Referenced Tests to Assess Comprehension Skills

Criterion-referenced tests or mastery tests deal with one or several of the reading subskills and specify the point at which the student has achieved mastery of that subskill or subskills. Some examples of comprehension subskills that can be evaluated by criterion-referenced tests are: location of the directly stated or implied main idea, location of significant or irrelevant details, ability to read and carry out directions, sequential ability, knowledge of cause-effect relationships, and knowledge of comparison-contrast relationships.

These tests differ from norm-referenced tests that are designed to compare a student's performance with the performance of other children who possess similar characteristics. As stated in Chapter 2, criterion-referenced tests may be used less frequently in the future because they view reading as a composite of separate skills rather than as a global, language-based process. (This latter view of reading is perhaps best reflected in the process-oriented measure of reading comprehension which was described and illustrated in the preceding section of this chapter.)

You will find a comprehensive list and description of standardized criterion-referenced tests in Chapter 2, and you are urged to refer to this chapter if you want more information on how to use them in assessing comprehension ability.

Using Individual and Group Diagnostic Reading Tests to Assess Comprehension Skills

As you may recall, standardized individual and group diagnostic reading tests were described in detail in Chapter 2. Any standardized diagnostic reading test is either an individually administered or group-administered reading test that tries to ascertain a student's specific reading skill strengths and weaknesses in the various word-identification and comprehension skills. Sometimes it also attempts to determine a student's instructional reading level.

Since most such tests focus on a student's competencies and weaknesses in the word-identification skills, they are normally not particularly well suited to assessing a child's comprehension skills. However, the various levels of the *Stanford Diagnostic Reading Test* may be fairly well suited for this purpose. (This test is described in detail in Chapter 2.)

Using the Traditional Cloze Procedure to Assess Comprehension Ability

The traditional cloze procedure can be used as one informal way to assess a student's comprehension ability and his/her ability to read and comprehend a selected textbook. Since cloze was described and illustrated in detail in Chapter 2, it is only briefly mentioned in this chapter. However, you will find in the next section a ready-to-use example of this device at the intermediate-grade reading level.

When the cloze procedure is used to ascertain a student's ability to comprehend reading material, it should always be used as a supplementary or alternative way to determine a student's independent, instructional, or frustration reading level. Furthermore, it must be considered as only a very tentative indicator of those reading levels.

When traditional cloze is used to determine a student's approximate reading levels, you count as correct only those completed blanks that are the same in the original passage, although incorrect spelling is not penalized. The following percentages can be used in estimating a student's independent, instructional, and frustration reading levels:

- *independent reading level—60 percent* or more of the blanks completed with the exact omitted word
- *instructional reading level—40 percent to 60 percent* of the blanks completed with the exact omitted word
- *frustration reading level—less than 40 percent* of the blanks completed with the exact omitted word

For adequate comprehension, a student's reading material should be on the independent or instructional reading levels.

Example of a Traditional Cloze Procedure That Can Be Used to Assess Comprehension Ability

Here is a ready-to-duplicate example of a traditional cloze procedure that can be used to determine a student's approximate reading levels, thus enabling you to provide the child with reading material that can be comprehended with ease.

Note: Every fifth word was deleted from the passage except proper nouns or unless a deletion in that position would be unduly difficult for the child to complete.

The answers are given at the end of this chapter.

TRADITIONAL CLOZE PROCEDURE

(Approximately Fifth-Grade Level)

Name_____ Grade_____ Teacher_____ Date_____

Read this passage about Judy Blume—the well-known young people's author—to yourself. Write a word in each blank that makes sense. When you have completed the passage, reread it to be sure that it is correct.

JUDY BLUME

Almost every student in the intermediate grades has read one of Judy Blume's books. They are considered to _____ very special because they _____ with many of the _____ that are most important _____ young people in a _____ truthful way. Many of Judy's _____ are based upon her _____ experiences when she was _____ up as a very _____ child.

Judy was born _____ Elizabeth, New Jersey, on February 12, 1938. _____ father, who was a dentist, _____ her mother had known _____ other since high school. _____ she was growing up, Judy _____ to be a timid _____ girl, but she loved _____ pretend that she was _____ famous, adventuresome person. Judy _____ extremely close to her fun-loving, warm-hearted _____ but not especially close _____ her rather reserved mother.

_____ she was growing up, Judy _____ her older brother and _____ spent several winters in Miami _____ her father stayed in New Jersey.

_____ she missed him, Judy _____ Florida with its ocean _____ swim in and its _____ sunshine. When she was _____ up, Judy also spent summers at camp where _____ learned to be an _____ swimmer and made many _____. When Judy grew up, _____ wanted to write realistic _____ for young people because _____ were no such books _____ when she was growing _____. She hoped that her _____ would help young people _____ and be able to _____ the problems that they _____. Today Judy lives in Santa Fe, New Mexico, and receives a thousand letters a month from her readers asking her questions they would never dare to ask their parents.

Using the Maze Technique to Assess Comprehension Ability

The *maze technique* can be used as a supplementary or alternative way to learn more about a student's comprehension ability. Most of the students we have tutored over the years have enjoyed completing a maze technique much more than they have a traditional cloze procedure. A maze technique can be used as a supplement to the graded oral reading paragraphs of an IRI or a traditional cloze procedure.

To construct a maze technique, select a passage of approximately 150 to 180 words from a basal reader story, supplementary reading materials, a content textbook, or a tradebook on the student's approximate instructional reading level. Then modify the passage by separating it into sentences. In place of about every fifth word, provide three alternative words. One alternative should be the correct word, another should be an incorrect word that is the same part of speech, and the third should be an incorrect word that is another part of speech. Then type or print the maze technique so that it can be duplicated.

The maze technique can be given either on an individual or a group untimed basis. Since research on the maze technique is limited, the findings from this procedure should be interpreted cautiously and used only as an alternative means of evaluating a student's comprehension ability. Here is one tentative way of interpreting the results of a maze technique:

- *independent reading level—80 percent* or more of the words correct
- *instructional reading level—60 percent to 80 percent* of the words correct
- *frustration reading level—less than 60 percent* of the words correct

Interestingly enough, a number of our students have been able to obtain 100 percent correct responses on the maze technique, partly because they have found it highly motivating to complete.

An Example of a Maze Technique to Assess Comprehension Ability

Here is a ready-to-use example of a maze technique at about the fourth-grade reading level. You can use it in its present form or as a model for constructing your own maze technique.

The answers are given at the end of this chapter.

THE MAZE TECHNIQUE
(Approximately Fourth-Grade Level)

Name_____ Grade_____ Teacher_____ Date_____

Read each sentence silently. Then circle the one word in each sentence that makes that sentence correct.

THE AMAZING PELICAN

one
The pelican undoubtedly is once of the most amazing
man

    always   among
birds alive today. The pelican is round the most ancient of
    dead   amount

an   alive
the bird species that is dead today, apparently first inhabiting
than   always

than   youth
an earth between 60,000,000 and 70,000,000 years ago.
the   yellow

        prairie's   its
One of the pelican's most remarkable features is red bill
        play's   run

    is
that can be as long as eighteen inches.
    so

The   fast   jumps
An pelican also has a flexible bag of flesh that sags
Thin   dressy   sly

under its bill.

       the   an
When an pelican dives to catch the fish, it gulps the fish
       ate   ate

© 1993 by The Center for Applied Research in Education

The Amazing Pelican, continued

and   fold
but water into its pouch, which can stretch enormously to
ant   when

fold   to   slips
hold up to seventeen pints of water. When the pelican sur-
happy   often   slowly

food,   and
faces with its catch of fowl, it closes its mouth but by com-
flying,   aunt

up   an
pression drains water ouch of its bill to trap the fish inside.
out   than

paper   manly
Certainly the pelican cannot be called a beauty bird. For
paint   beautiful

postman's   aunt
example, a pelican's neck always is in an twisted position
paints   a

pretty   only
since the eighth vertebra is abnormally joined to the one in
ate   of

ant   pour
front and behind so that the policeman can never hold its
but   pelican

nice
neck straight.
new

be   bird
However, the pelican is a unique and wonderful bell
in   bump

despite its appearance.

© 1993 by The Center for Applied Research in Education

193

How Comprehension Skills and Basic Study Skills Are Related

Comprehension skills and the most important study skills are closely related. Many of the assessment devices mentioned in this chapter and the teaching strategies mentioned in Chapter 6 are equally applicable to comprehension skills and the basic study skills. Many comprehension skills and study skills are best reinforced using content (expository) material.

Study skills often deal with those special strategies needed for effective comprehension and retention in the content areas of literature, social studies, science, and mathematics. Each of these content areas requires a somewhat different set of assessment and teaching strategies. Concrete evidence of this statement is found both in this chapter and in Chapter 6.

Ways to Evaluate Competency in the Various Study Skills

A number of the devices that have been described earlier in this chapter for the assessment of strengths and weaknesses in reading comprehension can also be used effectively in the assessment of competencies and weaknesses in the various study skills.

For example, portions of the observational checklists included in Chapter 2 can be useful for determining strengths and weaknesses in the various study skills. Such checklists enable you to know what to observe when trying to determine a student's abilities in various study skills.

Both survey reading/achievement tests and criterion-referenced tests can also be used for this purpose. Some of the survey reading/achievement tests are more useful for this purpose than others. For example, the *Iowa Test of Basic Skills* may be especially well suited for measuring a student's abilities in the study skills. You can construct your own criterion-referenced tests to determine a student's ability in the various elements of the reading-study skills. A process-oriented measure of comprehension can also be used to ascertain competencies in the reading-study skills. For example, the *Illinois Goal Assessment Program* (IGAP) uses some expository material at the intermediate and junior high school levels.

Examples of Group Reading Inventories to Assess Ability in the Study Skills

Many students in the intermediate grades, junior high school, and secondary school have great difficulty in comprehending and studying their social studies and science textbooks. A number of them simply do not have the special vocabulary and strategies required for effective study in these difficult content areas. You can use a variation of a group reading inventory to determine whether your students have the ability to read and study a content textbook effectively. Many students need to be taught the special reading-study skills needed for successful comprehension and retention in these content areas. A group reading inventory can help you determine the special reading skills that should be presented in a content area.

There are several different versions of group reading inventories. One such variation tries to determine if a group of students can use the various aids that are contained in the chosen content textbook. This informal inventory is usually given at the beginning of a course or semester. To construct this type of inventory, make up about twenty questions on the use of textbook aids, such as the table of contents, glossary, appendices, maps, index, boldface and italicized words, diagrams, pictures, tables, and graphs. The students then try to complete the inventory by using their textbook to answer the questions. Any textbook aids that a student does not have competency in should then be taught on a whole-class or small-group basis.

Another variation of a group reading inventory is designed to determine whether students can successfully understand and study a selected content textbook. To formulate this kind of inventory, choose a passage of about 1,000 to 2,000 words near the middle of the content textbook. The student then silently reads the passage and then answers an open-ended question such as "What was this passage about?" This open-ended question is an example of the popular retelling technique. The students then also answer some objective questions about this passage. These questions can evaluate a student's ability in reading skills such as: literal (explicit) and interpretive (implicit) comprehension, specialized vocabulary terms, main ideas, important details, irrelevant details, and applied reading.

The next type of group reading inventory is based on one specific chapter of the selected content textbook. This also is an open-book test that is given at the beginning of a class or semester. It is designed to determine whether a student possesses the reading skills required for effective comprehension and retention of content material. This type of informal reading inventory usually contains a matching vocabulary exercise that uses the most important specialized vocabulary terms included in the chapter. It also usually has literal (explicit) and interpretive (implicit) comprehension questions, applied questions, and questions about the main ideas and significant details from that content chapter. If a student does not perform well on such a test, the appropriate vocabulary terms and reading-study skills should then be presented.

The major purpose of each of these variations of the group reading inventory is to enable you to determine which important reading-study skills need to be presented to a group of students. You can find models of each of these variations of the group reading inventory in the following source:

Wilma H. Miller, *Reading Diagnosis Kit, Third Edition* (West Nyack, New York: The Center for Applied Research in Education, 1986, pp. 307–310.)

A Group Reading Inventory Model

The following is an example of a group reading inventory using textbook aids. Since it is specific to a particular junior high school science textbook, it should serve as a model for this type of inventory. Each variation of the group reading inventory should be constructed from the content textbooks that your students use.

EXAMPLE OF A GROUP READING INVENTORY ON USING TEXTBOOK AIDS

(Junior High School Level)

Name_____ Grade_____ Teacher_____ Date_____

1. On what page does the chapter "Two Problems in Ecology" begin?

2. On what page does Unit 5, "The Human Body: A Study of Yourself," begin?

3. According to the glossary in this textbook, what is the definition of <u>olfactory</u>?

4. According to the index of this textbook, on what page does "nucleic acid" first appear?

5. According to the glossary of this textbook, what does <u>omnivore</u> mean?

6. What are the answers to the two questions in Figure 17-5 on page 325 of this textbook?

7. How many units does this textbook contain?

8. In what year was this textbook published?

9. What animal is pictured on page 288 of this textbook?

10. According to Figure 20-5 on page 393 of this textbook, what is a synonym for <u>mandible</u>?

11. According to the chart on pages 544–545 of this textbook, about how many years ago did the Cenozoic Era begin?

12. According to the index of this textbook, on what pages does the topic "nitrogen-fixing bacteria" appear?

13. According to the glossary of this textbook, what does <u>periosteum</u> mean?

14. According to the diagram in Figure 22-4 on page 407 of this textbook, which is the largest of the following elements of the human circulatory system: arteries, veins, or capillaries?

15. What do you think is the answer to the question in Figure 18-10 on page 347 of this textbook?

Device for Assessing Ability in a Study Skill

Here is a ready-to-use device for assessing a student's ability in locating the implied main idea in a paragraph. It is mainly designed to show you how any specific study skill can be assessed by some form of assessment device. Any such device does not require a great deal of time to construct and is useful for informally assessing a student's ability in any study skill.

ASSESSMENT DEVICE FOR LOCATING THE IMPLIED MAIN IDEA IN A PARAGRAPH

(Approximately Fifth-Grade Level)

Name_____ Grade_____ Teacher_____ Date_____

Read this paragraph silently. After you have read it, put an X in front of the best statement of the <u>implied main idea</u>.

GORILLAS

Gorillas and people should be friends, since gorillas share many traits with humans. However, although a person cannot use his or her feet to grab things, a gorilla is able to do this very well. The gorilla has a smaller brain than does a human, but an adult gorilla is so strong that it could easily win a tug of war with six adult men. Gorillas have bigger muscles in their arms than in their legs, while humans have better developed leg muscles. In addition, gorillas have arms that are much longer than their legs, while that is not the case with humans. Although human and gorilla hands look similar, the thumb on a gorilla's hand is shorter in comparison to the rest of the fingers than is the thumb of a human hand. Under its dark hair, the skin of the gorilla is also dark.

Now put an X in front of the best statement of the <u>implied main idea</u>.

_____ Gorillas and humans are similar in a number of significant ways.

_____ There are significant differences in the physical characteristics of gorillas and people.

_____ The hand of a gorilla is very similar to the hand of a human.

ANSWERS TO "BEAVERS—A MARVEL OF NATURE"

Topic Familiarity
1. Yes, Yes, No, No, Yes
2. Yes, No, Yes, No, No
3. Yes, No, Yes, No, No

Constructing Meaning Questions
1. Yes, No, Yes, Yes, No
2. Yes, Yes, No, No, No
3. Yes, No, No, No, No
4. Yes, Yes, No, No, No
5. Yes, Yes, Yes, No, No
6. Yes, Yes, No, No, No
7. Yes, Yes, No, Yes, No
8. Yes, Yes, No, No, No

Reading Strategies
1. Yes, Yes, Yes, No, No
2. Yes, No, No, No, No

ANSWERS TO "JUDY BLUME"

be	appeared	warm
deal	little	growing
issues	to	many
to	a	she
very	was	expert
books	father	friends
own	to	she
growing	When	books
sensitive	and	there
in	mother	available
Her	while	up
and	Although	books
each	loved	understand
When	to	solve
		faced

NOTE: If you are going to use the formula for determining *reading levels* that was mentioned previously in this chapter, you can count only the *exact word* as being correct in each case. If you want to use the cloze procedure for some other purpose, any word that makes sense in context can be considered correct.

ANSWERS TO "THE AMAZING PELICAN"

one	sags	pelican
alive	the	beautiful
among	the	pelican's
the	and	a
alive	which	eighth
the	hold	with
years	of	and
pelican's	surfaces	pelican
its	food	neck
as	and	is
The	out	bird
flexible	the	

Ready-to-Use Strategies and Activities for Correcting Disabilities in the Word-Identification Techniques

"Learning to read" is the main emphasis in reading instruction in the primary grades, while "reading to learn" is emphasized in the intermediate grades and beyond. Therefore, it follows that a child who does not master the various word-identification techniques in the primary grades is certain to have reading disabilities of various kinds. Indeed, most of the disabled readers and learning-handicapped students we have tutored in both the primary and intermediate grades have had significant difficulties with one or more of the word-identification techniques. Several of the junior high school students my teacher-trainees have tutored still need additional instruction in the most important phonic elements, such as the short vowel sounds.

This chapter is designed to provide you with many strategies and ready-to-use activities that will help present and reinforce the word-identification techniques.

What Is Visual Perception Ability?

Since some students, especially some learning-handicapped students, have considerable difficulty with visual perception ability, it is important to explain exactly what elements constitute perception. Perception is the interpretation of incoming sensations by the brain, which selects, groups, organizes, and sequences them. When the eyes are stimulated, visual perception occurs. Meaningful interpretation of incoming visual sensations then leads to appropriate responses or actions. The perceptual aspects of reading are complex because the mind must act on a succession of stimuli in which both spatial and temporal patterns must be perceived.

The following terms are often used in the literature of perception and reading:

Figure-ground relationships. One unit or group of units that is perceived against a background only vaguely; for example, when reading, print is perceived clearly while the background of the printed page is seen only vaguely.

Discrimination. This is the ability to discriminate among visual stimuli. This ability normally improves with maturation. For instance, most children make the difficult discrimination between the letters *b* and *d* more easily with maturity.

Closure. The mind has a strong desire to fill in the missing parts or to perceive wholes.

Sequence. A student must understand the sequence of visual stimuli to be able to read. The child must learn the arbitrary conventions of left-to-right progression and reading from top to bottom.

Mind-Set. A student's mind-set helps him/her to anticipate what is going to occur next in reading. This mind set enables a student to make effective predictions while reading.

Here are the results of some studies on visual perception that you should consider in teaching this skill to all students, but perhaps especially to learning-handicapped students. (Eleanor J. Gibson, and Harry Levin. *The Psychology of Reading*, Cambridge, Massachusetts: MIT Press, 1975, pages 16, 195–197.)

1. Lower-case letters can be read more quickly than upper-case letters.

2. Initial letters can be perceived best visually, final letters next best, while middle letters cause the most difficulty for most students. This is one reason why initial consonants are often presented first in a beginning reading program.

3. Overall form or contour is not a very effective strategy in word perception. That is why the technique of *configuration* is not used very often.

4. Special features such as lines and curves in different positions are fairly important in word perception.

Ways to Improve Visual Perception Ability

There are a number of useful ways in which visual perception ability can be improved. They are most useful with a child who is very weak in visual perception ability but who has satisfactory visual channel. This often may be a learning-handicapped child who is functioning at the beginning or early primary-grade reading level.

Children who would probably profit from activities to develop visual perception ability can be identified by one or several of the visual perception tests described in detail in Chapter 2 of this *Handbook*. Visual perception ability can be improved by a number of different activities, programs, and activity sheets.

The following activities can be used to improve a child's ability in visual perception. They are included in order of increasing difficulty.

1. *Trace, copy,* and *reproduce* geometric forms. Although research does not conclusively show any relationship between geometric forms and reading achievement, it may be advantageous to use them with children who are very weak in visual perception ability. Use *tracing activities* with the child who has the most diffi-

culty, use *copying activities* with a child who does not have quite that much difficulty, and use *reproducing activities* with the child who has more competency in the area.

2. Use *templates* to help a child learn to draw the various geometric figures, such as the *circle, square, rectangle, triangle,* and *diamond.* A template can be made from cardboard, oaktag, linoleum, or plywood. Here is an example of a template for a triangle:

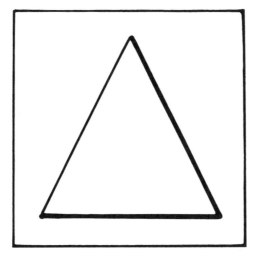

3. Assemble simple and then more difficult *jigsaw puzzles.* Teacher-trainees who have tutored kindergarten children with weak visual perception ability have constructed their own four-piece jigsaw puzzles using a picture glued to cardboard. You can also make more difficult jigsaw puzzles containing more pieces than that. You can use simple commercially available jigsaw puzzles also. Here is an example of a four-piece puzzle:

4. *Complete an incomplete picture.* Here is an example of such a picture; a cat without a tail:

5. Work with a commercially-available *pegboard*.

6. *String beads.* Many teachers have the child string beads copying a model after he/ she has developed proficiency in stringing them.

7. Perform all types of *tracing, cutting*, and *pasting activities*. All of these types of activities improve hand-eye coordination, an important aspect of visual perception ability.

8. *Locate and trace a figure in a ground* to improve ability in figure-ground relationships.

9. Work with a *balance beam*. The child can learn to walk both forward and backward on the balance beam in a toe-to-heel position.

10. Scribble and draw on a *chalkboard*. It is extremely helpful to have a chalkboard available for children both at school and at home.

11. Play the game *Angels on the Mat*. A variation of the game "Angels in the Snow," it is played on a mat on the floor instead of in the snow.

12. Suspend and swing a *ball* at eye level. This is called a *Marsden ball*, and the

child is to follow the swinging ball with his/her eyes. This is sometimes used in optometric training to improve ability in visual perception.

13. Catch and throw different sizes of *balls* and *beanbags*.

14. *Make his/her own body into the shape of a letter.* A very easy letter for the child to make is the letter *T*, for example.

15. *Combine geometric figures* into pictures.

16. Perform various kinds of *chalkboard exercises* such as dot-to-dot, incomplete pictures, drawing various geometric figures, and printing letters and words.

17. *Discriminate between non-look-alike letters.* Here is an example:

    w   c e w

18. *Discriminate between look-alike letters.* Here is an example:

    b   d b q

19. *Discriminate between non-look-alike words.* Here is an example:

    run   pen bun run

20. *Discriminate between look-alike words.* Here is an example:

    saw   was saw was

21. *Print simple scrambled words in correct order.* Here is an example:

    nur   run

    pujm   jump

Some Visual Perception Training Programs

There are several commercially available training programs for the improvement of visual perception ability. In general, the results of research studies with these programs have not shown significant improvement in the reading skills of the students who have been exposed to them. Such a program may well often improve a child's visual perception ability but not his/her reading achievement.

However, some elements of a visual perception training program may be of some value with learning-handicapped children at the beginning stages of reading if they have a satisfactory visual channel. Therefore, such a program can be recommended with reservations for such children if additional strategies and materials are used along with it.

In any case, here is a brief list of several visual perception training programs and a brief summary of the content of the programs.

1. *Frostig Program for the Development of Visual Perception* (Consulting Psychologists Press, Inc., 577 College Avenue, Palo Alto, California 94306). This program consists of workbooks and physical activities in the following areas of visual perception ability: figure-ground relationships, eye-hand coordination, form constancy, position in space, and spatial relations.

2. *The Slow Learner in the Classroom* by Newell Kephart (Columbus, Ohio: Charles E. Merrill Company, 1971). This program emphasizes such activities as the use of balance beams and trampolines (not recommended at this time due to the potential for injuries), pegboards and puzzles, a swinging (Marsden) ball, and scribbling and drawing geometric forms on a chalkboard.

3. *Techniques and Diagnostic Criteria for the Optometric Care of Children's Vision* by G. N. Getman (Duncan, Oklahoma: Optometric Extension Program Foundation, 1960). This program stresses such activities as the use of balance beams, templates and ditto masters, chalkboard training, sighting exercises, and charts and filmstrips.

The Role of Optometric Training in the Improvement of Visual Perception

Undoubtedly, mainly due to the leadership of G. N. Getman, a nationally-known optometrist, a number of American optometrists have developed visual perception training programs. Such training programs emphasize visual training in ocular motility, binocular coordination, stereopsis, orientation to distance, and shape in space. These programs often also include perceptual-motor tasks.

Are such training programs related to improved reading performance? According to research, the answer is *no*. However, I have had a number of graduate students tell me that in their personal experience the answer is *yes*. Such programs are usually fairly expensive and time-consuming to implement since parents must practice the exercises, which are first presented by the optometrist, at home. One parent whom I had in class said that the optometric training program for her eight-year-old son had cost several thousand dollars. However, she emphatically maintained that this program had resulted in improved reading performance for her son. Did the program result in her son's better reading ability? I honestly cannot answer this question. Perhaps the individual attention which he received both from the optometrist and from her helped him improve his reading. Perhaps his self-esteem improved from the additional help, which in turn resulted in improved reading skills. I have had other parents tell me essentially the same thing about their child and optometric training to improve visual perception ability.

In summary, I cannot recommend such a training program for the improvement of reading skills. However, I admit that it might be of some use for some children in certain circumstances and cannot be completely discounted.

Activity Sheets for Improving Visual Perception Ability

Here are several ready-to-duplicate activity sheets that can be used to improve a child's visual perception ability. Notice that only a few items are included in each activity sheet to avoid the distractions that can be harmful to learning disabled children. They were constructed to be as useful as possible with this type of child. You can duplicate and use them in their present form. However, more important, they can serve as a model for use in constructing your own activity sheets of this type.

ACTIVITY SHEET #1 FOR IMPROVING ABILITY IN VISUAL PERCEPTION

Name_____

Color the design in each box.

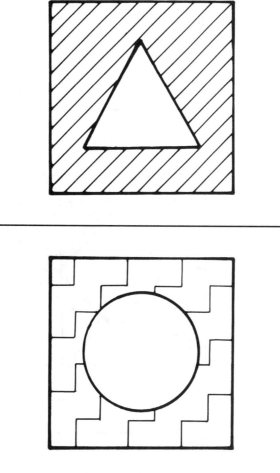

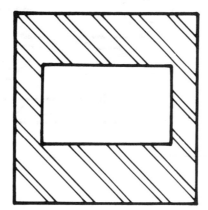

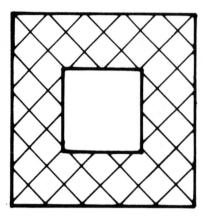

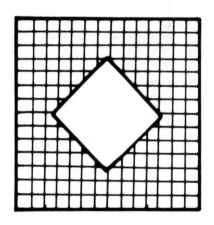

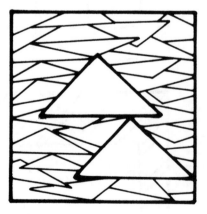

ACTIVITY SHEET #2 FOR IMPROVING ABILITY IN VISUAL PERCEPTION

Name_____

Put an X on the one that is the *same*.

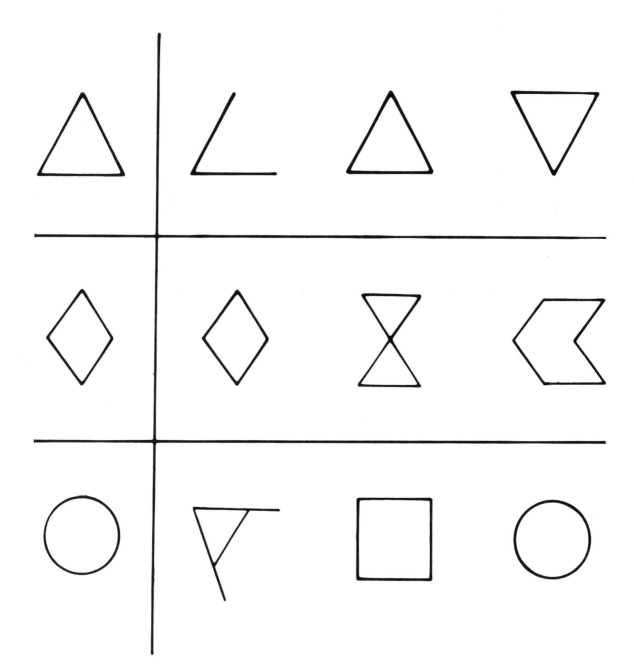

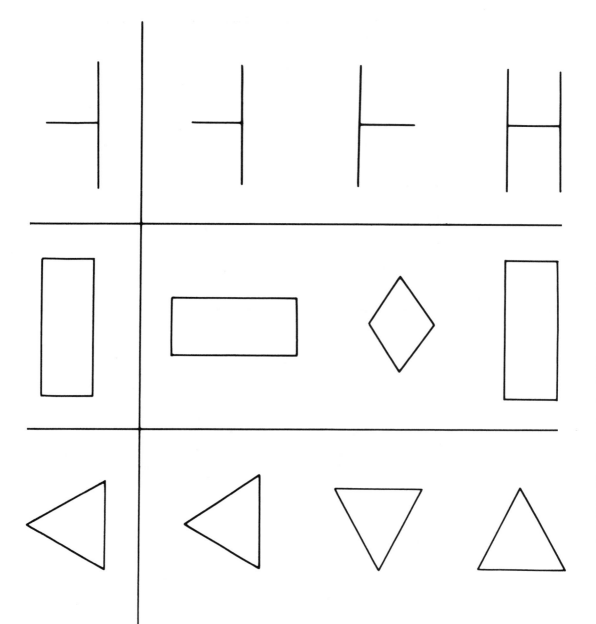

ACTIVITY SHEET #3 FOR IMPROVING ABILITY IN VISUAL PERCEPTION

Name _____

Finish each incomplete picture.

_____

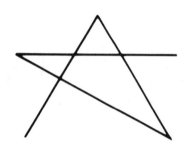

_____

_____

What Is Letter Identification?

Letter identification and *letter recognition* are both important to success in beginning reading activities. Although letter recognition is easier for most children than letter identification, it also is less significant to reading achievement. For example, the following is an example of *letter recognition*:

Put an *X* on the capital *F*.

S   F   R   E

On the other hand, this is an example of *letter identification*:

What is the name of this letter?
F

It is obvious that letter identification, not letter recognition, is required in actual reading. Therefore, although letter recognition activities may have some value as a beginning point in reading instruction, letter identification should receive the primary stress in initial reading instruction.

Although research has discovered that ability in letter identification is highly related to success in beginning reading, it is not a true prerequisite to early reading success. A number of emergent literacy activities such as reading to the child, the use of predictable books, the use of Big Books, the language-experience approach, various types of writing experiences, and the learning of environmental print can precede direct instruction in the letter names.

However, it is important for a child to learn the letter names early in the reading program for several reasons. A child needs to know the letter names in order to call them by a name in beginning reading activities. He/she cannot call a lower-case *a*, for example, a "circle and a stick." However, more important, a child who can identify the letter names probably has come from a home environment in which all reading-related activities such as reading to the child, scribbling and writing activities, and development of prior knowledge have been encouraged. In addition, the child who knows the names of the letters undoubtedly also has a good linguistic aptitude. Therefore, he/she learns both the letter names and sight words fairly easily.

A child obviously should have 100 percent competency in the knowledge of both the capital and lower-case letter names. Letter-naming is a very easy task for a child with good linguistic aptitude, and he/she seems to learn them almost effortlessly. However, it can be a very difficult task for some children, in particular with both learning-handicapped children and slow-learning children. For example, I have had teacher-trainees tutor hundreds of kindergarten children over the years. My teacher-trainees have attempted to teach their children to identify the capital and lower-case letter names. It has not been uncommon for the child to learn to identify four or fewer letter names in ten one-half hour sessions. Indeed, some children have learned only one or two letter names in ten sessions. This is the case even though the teacher-trainees have used all types of tactile activities, repetition, and overlearning.

Note: We have found that children who later were identified as learning handicapped had the greatest amount of difficulty in learning to identify the letter names.

In teaching the letter names it is important to teach *only one letter name at a time* if the child seems to have great difficulty. Tactile strategies such as the ones described in the next section of this chapter may be helpful although this is not always the case. If a child does not have a great deal of difficulty, it may be possible to teach two letter names at a time. If this is done, select two letters that do not resemble each other. For example, teach the following two letters at the same time:

e y

Do not teach the following two letters at the same time:

e c

Research has not found any one correct sequence in which to teach the letter names. Normally, the child is taught to identify the letters in his/her own first name first. As an example:

Billy

Some teachers prefer to teach the child to identify all of the lower-case letter names first, followed by all of the upper-case letter names. Other teachers present matching capital and lower-case pairs such as the following:

M m

Some teachers present letter names in terms of their usefulness. For example, such a teacher would present the letters *s* and *t* before presenting the letters *g* and *z* since the latter two letters are not seen as frequently. One possible exception to this would be the letters *X* and *x*, which are uncommon but are often used in reading readiness workbooks and tests.

The child also should learn the differences between a *letter* and a *word*. I have asked many kindergarten children to point to a word on an experience chart, and they have pointed to a letter. They do not understand this concept unless it is explained and illustrated to them.

It is also important for the young child to use the proper terms for the letters. For example, we use the terms *capital* and *lower-case*, although the term *upper-case* may also be used. We do not allow children to use the terms *big* and *little* (*small*) in place of the proper terms. For example, the *letters b* and *d* could justifiably be called *big letters* because they are ascenders, although they are lower-case letters.

Many kindergartens teach the letter names in D'Nealian script because of the potential help it may give the children in making the transition to cursive handwriting later. Although I am not opposed to this type of handwriting, I prefer block handwriting because parents can teach it properly in the home, it better matches the print found in the books that the children will read, and it is generally easier for young children to learn.

In summary, identification of all the upper-case and lower-case letter names is an important task for young children to learn. It is exceedingly difficult for many learning-handicapped children, and they must have much meaningful repetition of each letter name with overlearning if they are to be successful in this very important developmental task.

Improving Letter-Naming Ability in Isolation and in Context

There are a number of different strategies and materials we have used successfully in improving both letter-recognition and letter-identification abilities. Some of these activities stress these skills in isolation, while some stress them in word or story context. We have used all of the strategies and materials with hundreds of kindergarten-aged children in tutoring sessions. Although they have all been very successful, as stated earlier, some children have a great deal of difficulty with letter identification. These children require much concrete, meaningful repetition to insure that they learn all of the lower-case and upper-case letter names.

Flashcards

Flashcards can be successfully used for letter identification. Just print each capital and lower-case letter name on an individual card of tagboard about 2 inches by 2 inches with a marking pen. Then mix them up. Have the child identify each letter name as you hold it up. The child should state the letter's name and whether it is a capital or lower-case letter. You also can have the child match the capital and lower-case letters by placing them in pairs on a desk.

Puzzles

Puzzles can be used in having the child match each capital letter name with its corresponding lower-case letter name. Print each corresponding pair on a piece of tagboard about 2 inches wide by 6 inches long. Then cut apart each pair using a different type of cut. Place all of the puzzle parts into a large envelope. Have the child attempt to match each pair of letters by putting each puzzle together. As the child assembles each puzzle, have him/her give you the letter name and indicate whether it is a capital letter or a small letter. Here are several examples of such puzzles for letter matching.

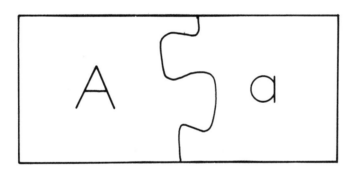

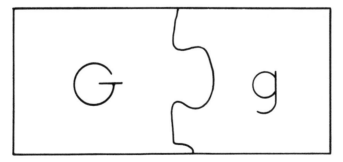

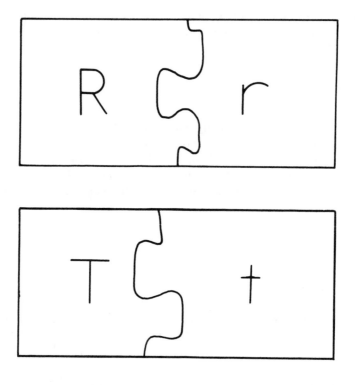

Tactile Strategies

We have found that various types of tactile activities are the most successful single strategy in helping children learn letter names if this task has proven very difficult for them. Unfortunately, this also is a very time-consuming strategy. However, usually it works quite well with learning-handicapped children or slow-learning children. We have used all of the following tactile strategies with equally good success.

Colored Chalk Sand Tray. Place sand in a flat pan such as a cake pan. Grind a piece of colored chalk to make the sand more attractive. Have the child draw the target letter name in the sand, saying its name aloud as he/she does so. Have the child use the terms *capital* and *lower-case.*

Colored Chalk Salt Tray. This tactile strategy is identical to the previous one except that salt is used instead of sand. Both seems to work equally well.

Instant Pudding. This tactile strategy probably has been the most effective. Prepare a package of instant pudding and place it in a flat pan (like a cake pan). Have the child draw the target letter name in the pudding, saying its name aloud as he/she does so. Have the child use the terms *capital* or *lower-case.* The child may lick his/her fingers after each letter is made. Chocolate pudding has been the favorite, although we have also used strawberry pudding successfully.

Macaroni. Have the child glue pieces of macaroni to a large piece of tagboard in the form of a target capital or lower-case letter. After each letter is formed, the child traces over it with his/her index finger, saying the letter name aloud. Have the child use the terms *capital* or *lower-case.*

Rice. The same procedure as above can be followed with rice.

Dried Beans. The same procedure as above can be followed with dried beans.

Finger Paints. Have the child spread finger paint over a sheet of butcher (shiny) paper. Have the child draw each target letter in the finger paint, saying the letter name as he/she does. The child should indicate whether the letter is a capital or lower-case letter. I have found finger paints to be fairly messy and, therefore, prefer to use instant pudding, which is less messy, and the child can lick his/her fingers with the pudding also. However, here are two receipes for finger paints.

Finger Paint Recipe #1

1/2 cup lump starch
1/2 cup cold water
1-1/2 cup boiling water
1/2 cup white soapflakes
1 tablespoon glycerin
food coloring

Dissolve starch in cold water. Add hot water and cook mixture until it is clear, stirring constantly. Add soapflakes and stir and remove from heat immediately. When cool, stir in glycerin and enough drops of food coloring to give the desired shades.

Finger Paint Recipe #2

1/2 cup cornstarch
1 cup cold water
1 envelope unflavored gelatin
2 cups hot water
1/2 cup mild soapflakes or detergent
Rit® dye
If Liquid Rit® Dye is used, increase the cornstarch to 3/4 cup.

Combine cornstarch and 3/4 cup of the cold water in a medium-sized sauce pan. Soak gelatin in remaining 1/4 cup cold water. Stir hot water into the starch mixture and cook over medium heat until the mixture comes to a boil and is smooth, stirring constantly. Remove from heat; blend in softened gelatin. Add soap or detergent and stir until thoroughly dissolved.

Divide into portions in jars or bowls. Stir in about 1 teaspoon Rit® powder or 1 tablespoon Rit® Liquid Dye for every cup of mixture.

If not used immediately, cover mixture tightly for storage. This recipe makes about 3 cups and can be multiplied.

Shaving Cream. The same procedure can be followed with shaving cream as with finger paints. However, shaving cream is less messy and probably preferable.

Hair Gel. Place some hair gel in a Zip-Loc® Freezer Bag. Spread some of the hair gel on a piece of butcher (shiny) paper. Have the child make each target letter in the hair gel, saying the letter name as he/she does so. Have the child indicate whether it is a capital or lower-case letter.

Pipe Cleaners. Have the child bend a pipe cleaner into the shape of each target letter. Then have the child trace over the pipe cleaner, saying the letter name aloud as he/she does so. Have the child indicate whether it is a capital or lower-case letter.

Clay. Have the child form each letter out of clay saying the letter name aloud as he/she does so. Have the child indicate whether the letter is a "capital" or "lower-case" letter.

Playdough or Magic Modeling Clay. Playdough can be used in the same manner as the clay described above. It can be either commercial or homemade playdough. Here is a recipe for homemade playdough or magic modeling clay.

Playdough or Magic Modeling Clay Recipe

2 cups salt
2/3 cup water
1 cup cornstarch
1/2 cup cold water

Mix salt and 2/3 cup water in a saucepan; place pan over low heat, stirring constantly until mixture is thoroughly heated. This will take about 3 or 4 minutes.

Remove from heat. Immediately mix cornstarch and 1/2 cup cold water and add this all at once to the hot salt and water mixture. Stir quickly to combine. Mixture should thicken to about the consistency of stiff dough. If the mixture does not thicken, place the pan over low heat again and stir about 1 minute or until the mixture starts to thicken.

Turn out on board or work surface and knead as you would bread dough to form a smooth, pliable mass. It can be used immediately, and it will keep pliable indefinitely if it is stored in a tightly closed container or wrapped in plastic or foil. This recipe makes 1-3/4 pounds.

Double batch:

Double recipe ingredients. Follow the directions given except keep saucepan over heat when adding cornstarch and water to the hot salt mixture.

How to color:

Food colors or tempera paint may be added while cooking, or they may be kneaded into the pliable base. Modeled objects may be painted when hard and dry to give the surface color.

How to dry:

Objects will dry and harden at room temperature in about 36 hours, depending on the thickness. To speed drying, preheat oven to 350°. Turn oven off and place object in oven on the wire rack to allow air circulation. Leave in oven until the oven is cold. When dry, surface may be smoothed by rubbing with sandpaper.

Magnetic Letters. Commercially available magnetic letters have been very successful in teaching letter names. Have the child identify each magnetic letter or have the child trace each magnetic letter with his/her index finger, saying the letter name aloud. Have the child indicate whether it is a capital or lower-case letter.

Oobleck. Help the child make oobleck following the recipe given here.

Oobleck Recipe

6-3/4 cups water
4 boxes cornstarch
Mix the ingredients together. A half batch is usually plenty.

Then have the child draw each letter in the oobleck, which is spread on a sheet of heavy paper such as butcher paper. Read the book *Bartholemew and the Oobleck* by Dr. Seuss either before or after the oobleck is used for letter naming. This has been a very popular tactile strategy with kindergarten children.

Alphabet Pretzels (Edible). Prepare the alphabet pretzel recipe according to the directions. Have the child form each target capital or lower-case letter out of the pretzel dough, saying the letter name aloud as he/she does so. Then bake the dough letters and allow the child to eat a baked dough letter if he/she is able to say its name.

Alphabet Pretzels (Edible) Recipe

1 cup lukewarm water
1 cake active yeast
  or 1 package dry yeast
4-1/2 cups all-purpose
  flour

2 teaspoons sugar
3/4 teaspoon salt
1 egg yolk beaten with
  1 tablespoon water
coarse salt

Preheat oven to 475°. Grease a cookie sheet. Slowly stir yeast into 1 cup lukewarm water, following package directions. Set aside.

Combine flour, sugar, and salt. Add to yeast mixture to form stiff dough. Turn dough out onto floured counter and knead 8 to 10 minutes or until it is smooth and elastic.

Oil a large bowl. Turn dough in bowl to oil both sides and then cover with clean damp cloth. Let rise in warm place until double in size.

Punch down and shape into letters. Place on cookie sheet. Baste each pretzel with egg yolk mixture. Sprinkle with salt. Let rise again until almost double.

Bake for 10 minutes or until golden brown and firm.

Letters of Dough (Inedible). Follow this recipe to make the inedible dough letters.

Letters of Dough (Inedible) Recipe

1 cup salt
2 cups flour
1 cup water

Put the ingredients in a mixing bowl. Mix together and then knead for ten minutes.

Have the child shape each target letter, saying its name as he/she does so. (We often have used the child's own first name in this tactile activity.)

Place the letters on an ungreased cookie sheet and bake 40 minutes at 325°. When the letters are cool, have the child paint them with watercolors. Bake again for 10 to 15 minutes. Varnish.

Mount on a board with white glue. Have the child trace each letter mounted on the board for additional reinforcement.

Cooking and Baking Activities

There are a number of cooking and baking activities that can be used to stress both letter identification and letter-sound relationships. Since most of these activities are highly motivating, they are also often very effective for these purposes.

Here is a sample of some of the cooking and baking activities that can be used for these purposes.

Recipes for all of the starred foods can be found in *Cook and Learn* by Bev Vietch and Thelma Harms (Menlo Park, California: Addison-Wesley, 1981).

The Letter A

applesauce*
apple salad*

The Letter B

biscuits*
bean salad*
banana bread
butter*

The Letter C

cole slaw*
cupcakes*

The Letter D

doughnuts (Have one tube-type refrigerator baking biscuit per child. Have the child gently flatten the biscuit and push his/her fingers through the center to make a hole. Heat one inch of cooking oil in an electric fry pan to hot, about 375°. Place doughnut in the oil and fry on both sides until it is golden brown. Remove the doughnut from the oil with tongs and have the child shake in a brown paper bag with powdered sugar.)

The Letter E

eggs*

The Letter F

fruit salad*
fritters*
french fries

The Letter G

grilled cheese
gingerbread man*

The Letter H

hamburgers
hush puppies*

The Letter I

ice cream*
Irish soda bread*

The Letter J

juice*
jelly beans
jam sandwich

The Letter K

kabob (Have the child thread cut pieces of fruit on a straw.)

The Letter L

latke* (potato pancake)
lasagna
lemonade*

The Letter M

meatballs
macaroni salad*
muffins*

The Letter N

navy bean soup
noodles
nachos (Place tortilla chips in a single layer on a cookie sheet. Sprinkle them with grated cheese and bake in a 400° oven until the cheese melts, usually about five minutes.)

The Letter O

oatmeal ("Three Bear's porridge")
omelet
orange juice

The Letter P

peanut butter*
popcorn
pasta
pizza*

The Letter Q

quince jelly
quesadillas
quick bread
(Any food item the child thinks would be "fit for a *queen*."

The Letter R

raisins
(hot) rice salad

The Letter S

salad*
soup*
stone soup (Make stone soup as described in *Stone Soup* by Marcia Brown. New York: Charles Scribner's Sons, 1947.)

The Letter T

tacos*
tortillas*
tomato catsup*

The Letter U

upside-down cake (use a packaged mix)

The Letter V

vegetable soup*
vanilla ice cream*

The Letter W

waffles*

The Letter X

(Have the child mix fresh fruits or vegetables.)

The Letter Y

yogurt*
yogurt shake*

The Letter Z

zucchini fritters*
zucchini muffins*

Some Suggestions for Constructing Games

Here are some ideas for constructing gameboards that should save you considerable time and effort. (These suggestions are adapted with permission from *The Reading Teacher's Almanac* by Patricia Tyler Muncy; West Nyack, New York: *The Center for Applied Research in Education*, 1991, pages 5–6.)

1. Construct any gameboard omitting the words to be practiced. After the gameboard has been laminated, add the words, letters, or phonic elements to be practiced, writing them along the pathway of the gameboard using a transparency pen. When the students have played the game a number of times and no longer need to practice those words or skills, wipe off the words or elements along the pathway. Then, you can use the gameboard over and over throughout the year for many purposes.

2. To avoid smearing words written on a gameboard's laminated surface, write the words on the pathway using a permanent fine-line pen, such as a Stanford's Sharpie™ pen. Later, when you are going to put new words or phonic items on the gameboard, spray hair spray on the words and wipe them off with a soft cloth. The permanent ink is easily removed and the gameboard is ready for you to write new words.

3. Papermate Fine-Line Flair™ Pens work well for writing words on game cards. This type of ink will not bleed through to the back side of items made with lightweight materials.

4. Stanford's Sharpie™ Fine-Point Pens work well for outlining drawings on gameboards because they will not smear when you color in pictures with markers.

5. Permanent ink felt-tip markers are good for coloring in pictures on gameboards made on posterboard. It is most effective to color the picture once with the permanent markers and then go back and color them in again.

6. Watercolor felt-tip markers work the most effectively for games constructed on lightweight cardboard.

7. Crayon can be used for coloring games that are to be laminated, only if the crayon is applied lightly. Heavy application will result in melted streaks of crayon wax when the object is laminated.

8. A good set of colored pencils is helpful in constructing teacher-made games. Two excellent sets are the Prismacolor™ colored pencil set and the Venus™ colored pencil set. These brands can be purchased through school supply catalogs and through office supply stores.

9. If you want to erase lines from posterboard games under construction, use a gum eraser as it will not leave markings.

10. Use only rubber cement for gluing things to a gameboard before laminating. When laminated, the glue marks will not show. If white school glue is used, the glue will show through when it is laminated.

Activities and Games for Reinforcing Letter Names

There are a number of activities and games that can be used to reinforce both the recognition and identification of capital and lower-case letters. They undoubtedly are most useful with children who demonstrate difficulty in learning the letter names and need additional meaningful reinforcement to learn them.

Letter Cut-Outs. Cut target capital letters out of construction paper or tagboard. Each letter should be about ten inches high. If the child is able to do so, he/she can cut the target letter himself/herself. Have the child look through old magazines to locate pictures of objects which begin with the target letter; e.g., pictures for the capital *T* might be *turkey*, *table*, *toy*, *truck*, and *teddy bear*. Have the child glue each of the pictures to the large cut-out letter. Place a string on a large cutout *T* with the glued-on pictures to make a necklace that the child can wear.

Visual Closure Cards. Cut strips from white posterboard about 5 inches by 20 inches and "start" four letters per card. Make only the first stroke. Make dots to show the remaining strokes in the following color coding: 1—green, 2—blue, 3—red, and 4—brown. Cover each card with clear self-stick vinyl. Have the child complete each incomplete letter by connecting the dots in the same color code as the writing strokes. Here are several examples of this type of visual closure activity.

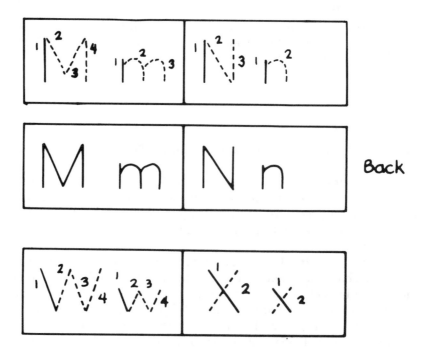

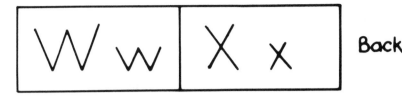

Stringing Letters. Obtain a box of large macaroni (ziti or rigatoni). With fine-line felt-tipped pens, write large capital and lower-case letters on the macaroni. Make five of each capital and lower-case letter. Print the consonants in black and the vowels in red. Dip the ends of pieces of heavy yarn into glue to make the letter stringing easier. When they are still somewhat wet, roll the ends of the yarn to form permanent points.

Have the child string the letters of the alphabet in correct order on the yarn—all capital letters and all lower-case letters. Have the child subsequently pair the letters and make words of the letters on various pieces of yarn.

Newspaper Letters. Provide the child with various pages of a daily newspaper in order to locate a target letter or letters. Have the child circle each letter with a felt-tipped pen. An alternative is to let the child cut out the target letter or letters and paste each letter to a sheet of paper to form a collage.

Octopus. Have the child trace a circle about six inches in circumference and then cut it out. Then have the child paste on eight round stickers around the circle. Have the child paste on eight strips to form tentacles. This requires one-to-one correspondence. Have the child glue confetti on the letter *O*. This is a very effective way in which to teach the letter *O*.

Pig. Have the child trace and cut out a large pig. Have the child then use a felt-tipped pen to write as many words as he/she can that begin with the letter *p*. The child should be allowed to use invented spelling.

Concentration. Construct capital and lower-case letter cards out of tagboard. Make two sets of identical cards. Begin with five pairs of cards. Place the cards in two sets face down on a flat surface. Have the child turn up a card in one set and try to find the card that matches in the other set. When a match is made, have the child say the letter name and keep the card. Points or prizes can be given for the number of cards each student has.

Bang. Cover a Pringle® potato chip can with red self-stick vinyl. Attach heavy string through the plastic lid and print the letters *B A N G* on the can. Cut tagboard into cards about 1 inch by 2 inches and print the capital and lower-case letters on the cards. Print the word *BANG* on a few of the cards. Have the child take turns drawing a card and saying each letter name. If the child can correctly say the letter name, he/she can keep the letter card. If a child draws the word *BANG*, he/she must return all the cards to the can. The first child to collect ten cards is the winner of the game.

Bingo. Construct Bingo cards out of tagboard that are divided into 8 or 16 squares. Write a capital or lower-case letter in each square with a felt-tipped pen. As the caller says the letter name, have the child place markers of some type on their card. When a complete row—either horizontal, vertical, or diagonal—is covered, the child calls out "Bingo." To win, the child must be able to repeat each letter name as he/she takes off the chips to prove that he/she has won.

Letter Card Matching Game. Make two decks of both the capital and lower-case letters on construction paper cards. The cards should be about 2½ inches by 3 inches. Make a ¼-inch border on one edge. This shows the child the bottom edge so that the letters will be placed right side up. Cover the cards with clear self-stick vinyl. The dealing deck can be red, while the drawing deck can be blue. The target letters are dealt out to two to four players from the red deck. The blue deck will be the drawing pile. Each child draws from this pile and lays the card down so that all players can see the letter. The player who has the matching letter card lays down the card, says the letter, and keeps both cards. The first child to use all the dealt cards wins if he or she has picked up the most cards.

Alphabet Apple Tree. Cut the illustrated tree design using a piece of tagboard about 15 inches by 10 inches. Print the upper-case alphabet on the tree. Then cut tagboard into small pieces about 1½ inches by 1 inch. These small pieces of tagboard can be in the shape of apples. Print the lower-case letters on the small pieces of tagboard. Put the tree on a flat surface, and have the child take the apples and match the letter on each apple with its capital letter counterpart on the tree. The teacher or another child can check the work.

What Letter Is Missing? Fold eight pieces of tagboard about 4 inches by 10 inches in order to make 2-inch by 10-inch rectangles. Using a ruler, draw a line every two inches as shown in the illustration. Copy the upper-case or lower-case letter names on the tagboard pieces in any sequence that you wish to stress. Cut out the squares that would cover the letters if folded over. On the back of the blank letter spaces copy the letter that has been omitted, so if it is folded over it will show the correct letter. Have the child take one strip at a time and look at the letters. Have the child find the missing letters from the letter cards and place them in the blank spaces. Then have the child fold over the squares to see if he/she is correct.

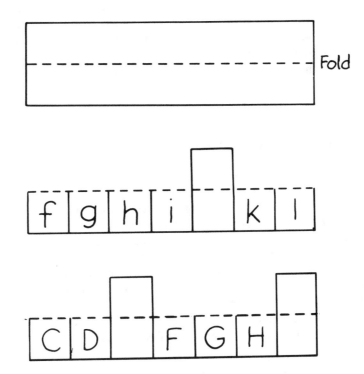

Matching Letter Names on Various Holiday Themes. Print upper-case and lower-case letter names on pumpkins and ghosts and have the child match each pair. You also can print the letter pairs using other holiday themes, such as: Pilgrims and Indians, presents and bows, or hearts and arrows. In each case, the child must match the upper-case and lower-case letter names.

Old Maid Letter Name Game. Print the upper-case and lower-case letter names on 2-inch by 2-inch square colored construction paper or tagboard. Make a card with an "old maid" on it. Have the children take turns picking a card and saying the letter name on it. If the child says it correctly, he/she is able to keep the card. If not, the card goes back into the pile. If the child picks the old maid card, he/she must put all of his/her cards back into the pile. The winner is the child who has the most cards.

Letter Chairs. Have children sit on chairs that are lined up behind each other. Begin at the front of the line and show a card with an upper-case or lower-case letter name printed on it. If the child can give the letter name correctly, he/she is able to stay in the chair. If a wrong answer is given, the child goes to the end of the line and all of the other children move up. Children try to stay at the front as long as they are able to be the "captain."

Letter Name Basketball. Use a soft foam basketball and hoop. Hang the hoop at an appropriate place and height for the children. Divide the group into two teams. Hold up a flashcard with a capital or lower-case letter name on it to the first team member in Team A. If the child can correctly give the letter name, he/she is able to try to shoot a basket. If the child makes the basket, he/she earns two points for his/her team. If the basketball hits the rim of the basket, the child earns one point. This child then goes to the end of the line in his/her team. Continue this same procedure with Team B. Keep playing until all of the team members have had a chance to shoot at the basket.

Jump-Up. Put a list of capital or lower-case letters on the chalkboard or an experience chart. Prepare two cards for each letter on the board. Give each child two to four letter cards, each of which should be different. Point to one letter on the board or paper. The children with that letter card jump up and say the letter name. The child who says it first gets the other child's card. The winner is the child with the most cards at the end of the game.

Using Predictable Books and Language-Experience Stories to Improve Letter-Name Knowledge

Predictable books and language-experience stories can be used effectively both to present and to reinforce letter-naming ability. Teaching and reinforcing letter names in sentence context and story context is in keeping with the contemporary whole-language philosophy. However, it is often necessary to teach both letter recognition and letter identification in isolation as well as in context with learning-handicapped children, slow-learning children, and immature children. They seem to profit best from this type of instruction.

The next major section of this chapter, which is devoted to sight words, contains a comprehensive list of predictable books that can be used for instruction and reinforcement in both letter identification and sight-word instruction. It also contains a detailed description about how to implement the language-experience approach. This approach can be used effectively in presenting both letter identification and sight-word recognition.

Tradebooks for Teaching and Reinforcing Letter Names

Here is a brief list of tradebooks that can be read by you to present and reinforce letter names for children at the beginning stages of reading instruction. They are just illustrative of the many books that could be used for this purpose.

The Letter A

About Animals, by Richard Scarry. New York: Golden Press, 1976.

Ants, by Diana Ferguson, illustrated by Reginald Davis. New York: Wonder Books, 1977.

Apples: How They Grow, by Bruce McMillan. Boston: Houghton Mifflin, 1979.

The Letter B

Ask Mr. Bear, by Marjorie Flack. New York: Macmillan, 1932.

Benjamin's Book, by Alan Baker. New York: Lothrop, Lee and Shepard, 1982.

Teddy Bears 1 to 10, by Susanna Gretz. Chicago: Follett, 1969.

The Letter C

Carousel, by Donald Crews. New York: Greenwillow Books, 1982.

Clifford, The Small Red Puppy, by Norman Bridwell. New York: Scholastic, Inc., 1972.

Corduroy, by Don Freeman. New York: Penguin Books, 1977.

The Letter D

Dinosaur Bones, by Stan and Jan Berenstein. New York: Beginner Books, 1980.

The Dinosaur World, by Edwin H. Colbert, illustrated by George and Paul Geygan. New York: Stravon Educational Press, 1977.

Harry, the Dirty Dog, by Gene Zion, illustrated by Margaret Bloy Graham. New York: Harper & Row, 1956.

The Letter E

Eggs, illustrated by Esme Eve. New York: Wonder Books, 1971.

Little Elephant, by Arnold Lobel. New York: Scholastic, Inc., 1981.

The Little Engine that Could, by Watty Piper, illustrated by George and Doris Hauman. New York: Scholastic, Inc., 1961.

The Letter F

Frog in the Meadow, by Joanne Ryder, illustrated by Gail Owens. New York: Harper & Row, 1979.

The Foolish Frog, by Pete Seeger and Charles Seeger, illustrated by Miloslaw Jagr. New York: Macmillan, 1973.

The Story of Ferdinand, by Munro Leaf, illustrated by Robert Lawson. New York: The Viking Press, 1936.

The Letter G

The Gingerbread Man, by Ed Arno. New York: Scholastic, Inc., 1967.

Green Eggs and Ham, by Dr. Seuss. New York: Beginner Books, 1960.

In Granny's Garden, by Sarah Harrison and Mike Wilks. New York: Holt, Rinehart, and Winston, 1980.

The Letter H

How, Hippo!, by Marcia Brown. New York: Charles Scribner's Sons, 1969.

Humpty Dumpty, illustrated by Stephan Weatherhill. New York: Greenwillow Books, 1982.

The Little Red Hen, by Paul Galdone. New York: Scholastic, Inc., 1973.

The Letter I

The Indoor Noisy Book, by Margaret Wise Brown, illustrated by Leonard Weisgard. New York: W. R. Scott, 1942.

Ira Sleeps Over, by Bernard Waber. Boston: Houghton Mifflin, 1972.

Let's Look at Insects, by Deborah Manley, illustrated by Annabel Milne and Peter Stebbing. New York: Derrydale, 1977.

The Letter J

Giant Jam Sandwich, by John Vernon Lord with verses by Janet Burroway. Boston: Houghton Mifflin, 1973.

Jump Frog Jump, by Robert Kalan. New York: Greenwillow Books, 1981.

This Is the House that Jack Built, illustrated by Iris Simon. New York: Dandelion Press, 1979.

The Letter K

Katy-No-Pocket, by Emmy Payne, illustrated by H. A. Rey. New York: Scholastic, Inc., 1972.

Kenny's Crazy Kite, by Arnold Shapiro, illustrated by Karen Acost. Los Angeles: Price/Stern/Sloan, 1978.

My Kitchen, by Harlow Rockwell. New York: Greenwillow Books, 1980.

The Letter L

The Grouchy Ladybug, by Eric Carle. New York: Scholastic, Inc., 1977.

Leo the Lop, by Stephan Cosgrove, illustrated by Robin James. Bothell, Washington: Serendipity Press, 1977.

Light, by Donald Crews. New York: Greenwillow Books, 1981.

The Letter M

City Mouse—Country Mouse, illustrated by Marian Parry. New York: Scholastic, Inc., 1970.

Mouse Soup, by Arnold Lobel. New York: Harper & Row, 1977.

Tell Me a Mitzi, by Lore Segal, illustrated by Harriet Pincus. New York: Farrar, Straus, and Giroux, 1970.

The Letter N

Miss Nelson Is Missing, by Harry Allard and James Marshall. Boston: Houghton Mifflin, 1977.

Noisy Nora, by Rosemary Wells. New York: Scholastic, Inc., 1973.

There's a Nightmare in My Closet, by Mercer Mayer. New York: Dial Press, 1968.

The Letter O

Oliver, by Syd Hoff. New York: Harper & Row, 1960.

Over in the Meadow, illustrated by Paul Galdone, based on the original by Olive A. Wadsworth. Englewood Cliffs, New Jersey: Prentice-Hall, 1986.

Thy Friend, Obadiah, by Brinton Turkle. New York: The Viking Press, 1969.

The Letter P

Each Peach Pear Plum, by Janet and Allen Ahlberg. New York: Scholastic, Inc., 1978.

Pickle, Pickle, Pickle Juice, by Patty Wolcott, illustrated by Blair Dawson. New York: Scholastic, Inc., 1975.

Pig, Pig Grows Up, by David McPhail. New York: Scholastic, Inc., 1980.

The Letter Q

Q Is for Duck: An Alphabet Guessing Game, by Mary Elting and Michael Folsom, illustrated by Jack Kent. New York: Clarion Books, 1980.

The Queen Wanted to Dance, by Mercer Mayer. New York: Simon and Schuster, 1971.

Quilts in the Attic, by Robbin Fleisher, illustrated by Ati Forberg. New York: Macmillan, 1978.

The Letter R

Applebaums Have a Robot!, by Jane Thayer, illustrated by Bari Weissman. New York: William Morrow, 1980.

Little Red Riding Hood, told by Mabel Watts, illustrated by Les Gray. Racine, Wisconsin: Golden Press, 1979.

Rain Rain Rivers, by Uri Shulevitz. New York: Farrar, Straus, and Giroux, 1969.

The Letter S

My Snail, by Herbert H. Wong and Matthew F. Vessel, illustrated by Jean Day Zallinger. Reading, Massachusetts: Addison-Wesley, 1976.

The Stickleback, by Sacha van Dulm and Jan Reim. Woodbury, New York: Barron's, 1979.

Swimmy, by Leo Lionni. New York: Pantheon, 1968.

The Letter T

The Bear's Toothache, by David McPhail. New York: Penguin Books, 1972.

Tikki Tikki Tembo, retold by Arlene Mosel, illustrated by Blain Lent. New York: Scholastic, Inc., 1968.

The Truck Book, by Robert L. Wolfe. Minneapolis, Minnesota: Carolrhoda Books, 1981.

The Letter U

My Red Umbrella, by Robert Bright. New York: W. Morrow, 1959.

Umbrella, by Taro Yashima. New York: The Viking Press, 1958.

Upside-Downers, by Mitsumasa Anno. New York: Walker/Weatherhill, 1971.

The Letter V

A Day in the Life of a Veterinarian, by William Jaspersohn. Boston: Little, Brown and Company, 1978.

The Night Vegetable Eater, by Elke and Ted Musicant, illustrated by Jeni Bassett. New York: Dodd, Mead and Company, 1981.

What Can She Be? A Veterinarian, by Gloria and Esther Goldreich, photographs by Robert Ipcar. New York: Lothrop, Lee, and Shepard, 1972.

The Letter W

Where the Wild Things Are, by Maurice Sendak. New York: Harper & Row, 1963.

Whistle for Willie, by Ezra Jack Keats. New York: The Viking Press, 1964.

Willaby, by Rachel Isadora. New York: Macmillan, 1977.

The Letter X

The Box Book, by Celia Maloney, illustrated by Carolyn Bracken. Racine, Wisconsin: Golden Press, 1978.

Little Max, the Cement Mixer, by Renee Bartkowski, illustrated by Robert Doremus. Chicago: Rand McNally, 1975.

The Skeleton Inside You, by Philip Balestrino, illustrated by Don Bolognese. New York: Scholastic, Inc., 1971.

The Letter Y

Little Blue and Little Yellow: A Story for Pippo and Ann and Other Children, by Leo Lionni. New York: I. Obolensky, 1959.

What Does the Rooster Say, Yoshio?, by Edith Battles. Chicago: Albert Whitman, 1978.

Yertle the Turtle and Other Stories, by Dr. Seuss. New York: Random House, 1958.

The Letter Z

Animals in the Zoo, illustrated by Feodor Rojankonsky. New York: Alfred A. Knopf, 1962.

We Need a Bigger Zoo, by Eve Bunting, illustrated by Bob Barner. Lexington, Massachusetts: Ginn and Company, 1974.

Songs and Fingerplays for Reinforcing Letter Names

Here are some songs and fingerplays that can be used to reinforce letter names. These are just illustrative of some of the songs and fingerplays that you can use for this purpose.

The Letter A

Apples

I opened an apple and what did I see?
A little green worm, looking at me!
Apples, apples, good to eat.
Apples hide a special treat.

The Letter B

"Row, Row, Row Your Boat"

Row, row, row, your boat,
   Gently down the stream.
Merrily, merrily, merrily, merrily
   Life is but a dream.

Teddy Bear

Teddy bear, Teddy bear, turn around.
Teddy bear, Teddy bear, touch the ground.

Teddy bear, Teddy bear, show your shoe.
Teddy bear, Teddy bear, that will do.
Teddy bear, Teddy bear, go upstairs.
Teddy bear, Teddy bear, say your prayers.
Teddy bear, Teddy bear, turn out the light.
Teddy bear, Teddy bear, say good-night.

The Letter C

Caterpillar

Caterpillar, caterpillar,
Brown and furry. *(Move cupped hand up arm.)*
Winter is coming and
You'd better hurry! *(Move hand faster.)*
Find a big leaf
Under which to creep; *(Mold one hand over the other.)*
Spin a cocoon in which to sleep. *(Put hands beside face; close eyes.)*
Then when spring time comes,
One fine day,
You'll be a butterfly,
And fly away! *(Move arms as if flying.)*

The Letter D

Six Little Ducks

Six little ducks that I once knew—
Fat ones, skinny ones, wet ones, too.
But the one little duck with the feather on his back
He ruled the others with a quack, quack, quack.

The Letter E

The Elephant

The elephant has a trunk for a nose *(Pretend an arm is the elephant's trunk.)*
And up and down is the way it goes. *(Move arm up and down.)*
He wears such a saggy, baggy hide,
Do you think two elephants would fit inside?

The Letter F

Put Your Finger in the Air

Put your finger in the air, in the air.
Put your finger in the air, in the air.
Put your finger in the air and leave it right up there.
Put your finger in the air, in the air.

The Letter G

Gobble, Gobble, Gobble

He's big and fat and gobble, gobble, gobble.
He spreads his tail and gobble, gobble, gobble.
But when Thanksgiving Day is here
Then it's our turn to gobble, gobble, gobble.

The Letter H

Homes

Here is a house for a robin. *(Open hand.)*
Here is a hive for a bee. *(Close hand.)*
Here is a hole for a bunny. *(Make a circle with fingers.)*
Here is a home for me. *(Gesture around.)*

The Letter I

Insect Parts

Head, thorax, abdomen,
Head, thorax, abdomen,
Head, thorax, abdomen,
Two antennae and six little legs,
Head, thorax, abdomen.

The Letter J

Two Little Blackbirds

Two little blackbirds
Sitting on a hill
One named Jack,
One named Jill.
Fly away, Jack.
Fly away, Jill.
Come back, Jack.
Come back, Jill.
(The hands should be used to show the motions of birds.)

The Letter K

Kookaburra

Kookaburra sits on an old gum tree.
Merry, merry king of the bush is he.
Laugh, Kookaburra, laugh Kookaburra.
Gay your life must be.
(A kookaburra is an Australian bird with a unique call that kills snakes.)

The Letter L

Leaves

Like a leaf and a feather
In the windy weather,
We will whirl and twirl about
And then sink down together.

The Letter M

Five Little Monkeys

Five little monkeys jumping on the bed—
One fell off and bumped his head.
Went to the doctor and the doctor said,
"No more monkeys jumping on the bed."

The Letter N

One, Two, Buckle My Shoe

One, two, buckle my shoe.
Three, four, shut the door.
Five, six, pick up sticks.
Seven, eight, lay them straight.
Nine, ten, a big fat hen.

The Letter O

Open, Shut Them

Open, shut them; open, shut them.
Give a little clap.
Open, shut them; open, shut them.
Lay them in your lap.
Creep them, creep them, creep them, creep them.
Right up to your chin.
Open wide your little mouth
But do not let them in.

The Letter P

Pancake

Mix a pancake,
Stir a pancake,
Pop it in a pan.
Fry a pancake,
Toss a pancake,
Catch it if you can.

The Letter Q

Bells are ringing, people singing, chickens clucking, ducks are ducking,
Noises all around, but (Mr.) Q not a sound.
Whistles wailing, wheels going, cows are mooing, trucks are moving,
So much to be heard, but (Mr.) Q not a word.
Rain is pouring, bodies snoring, rockets shooting, horns are tooting,
What a noisy world, but (Mr.) Q you're so quiet.*

The Letter R

It's Raining

It's raining, it's pouring,
The old man is snoring.
He went to bed and he bumped his head,
And he couldn't get up in the morning.

The Letter S

Eensy-Weensy Spider

The eensy-weensy spider
Went up the water spout. *(Put index fingers to thumbs to make spider climb.)*
Down came the rain
And washed the spider out. *(Swish hands downward.)*
Out came the sun
And dried up all the rain. *(Have hands meet above head.)*
And the eensy-weensy spider
Went up the spout again. *(Make the spider climb up again.)*

The Letter T

I'm a Little Teapot

I'm a little teapot
Short and stout.
Here is my handle. *(Crook arm and put hand on hip.)*
Here is my spout. *(Extend the other arm out.)*
When I get all steamed up
Hear my shout.
"Just tip me over
And pour me out!" *(Bend over as if pouring.)*

---

*Adapted from songs on the following records: Alpha Time: *Songs of the Letter People.* New Dimensions in Education, 83 Keeler Avenue, Norwalk, Connecticut 06856. Copyright 1972 Claro Music Corporation (ASCAP).

The Letter U

Under the Spreading Chestnut Tree

Under the spreading chestnut tree *(Spread arms out; touch chest, head [nut], fingers together over head.)*
We were as happy as could be *(Hug self and rock back and forth.)*
With our banjoes on our knees *(Strum banjo; slap knees.)*
Under the spreading chestnut tree. *(Repeat first step.)*

The Letter V

Going to St. Ives

As I was going to St. Ives
I met a man with seven wives.
Every wife had seven sacks,
Every sack had seven cats,
Every cat had seven kits.
Kits, cats, sacks, and wives.
How many were going to St. Ives?

The Letter W

Wee Willie Winkie

Wee Willie Winkie
Runs through the town
Upstairs and downstairs
In his nightgown.
Rapping at the window
Crying through the lock
Is everyone into bed?
It's almost eight o'clock.

The Letter X

Jack in the Box

Jack in the box *(Make a fist with the thumb on top.)*
Sits so-o-o still.
Will he come out?
Yes! He will. *(Raise thumb up quickly.)*
Jack in the box *(Reform fist with the thumb on top.)*
Sits so-o-o still,
Will he come out?
No! He won't. *(Shake head.)*

The Letter Y

Yankee Doodle

Yankee Doodle went to town.
Riding on his pony.
Stuck a feather in his hat
And called it macaroni.

The Letter Z

The Zoo

This is the way the elephant goes, *(Clasp hands and move arms back and forth.)*
With curly trunk instead of nose.
The buffalo, all shaggy and fat,
Has two sharp horns in place of a hat. *(Point fingers out from forehead.)*
The hippo
Lets you see what is in. *(Open and close hands to make mouth movements.)*
The wiggly snake upon the ground
Crawls along without a sound. *(Weave hands back and forth.)*
But monkey see and monkey do
Is the funniest animal in the zoo. *(Put thumbs in ears and wiggle hands.)*

What Is Sight-Word Knowledge?

Sight words can be described in a number of different ways. They can be designated as those which a reader recognizes immediately upon seeing them. They are those words a reader does not have to stop and analyze by using some other word-identification technique such as phonic analysis or structural analysis. In addition, many sight words also do not have a regular sound-symbol relationship. Therefore, these kinds of words cannot be analyzed effectively but are most effectively recognized as a *total unit.* Some examples of sight words are *have, of, off, mother, through,* and *father.*

Sight-word recognition consists of such subskills as recognizing a word by its total unique shape, its first few letters, its special characteristics such as *ascenders* (*b, h, f*), descenders (*g, p, y*), or its length. *Configuration* or drawing a frame around the word is another subskill of sight-word recognition. Here is an example of configuration:

You should understand that some subskills of sight-word recognition may provide irrelevant or unimportant cues to word identification. One such irrelevant cue was said to be configuration. Configuration was emphasized in the past in beginning reading programs. However, reading teachers noticed that many beginning reading words had a similar configuration such as the words *son, man, run, van,* and *won.* Therefore, configuration received very little stress for a long time. However, it is again receiving increasing emphasis at this time. Another unimportant cue is the *double o* in the word *look* which was said to "appear as two eyes." However, a number of other words such as *book, cook, took,* and *hook* also have a *double o* in the same position. One other irrelevant cue presented in the past was the incorrect practice of having a child look for small words in a larger word. It can be seen that this technique certainly is incorrect in locating the words *fat* and *her* in the word *father.*

To be an effective reader a child must have a large stock of sight words which can be recognized instantly. Often these are the words that comprise a sight-word list (described later in this section). In addition, a number of words first decoded by using another word-identification technique, such as phonic analysis or structural analysis, should eventually become part of a child's stock of sight words. Many reading teachers believe that a child may need 120 to 140 meaningful exposures to a word before it becomes part of his/her sight-word bank. Some disabled readers or learning-handicapped students may need many more exposures than that before a sight word is recognized instantly.

Note: Some sight words can be exceedingly difficult for learning-handicapped students to learn to recognize. Therefore, such a child may need to use a unique strategy such as the tracing strategies described later in this chapter to master an especially difficult-to-learn sight word.

The most common sight words are found in a number of different sight-word lists. There is considerable overlap among all of the lists, although the words contained on the lists do vary somewhat depending upon the sources from which they were taken (children's reading or writing or a combination of both).

The most common, and a very useful, sight-word list is the *Dolch Basic Sight Word List,* which was formulated by the late Edward Dolch of the University of Illinois in 1941. Although it might seem dated, it is not; the words in it are comparable to those contained in the newer word lists. This list of 220 service words is supposed to make up about 70 percent of the words found in most first readers and about 65 percent of the words contained in many second and third readers. As is the case with all the sight-word lists, most of the words contained in the *Dolch Basic Sight Word List* are structure or function words, meaning that they have no referent. Structure or function words are normally more difficult for most children to remember than are content words which have a concrete referent. Learning-handicapped children usually find those words especially difficult to learn. Examples of structure or function words are *of, through,* and *should.* Examples of content words are *mother* and *tractor.*

Although my teacher-trainees have used the *Dolch* list in various tutoring situations, I could not obtain permission to reprint it in this *Handbook.* However, you may obtain it for a nominal cost from the following source:

Garrard Publishing Company
1607 North Market Street
Champaign, IL 61820

Here is a way to determine a child's approximate instructional reading level (explained and illustrated in detail in Chapter 3) determined by their performance on the *Dolch Basic Sight Word List.* (See Maude McBroom, Julia Sparrow, and Catherine Eckstein, *Scale for Determining a Child's Reader Level.* Iowa City, Iowa: Bureau of Publications, Extension Service, University of Iowa, 1944, p. 11.

Words Recognized	Reading Level
0–75	Preprimer
76–120	Primer
121–170	First Reader
171–210	Second Reader
Above 210	Third Reader or above

Edward B. Fry, Professor Emeritus of Rutgers University, has compiled an updated version of the *Instant Word List*, which he first compiled in 1957. This word list was revised in 1980 based on a modification of the Carroll (American Heritage) data. The first one-hundred words make up half of all written material, and the three-hundred words together comprise 65 percent of all written materials. Fry has graciously given all textbook authors permission to reprint his revised *Instant Words* in the hope that this word list will aid in the improvement of reading instruction. Here is a copy of *Fry's Instant Word List*:

FIRST HUNDRED

Words 1–25	Words 26–50	Words 51–75	Words 76–100
the	or	will	number
of	one	up	no
and	had	other	way
a	by	about	could
to	word	out	people
in	but	many	my
is	not	then	than
you	what	them	first
that	all	these	water
it	were	so	been
he	we	some	call
was	when	her	who
for	your	would	oil
on	can	make	its
are	said	like	now
as	there	him	find
with	use	into	long
his	an	time	down
they	each	has	day
I	which	look	did
be	do	more	get
this	how	write	made
have	their	go	may
from	if	see	part

Common suffixes: -s, -ing, -ed, -er, -ly, -est

If you want more than the three-hundred sight words, the following is a list of three-thousand sight words: Elizabeth Sakiey and Edward B. Fry, *300 Instant Words*. Providence, Rhode Island: Jamestown Publishers, 1984.

Words 101–125	Words 126–150	Words 151–175	Words 176–200
over	say	set	try
new	great	put	kind
sound	where	end	hand
take	help	does	picture
only	through	another	again
little	much	well	change
work	before	large	off
know	line	must	play
place	right	big	spell
year	too	even	air
live	mean	such	away
me	old	because	animal
back	any	turn	house
give	same	here	point
most	tell	why	page
very	boy	ask	letter
after	follow	went	mother
thing	came	men	answer
our	want	read	found
just	show	need	study
name	also	land	still
good	around	different	learn
sentence	form	home	should
man	three	us	America
think	small	move	world

SECOND HUNDRED

Common suffixes: -s, -ing, -er, -ly, -est

THIRD HUNDRED

Words 201–225	Words 226–250	Words 251–275	Words 276–300
high	saw	important	miss
every	left	until	idea
near	don't	children	enough
add	few	side	eat
food	while	feet	face
between	along	car	watch
own	might	mile	far
below	chose	night	Indian
country	something	walk	really
plant	seem	white	almost
last	next	sea	let
school	hard	began	above
father	open	grow	girl
keep	example	took	sometimes
tree	begin	river	mountain
never	life	four	cut
start	always	carry	young
city	those	state	talk
earth	both	once	soon
eye	paper	book	list
light	together	hear	song
thought	got	stop	being
head	group	without	leave
under	often	second	family
story	run	late	it's

Common suffixes: -s, -ing, -er, -ly, -est

Presenting and/or Reinforcing the Words in a Sight-Word List or in a Basal Reader in Isolation

There are a number of different strategies, materials, and games we have used very effectively in improving the sight-word knowledge of hundreds of students. Although all of the strategies have been successful with different types of children, as stated earlier some children have extreme difficulty with retaining the sight words presented to them. Such children often are learning-handicapped children. These children require much concrete, meaningful, interesting repetition to insure that they master all of the important sight words in a word list or in the basal readers they are required to read.

A Special Statement for Teachers of Learning-Handicapped Students. Here are some unique considerations you should consider carefully in presenting and/or reinforcing sight words to learning-handicapped children:

- *Tracing* or *kinesthetic strategies* may be helpful in helping this kind of child learn difficult-to-retain sight words.
- *Overlearning with much concrete, meaningful repetition* is especially important to help this kind of child learn difficult-to-retain sight words.
- *Comparison with previously learned words* can also help this type of child to retain difficult sight words.
- *Avoid distractions on activity sheets* for these children. An activity sheet should focus on only one concept at a time.

Tracing or Kinesthetic Strategies

Many of the tracing or kinesthetic strategies described in detail for helping children to remember difficult-to-retain letter names are equally applicable in helping a child retain difficult sight words. These tracing strategies are generally most effective with learning-handicapped children or severely disabled readers. These are children who often cannot seem to remember sight words that are taught by a conventional method. Since tracing is very time consuming, it should only be used with sight words that seem especially difficult for a child. For the same reason, tracing only should be used as long as absolutely necessary.

The following are some tracing strategies which were described earlier in the chapter that can be used in helping children to remember difficult sight words:

- Colored chalk sand tray
- Colored chalk salt tray
- Instant pudding
- Finger paints
- Shaving cream
- Oobleck

In each case, the child should print the target sight word in the material, saying it aloud as he/she forms it. Have the child trace the sight word in the material as many times as necessary to retain the word. Have the child also use the word in a sentence.

- Macaroni
- Rice
- Dried beans
- Cheerios™
- Pipe Cleaners

In each case, have the child glue the material to a piece of tagboard. Then have the child trace the sight word, saying it aloud. Have the child trace the word enough times to insure that he/she has mastered it. Then have the child use the word in a sentence.

- Clay
- Playdough
- Magic modeling clay
- Alphabet pretzels (edible)
- Letters of dough (inedible)

In each case, have the child form the target sight word out of the material. Have the child trace the word sufficient times to insure mastery. Have the child use each sight word in a sentence.

- *Magnetic Letters*—As described earlier in the chapter, the child should form each target sight word out of the commercially available magnetic letters, saying the sight word aloud as he/she does so. Each sight word should be used in a sentence. The child can also form an entire sentence using magnetic letters. This type of activity is used in the contemporary Reading Recovery Program, an early intervention program for at-risk readers in first grade which is described later in this chapter.

Flashcards

Flashcards are a traditional, but still useful, way of improving a child's ability in sight-word recognition. Simply print, or have the child print, the target sight words on small flashcards constructed out of tagboard. You can also use words from the child's language-experience stories. All of the target words can serve as the child's *word bank*. (See the section later in this chapter on the language-experience approach.) Have the child review the target sight words individually or with a partner to attain immediate recognition. The flashcards can also be used in some of the games included later in this section.

Word Puzzles

Word puzzles can be used to have the child match difficult-to-retain sight words. Print each pair of sight words on a piece of tagboard about 2 inches wide by 8 inches long. Then cut apart each pair using a different type of cut. Place all of the puzzle parts into a large envelope. Have the child attempt to match each pair of sight words by putting each puzzle together. As the child assembles each puzzle, have him/her say the sight word and use it in a sentence. Here are a few examples of such puzzles for sight word matching.

Activity Sheets for Improving Sight-Word Knowledge

Here are ready-to-duplicate activity sheets and word searches you can use to reinforce sight-word knowledge. You can duplicate and use any of these reproducible examples or use them as models for constructing your own materials. The answers are given at the end of the chapter.

Note: If you are going to use any of the activity sheets included in this section with a *learning-handicapped child,* you may want to include only *a few examples* of each activity on a page to make it easier for him/her.

ACTIVITY SHEET FOR LEARNING DIFFICULT SIGHT WORDS USING VISUAL AND KINESTHETIC SKILLS

(First-Grade Level)

Name_____ Grade_____ Teacher_____ Date_____

Look at each of the words on this sheet. Fill in each missing letter. Then write the word. The first word has been done for you.

one	they
o_ne_	th_y
o_ne	t_ey
o_ne	the_
_o_ne_	__ey
	____

have	word
h_ve	w_rd
ha_e	wo_d
_ave	_ord
h__e	w__d
____	____

were

w__re

we__e

wer__

w____e

_____

many

m__ny

ma__y

__any

m____y

_____

about

ab__ut

a__out

abou__

ab____t

_____

then

th__n

t__en

the__

____en

_____

been

__een

b__en

bee__

b____n

_____

could

c__uld

__ould

cou__d

c____ld

_____

ACTIVITY SHEET FOR LOCATING AND WRITING DIFFICULT SIGHT WORDS

(First-Grade Level)

Name_____ Grade_____ Teacher_____ Date_____

Look at the word on each line. Then put a circle around each letter after it to make the word. Then write the word on the line. The first one is done for you.

1. the   r   (t)   o   a   (h)   p   (e)   _____ the

2. your   y   x   v   o   u   s   r   _____

3. do   r   x   a   d   u   o   t   _____

4. of   o   c   q   f   r   z   p   _____

5. some   s   o   a   b   m   t   e   _____

6. who   f   w   t   h   t   o   s   _____

7. are   a   c   r   y   p   s   e   _____

8. said   s   e   a   o   i   d   q   _____

9. now   i   n   o   m   y   w   b   _____

10. first   f   i   a   r   s   m   t   _____

ACTIVITY SHEET FOR LOCATING HIDDEN SIGHT WORDS

(Second-Grade Level)

Name_____ Grade_____ Teacher_____ Date_____

In each line first look at the word on the left. Then try to find this word wherever it is hidden on the same line. Circle each of the hidden words. The first line is done for you.

1. know	bt(know)rs	vriwot	(know)crt	fap(know)
2. great	greatsmk	thgreato	ygreat	nggreati
3. also	poalso	uioalso	alsoso	walsoy
4. through	rthroughp	througher	bethrough	knthrough
5. does	frdoes	doesnw	fedoes	atdoes
6. read	rreader	yiread	readpt	creadi
7. turn	turnce	wereturn	fcreturnd	returnop
8. learn	learny	blearnn	learnhr	telearn
9. high	alhigh	highins	prhigh	highmas
10. boy	boyeye	reboy	boysrt	olboy

© 1993 by The Center for Applied Research in Education

11. point	rpoints	pointes	fpointed	sepoint
12. found	wfounds	refounds	wufound	msfoundr
13. air	reair	sairs	airmas	alair
14. why	rewhy	whyer	whybras	fxwhyqr
15. form	airform	tuforms	preformxt	torform
16. again	againer	reagain	saragain	againop
17. page	pagers	fixpage	pagewer	pagedbit
18. move	movein	dismove	moveof	movegno
19. enough	menoughm	nevenough	emough	alenough
20. who	rfew	tawho	whoers	waoudh

SIGHT-WORD SEARCH

(Third-Grade Level)

Name_____ Grade_____ Teacher_____ Date_____

There are 8 words hidden in this puzzle. The words go across, down, backwards, and upside down. Circle all the words that you can find in this puzzle.

w	r	p	o	t	f	t	y	s	u	l	m	i	p	q
z	p	p	q	l	r	i	v	e	r	m	o	y	s	v
r	m	o	u	v	p	y	z	z	i	f	f	t	c	a
t	r	e	a	l	s	m	i	j	k	f	c	o	r	y
c	c	b	d	r	y	x	x	l	p	g	n	u	o	y
b	c	e	r	y	o	e	q	g	r	s	u	m	n	p
b	o	d	y	h	q	w	x	i	p	r	t	u	v	z
a	c	r	y	f	g	c	r	a	g	n	o	s	q	t
l	i	p	q	v	w	x	z	y	m	p	u	y	s	m
e	c	o	l	o	r	m	y	f	g	p	l	s	t	f
r	e	f	m	i	g	h	t	q	c	b	l	e	f	v
c	x	f	l	j	k	r	s	i	j	l	p	e	x	r
e	i	x	r	j	p	u	z	p	u	r	o	y	b	c
m	n	r	d	o	z	b	e	o	u	c	y	e	g	j
r	z	l	w	v	x	b	p	g	q	h	o	y	r	e
j	y	a	j	w	l	b	o	c	f	w	r	g	i	m

© 1993 by The Center for Applied Research in Education

Hidden Words

example	body
river	song
young	color
real	might

RAPID VISUAL TRACKING

(Fifth-Grade Level)

Name_____ Grade_____ Teacher_____ Date_____

The word <u>enormous</u> appears 49 times in this activity sheet. Move your eyes from left to right as rapidly as possible, and circle the word <u>enormous</u> each time you see it.

enormous

encourage enormous mantel ordeal enormous

scorn petunias vehicle urgent enormous prowl

loft sulphur vault enormous ledge liver shaft

enormous surrey zoom yonder waver enormous

meal numb fleece coyote crab extend enormous

evaporate indicate low enormous mare octopus

rustic swarm sponge papoose enormous prim

shreds tranquil twirl enormous tornado

wilderness vinegar staff wheeze enormous

skeleton turban terminal picket prairie enormous

license frantic ancient gadget advantage beetle

century enormous exasperate cupboard

commotion fatigue enormous indignant hoist

enormous horizon gun enormous lasso pouch

enormous reservoir rhythm enormous prey scorn

attention enormous swagger enormous vanish

threat enormous swarm enormous sponge

simmer staff tournament topple sulphur

enormous yonder wedge enormous vein wheeze

enormous zoom production enormous prospect

gleefully fleece fiord enormous hermit heron

intensely enormous hunch goal gnash enormous

horizon enormous gaping lithe mantel khaki

lather picket enormous prop pioneer enormous

sufficient tinderbox vault enormous vehicle wield

vision wicker stampede enormous toast enormous

trample spell strictly enormous enormous

production rehearse lunge enormous malicious

obviously enormous opportunity orphan

enormous reef reproach enormous sausage

solution enormous swarm enormous tundra vast

writhe enormous warehouse vigorous enormous

fleece enormous gnaw flank gesture homestead

gaping goal enormous insult enormous interfere

ordeal international

Strategies and Games for Teaching and/or Reinforcing Sight-Word Knowledge in Isolation

The following are strategies and games you can use to present and practice sight-word knowledge in isolation. You can use any of these suggestions and games in their present form or modify them any way you wish dependent on the needs of your students.

Effective Teaching Strategy

Here is a useful three-step method for teaching sight words to children:

1. ***Seeing.*** Write the word on the chalkboard and pronounce it. Draw attention to such features of the word as initial consonants and word endings which are similar to words which have been presented earlier. Use each word in a sentence so that its meaning can be deduced from the sentence. When children are more proficient readers, they will not need such a detailed introduction to new words.

2. ***Discussing and defining.*** When the meaning of the new word is unfamiliar to the students, you should discuss the word in detail. Students should draw upon their prior knowledge to determine the meaning of the word, and they should consult the dictionary if they are not sure of the meaning of the word.

3. ***Using and writing.*** Have the students use the new word in their speaking and writing. Ask one or more several students to give a sentence containing the word and write each of these sentences on the chalkboard, chart paper, or the overhead projector. Children at the initial stages of reading may want to include the words in their word banks. New words become mastered in two main ways: through repeated exposure when they recur frequently in sentences and stories that the children read and when they are used frequently in children's writing.

Screen Board

A screen board is a device that can help children remember difficult sight words. A screen board is made by attaching wire screening to a frame made of four boards and securing the screen with book tape to cover the rough edges. The child then puts light-weight blank paper on top of the screen board. The child copies the sight word to study from a word card by writing on the paper with crayon. Writing with crayon on the screen provides a raised texture which the child can trace with a finger while saying the sight word. Here is an illustration of a screen board:

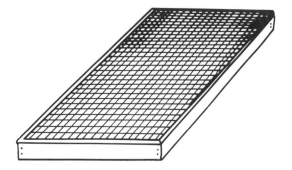

The Fernald Tracing Method

This method of teaching sight words in isolation is more effective with older disabled readers in the upper primary grades than are the tracing strategies mentioned earlier. It is an example of a VAKT method. Very briefly, here is how the Fernald Tracing Method can be implemented:

1. A disabled reader chooses a word he/she wishes to learn to recognize, and the reading teacher then writes it in manuscript or cursive handwriting, depending on the child's age, with a dark crayon on a piece of posterboard in syllables as he/she traces it. The child then attempts to write the word on a piece of paper without looking at the model. If he/she cannot do so, the child retraces the word saying it aloud. The child does this until he/she can write the word correctly. When the child has written it, he/she copies it on an index card and files it in a box for further study. The child also uses the word in a sentence or story.

2. At the second stage of remediation, the disabled reader writes each word he/she wishes to recognize saying the word to him-/herself in syllables as it is being written. The child writes each newly learned word on an index card and files it in a box. The child then uses the word in a sentence or story.

3. At the last stage of remediation, the disabled reader is able to read or write the words without tracing them or writing them from copy. The child continues to file the newly learned words in the box and to use them in sentences and stories.

The Tape Recorder as an Aid to Teaching Sight Words

Write a sight word on each word card constructed out of pieces of tagboard about 3 inches by 6 inches. Put a number on the other side of each card. Put eight cards in each envelope, and number the envelopes to correspond with the narrative on each paper. Prepare the tape by recording the following: "Now you will be given some words to be learned. Take the words from envelope number one. Put them in a pile on the table so that the numbers are showing. Number one should be on top, number two under number one, number three under number two, and so on. Turn the tape recorder off after you have done this. Then turn the tape recorder on again and turn over card number one. The word is have—have. Now you say it. Now listen to this sentence using the word have. 'I have a dog.' Now take your practice sheet and write the word have beside the number one. You may look at the card if you want to. Turn the tape recorder off after you have done this. Then turn the tape recorder on again and look at the word that you have just written. It is spelled h-a-v-e. Say it again. Now turn over card number two." This same procedure is followed for each additional word.

Pantomiming Sight Words

Have the child pantomime sight words that are difficult to illustrate in any other way. Verbs and prepositions especially lend themselves to pantomiming or illustrating by actions. Here are some sight words that can be pantomimed effectively: *work, play, laugh, smile, walk, run, under, over,* and *between.*

Animal Tachistoscope

A hand tachistoscope can be a very effective way to enable students to practice sight words. The tachistoscope can be constructed in the traditional way illustrated later. However, it also can be made in the shape of any animal, such as a monkey, bear, or giraffe. It also can be made on a holiday theme such as a ghost, a pumpkin, or a heart.

How to construct a tachistoscope in the form of a monkey. Trace a monkey pattern on a sheet of tracing paper. Place the tracing paper on top of a sheet of carbon paper. Place these on top of a piece of white posterboard. Trace over the tracing to transfer the monkey drawing on the tracing paper to the posterboard. Remove the tracing paper and the carbon paper. Use a black fine-line pen or black felt-tipped pen to outline the drawing. Color the monkey with a black marker or with colored pencils. Cut out the monkey and laminate it. Trim the laminating film from the cut-out monkey. Using an art knife, cut two horizontal slots, about 2½ inches long and 1 inch apart on the monkey's chest or stomach. Cut a piece of white tagboard into strips about 2 inches by 12 inches and laminate them. (See illustrations.)

Procedure for use. Choose sight words that need practice. Using a marking pen print the sight words on the laminated plastic strip, one under the other and about 1 inch apart. Put the word strip behind the monkey tachistoscope and thread it through the bottom slot and then back through the top slot. To use, slide the word strip up to expose a word. Have a child read the word. Then pull the word strip up to expose the next word and call on another student to read the word. Continue in this manner.

When finished with the sight word practice on the monkey tachistoscope, remove the word strip and wipe off the words with a damp paper towel. New words can then be written on the word strip. After some practice, a child can use the tachistoscope for independent practice with sight words.

Sight Words on Dice

Have the child assemble a sentence from words that are printed on dice. The child can throw the dice and then try to form a sentence. To construct the dice, words of a particular part of speech should be printed on each die. See the following illustrations:

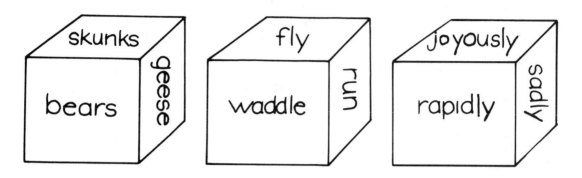

These words are printed on the other three sides of the dice in the illustration:

chipmunks	glide	slowly
porcupines	walk	quickly
ducks	swim	happily

Word Sort

A word sort may be appropriate for children who are reading on the upper primary-grade level. A word sort is a type of categorization activity based upon feature analysis and induction. A child categorizes words in a word sort by grouping them in terms of a common feature, such as physical appearance, grammatical function, or related meaning. In a word sort a child must discover for him-/herself the features the words have in common. In the *open word sort* no criterion is given in advance, and the child must determine the class of related features him-/herself.

To use an open word sort write a number of different sight words that have a distinctive feature in common on small word cards made of posterboard. This group of word cards then comprises one word sort. Additional cards can be made that have other common features. The child then tries to group all of the word cards into the appropiate categories on the basis of the distinctive features.

Here are some sight words that can be used in this activity:

moose	hood	book	goose	balloon	stood	hook
rough	through	bought	enough	though	thought	bought
ring	wing	thing	sting	bring	spring	fling
every	even	oven	ever	very	never	evening

Magic Words

To help a child remember a sight word, have him/her paint the target word on the chalkboard with a wet paintbrush. Have him/her watch the word disappear letter by letter as the chalkboard dries. This will help the child remember the sequence of letters in the sight word.

TV Flashcards

Draw television card patterns onto white posterboard. Color the television—except the screen—dark brown. Leave the television screen white. Use a black pen to outline all of the lines and details on the television sets. Then laminate and cut out each of the television cards. Use a black pen to print a different vocabulary word in the center of each television flashcard. (See illustration.) Have the child work with a partner or alone reviewing the target sight word using the television flashcards. The TV flashcards can be used over again by simply wiping off the words and printing new words on each card.

Word Processor

The word processor or typewriter can be a useful tool for children in the upper primary grades in learning to remember difficult sight words. I have used this type of device myself many times in tutoring sessions. The word processor or typewriter is effective in teaching sight-word recognition because it emphasizes left-to-right progression and adds tactile reinforcement to sight-word recognition. Both devices are highly motivating for children to use, adding to their effectiveness.

Grab Bag Technique

The grab bag technique also can be used to improve sight-word recognition. Print difficult sight words on posterboard cutouts that represent any type of seasonal theme, such as fall leaves, pumpkins, flags, snow people, Valentines, or shamrocks. Put all of the sight words in a bag, and have the child choose a word card from the bag and try to pronounce it. If he/she is able to do so correctly, the child can keep the word card. If not, it is placed back in the bag. At the end of the game, the child with the most word cards wins.

Vocabulary Sewing Cards

Vocabulary sewing cards can be used as a way of reinforcing difficult-to-remember sight words. Print each sight word on a piece of cardboard, pricking small holes in each letter of the word. Then have the child sew through the holes with yarn to make each of the words appear.

Word Wheel

A variation of a word wheel can be constructed to provide reinforcement of hard-to-remember sight words. To make such a device, print each sight word near the outside edge of a circular piece of posterboard. Fasten a slightly smaller circular piece of tagboard with a window to the larger piece using a paper brad. As the child turns the outside circle, a sight word comes into view through the window. (See illustration.) Have the child say each of the words.

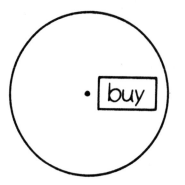

The Language Master®

The Language Master® is a machine that uses large cards with strips of magnetic tape placed on them. The child can look at the card, try to identify the word, place the card in the machine, and listen through earphones as the machine says the sight word. According to reading teachers who use it, the Language Master® seems to be most effective when the reading teacher or the child makes the word cards with blank cards that accompany the machine. The Language Master® has been used successfully with learning-handicapped children. The Language Master® can be purchased from the following source:

Bell and Howell Company
Audio-Visual Products Division
7100 McCormick Road
Chicago, IL 60645

Crossword Puzzle

A crossword puzzle can be used to emphasize sight words. Here is a ready-to-duplicate crossword puzzle you can duplicate and use if it seems applicable. The answers are given at the end of the chapter. You now can also purchase computer software programs to construct crossword puzzles very easily.

CROSSWORD PUZZLE
(Approximately Third-Grade Level)

Name_____ Grade_____ Teacher_____ Date_____

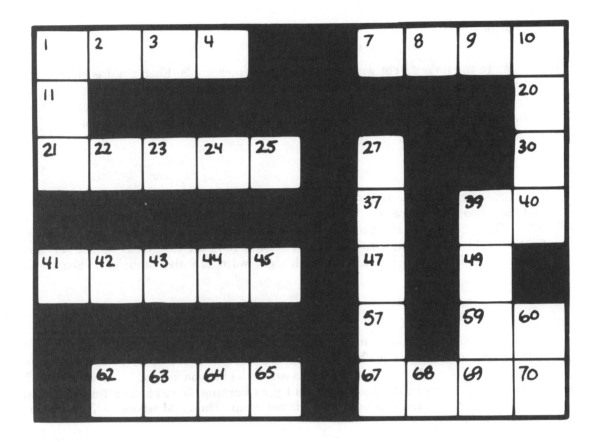

Across
1. this is fun to read
7. the opposite of soft
21. the opposite of old
41. the planet on which we live
62. the opposite of right
67. what a child can do on a horse

Down
1. not a *girl*, but a _____
10. the contraction for *do not*
27. a fish can swim in this
39. a group of cattle
60. not *she*, but _____

Scrambled Words

Write the target sight words on different colors of construction paper—write one word to a color. Cut the letters apart and rearrange the letters to a word. Have the child arrange the letters in proper sequence. Then have him/her pronounce the word and use it correctly in a sentence.

Sight It

Write the target sight words on 3-inch by 5-inch cards. Each child is then given eight sight word cards to hold. You then call out a word. Each student with that word card lays it down on his/her desk. The winner is the first child to lay down all eight cards. The game continues with the other students until all of the cards are laid down.

Cover It All

Construct game cards about 5 inches by 8 inches. Each game card should be squared and have about ten words on it. Each child is given a 5 x 8 card. You then call out a sight word. The child marks the game card as is done in Bingo except each card must be filled for the child to be a winner. The winner should read off the words on his/her card as a verification of the win. If you wish, each sight word can also be used in a sentence.

Hunting for Sight Words

Give a sight word card to all but one of the children who are to play this game. As soon as each child knows his/her word, he/she holds the card up so that it can be seen by the other children. When all of the cards are in sight, you pronounce a word held by one of the children. The child who has no card goes hunting. If he/she can find the word, that child may read it aloud and take it to his/her chair. The child whose card has been taken is now the *hunter*.

Sight Word Ticket

Have the class choose a sight word for the day. Each child writes the word on an index card to take home. Each child reads and spells the word to his/her parents and also writes a sentence using the word. The child can also illustrate the word. The child may add the word to a list on a long piece of shelf paper that is displayed on the refrigerator at home. To extend the activity and foster responsibility, ask each student to bring the word card back to school the following day as their "ticket" to get in the classroom. Each child can read the word to you upon entering the classroom and file it in a special file box.

Sight Word Tic-Tac-Toe

Play this unusual variation of tic-tac-toe by arranging nine chairs in the center of the room in a tic-tac-toe formation. Divide the children into two teams—the *X*s and the *O*s. Flash a target sight word. A child must say it correctly. If the sight word is pronounced correctly, the child takes a card with an *X* or *O* depending on his/her team and selects a chair to sit on. The first team to get three *X*s or *O*s in a row is the winner.

Newspaper Relay

Obtain copies of a newspaper. Give each student the same page from that newspaper and let each child circle in red all of the Dolch sight words he/she can in an allotted time. They will need a copy of the *Dolch Basic Sight Word List* or part of the list in order to play this game. The time limit might begin with five or ten minutes and continue down to one minute.

Sight Word Airplane

To construct this game, cut an oatmeal carton in half and decorate it to represent an airplane hangar. You also need construction paper and a set of 1-inch by 2-inch word cards with sight words printed on them with a marking pen.

Draw a spiral path on a sheet of paper with the airplane hangar at the end of the path. Divide the path into sections in which are printed sight words. Two players should have an object that represents an airplane and duplicate sets of cards with the same words that are on the path. The game begins with the airplanes at the end of the path and each player's cards placed face up. The first player reads the words on his/her top card. If the word is the same as the one in the first space of the path, his/her airplane is moved to that space. If it is not, the child may not move. His/her card is placed on the bottom of the deck and the other player takes his/her turn. The winner is the child whose airplane reaches the hangar first.

Feed the Monkey

To construct this game, cut out a large stand-up figure of some favorite animal. A monkey works effectively for this game. Give the monkey a big, wide-open mouth behind which a paper bag is stapled. Print sight words on small cards that are shaped like bananas.

Let the children take turns selecting cards and identifying the sight words. When the child has identified the sight word correctly (and used it in a sentence if you wish), he/she can put a banana into the monkey's mouth (and into the paper bag). When a word identification is not correct, you can show that word to all of the children, identify it, and then put it back with the other uneaten bananas. Once all of the sight words have been fed to the monkey, the words can be renamed and counted to see how well the monkey has been fed.

For a variation, only the words correctly identified the first time will be fed to the monkey. These words can then be counted, and you may mention that the monkey probably still is hungry. To solve the problem, uneaten bananas can be examined and correctly identified by the group of children. Following this procedure, all of the bananas can again be identified by individual children and fed to the monkey.

Magician's Hat

Make a paper "magic hat" or use a real hat. Print target sight words on small rabbit-shaped cards. Select a child in need of practice to be the magician. The magician then must pull a rabbit from the hat and identify the word on the card.

Pick-a-Chip

Divide the words on a basic sight-word list into four sections of fifty-five words each. Type or write the sight words on folder labels or masking tape and place these on poker chips of four colors. Put the chips in four small boxes of matching colors. A child begins the game by choosing a color and giving a spinner a whirl. The child picks as many chips from his/her color section as the spinner indicates. If the child fails to say one of the words, he/she is told what it is. However, this child must return the chip to the box and pass the spinner to the next player. The winner of the game is the child who has acquired the most chips. The game can be played with three or four children.

Pack of Trouble

Construct word cards with the sight words you wish to stress written on them. Flash each word card to an individual child and ask him/her to pronounce the words as quickly as possible. When a child misses a word, he/she is given that sight word and makes a copy of it to keep. The child then gives the original word back to you. Each child then develops his/her own "pack of trouble words" that he/she can use for study with another child or with a small group. As soon as the child masters a word, he/she may give it back to you. The idea of this game is to keep the pack of trouble words as small as possible.

Sight-Word Basketball

Obtain a soft foam basketball and hoop. Hang the hoop in an appropriate place and height for the children. Divide the class into two teams. Hold up a flashcard with a sight word on it to the first team member in Team A. If the child can correctly tell you the word and use it in a sentence, he/she is allowed to try and shoot a basket. If the child makes a basket, he/she earns two points for his/her team. If the child hits the rim of the basket, he/she earns one point. Continue this same procedure with Team B. Keep playing until all of the team members have had a chance at the basket.

Word in the Box

Obtain a large box containing word cards with difficult sight words printed on them. Have the children sit in a circle around the box. You may either read or play a tape recording of a story. Before hearing the story, each child is given a card on which there is a word from the story. When that word is read in the story, the child says "_____ goes in the box" and throws the word in the box. The child then is given another word so that he/she may continue to play the game.

Sight-Word Checkers

Have a pair of children play checkers as usual, but a child must read a word in order to move to another space on the checkerboard. Print each sight word in two directions so that both players can always see them. Vary the checkerboards to include sight words that are causing problems for certain children.

Musical Words

Place the sight words a group of children needs to work on in a box or a bag. Have the children sit in a circle and start passing the box around while a record plays. Whatever child has the container when the music is stopped by you must pick out a word card and read the sight word printed on it. The game continues until there is only one person remaining. The winner must be able to read at least five of the words.

Find the Bones

Print a sight word on each posterboard bone, which is about 2 inches by 4 inches. Hide the bones around the classroom. Have each child find a bone and then say the sight word correctly and use it in a sentence or else he/she loses the bone. The child who has the most bones wins the game.

Peppermint Tree

Tack pieces of wrapped hard candy to a picture of a tree on the bulletin board. Then write a list of ten sight words the children are finding difficult. If a child can read all ten of the words, he/she is allowed to go to the "peppermint tree" for a peppermint or other piece of hard candy.

Dragon Hunt

Draw a picture of a dragon in the middle of a large sheet of posterboard. Put a row of small circles from start to finish intertwined around the dragon. Laminate the gameboard. Write sight words on index cards and put them in a Ziploc™ bag that is taped to the back of the posterboard. Each player in turn selects a card and reads the word. If he/she is correct, the child moves one space (with a button as a marker) on the small circles. If the card has a star in the corner, the child is allowed to move an extra space. The first child to finish wins the game.

Treasure Chest

Make a "treasure chest" by wrapping a box in gold or silver paper. Cut coins out of cardboard and print one sight word on each coin. The student may put each sight word he/she is able to read into the treasure chest. Then the treasure can be taken home to show to the child's family.

Presenting and/or Reinforcing Words in a Sight Word List or in a Basal Reader in Context

There are a number of strategies and materials that stress sight-word knowledge in context which we have used effectively to improve this word-identification technique in hundreds of students. Presenting and reinforcing sight-word knowledge in context is in keeping with the whole-language philosophy that is widely used in primary-grade and intermediate-grade classrooms today. Such techniques often are extremely successful with above-average, average, and some disabled readers at these levels. However, a number of children who have great difficulty retaining important sight words still benefit from some instruction and practice of sight words in isolation. Even these children, however, can make excellent improvement in retaining sight words when they are presented in the context of language-experience stories and predictable books. The Reading Recovery Program (described in detail shortly) clearly illustrates this fact.

Wide Reading

Wide reading is undoubtedly the single most effective way of improving sight-word knowledge at both the primary-grade and intermediate-grade reading levels. The more widely that a child reads from a variety of materials, the larger his/her stock of sight words. Wide reading also effectively improves a child's comprehension ability.

Such wide reading can take place in predictable books, language-experience stories, tradebooks of various types, content textbooks, and children's magazines and newspapers. It is obvious that reading is a skill that best improves with motivated practice. That is why a good reader who enjoys reading for pleasure and information usually improves his/her reading skills much more than a reluctant or disabled reader who does not read extensively either for pleasure or for information.

The Language-Experience Approach

The language-experience approach is an extremely effective way of presenting and practicing sight words. We have found it particularly appropriate for children in the primary grades who have great difficulty in retaining sight words. Besides being effective in stressing sight-word identification, it is highly motivating for the children who use it. My teacher-trainees have used it successfully with thousands of kindergarten and primary-grade children since 1964.

Here is a brief description of how this approach can be implemented with one child or several children who are reading at about the same level:

1. The child must first be motivated for the dictating (and later, self-writing) of the story. We have found some type of hands-on activity to be the most effective type of motivation. My teacher-trainees have used such activities as these for the motivation: taking an excursion to some interesting place such as a forest preserve, a zoo, a candy factory, a doll museum, a pet shop, a greenhouse, a shopping center, a toy store, a circus, a pig farm, a dairy farm, and a police station; baking cookies; frosting cupcakes; making a gingerbread person; constructing a kite and then flying it; seasonal construction activities such as a Thanksgiving turkey, a jack-o'-lantern and a snow person. We have found that the child often needs some type of hands-on activity to give him/her a specific topic to dictate or write about. Such an activity also helps the child dictate or write the story in the correct sequence.

2. You and the child should have an interesting preliminary discussion in which the language-experience story is structured loosely.

3. The child then dictates or writes the experience story. At the very initial stages of writing, I prefer to have the child dictate the story the majority of the time. Other emergent literacy specialists prefer to have the child write the story using scribbling, letter strings, inventive spelling, or conventional spelling. Although scribbling and letter strings are acceptable, dictation at this stage allows the child to see written standard English, to read the stories of other children, and to take the story home to read to his/her parents.

In any case, you can ask a few leading questions being careful not to structure the story too much. The story can be transcribed on a piece of chart paper, a sheet of ordinary paper that is lined larger than normal, or on an index card. The child can write the story on unlined paper first and then later write it on lined paper. I recommend that the story be transcribed as the child has dictated it, although it may be altered slightly if this is done *very carefully* and *tactfully*, and if you have good rapport with the child.

4. If you want, you can later type the language-experience story with a primary typewriter, copy it over on a large sheet of chart paper, or put it on a ditto master so that it can be duplicated and used for a number of different purposes. Since it takes a great deal of time to transcribe the individual stories, some reading teachers use a parent volunteer to type some or all of the individual experience stories.

Note: Steps 3 and 4 can effectively be done on a word processor. The word processor (computer) has been used successfully in a number of reading improvement programs both to record the children's dictated experience stories and to help them in the writing of the stories. A number of the following steps also can be adapted to the use of the word processor. I have seen children in first grade, for example, write wonderful, creative stories using a computer in the IBM program, *Writing to Read.*

5. After the child has dictated a language-experience story, you can read it aloud for the child. If the child wrote the story, he/she can try to read it aloud him-/herself. Later the child and you can read a dictated story together, and the child should be encouraged to read it alone as soon as possible.

6. The child then underlines or circles all the words recognized.

7. A word bank can be made from a child's dictated or written stories. Each selected word is written on a card of some kind. All the cards are put into a large envelope, an index box, or a shoe box. The words can be used later as flashcards or for other purposes such as alphabetizing, putting into categories, or using in reading games.

8. Most of the time a child illustrates each page of his/her experience stories. My teacher-trainees have had their tutees use marking pens, crayons, watercolors, colored pencils, finger paints, or tempera paints. All of the illustrations can be used in the child's experience booklet. If a book is not made, the illustration can be attached to the story in some way.

9. Most of the time, children's dictated or written stories can be bound into a booklet that can be read by other children in the classroom or taken home to read to their parents. The book can be laminated for durability and attractiveness. An interesting cover also can be made for the booklet. If you wish, you can buy prebound blank experience books from the local book store or order prebound books with blank pages, on which the child can dictate or write stories, from the following address:

Treetop Publishing
220 Virginia Street
Racine, WI 53405

Note: Dictating and writing stories is extremely useful in teaching both sight-word knowledge and beginning phonic analysis and structural analysis skills, and comprehension skills because it integrates the teaching of reading and writing, capitalizes on a child's own experiences and language, and is highly motivating. I cannot recommend it too highly for use with all children at the emergent literacy level and with disabled readers (including learning-handicapped children) in the primary and intermediate grades. It has even been used successfully with severely disabled readers at the secondary and adult levels.

The following resources are highly recommended for additional information on dictating and writing experience stories:

Allen, Roach Van and Claryce Allen, *Language Experience Activities*. Boston: Houghton Mifflin Company, 1982.

Evans, Joy and Jo Ellen Moore, *How to Make Books with Children*. Monterey, California: Evan-Moor, 1985. (This is a practical resource with ideas for books and illustrations for book covers.)

Evans, Joy, Kathleen Morgan, and Jo Ellen Moore, *Making Big Books with Children*. Monterey, California: Evan-Moor, 1989. (This is a practical resource with ideas for making big books and illustrations for book covers.)

Hall, MaryAnne, *Teaching Reading as a Language Experience*. Columbus, Ohio: Charles E. Merrill Publishing Company, 1981.

Lee, Dorris and Roach Van Allen, *Learning to Read Through Experience*. New York: Appleton-Century-Crofts, 1963.

Storm, Mary Pat and Kathy Theis, *The Language Experience Approach to Reading: A Workshop for Parents*. Bloomington, Illinois: Illinois Reading Council Parents and Reading Committee.

Using Reading Recovery Strategies, Predictable Books, and Big Books to Increase Sight-Word Knowledge

A number of the strategies and materials currently being used in the modern, successful Reading Recovery Program can be adapted and used by any reading teacher who is working with children at the emergent literacy level (kindergarten or first-grade reading level). They may well be effective with learning-handicapped children who also are functioning at that level. This part of the chapter describes those strategies and materials you can adapt and use to improve the word-identification and comprehension skills of your children.

Reading Recovery

Reading Recovery is an intervention program designed to help at-risk children in first grade develop the relevant reading strategies that should help them learn to read at grade level and to continue making reading progress throughout their school career.

Reading Recovery originated in New Zealand more than twenty years ago under the direction of Marie Clay with collaboration from Don Holdaway. Since it was found to be successful there in improving the reading skills of young at-risk children, it was begun in this country at Ohio State University in the early 1980s. It now is found in most areas of the United States as well as in many other countries. According to a number of research studies, it is a very effective way to prevent young at-risk children from becoming older disabled readers.

Here is a very brief description of some of the major characteristics of Reading Recovery: It is conducted in first grade only, usually with the lowest eight children in the class in reading. These children are recommended for testing by their first-grade teacher. A trained Reading Recovery teacher then gives each recommended child the *Diagnostic Survey*, an individually administered test designed to assess such areas of emergent literacy as writing words from dictation, identifying all of the capital and lower-case letter names, a sight-word test of twenty words, and a concepts-about-print test that evaluates such understandings as the title and author of a book, knowledge of the concepts of *letter* and *word*, where to begin reading a page of print, and the match of speech and print.

A teacher must have an intensive, specialized training program to be able to be a Reading Recovery teacher. The entire program consists of a tier of specialists, each of whom has a unique type of training. There is a university-trained specialist in Reading Recovery who probably has received his/her training at a major Reading Recovery center. Such persons train Reading Recovery Teacher Leaders. This is a teacher who has attended the University Center in Reading Recovery full time for a full academic year in addition to attending summer workshops. Besides attending classes in Reading Recovery, this person must teach Reading Recovery skills to at least four at-risk children in first grade. After his/her training and supervision, the teacher leader is qualified to teach a class in Reading Recovery to twelve teachers from his/her area. The cost of their education and materials normally is paid for by the teacher's school district. Such a teacher must be an experienced primary (often first-grade) teacher who is recommended by his/her principal. This teacher in training usually attends a one- or two-week workshop before the school year begins and also attends a weekly evening class in Reading Recovery. He/she usually must teach four children in his/her first grade the Reading Recovery strategies. In addition, the teacher-in-training must bring one of his/her students to the University to engage in a Reading Recovery lesson "behind the glass" (a one-way mirror) which is critiqued by the teacher leader and the other class members. The teacher leader also makes periodic visits to observe and critique each Reading Recovery teacher-in-training during the school year. Usually the teachers must also attend a workshop at the close of the school year. The teacher-in-training receives graduate credit from the University for the academic work.

Thus, you can see that Reading Recovery is an intensive, structured, and fairly expensive program to implement. Sometimes two Reading Recovery teachers share one first-grade class of children. Each teacher teaches the class one-half of the school day and tutors four at-risk children during the other half. Sometimes Reading Recovery is combined in some way with Chapter I reading to conserve resources.

Here are some of the reasons why Reading Recovery has resulted in many children making good progress, thus enabling them to be "discontinued" from the program after about twelve to sixteen weeks. According to research, such children are then reading at least at grade level and are able to maintain their progress throughout the elementary school.

1. Reading Recovery strategies and materials are presented to children in first grade before they have had the opportunity to learn and practice incorrect strategies. In addition, they usually have not developed the negative attitudes toward all reading activities often manifested by older disabled readers.

2. Reading Recovery teachers are well trained and thoroughly understand the reading process. They are extremely competent in observing a child's reading behaviors and in knowing how to help a child learn relevant reading strategies. Thus, in a sense, each child's reading program is individualized and is well suited to his/her unique reading strengths and weaknesses.

3. Reading Recovery primarily uses elements of the whole-language approach, such as predictable books. Any predictable book, some of which are listed later in this chapter, provides children with an optimum opportunity for reading success because of its repetitive language patterns and interesting story content.

4. In the Reading Recovery Program phonic analysis and structural analysis skills are taught in the context of whole language as the need arises instead of in isolation as is the case in the typical basal reader or formal phonic lesson.

5. The child receives his/her Reading Recovery training on a one-to-one basis. Normally one-on-one intervention results in increased achievement for the tutee. Usually a

child's unique reading needs are met much better in an individual setting than in either a group or total-class setting.

6. The child's Reading Recovery teacher attempts to integrate that program with his/her regular first-grade reading program. The Reading Recovery teacher tries to be sure that this training is continued in the child's regular reading instruction. In addition, the training is carefully supervised on a regular basis by the teacher leader.

Thus, you can see that Reading Recovery is a complicated program. However, a regular classroom reading teacher, a special reading teacher, or a teacher of learning handicapped children can adapt some of the Reading Recovery (whole-language strategies effectively to their own students. For more information on Reading Recovery, consult the following sources, among others:

Marie M. Clay, *An Observation Survey of Early Literacy Achievements*. Portsmouth, New Hampshire: Heinemann, 1993.

Marie M. Clay, *Reading Recovery: A Guidebook for Teachers-in-Training*, Portsmouth, New Hampshire: Heinemann, 1993.

Gay Su Pinnell, Mary D. Friel, and Mary Estice, "Reading Recovery: Learning How to Make a Difference," *The Reading Teacher*, 42 (January 1990), pp. 282-295.

Using Such Effective Strategies with Your Own Students

From examination of the material about the Reading Recovery program, you probably have already formulated some tentative ideas about strategies and materials that might apply to some of the children with whom you work.

Here is a brief summary of some of the effective strategies most relevant for use with children in kindergarten and first grade who are at the emergent literacy stage. Many emergent literacy teachers are already using a number of these strategies, since they are commonly used in any whole language program. Many of these concepts probably are equally applicable for older students who are functioning at approximately this level. In addition, this chapter contains a list of some of the predictable books that can be used successfully in any emergent literacy program.

1. It is important that a child know how to recognize and identify all of the upper-case and lower-case letter names fairly early in the emergent literacy program although not necessarily at the very beginning stage. Reading Recovery programs use magnetic letters as one strategy for teaching letter names. As you know, this chapter has provided you with many practical suggestions and materials for helping children learn the letter names.

2. It is very important that beginning readers have accurate concepts about print. A child should understand such features of the reading process as the title and author of a book, the concept of letter and word, where on a page to begin reading, and the function of punctuation marks.

3. *Predictable books* (little books) are principle reading materials in the Reading Recovery program. Predictable books are useful at the beginning stages of reading because their repetitive language patterns make them easier for a child to read. Therefore, the child is motivated from the outset by feeling that he/she indeed can really read. In addition, such books are often more motivating than are many beginning basal reader stories.

4. Each predictable book should be read to the fluency level by the child. In a typical Reading Recovery lesson the child always reads for fluency a predictable book which he/she was first introduced to the previous day. It is exceedingly important that a beginning reader with difficulties read and reread materials to the fluency level so that he/she can

experience complete success with them. This not only builds the child's self-confidence but also helps him/her learn many sight words.

5. It is important for you to be thoroughly knowledgeable about the reading process and to be a careful observer of a child's specific reading strengths and weaknesses. You are usually most effective when you have a comprehensive understanding of all of the facets that comprise the complex reading process, including graphophonic analysis (phonic analysis), syntactic clues (grammar or language structure clues), semantic clues (context clues), and the various elements of comprehension.

An effective reading teacher also must be able to quickly observe a child's reading weaknesses and act upon this diagnosis by providing the correct reading strategies to help the child overcome these weaknesses.

6. The strategies used in the Reading Recovery program are mainly those strategies used by all good readers. You can help a child become aware of useful strategies by making comments such as these:

- "You said ＿＿＿ and read ahead to figure out a word that you didn't know."
- "You tried to be sure that your reading made sense."
- "You read the sentence again and figured out the word that you didn't know."
- "You read the material aloud as though you really understood it."
- "I liked the way you always made sure that your reading made sense."

7. The Reading Recovery program teaches the child to be aware of and to use multiple cuing systems while reading. Normally a child should use these cuing systems simultaneously. Here are the three major cuing systems of which the child should be aware and should use:

—Does the word make sense there? (a semantic or meaning cue)

—Does the word seem to sound right there? (a syntactic or grammar cue)

—Are these the letters I would have expected to see in the word I predicted? (graphophonic cue)

Some children, especially if they have been taught reading by a phonic program, rely too much on graphophonic cues and do not pay much attention to the meaning of the passage. You can then ask questions to help the child focus on the meaning and language structure of the material. On the other hand, if a child pays little attention to graphophonic cues and relies too much on semantic and syntactic cues, you can ask questions and point out graphophonic elements such as word beginnings, word middles, and word endings.

A child always should be encouraged to self-correct as well as to monitor his/her reading for understanding. Good readers self-correct and monitor their reading to be sure it makes sense much more effectively than do poor readers. Here are some sample comments and responses you should find helpful in encouraging a child to use the various cuing systems effectively:

Semantic (Meaning) Cues

- Does that word make sense there?
- What word would make sense there?
- Is ＿＿＿＿＿＿＿ a real word?
- You said the word ＿＿＿＿＿＿＿. Does that make sense in the sentence?
- Try that sentence again and think about a word that would make sense there.
- What is a ＿＿＿＿＿＿＿?

- Could a person really do that?
- Can you think of a word that would make sense there?
- Look at the picture. Does it help you figure out what the word might be?
- How does a fairy tale usually begin?

Syntactic (Language Structure or Grammar) Cues

- Would that word fit in the sentence there?
- Does that word sound right at that place in the sentence?
- Try it again and think what word would fit in the sentence.
- Try reading ahead for a clue to the word that you don't know.
- Does that word sound all right in the sentence at that place?
- Reread that part again to be sure that all of the words make sense the way they are written.
- How does that sound to your ears?
- Would a word like that fit in that place in the sentence?
- Do people talk that way?
- Read it again to check on all of the words.

Graphophonic (Symbol-Sound) Cues

- What letter do you see at the beginning (end) of that word? What sound does it make?
- How does that word look like the word _____? How is it different?
- Are these the letters you expected to see in that word? Are these the sounds in the word that you predicted them to be?
- Do you think the word looks like _____?
- Look at the letters. Could the word be _____ or _____? (In this case the child then has two words from which to choose.)
- Can you think of a word that makes sense there and starts with those letters?
- If the word were _____, what letter(s) would you expect to see at the beginning?
- Since the vowel is in the middle of that short word, what sound do you think it probably makes?
- Since that word has an *e* at the end, what sound do you think this vowel in the middle makes? I think that you can probably sound out that word for yourself.
- What sound does the letter _____ usually make?
- What sound does the letter *c* usually make when it is followed by an *e*?
- Can you think of a word that begins with those letters and still makes sense there?
- The word might be _____, but look at which letters that it starts with.
- Can you think of a word that starts with a _____ that might make sense in that sentence?

Note: ALL of the questions in the three previous sections are included for illustrative purposes. You can adapt any of them and formulate many additional similar questions to help a child use the three cuing systems.

8. It is exceedingly important that the instruction of reading and writing be integrated whenever possible. Reading Recovery requires a child to write his/her own sentence during each lesson. This sentence often relates to the tradebook the child has just read. Usually the child is encouraged to spell each word in the sentence as he/she hears it with you prompting or helping the child with difficult parts. White correction tape is also often used so that the child can write each word correctly in his/her sentence. Sometimes an Elkonin box is used to help the child segment the word phonetically. Here are two examples of words written in Elkonin boxes:

j	u	m	p

th	i	n

9. The effective reading teacher must be able to keep good records of a child's reading progress. This includes a complete record of the predictable books read and an up-to-date record of his/her reading strengths and weaknesses. The recordkeeping in this program is indeed very complex.

Very briefly, the cue sources evaluated in Reading Recovery include the following (as demonstrated to several of my classes by Susan Almeida, a trained Reading Recovery Teacher Leader at Illinois State University):

V—Visual
M—Meaning
S—Structure

In addition, each lesson is evaluated by the teacher using the following elements of miscue analysis:

—Accurate Reading (place a checkmark over each correct word)

—Substitutions

—Repetitions

—Self-Corrections

—Omissions

—Insertions

—Told by the Teacher

—Appeal (The child looks at the teacher for assistance)

—TTA (the teacher says "Try that again")

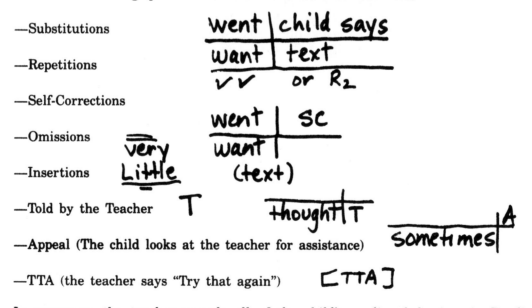

In summary, the teacher records all of the child's reading behaviors in Reading Recovery.

Note: Since the recordkeeping in Reading Recovery is so complicated, I recommend a simpler way of recording oral reading miscues, such as the method described in detail in Chapter 2.

10. Both the whole-language philosophy and Reading Recovery recommend that the reading skills such as sight words, phonic analysis, structural analysis, and comprehension skills be taught in the context of whole language instead of in isolation. This is a good recommendation for many children at least a good portion of the time. However, it is necessary to teach some elements of phonic analysis, structural analysis, and comprehension in isolation part of the time, at least for some children. This is particularly the case with learning-handicapped children. However, even mainstreamed children may need to have the short vowel sounds isolated, for example, to be able to discriminate effectively between them. Reading Recovery certainly helps children learn sight words effectively; however, sight words sometimes need to be reinforced in isolation for learning-handicapped children.

A List of Predictable Books that Can Be Used at the Emergent Literacy Stage

The following is a list of predictable books that can be used in any emergent literacy program for the reasons mentioned earlier. Some of them undoubtedly are used in a typical Reading Recovery program. They are in an easy-to-difficult sequence.

Carle, Eric. *Have You Seen My Cat?* Picture Book Studio, 1987.
Hutchins, Pat. *One Hunter.* Greenwillow, 1982.
Wildsmith, Brian. *All Fall Down.* Oxford, 1983.
Martin, Bill. *Brown Bear, Brown Bear, What Do You See?* illustrated by Eric Carle. Holt, Rinehart and Winston, 1984.
Peek, Merle. *Roll Over.* Clarion, 1981.
Tafuri, Nancy. *Spots, Feathers, and Curly Tails.* Greenwillow, 1988.
Raffi. *Five Little Ducks.* Illustrated by Jose Aruego and Ariane Dewey. Crown, 1989.
Tafuri, Nancy. *The Ball Bounced.* Greenwillow, 1989.
Browne, Anthony. *I Like Books.* Knopf, 1988.
Hellard, Susan. *This Little Piggy.* Putnam, 1989.
Lindgren, Barbro. *Sam's Cookie.* Illustrated by Eva Eriksson. Morrow, 1982.
Lindgren, Barbro. *Sam's Wagon.* Illustrated by Eva Eriksson. Morrow, 1986.
Campbell, Rod. *Henry's Busy Day.* Viking, 1984.
Kraus, Robert. *Herman the Helper.* Illustrated by Jose Aruego and Ariane Dewey. Windmill, 1974.
Roffey, Maureen. *Home Sweet Home.* The Bodley Head, 1982.
Asch, Frank. *Just Like Daddy.* Prentice-Hall, 1981.
Campbell, Rod. *Dear Zoo.* Four Winds, 1982.
Galdone, Paul. *Cat Goes Fiddle-i-Fee.* Clarion, 1988.
Stobbs, William. *Gregory's Garden.* Oxford, 1987.
West, Colin. *Have You Seen the Crocodile?* Harper & Row, 1986.
Bang, Molly. *Ten, Nine, Eight.* Greenwillow, 1983.
Gerstein, Mordicai. *Roll Over!* Crown, 1984.
Rockwell, Anne. *Cars.* Dutton, 1984.
Stadler, John. *Hooray for Snail!* Harper & Row, 1984.
Ward, Cindy. *Cookie's Week.* Illustrated by Tomie de Paola. Putnam, 1988.
Wheeler, Cincy. *Marmalade's Nap.* Knopf, 1982.
Ziefert, Harriet. *Thank You Nicky!* Illustrated by Richard Brown. Viking Penguin, 1988.
Barton, Byron. *Dinosaurs, Dinosaurs.* Crowell, 1989.
Hellen, Nancy. *The Bus Stop.* Orchard Books, 1988.
Barton, Byron. *Buzz Buzz Buzz.* Macmillan, 1973.
Burningham, John. *The Baby.* Crowell, 1975.
Burningham, John. *The Dog.* Crowell, 1975.

Crews, Donald. *Then Black Dots.* Greenwillow, 1986.

Keller, Holly. *Then Sleepy Sheep.* Greenwillow, 1983.

Kraus, Ruth. *The Carrot Seed.* Illustrated by Crockett Johnson. Harper & Row, 1945.

Stadler, John. *Three Cheers for Hippo.* Crowell, 1987.

Wescott, Nadine Bernard. *Peanut Butter and Jelly.* Dutton, 1987.

Alexander, Martha. *Blackboard Bear.* Dial, 1969.

Jonas, Ann. *Two Bear Cubs.* Greenwillow, 1982.

Tolstoy, Alexei. *The Great Big Enormous Turnip.* Watts, 1968.

Brown, Margaret Wise. *Goodnight Moon.* Harper & Row, 1947.

Carle, Eric. *The Very Busy Spider.* Philomel, 1984.

Ehlert, Lois. *Planting a Rainbow.* Harcourt Brace Jovanovich, 1988.

Serfozo, Mary. *Who Wants One?* Illustrated by Keiko Narahashi. Macmillan, 1989.

Alexander, Martha. *We're in Big Trouble, Blackboard Bear.* Dial, 1980.

Bonsall, Crosby. *And I Mean It Stanley.* Harper & Row, 1974.

Hutchins, Pat. *Happy Birthday Sam.* Viking Penguin, 1978.

Mayer, Mercer. *There's a Nightmare in My Closet.* Dial, 1968.

Minarik, Else Holmelund. *A Kiss for Little Bear.* Illustrated by Maurice Sendak. Harper & Row, 1968.

Bridwell, Norman. *Clifford the Big Red Dog.* Scholastic, 1985.

Galdone, Paul. *The Little Red Hen.* Clarion, 1972.

Johnson, Crockett. *Harold and the Purple Crayon.* Harper & Row, 1965.

Lobel, Arnold. *Mouse Soup.* Harper & Row, 1972.

Udry, Janice May. *Let's Be Enemies.* Illustrated by Maurice Sendak. Harper & Row, 1970.

Asch, Frank. *The Last Puppy.* Prentice-Hall, 1980.

DePaola, Tomie. *Charlie Needs a Cloak.* Prentice-Hall, 1973.

Jonas, Ann. *The Trek.* Greenwillow, 1985.

Lionni, Leo. *Little Blue and Little Yellow.* Aston Honor, 1959.

Shulevitz, Uri. *Dawn.* Farrar, Straus, Giroux, 1974.

Brown, Ruth. *The Big Sneeze.* Lothrop, Lee, Shepard, 1985.

Burningham, John. *Mr. Gumpy's Outing.* Holt, Rinehart & Winston, 1970.

Lobel, Arnold. *Frog and Toad Are Friends.* Harper & Row, 1970.

Murphy, Jill. *What Next, Baby Bear?* Dial, 1984.

Allen, Pam. *Who Sank the Boat?* Coward-McCann, 1982.

Crowe, Robert L. *Tyler Toad and Thunder.* Illustrated by Kay Chorao. Dutton, 1980.

Heine, Helme. *The Most Wonderful Egg in the World.* Atheneum, 1983.

Hoberman, Mary Ann. *A House Is a House for Me.* Viking, 1978.

Hutchins, Pat. *The Very Worst Monster.* Greenwillow, 1985.

Kuskin, Karla. *Dogs and Dragons, Trees and Dreams.* Harper & Row, 1980. (A book of poems)

Reinl, Edda. *The Three Little Pigs.* Picture Book Studio, 1983.

Rice, Eve. *Peter's Pockets.* Illustrated by Nancy Winslow Parker. Greenwillow, 1989.

Tresselt, Alvin. *The Mitten.* Illustrated by Yaroslava. Lothrop, Lee & Shepard, 1964.

Zemach, Margot. *The Little Red Hen.* Farrar, Straus & Giroux, 1987.

Zolotow, Charlotte. *I Know a Lady.* Illustrated by James Stevenson. Greenwillow, 1984.

What Is Auditory Discrimination?

Auditory discrimination is the child's ability to differentiate between phonemes (sounds). Good auditory discrimination ability is important to success in most beginning reading approaches, perhaps especially the basal reader approach and phonic approaches.

A child can have good auditory acuity (hearing) and still be unable to discriminate between sounds. However, it is obvious that a child with inadequate auditory acuity cannot have good auditory discrimination. Some learning-handicapped children have great difficulty with the auditory modality or channel, thus causing them to have inadequate auditory discrimination.

Auditory discrimination ability is usually more difficult for most children than visual perception ability. One exception is the learning-handicapped child who has an inadequate visual modality (channel).

Any child who is able should have at least a minimal competence in auditory discrimination. This should enable him/her to experience greater success with phonic elements and generalizations. The following activities can help your students achieve competence in auditory discrimination.

Strategies for Improving Ability in Auditory Discrimination

Here are a few activities for improving skill in auditory discrimination. You undoubtedly can think of other useful strategies yourself.

1. Read *nursery rhymes* to the child. Have the child listen for and then repeat the rhyming patterns found in this material.
2. Read *predictable books*, such as those listed earlier, to the child and have him/her read along with you. This is an example of teaching auditory discrimination in a whole-language context.
3. Pronounce pairs of words orally or on cassette tape. Some word pairs should be alike, while others should be different. Have the child tell you or record on tape whether each word pair is the same or is different. Here are several word pairs that can be used for this purpose:

fell—fill	tub—tug
top—tip	cat—mat
well—will	pick—kick

4. Show the child some objects. All but one of the objects should begin with the same sound. Have the child point out the object that begins with a different sound. Here are some objects for the phoneme /d/: duck, doll, *ball*, dish, dog.
5. Obtain pictures that represent minimal pairs of words. Place each pair of pictures on a table and have the child point out the one of two pictures whose word you say. For example, from the pair *cat* and *rat*, ask the child to point to the picture of the cat.
6. Have the child practice rhyming words. Illustrate the concept of rhyming by modeling examples. A number of children at the emergent literacy stage can rhyme words but do not know what the term *rhyming* means.

What Is Phonic (Graphophonic) Analysis? _____

Phonic (graphophonic) analysis can be defined as using phonic elements in a word to determine its pronunciation and meaning. Many reading teachers believe that competency in phonic analysis is absolutely necessary for success in beginning reading. Phonic analysis probably has received more stress in the past in beginning reading programs than any other technique of word identification. Should this have been the case?

Phonic analysis is a very important technique of word identification that should be taught to all children who have the requisite auditory discrimination skills to be able to profit from it. However, I believe reading teachers probably have taught too many phonic elements and rules in isolation to too many students in the past.

Note: One possible exception to this statement is the learning-handicapped child, who well may profit from a structured program of phonic analysis with much concrete repetition *if* that child has the requisite auditory discrimination skills. A learning-handicapped child may need the structure of some kind of formal phonic approach.

Phonic analysis is rarely used by good readers in the intermediate grades and above. Most adult readers rarely, if ever, use phonic skills. Most of the most common phonic elements and phonic rules are taught to the typical child by the end of the third-grade reading level. Thus, phonic analysis can be a very useful technique for identifying unknown words at this level. However, it is less useful at the middle-upper reading levels and secondary and adult levels. At these levels, semantic (meaning) clues and structural clues are much more effective. I have found in testing the phonic skills of many children in the intermediate grades that although they cannot provide the definition of phonic elements or rules, they usually can apply them. Therefore, when my teacher-trainees tutor older disabled readers in the intermediate grades and junior high school, they stress only the most important phonic elements—such as long and short vowel sounds, consonants, and consonant blends—if they have not been previously mastered.

You should also realize that phonic analysis is usually most helpful when it is combined with semantic clues. For example, note how the addition of the beginning consonant in this sentence greatly helps the reader in deducing the omitted word:

Betsy would like to receive a d_____for her birthday.
necklace
doll
ring

It is possible for a person to be a competent reader with no ability at all in phonics. This obviously is exemplified by a hearing-impaired person. If a child has truly failed at learning phonic elements and rules, he/she probably should have most of the emphasis in the reading program placed upon sight words and use of semantic clues with some emphasis placed on tracing strategies. Again, the possible exception to this is the learning-handicapped child, if he/she has an adequate auditory channel.

Since phonic analysis is so complicated, entire books have been written on it. Therefore, this chapter contains only a cursory discussion of it. If you want further detail about graphophonic analysis, here are several resources you can consult:

Fry, Edward B., Jacqueline Kress, and Dona Fountoukidis, *The Reading Teacher's Book of Lists*, Third Edition. Englewood Cliffs, New Jersey: Prentice-Hall, 1993.

Heilman, Arthur, *Phonics in Proper Perspective*. Columbus, Ohio: Merrill Publishing Company, 1989.

Hull, Marion A., *Phonics for the Teacher of Reading*. Columbus, Ohio: Merrill Publishing Company, 1989.

Rinsky, Lee Ann, *Teaching Word Attack Skills*. Dubuque, Iowa: Scarisbrick Gorusch Publishers, 1993.

In addition, *basal reader manuals* also contain much information about the teaching of phonic elements and rules.

Phonemes and Graphemes

Phonemes can be defined as the sounds that occur in a language. There are about forty-four or forty-five phonemes in English, depending on whom you ask. A phoneme is conventionally written as a letter, or phonetic symbol between slash marks: /d/. A *grapheme* is the written symbol for a phoneme or sound. A grapheme can be composed of one or more letters. For example, it takes the two letters *c* and *h* to represent either phoneme /ch/. There are about 251 graphemes in written English. Thus, you can see that English does not have a regular, direct phoneme-grapheme relationship as do some languages.

Consonants

A *consonant* is caused when the outgoing breath stream is obstructed by an organ of speech. The organs of speech are the hard palate, the larynx, the soft palate, the tongue, the teeth, the lips, and the vocal cords. When the obstruction is complete, the resulting sounds are known as *plosives* or *stops*. Those in which the obstruction is partial are called *continuants*. Consonants are also classified as *voiceless* or *voiced*, depending on whether or not the vocal cords vibrate while producing the sound. Here are examples of plosives:

p _p_in	*b* _b_oy
t _t_oy	*d* _d_ay
k _k_ite	*g* _g_ame

These nasal sounds are one type of continuant:

m _m_other	*n* _n_ow

Fricatives are continuants made when the outgoing breath stream escapes with audible friction:

f _f_armer	*v* _v_ine
s _s_ay	*z* _z_ebra
h _h_er	
th _th_in	*th* _th_ere
ch _ch_urch	*j* _j_ump
sh _sh_ip	

The *liquids* are as follows:

r _r_ain	*l* _l_ion

The *glides* are as follows:

y _y_ear	*w* _w_indow

Consonant Blends

A *consonant blend* consists of two or, less often, three consonant letters that appear together. Each consonant contains some element of its own sound while blending with that of the others. Although most consonant blends occur at the beginning of words, they also can be found at the end.

bl _bl_ack	*br* _br_own	*cl* _cl_ear
cr _cr_eam	*dr* _dr_eam	*fl* _fl_ood

fr *fr*iend	*gl* *gl*ass	*gr* *gr*eat
pl *pl*ay	*pr* *pr*etty	*sc* *sc*are
sk *sk*y	*sm* *sm*ile	*sn* *sn*ow
sp *sp*in	*spl* *spl*ash	*spr* *spr*ing
st *st*op	*str* *str*ing	*sw* *sw*im
tr *tr*ay	*tw* *tw*in	

Consonant Digraphs

A *consonant digraph* is composed of two consonant letters that record a single sound that is different from the sound that either letter would record separately. Here are some examples of consonant digraphs:

th *th*in (voiceless)	*th* *th*ose (voiced)
sh *sh*ip	*ch* *ch*ur*ch*
wh *wh*at	*ph* *ph*ase
ng si*ng*	*gh* tou*gh*

Vowels

Vowels result when the organs of speech modify the resonance chamber without impeding the flow of the outgoing breath. All vowels are voiced, and there are no nasal vowels in English. One vowel is distinguished from another by the quality of its sound.

a m*a*ke	*a* *a*pple	
a t*a*ll	*a* *a*rm	*a* *a*ir
a f*a*ther		
e w*e*	*e* p*e*t	*e* *e*arn
e h*e*rd	*e* w*e*ar	*e* s*e*rgeant
i *i*ce	*i* *i*t	*i* b*i*rd
o r*o*pe	*o* st*o*p	*o* *o*ften
o *o*r	*o* w*o*rm	
u *u*se	*u* j*u*ice	*u* n*u*t
u f*u*r		
y fl*y*	*y* bab*y*	*y* m*y*th
w co*w* (diphthong)		

The Schwa Sound

The *schwa sound* is the unstressed vowel sound in a word of more than one syllable. Any one of the five vowel letters can be the schwa sound when it is found in an unaccented syllable. The schwa sound has a sound very much like that of the short *u*. Here are some words that contain a schwa sound:

a comm*a*	*e* lab*e*l	*i* penc*i*l
o butt*o*n	*u* min*u*s	

Diphthongs

A *diphthong* is composed of two vowel sounds that together record one sound that is different from the sound that either of the vowels would have recorded alone. Here are some examples of words containing a diphthong:

ow h*ow*	*oi* b*oi*l	*oy* b*oy*	*ou* m*ou*se

Vowel Digraphs

A *vowel digraph* occurs when two adjacent vowel letters record one sound. Here are some examples of words that contain a vowel digraph:

ai tr*ai*n	*ay* s*ay*
ee b*ee*t	*ea* s*ea*t
oa b*oa*t	*oe* t*oe*
oo c*oo*k	*oo* g*oo*se
ow cr*ow*	
ui j*ui*ce	

Phonograms

Phonograms or *graphemic bases* are groups of vowel and consonant letters that are often learned and pronounced as a unit. Here are some examples:

all f*all*	*ill* w*ill*
ick p*ick*	*igh* h*igh*
ight s*ight*	*ank* b*ank*
ink p*ink*	*ate* pl*ate*

Homophones (Homonyms)

A *homophone* is a word that is pronounced the same as another word but has a different spelling and meaning. Here are some examples:

bear	bare
beat	beet
blue	blew
brake	break
cheep	cheap
forth	fourth
lessen	lesson
made	maid
sail	sale
wood	would

Homographs

Homographs are words that have the same pronunciation and spelling but different meanings. For example:

I *can* ride to school on a bicycle.
My mother brought a *can* of fruit for lunch.

Strategies, Materials, and Games for Improving Ability in Phonic (Graphophonic) Analysis in Isolation and in Context

There are numerous strategies, materials, computer programs, commercially available games, and teacher-made games for improving ability in phonic (graphophonic) analysis. Since they could comprise a chapter by themselves, we can include only some of the most useful examples in this part of the chapter. You can find many additional suggestions in other professional books on reading instruction and in basal reader manuals.

Mnemonic Devices

Mnemonic devices can be useful in teaching important elements of phonic analysis, especially to learning-handicapped children. A mnemonic device normally involves teaching the child a key word for each different consonant phoneme and vowel phoneme. Each key word also can be illustrated by a picture of an object. For example, these may be the key words for the short vowel phonemes: *apple, egg, igloo, top,* and *umbrella.* One of my former graduate students, Kay Gillespie, who teaches young learning-handicapped and educable mentally handicapped children near Peoria, Illinois, has developed the following system which has proven effective.

First, she sends the following letter home to parents:

Dear Parents,

We are working on beginning consonant sounds and short vowel sounds. In order to help each child, we are associating *one* picture symbol with each letter. The letter in the picture is part of the object. The initial (front) sound of the pictured object is the letter. This provides a cue that aids in the sound-symbol association. For instance, <u>B</u>, <u>b</u> has the picture symbol: boy kicking a ball. Attached is a sound-symbol worksheet. You can help your child: (1) find the picture symbol in the magazines, (2) hunt for the letter in common words, and (3) listen for the sound.

Then she prepares worksheets (see the samples shown here) and attaches a copy of each page to the letter sent home to parents.

ă	ăpple	b	1. boy 2. kicking a ball (kicks it the way we read)
c	cough	d	1. door knob 2. shut the door
e	elephant	f	fighter
g	glasses	h	hospital (see the smokestack)
ĭ	insect	j	jumper
k	Kangaroo	l	line of children (like in a fire drill)
m	mountains	n	nail

ŏctopus	1. pipe 2. with smoke coming out
1. queen 2. with hair flipped, straight and curled	rip
snake	top (spin it!)
ŭpside - down ŭmbrella	valentine
witch (she is trying to scare you!)	X is an extra letter as far as I can see. Sometimes it says "ks"; sometimes it says "z" (box -- xylophone)
yard (see the yard by the sidewalk and street)	zig zag zipper

ā ē ī ō ū The long vowels are written in green to remind child to go ahead and say it as he/she would say it in the alphabet.	ch cough got so bad, had to go to the hospital. Now it says: ch! ch! ch!	sh snake in hospital says "sh." Don't tell anyone I'm here.

Other reading specialists also have used mnemonics successfully in teaching beginning reading to children who have had difficulty learning symbol-sound correspondences. For example, L.C. Ehri, N.D. Deffner, and L.S. Wilce found that picture mnemonics, in which the letter to be learned was highlighted in a picture of a word, was very effective. (See their article "Pictorial Mnemonics for Phonics" in *Journal of Educational Psychology*, 76, December 1985, pages 880-893.)

Strategies

1. Joan M. Harwell (*Complete Learning Disabilities Handbook*. West Nyack, New York: The Center for Applied Research in Education, 1989 pages 119-123) uses a strategy for teaching beginning phonic elements to learning-handicapped children that you may want to consider reading about. She stated that if a student has acquired few or no sounds from prior instruction, the process usually takes about twenty consecutive days, with the longest being forty days that it ever has taken. She further wrote that the teacher may work with one student at a time for 30 minutes daily, but that it was possible to work with up to four beginning students at a time. She stated that it was necessary to give adequate blending and feedback time to each student. Very briefly, here is how her system is used:

- Print each alphabet letter on the chalkboard or on a sheet of paper. *Say:* "The letter's name is *a*. Repeat, please." Be sure that the students repeat, "The letter's name is *a*," rather than just saying *a*.
- *Say:* "The letter's sound is_____." (Give the short *a* sound.) Simultaneously, draw an apple on the chalkboard or on their paper. If you're working with a group, the children can draw their own apple. Do not allow them to say, "The letter's sound is *apple*."
- *Say:* "Apple is a word that starts with_____(again pronounce the short *a* sound—really overemphasize it), but it takes five letters to spell *apple*." Write *apple*, point, and count to the five letters, then repeat, "The letter's sound is_____."

Harwell continues this same procedure for each of the other symbol-sound relationships.

2. The Orton-Gillingham Approach. This is a VAKT approach that can help a child recognize the more difficult sight words. A complete description of this approach can be found in the following book as well as in other sources: Anna Gillingham and Bessie Stillman, *Remedial Training for Children with Specific Disability in Reading, Spelling, and Penmanship* (Cambridge, Massachusetts: Educators Publishing Service, 1968).

Very briefly, here is how the technique is used:

- **Association I.** Show the child a Phonetic Drill Card (available from Educators Publishing Service, 75 Moulten Street, Cambridge, Massachusetts 02138), and say the name of the letter written on it. Have the child repeat the letter name until he/ she has mastered the association.
- **Association II.** Make the sound represented by the letter, and ask the child to tell you the name of the letter that has this sound.

- *Association III.* Print the letter with a dark crayon on a piece of tagboard, and have the child trace over the letter with his/her index finger. Then the child is to copy the letter and write it from memory.

Note: The Fernald Tracing Method can also be very useful with learning-handicapped students who are reading at the upper primary-grade or intermediate-grade levels. Such students may well benefit from the use of a VAKT Method.

3. The *tape recorder* can be used in a number of different ways to teach or review phonic elements. For example, tape record a number of words for the child in order to determine whether he/she hears the long or short vowel sound. The following can be recorded on tape: "Number your paper from 1 to 20. Turn the tape recorder off until you have done this. Then turn the tape recorder back on. Now you will hear some words pronounced. As you hear each word, write *long* or *short* after the number of that word. Here are the words: number 1—pet, number 2—cake, number 3—fast," etc. You want to have the child mark each blank with a breve (˘) or a macron (—) if the child has learned diacritical marking. This type of exercise also can be done with initial consonants, consonant blends, consonant digraphs and the hard and soft sounds of *c* and *g* among other phonic elements.

4. There are several strategies that will help a child blend the various sounds together, often a difficult skill. Use analogies between blending and other activities, such as ice skating. Put large letters on the floor and have the child "skate" from one to another while saying the letter sounds out loud or have the child stretch a rubber band between words. You also can use letter tiles or other movable letters that may be gradually moved apart while a word is sounded slowly, and then brought back together as the entire word is pronounced. Teach the child to use his/her voice to "slide" through the sounds of unfamiliar words.

5. One *every-pupil response technique* that has relevance to phonic instruction is to give each child three cards on which are printed the numbers 1, 2, and 3, or the words *beginning, middle,* and *end.* As you say words, have each child respond by holding up the appropriate card. For example, "I am going to say some words that have the *t* sound in them. If you hear it at the beginning of the word, hold up your number 1 card; if you hear it in the middle of the word, hold up your number 2 card; and if you hear it at the end, hold up your number 3 card."

6. *Give a sentence orally.* Then have a group of children say as many words as possible that begin with the same sound as the last word in the sentence. The children also can make up sentences for this activity. Here is an example: "I have a very nice mother and father." Words for this activity then might be: *fast, for, first, fat, far,* and *fall.*

7. Obtain a number of shoe boxes. Print an initial *s* (sock), consonant blend with initial *s* (slipper) or consonant digraph with initial *s* (shoe) on each shoe box. Then obtain a number of small objects that begin with these various sounds. Have a group of children *sort the objects* by placing each object into the correct box according to the initial sound.

8. Provide a *mail-order catalog* for two children. Have a separate sheet listing initial sounds or consonant blends in a random order. Have each of the two players take turns trying to locate pictures in the catalog that begin with the proper sound.

9. Have each child in a small group *print each of the vowel letters, a, e, i, o, u, y* on a small card. Then pronounce a number of words as each pupil holds up the correct vowel card for each word.

10. *Make a large tagboard circle.* Print consonant blends and/or consonant digraphs around the circle. Have a group of children sit around the circle and take turns flipping a

coin in the air and letting it land on the tagboard. Have the child say a word containing the consonant blend or digraph on which the coin landed.

11. *Draw three boxes or circles* on the chalkboard or on a duplicating master. Write consonants in the first box or circle, vowels in the second, and consonants in the third. Have each child make words by using a letter from each box to make the beginning, middle, and final sounds of a word. Have the child write the blended words on a sheet of paper or on the duplicating master.

12. *Make a phonic tree* by placing a small tree branch in a jar of sand. At the top of the tree attach a card with the letter or letters to be stressed. Have the children hang pictures of words beginning with the selected phonic element on the tree branches. Word cards may be hung from the tree branches instead if desired.

13. Have a group of children *make and use a code* in which numbers are substituted for vowels. For example:

a—1
e—2
i—3   M6 d4g 3s b3g 1nd t1n.
o—4   My dog is big and tan.
u—5
y—6

14. This activity requires the use of a *dart and target set.* Place cards with one phonogram on each spot on the target and paste a consonant blend or consonant digraph on each dart. Have the child hit a phonogram with the dart and pronounce the word formed by the consonant blend or consonant digraph and the phonogram. Give the child a point for each correctly formed word.

15. Have the child search for and circle a designated phonic element or elements in a *school newspaper or local newspaper.* Suitable phonic elements for this activity are: consonant digraphs, diphthongs, vowel digraphs, phonograms, the schwa sound, and r-controlled vowels.

16. *Word wheels* can be used to practice the attachment of an initial consonant or later a consonant blend to various phonograms. A word wheel is made by cutting two circles of tagboard, one of which is slightly smaller than the other. The two disks can be fastened with a brass fastener. Print phonograms on the larger disk, while the initial consonant or consonant blend is printed on the smaller disk. (See illustration.) The smaller disk then is spun, and the child pronounces each of the newly formed words. For example, a word wheel using the consonant *t* can be used to form the words: *tell, till, tall, tack, ten,* etc. You may also purchase commercial word wheels.

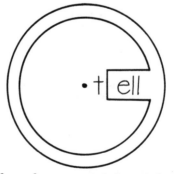

17. *Make a number of cards each one containing eight phonograms.* In addition, make a number of small cards of tagboard and print a consonant or consonant blend on each. Each child participating in this activity selects a small card from the deck of cards and attempts to place it in front of a phonogram to form a word. The child must pronounce the

formed word correctly. The first child to form eight words on the card correctly wins this activity.

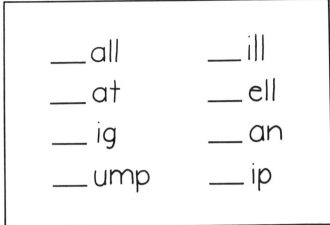

18. *The teacher prints a consonant on each of several wooden clothespins.* Have the child locate pictures in magazines of objects whose names begin with each of the consonants written on the clothespins. Have the child cut out the pictures and clip them in the appropriate clothespin.

19. Fold a piece of paper into thirds. At the top of each part (three on the front, three on the back), print a word with an initial blend or digraph. Then underline the blend or digraph. Have the child find pictures of objects whose names begin with the same blend or digraph printed at the top of each section of the paper and paste them in the appropriate place.

20. *Print a list such as the following on the chalkboard,* a transparency, or a duplicating master. Have the child make words using the diphthongs/digraphs provided.

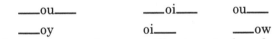

21. *Draw a stimulus picture such as a sailboat* on tagboard and cut it out. Make a word strip about 1½ inches by 10 inches. On the word strip write words that contain the word family. The word family letters are to be written in red, while the other letters should be written in black. Cut two slits in the sailboat about 1⅝ inches wide and ½ inch apart. Insert the word slip and have the child say each of the formed words.

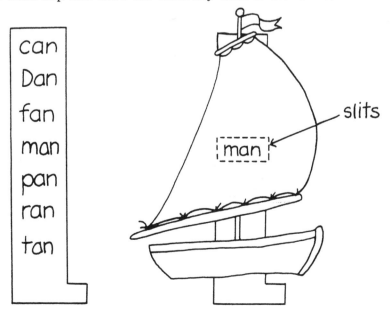

22. To construct *family wheels*, cut 3-inch by 5-inch posterboard strips. Cut disks three inches in diameter. Print the word family letters in red and cut out a one-inch window to the left of the letters. Attach the wheel disks with the paper brad so that one edge is shown in the window. Print the appropriate consonants in the window in black letters. Remove the disks to laminate them and then reassemble with the paper brad.

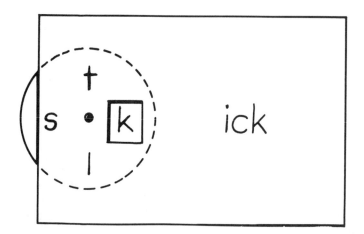

23. *The animal tachistoscope* described in this chapter's section on sight-word knowledge can easily be adapted to teaching various phonic elements. Make word strips containing words with the phonic element you want to stress for a child. For example, a word strip for the diphthong/digraph *oy* may contain these words: *boy, coy, enjoy, joy, toy, Roy,* and *soy.*

24. Here are some activities that can be used with learning-handicapped children who often reverse words, parts of words, and the order of words in sentences:

- All of the tracing activities mentioned earlier in this chapter.
- Cover a word with a card that is moved slowly to the right so that the letters are exposed in proper sequence.
- Underline the first letter in a word in green and the last letter in red. Tell the child to start on green and to stop on red.
- Expose a line of print a little at a time by means of a card or an opening cut in a card or by opening a zipper.
- Have the child use a computer, word processor, or typewriter. Such a device encourages sight-word knowledge, phonic ability, spelling ability, and writing ability.

Activity Sheets for Reinforcing Phonic Analysis

Here are several ready-to-duplicate activity sheets to use with your students to reinforce various elements of phonic analysis. You can duplicate and use them in their present form if they seem appropriate to the needs of your students, or you can use them as a model. The answers are given at the end of the chapter.

ACTIVITY SHEET FOR DOUBLE CONSONANT SUBSTITUTION

(Approximately Second-Grade Level)

Name_____ Grade_____ Teacher_____ Date_____

In each row of words exchange the initial consonant sound and write the two new words that are formed in the blanks. The first one is done for you.

1. send	lake	lend	sake
2. house	men		
3. kind	will		
4. big	did		
5. sat	pick		
6. car	fat		
7. camp	ran		
8. main	pail		
9. band	hat		
10. play	date		
11. mad	hat		
12. bail	hall		
13. tan	rail		
14. wag	sail		
15. came	take		
16. rate	hay		
17. tar	cake		
18. bank	rang		
19. say	dad		
20. tack	bake		

ACTIVITY SHEET FOR INITIAL CONSONANTS

(Late First- or Early Second-Grade Level)

Name_____ Grade_____ Teacher_____ Date_____

1. In each blank space write a letter to make a word that names <u>a living thing</u>.

____irl	____ear	____at	____oat
____eer	____ion	____orse	____ox
____ird	____ouse	____ig	____ish
____og	____an	____oy	____ow

2. In each blank space write a letter to make a word that names <u>something that can be found in a school</u>.

____eacher	____oor	____aper	____ight
____esk	____indow	____oys	____able
____ook	____irls	____ym	____ish
____encil	____aste	____ooms	____athroom

3. In each blank space write a letter to make a word that names <u>something or someone that you can have fun with</u>.

____uppy	____oy	____itten	____ook
____icycle	____ather	____all	____other
____uppet	____agon	____ite	____ister
____at	____et	____irl	____og

ACTIVITY SHEET FOR INITIAL CONSONANTS AND VOWELS

(Second-Grade Level)

Name_____ Grade_____ Teacher_____ Date_____

1. Make words that name something good to eat. Put the first letter from a word on the left in the correct blank on the right. The first one is done for you.

ask   _p_ie   pail   ____pple

come   ____ookie   rake   ____amburger

help   ____aisins

2. Make words that name an animal you might see at a zoo. Put the first letter from a word on the left in the correct blank on the right.

make   ____ion   best   ____ear

table   ____iger   lake   ____eal

seven   ____onkey

3. Make words that name something you might see in a kitchen. Put the first letter from a word on the left in the correct blank on the right.

pink   ____ork

father   ____ink

ring   ____efrigerator

several   ____ish

duck   ____an

4. Make words that name something a child might get for his or her birthday. Put the first letter from a word on the left in the correct blank on the right.

pay   ____icycle

bake   ____oy

dime   ____all

turkey   ____ame

give   ____uppy

5. Make words that name something a child could wear. Put the first letter from a word on the left in the correct blank on the right.

paper   ____ittens

candy   ____ocks

save   ____oat

mouse   ____acket

jelly   ____ants

ACTIVITY SHEET FOR DIPHTHONGS
(Third-Grade Level)

Name_____ Grade_____ Teacher_____ Date_____

Read this story about a child who wanted to buy his mother a special present for Mother's Day. The story contains four words with a diphthong. As you read each word with a diphthong in this story, underline it. When you have finished reading the story, print the first letter of each word containing a diphthong *in order* on the short lines after the story. If you have correctly located all of the words containing a diphthong, your word will answer this question: What Mother's Day gift did the child buy his mother?

What Present Should I Choose?

I have to make a very important decision. I want to buy my mother a very special present for Mother's Day, but I don't know what to give her. I could buy her a new dress, but she is a proud woman and might not like the dress that I chose. I might be able to buy a large round ring for her middle finger, but she probably wouldn't wear it anyway. I want to get her something that she will really like and be able to use.

I think that she might like a bouquet of fresh flowers, but they probably would wilt in several days anyway. I would take her on a trip to visit the mountains if I could since she likes them, but I don't have nearly enough money to do that.

I wonder what present I should buy for my mother.

What Present Did the Child Buy?

____ __e__ ____ ____ __u__ ____ __e__

ACTIVITY SHEET FOR OMITTED VOWELS
(Fifth-Grade Level)

Name_____ Grade_____ Teacher_____ Date_____

Read this story about the intelligence of whales. Notice that vowel letters have been omitted from some of the words. As you read the story, print the omitted vowel in each space. You may use a dictionary for help. When you have finished, reread the story to be sure it is correct.

Are Whales Really Highly Intelligent?

As y___u ___ndoubtedly know, altho___gh wha___les

l___ve in the ___cean lik___ fish, th___y are

m___mmals like h___man beings. Mammals ___re

w___rm-blooded with a b___dy t___emperature wh___ch

remains qu___te const___nt. A mamm___l also is an

an___mal that has l___ngs and bre___thes air. The

b___bies of all mammals ___re born al___ve inste___d of

being h___tched fr___m eggs. All m___mmal babi___s

dr___nk m___lk fr___m their m___thers. However,

wh___les ___re mammals who l___ve ___n the

sea—s___a mammals.

Th___re ___re some sci___ntists who believe th___t

s___me types of whales m___y be as ___ntelligent as

p___ople. However, th___re are ___ther scientists who

b___lieve that wh___les ___re m___re intelligent than

people, and s___me wh___ fe___l that they ___re no

more intelligent th___n d___gs.

Certainly, some wh___les h___ve v___ry large

bra___ns. The sp___rm whale, f___r ___xample, h___s

the largest bra____n ____f ____ny animal th____t h____s

ever lived. It c____n we____gh up to tw____nty pounds,

wh____ch is four times b____gger than the l____rgest human

brain. H____wever, a larger bra____n does not n____cessarily

m____an a m____ore intelligent brain.

Sc____entists also h____ve st____died the str____cture of

wh____le brains. The fr____nt of m____ny whale brains

____s v____ry larg____, th____s p____ssibly infl____encing

their th____nking ____bility. However, sci____ntists d____

n____t kn____w wh____t whales use th____s part of their

brain f____r.

In ____ddition, s____nce whales h____ve a v____ry

d____fferent type of ____xistence th____n h____mans, it

____s d____fficult to d____termine j____st what

c____nstitutes ____ntelligence ____n the____r

____nvironment. If hum____ns ____ver do le____rn to

c____mmunicate w____th whales, scientists m____y le____rn

that whal____s ____re n____t m____re or l____ss

intell____gent than w____ are, b____t r____ther just v____ry

differ____nt fr____m hum____ns.

Games for Phonic Analysis

1. The Magic E. You need 3-inch by 5-inch index cards for this activity. On the left half of the front of each card print a word that can be changed by adding an *e* to the end. For example, words such as *hid, rid, rat, cut, past,* and *plan* can be changed by adding a final *e*, making the vowel sound long rather than short.

Fold over an inch-wide vertical flap. On the folded flap (back of each card) print the letter *e*. Unfold the card and direct the child to read the word. Then have the child fold the card so that the *e* appears and read the new word.

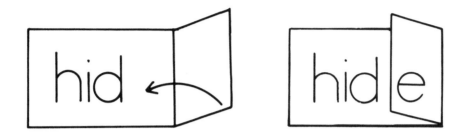

2. Circle Vowel Game. Have the children form a circle around the teacher. The teacher, acting as the leader, bounces a ball to a child and calls out a long or short vowel sound. The child who catches the ball tries to say a word containing the long or short vowel. If he/she can, that child bounces the ball to another child while calling out a long or short vowel. If he/she was not successful, the ball is returned to the teacher, and the teacher starts again. This can be a small-group activity or a whole-class activity.

3. Beanbag Game. The beanbag game may be played by two or more players. Construct a beanbag target by cutting six holes in a heavy sheet of 24-inch by 36-inch tagboard. Use heavy tape to attach a stand to the back of the board. Print a consonant blend by each hole. Each player attempts to toss a beanbag through any hole. To win, the player must toss the beanbag through the most holes and then correctly say a word beginning with each consonant blend. The game could be adapted to other phonic elements, such as initial consonants or consonant digraphs.

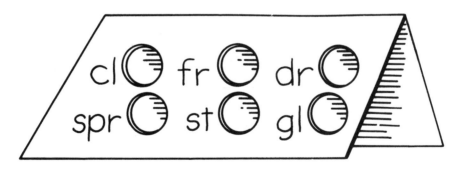

4. Rhyming Worm. Construct a word worm for displaying rhymes. Each hump on the worm should have a word that rhymes with the words printed on the other humps. Any phonograms you are stressing can be written on the word worm. The word worm can grow as children add new rhyming words.

5. Treasure Hunt Game. To construct this game, make forty word cards with one r-controlled vowel word on each, a Treasure Hunt gameboard, and four cards to represent rafts. Here are some suggested words:

ur	**ir**	**er**	**ar**
turn	sir	thermometer	car
burn	twirl	perhaps	part
urge	stir	kernel	ark
urn	bird	other	bark
plural	thirst	mother	mark
blurt	first	perform	tart
purr	whirl	dresser	large
hurt	third	her	warn
urgent	birth	father	park
fur	skirt	herd	star

Here is an example of a word card:

To play the game, two to four players are needed. Cards are shuffled and placed at appropriate r-controlled vowel island points. The first player begins by proceeding to the first island. He/she selects one card, says the *r*-sound at the top of the card and then the word. If the word is pronounced correctly, the child moves his/her raft to the next island. If the word is mispronounced, the child leaves his/her raft where it is. Used cards are placed at the bottom of each pile. A recorder keeps track of the number of times a child visits an island. The child who has visited all islands three times wins the game.

Here is a sample gameboard:

6. Y Tree. The purpose of this game is to provide practice in identifying *y* as a consonant and a vowel. Select a large piece of posterboard and attach brown felt cut in the shape of a tree without leaves. Cut green felt leaves that can be attached to the tree. To each of the leaves attach a word that begins with *y* or contains a *y* used as a vowel. Place all the leaves with words on them in a large envelope. Have the child select a leaf from the envelope, pronounce the word, and decide whether the *y* is a vowel or a consonant. When the *y* is at the beginning of a word, it acts as a consonant, and the leaf will be placed on the tree. All the words that have a *y* acting as a vowel will be placed on the ground beneath the tree.

7. *Sound Block.* On each side of an alphabet block or a small building block print or paste one of six letters that the children have studied. Have a group of children sit in a circle on the floor. Have one child come to the center of the circle and toss the block on a square of felt or other soft material. As soon as the block stops, the child in the center names the letter and calls on another child to name a word that begins with the sound that letter represents. If correct, that child may have the next turn to toss the block. If incorrect, the child in the center calls on someone else to answer.

8. *Typewriter (Word Processor).* Prepare eight letter cards. On each card print one of the consonants to be reinforced. Place eight chairs in a row facing the class. Select eight children to sit on the chairs, each child holding one of the letter cards facing the class. The row of cards are to be like a row of typewriter keys. When the child hears a word that ends with the sound that their letter stands for, he/she should stand up. You pronounce a word that ends with one of the sounds represented by the letters on the cards. The child holding that letter stands up.

9. *Junk-Mail Search.* Using junk mail from home, ask the children to find all of the words that begin with a certain consonant blend. Have the child circle or underline each word containing that blend. This same activity can be used for any phonic element such as consonants, consonant digraphs, and diphthongs.

10. *File Folder Tic-Tac-Toe.* Make a typical tic-tac-toe grid on a file folder, with graphemic bases (phonograms) in each square. Print cards with initial consonants on them. To be able to place a marker in a square, the child must draw a consonant card and combine it with the graphemic base (phonogram) to form a word.

11. *Supermarket.* To prepare this game, you need five large shopping bags labeled *a, e, i, o,* and *u,* and many empty containers (boxes, cartons, or cans) of foods whose names include the vowel sounds being studied. Have the children playing this game sort the food items into the correct shopping bag. Explain whether the children are to listen for and sort by long or short vowel sounds. Here are some suggested foods:

long vowels

potatoes	peaches	beets	pineapple
cake	peas	seeds	rice
raisins	beans	cheese	yogurt

short vowels

apples	ham	olives	muffins
jam	chips	butter	cabbage
eggs	popsicles	gum	apple butter

12. Ring-a-Blend. To construct this game, make a gameboard from a four-inch thick piece of styrofoam that measures 30 inches by 20 inches. Push nine large primary pencils (or similar objects) into the styrofoam in three equally spaced rows. Next to each pencil, attach to the styrofoam small cards with consonant blends written on them. You can change the cards when needed. From a distance of four to eight feet, a player tries to ring the pencils with plastic rings. (Rings can be cut from plastic lids.) A player scores five points for ringing a pencil. He/she scores an extra three points if he/she can give a word for the consonant blend represented by that pencil.

13. Bonus Game. Give the child a list of words. Have the child cut out pictures from magazines containing the same vowel sounds as the words. Each child is given 15 minutes to do this. At the end of 15 minutes, each child shows his/her pictures and tells the vowel sounds they have. For bonus points have the child use each word in a sentence. The emphasis of this game is on using each word in a sentence.

14. Beach Ball Bounce. Purchase a plastic beach ball that is divided into different colored sections. On each section, print a consonant with a black permanent marker. The children take turns bouncing the ball to one another. The person who catches the ball must say one word that begins with the consonant his/her right thumb is on and one word that begins with the consonant his/her left thumb is on.

15. Taxi. Build a small village of letters with the help of the children. There can be several streets in Alphabet Village. Tall Street can consist of those letters that extend above the line (*b*, *d*, *f*, *h*, *k*, *l*, and *t*); Low Street can consist of those letters that extend below the line (*j*, *p*, *q*, *y*, and *g*); Friend Street can consist of those letters that go together to make a sound (*ch*, *sh*, *th*, *ng*, and *wh*); Vowel Street will have the vowels; Main Street can consist of any letter left over. One child acts as the taxi driver. The other children ask the driver to take them to any word they want. The driver must drive them to the house whose letters begin that word.

16. Old MacDonald. Have the children sing the names of the five vowels in order in the song "Old MacDonald Had a Farm." When they reach the "animal sound," they use the short sound of each vowel. For example:

> Old MacDonald had a farm,
> a-e-i-o-u.
> And on his farm he had some letters,
> a-e-i-o-u.
> With an ă ă here and an ă ă there,
> Here an ă, there an ă,
> Everywhere an ă ă.
> Old MacDonald had a farm,
> a-e-i-o-u.

Continue through four more verses using another vowel sound each time.

What Is Structural (Morphemic) Analysis?

Structural or morphemic analysis means using word structure or word parts to determine the pronunciation and meaning of unknown words that are encountered during reading.

This word-identification technique can be very helpful in improving a child's meaning vocabulary, especially if it is used along with semantic analysis and phonic analysis. Although it can be helpful at the primary-grade reading level, it is usually more helpful in the intermediate grades and above when students add many new words to their vocabulary.

Structural or morphemic analysis is composed of a number of different subskills. One important subskill is attaching a prefix or suffix (affix) to a base or root word to form a derivative. This word-identification technique also deals with *inflections*, which are changes in a word that are made for grammatical reasons. For example, an inflection occurs when the singular form of the word *doll* is made into the plural form *dolls* by adding the suffix *s*.

Structural analysis uses the term *morpheme*, which is the smallest unit of meaning in a language and can be either free or bound. A *free morpheme* is a group of letters that comprise any meaningful word, such as these: *lake, tree,* or *horse.* A *bound morpheme* is composed of one or more letters that have a meaning but cannot function in isolation as do actual words. A few examples of bound morphemes are the *ed* in the word *hunted,* the *re* in the word *replay,* and the *s* in the word *ducks.*

Some other subskills of structural or morphemic analysis are: understanding the use of compound words, syllabication, stress, and word origins. Even though contractions are usually considered a part of structural analysis, they usually should be learned as sight words, especially at the initial stages of reading instruction. It usually is less useful for a child to determine from what two or three words the contraction was formed than to learn it as a sight word.

Note: With the current emphasis on reading as a global, language-based process that stresses comprehension of what is read from the beginning, in many cases structural analysis should be presented and practiced as much as possible in the context of meaningful reading. However, especially with learning-handicapped students, the various elements of word structure can be taught and reinforced to some extent in isolation and in phrase context. Although structural analysis is sometimes more useful than phonic analysis since it deals with larger, more meaningful word elements, this is not always the case with learning-handicapped students, especially if they have good auditory discrimination.

The study of the most useful prefixes, suffixes, word roots, and word origins may be a useful part of structural analysis since this type of study can add many words to a child's meaning vocabulary, consequently adding to his/her comprehension ability.

Here is a list of the more common prefixes and their meanings:

Prefix	Meaning	Example
ab-	from, away	abstract
ante-	before	antebellum
anti-	against	antiwar
be-	by	beside
bene-	good	benediction
by-	near, aside	bypass
circum-	around	circumnavigate
col-	with	collaborate
contra-	against	contraception
counter-	opposite	counteract
de-	down, with	dehumidifier
dia-	through, across	diagnose

dis-	not, do the opposite of	disagree
e-	out, away	eject
em-	in	embrace
en-	in	enclose
ex-	out	exhaust
extra-	outside	extracurricular
hyper-	over	hyperactive
hypo-	under	hypothyroidism
im-	into	immerse
in-	into	include
inter-	among, between	intermission
intra-	within	intramural
intro-	inside	introject
micro-	small, short	microscope
post-	after	postdate
pre-	before	preamble
pro-	before	prognosis
re-	back, again	recall
retro-	back	retrospective
sub-	under	subcontract
super-	over	superimpose
tele-	distant	telegram
trans-	across	transatlantic
un-	not	unhappy
under-	below	underground
with-	back, away	withhold

Here is a list of some of the more common suffixes and their meanings:

Suffix	Meaning	Example
-ance	state or quality of	annoyance
-ant	one who	immigrant
-arian	one who	librarian
-en	made of	wooden
-ent	one who	superintendent
-er	one who	teacher
-ful	full of	thankful
-hood	state or quality of	childhood
-ion	state or quality of	champion
-ism	doctrine of	capitalism
-less	without	thoughtless
-man	one who works with	cameraman
-mony	product or thing	matrimony
-ness	state or quality of	happiness
-ship	state or quality of	friendship
-ular	relating to	granular
-ward	direction	backward

Here is a list of some of the more common word roots and their meanings:

Root	Meaning	Example
aer	air	aerial
anthr	human	philanthropist
astr	star	astronaut
aud	hear	audience
bibl	book	bibliotherapy
bio	life	biography
cardi	heart	cardiologist
cred	believe	discredit
dem	people	democracy
dict	speak	predict
dogma	opinion	dogmatic
esth	feeling	anesthetist
fac	make, do	manufacture
gen	birth, race	generation
geo	earth	geology
gyn	woman	gynecologist
hydr	water	hydroelectric
kine, cine	movement	kinetic
loc	place	locate
log	word	apology
miss	send	missile
mot	move	motor
ped	foot	pedestrian
port	carry	transport
psych	mind, soul	psychology
spec	see	spectator
tract	pull, drag	tractor
urb	city	suburban
vid	see	video

Structural analysis often is the most useful when it is used along with semantic analysis and/or phonic analysis. For example, if a child attacks a polysyllabic word structurally, he/she first must be able to decode each of the syllables phonetically and then blend them into a recognizable word in his/her meaning vocabulary. After the word has been analyzed both phonetically and structurally, the child must then employ semantic analysis to determine whether it makes sense in sentence context.

Some reading specialists do not believe that traditional syllabication is very useful in word identification or even in spelling today, considering the widespread use of computers. One such reading specialist is Patrick M. Groff, who believes that it usually is more helpful to divide a word into "chunks" of meaning rather than into syllables that match those found in a dictionary. For example, Groff might "chunk" the word *butter* as *butt/er* instead of the syllabic division *but/ter* which is the more common one. (Groff, "Teaching Reading by Syllables," *The Reading Teacher*, 84, May, 1981, pp. 659–664). I probably agree with Groff to an extent.

As you know, some elements of structural or morphemic analysis are taught and practiced near the beginning stages of reading instruction. Whole-language instruction attempts to provide such instruction and reinforcement within the context of whole language such as predictable books, tradebooks, and experience stories. In any case, such simple suffixes as *-s, -ed,* and *-ing* can be added to regular base or root words in first grade. The identification and division of compound words such as *snowflake, cowhand,* and *strawberry* also can be taught at this level.

Simple prefixes such as *un-* and *re-* are presented and practiced in the later primary grades. Other useful prefixes and their meanings are emphasized in the intermediate grades.

Syllabication, stress, and word origins and their meanings are emphasized in the intermediate grades and beyond. Syllabication generations usually should be presented by using known words and should be practiced on unknown words. Consistent stress generalizations are often presented in the intermediate grades also. Above-average readers in the intermediate grades often find the study of word roots (etymology) stimulating.

There are many structural and stress generalizations that can be presented to children. However, the following are perhaps the most useful ones:

1. Each syllable must contain at least one vowel, and the syllable is the unit of pronunciation.

2. When two consonants are found between two vowels, the word is divided between the two consonants (VC/CV pattern, *tur/key*).

3. When one consonant is located between two vowels, the first syllable usually ends with a vowel, and the second syllable usually begins with the consonant. This makes the vowel in the first syllable long, and that syllable is said to be open (CV/C pattern, *ti/ger*).

4. A compound word is divided between the two small words that comprise it (*snow-plow*).

5. When a word contains two vowels together, the word is divided between the two vowels unless they form a diphthong (CV/VC pattern, *cru/el*).

6. Suffixes that begin with a vowel usually form a separate syllable. However, that is not true of *-ed* except when it is preceded by *t* or *d* (*buy/ing*).

7. Prefixes usually form a separate syllable when they are added to a word (*un/happy*).

8. Certain letter combinations at the end of words form a final syllable. Some examples are *-ble, -cle, -dle, -gle, -kle, -ple, -tle,* and *-zle* (*cir/cle*).

9. When the first vowel in a word is followed by *ch, sh,* or *th*, these consonant digraphs are not divided when the word is divided into syllables (*wash/es*).

10. When there is no other clue in a two-syllable word, the stress is usually placed on the first syllable (*'but/ter*).

11. In inflected or derived forms of words, the primary stress usually falls on or with the root word (*'play/er*).

12. If *a-, be-, de-, ex-, in-,* or *re-* is the first syllable in a word, it usually is unstressed (*a/'bout*).

13. Two vowel letters together in the last syllable of a word may be a clue to the stressed final syllable (*im/'peach*).

14. When there are two of the same consonant letters within a word, the syllable before the double consonants usually is stressed (*'letter*).

15. The primary stress usually occurs on the syllable before the suffixes *-ion, -ity, -ic, -ical, -ian,* or *-ious,* and on the second syllable before the suffix *-ate* (*tu/'i/tion*).

16. In words of three or more syllables, one of the first two syllables usually is stressed (*per/'cep/ti/ble*).

The stress generalizations and examples were adapted from the following source: Carol Winkley, "Which Accent Generalizations Are Worth Teaching?" *The Reading Teacher*, 20 (December 1966), pages 219–225 and 253.

Strategies, Materials, and Games for Improving Ability in Structural (Morphemic) Analysis in Isolation and in Context

There are many strategies, materials, computer programs, commercially-available games, and teacher-made games for improving ability in structural (morphemic) analysis. Since there are so many only the most useful are included here. You can find many additional suggestions and materials in other professional books about reading instruction as well as in basal reader manuals.

Strategies

Numerous strategies can be used to improve ability in structural (morphemic) analysis. This part of the chapter contains only a sampling of such activities. Many of the activities are equally adaptable for use in either the primary or intermediate grades, while some lend themselves better to either the primary or intermediate level.

The single best way to improve ability in the use of structural analysis is for the child to read widely from a variety of interesting materials at his/her independent or instructional reading levels. This strategy also is in keeping with the whole-language philosophy, which states that reading skills improve the most in the context of whole language. The child can learn, for example, many new vocabulary words by reading material containing prefixes and suffixes which give clues to word meaning.

Computer software. Some computer applications are especially useful in improving ability in structural analysis and vocabulary improvement. Structural elements, such as the knowledge of the meaning of prefixes, suffixes, and word roots, are effectively reinforced by computer programs. Appendix I of this *Handbook* contains a list of computer software manufacturers and distributors.

The language-experience approach. This approach is useful for teaching and practicing various elements of word structure, such as simple suffixes. Experience stories can be used for this purpose as early as the emergent literacy level.

Playdough and clay. To give practice in inflectional endings at the emergent literacy level, have the child use clay or playdough to construct objects that indicate comparatives and superlatives. For example, have the child use either medium to illustrate the following:

big, bigger, biggest
large, larger, largest
short, shorter, shortest
tall, taller, tallest
little, littler, littlest

The same concept can be illustrated by having the child fold a sheet of 12-inch by 18-inch newsprint or manila paper into thirds. Have the child print words such as the following on each third of the paper: *big, bigger, biggest; little, littler, littlest; long, longer, longest; small, smaller, smallest.* Then have the child draw pictures to illustrate each of the comparisons.

Word cards. For practice in compound words, print the two halves of a number of compound words on word cards made of tagboard. For example, *fire* is printed on one word card and *fly* is printed on another word card. Give each child in a group or in the entire class one word card. Each child is to find his/her word partner. Each pair of pupils then holds up their two word cards and pronounces the compound word to the rest of the group or class.

Frogs and lily pads. To give practice in recognizing small words in compound words, make several lily pads out of green construction paper. Print the last half of a compound word on each lily pad and make a slit in each lily pad above the word. Construct several frogs out of brown construction paper and print the first half of a compound word on each frog to match the lily pads. When cutting out each frog, leave a piece of construction paper sticking out on the bottom (as a tab) so that it can be placed into the slit cut in the lily pad. Put the frogs and the lily pads in two different piles on a table. Have the child match the frogs with the correct lily pads to form a true compound word.

Compound word race. Write parts of compound words on the chalkboard. Give each child a sheet of paper. Have the children write down as many compound words as they can using different combinations. After a specified time period, have the children count their words. The child who has written the most correct compound words is the winner.

Tying words together. For this activity, you need a sheet of 8-inch by 10-inch posterboard, a felt-tipped pen, scissors, and ten pairs of 16-inch shoestrings. Print the first half of appropriate compound words on the left of the board and the second half of the words on the right of the board. Punch holes by each of the word halves. Have the child thread a shoelace through the hole beside each compound word half to its corresponding word to form a complete compound word. Have the child continue until he/she has matched all of the words and formed compound words.

Magnetic compounds. To provide practice in forming compound words, print each part of a number of compound words on small word cards. Then attach a paper clip to each word card. Have the child pick up two word cards that form a true compound word with a horseshoe magnet. Have the child pronounce the word and write all of the formed compound words on a sheet of paper.

Real or make-believe. Write a number of compound words on the chalkboard, a transparency, or ditto master. Some of these compounds should be actual, and others should be make-believe. Have the child write all the words in two columns on a sheet of paper—those that are true compounds and those that are not. Here are some words you could use in this activity:

Real Compound Words	Make-Believe Compound Words
cowhand	dogpaws
blackberry	bearfur
bedroom	houseroof
headlight	treebark
windowpane	carwheels
doorknob	monkeytail
blueberry	fishscales
playground	mailstamp
railroad	bookcover
snowflake	chairleg

Illustrated compounds. Have the child select compound words that can be illustrated in a humorous way. Have the child write each compound word and then illustrate it. Some compound words that can be illustrated in this way are *jellyfish, bullfrog, catfish, cowpuncher, dragonfly, floodlight, greenhorn, horsefly, knothole, pigtail, ponytail, toadstool, wildcat,* and *wishbone.*

Humorous homographs. For an activity appropriate to intermediate grades, have the child write a humorous paragraph or story containing homographs that have different pronunciations depending upon the placement of the accent (stress). Then have the student read the material aloud, using the wrong pronunciation. Here are some homographs the student can use in this activity: *commune, console, converse, incense, minute, present, refuse, conduct, address,* and *subject.*

Contraction practice. The tape recorder can be used in the reinforcement of contractions. For example, give each child a numbered sheet of paper on which two to four contractions appear to the right of each number.

1. they'll	I've	you've	she's
2. wouldn't	I'm	they'd	couldn't
3. shouldn't	we'll	they're	I'll

Tape record sentences and have the children circle the contraction they hear in the sentences. In numbers 1, 2, and 3 above the sentences could be as follows:

1. I hope that you've already gone to the grocery store.
2. My mother couldn't go with me to the zoo.
3. I'll be home as soon as I can.

The child also can listen to a tape-recorded conversation. In this activity he/she should write the two or three words from which the contraction was made on his/her sheet of paper.

Contraction crossword. Contractions can be reinforced by the use of a crossword puzzle. As mentioned earlier, crossword puzzles now can be constructed with a computer program. For contraction practice, the words under *across* and *down* on the crossword puzzle are written in complete form, and the child prints the appropriate contractions on the puzzle.

Matching contractions. Obtain a large piece of tagboard. Print contractions in a column on the left side of the tagboard. Print the words from which the contractions were formed on the right side of the piece in random order. Punch holes beside the words on each side and place paper brads in the holes. Attach yarn to to the brads beside the contractions. Have the child attach the yarn from each contraction to the brad beside the words from which it was formed.

Animal affixes. In an activity for reinforcing affixes, obtain large sheets of construction paper or tagboard. Draw various animals—such as a donkey, monkey, dog, fox, rat, or cat—without their tails—on each sheet. On the body of each animal print a root word. Make various tails and print a suffix on each tail. Have the child pin a suffix to an animal in the correct position and read the derived word aloud.

Affix file. Have the child develop an affix card file. This file should contain affixes, their meanings, their origins, and sentences using the affixes. The file gives children a source of practice activities. The file can be made of index cards and put in a notebook or file box.

Team word building. Divide the class into two teams. Give each team one-half of a stack of cards with appropriate root words. Team A holds up a card and says "Send _____ over." That person must give four words using the root word plus an affix or go over to Team A. If he/she can give four correct words, the child selects a player from Team A to join his/her team. The game ends when the cards run out or when the players are all on one side.

Focused graffiti. Cover an area with butcher paper. Label the paper with some element of structural analysis, such as contractions, prefixes, suffixes, or compound words. Throughout a week in their free time, have children write their contributions on the paper. Have the entire class discuss and evaluate the "graffiti" at the end of the week.

Newspaper words. Make three columns on a large sheet of paper and label them *prefixes, suffixes,* and *root words.* Have children cut words out of a newspaper and paste them into the appropriate columns.

Learning long words. Select ten one-syllable words and write the words in a column down the left side of a sheet of notebook paper. Have the child think of two-, three-, and four-syllable words that have the same meaning or nearly the same meaning as the one-syllable word. Have the children work with a partner on this activity and allow a day or two to complete the task. Encourage the children to use a reference book, such as a thesaurus, for help. Here are some examples:

woods	forest	underbrush	vegetation
join	unite	congregate	affiliate

Suffixes in sentences. Make sentence cards and several suffix cards that can be used in a number of sentences. Make the activity self-correcting by placing identical symbols on the backs of cards that match correctly. Here is an example of this activity:

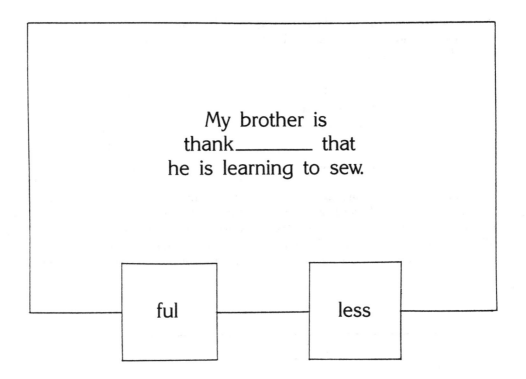

My brother is
thank_____ that
he is learning to sew.

ful

less

Suffix grid. Make a grid on the chalkboard and have each child in a group add the appropriate suffix to the base or root word and then pronounce the word.

	er	est	ly
quick			
slow			
light			
strong			

Missing morphemes. Print sentences or a paragraph on the chalkboard or a duplicating master that are variations of the cloze procedure that have deleted morphemes instead of words. Have the child complete these variations of the cloze procedure. Here is an example:

Know_____ as much as possible about zoo_____ certain_____ is very interest_____. The animal_____ who live in zoo_____ often do clever things that almost make them seem like human being_____. Many zoo_____ are now fair_____ nice places for animal_____, and zoo_____ are get_____better all the time.

Scrambled syllables. Write words in the form of scrambled syllables on the chalkboard or a duplicating master. Have the child place the syllables in order and write each word. For example:

di cate in	indicate
ter i hel cop	helicopter
deav or en	endeavor
nel chan	channel
pa ble ca	capable

Puzzles. Reinforce prefixes, suffixes, and compound words with puzzles. Print a derivative or compound word on a piece of tagboard with a marking pen. Cut each piece apart between the root word and affix or between the two small words in the compound words using a different type of cut for each. The puzzles can be laminated if you wish. Have the child reassemble each of the puzzles and pronounce the completed word.

Word octopus/tree. Either a tree or an octopus can be used to illustrate the relationship between word roots and derivatives. Make either a tree or an octopus on the chalkboard or a transparency. After several students have examined the tree or octopus, have them construct their own tree or octopus on a sheet of paper. Here are some root words that can be used in this activity:

happy, love, play, man, teach

Etymology. Some above-average readers in the intermediate grades may enjoy the study of etymology or word origins. If a child wants to learn about word origins, here are several good resources:

Adelson, Leone. *Dandelions Don't Bite: The Story of Words.* New York: Pantheon, 1972.

Funk, Charles E. *Thereby Hangs a Tale: Stories of Curious Word Origins.* New York: Harper, 1985.

Funk, Wilfred. *Word Origins and Their Romantic Stories.* New York: Crown, 1987.

Klausner, Janet. *Talk About English: How Words Travel and Change.* New York: Thomas Y. Crowell Junior Books, 1990.

Kohn, Bernice. *What a Funny Thing to Say!* New York: Dial, 1974.

Sarnoff, Jane, and Reynold Ruffins. *Words: A Book About the Origins of Everday Words and Phrases.* New York: Scribners, 1981.

Steckler, Arthur. *101 Words and How They Began.* New York: Doubleday, 1979.

More word stories. For an activity that stresses etymology or word origins, write several questions on the chalkboard or a ditto master that children are to try to answer. This activity should be used mainly with above-average readers in the upper-intermediate grades. Here are several examples:

- What is a *barometer* used to measure in meteorology?
- What does a *bibliophile* enjoy doing?
- What is used for energy in a *hydroelectric* plant?
- What type of physician is a *podiatrist?*
- What does the word *evacuate* mean?

Prefix disks. Construct prefix disks using specialized vocabulary, such as is found in a content area. Such disks can be constructed from two circular pieces of tagboard. Print the prefix on the smaller disc, word roots on the larger disc, and fasten the two discs together with a paper brad as shown in the illustration.

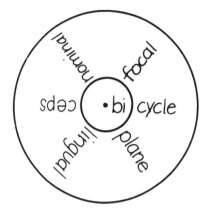

Activity Sheets for Reinforcing Structural Analysis

Here are several ready-to-duplicate activity sheets. You may reproduce these activity sheets as they are, or modify them to suit your particular needs. In addition, you can use them as models in constructing your own activity sheets. The answers are given at the end of this chapter.

CONSTRUCTING COMPOUND WORDS

(Third-Grade Level)

Name_____ Grade_____ Teacher_____ Date_____

There are two compound words under the blank in each sentence. <u>Put part of one word</u> <u>and part of the other word together to make a new compound word.</u> The new compound word must make sense in the sentence. The first one has been done for you.

1. My mother is going to put wallpaper in the ___bathroom___ tomorrow.
   bathrobe/classroom

2. Our puppy chewed a large hole in a _____ when she was left
   dishpan/tablecloth
   alone yesterday.

3. If a person sees a _____, that person is supposed to have good luck.
   blueberry/birdhouse

4. There was a big _____ in my bedroom last evening that
   dragonfly/housebroken
   kept me from going to sleep.

5. Jeff usually does his reading _____ pages very carefully.
   workhorse/bookcase

6. I like to read the comics in the _____ every day.
   newscast/paperback

7. My grandfather likes to watch the purple martins fly in and out of the

   _____ that he built.
   hummingbird/greenhouse

8. The _____ we made yesterday melted nearly right away since
   snowstorm/mailman
   it got warm in the afternoon.

9. The _____ is a make-believe person who is supposed to help
   sandbox/policeman
   children fall asleep at night.

10. We saw a beautiful black and gold _____ on our way to school
    buttermilk/dragonfly
    yesterday.

11. I don't really like to do my _____ on the weekends.
    homemade/workday

12. My family was lucky enough to see a _____ when we were
    sailboat/jellyfish
    fishing in Florida last winter.

ACTIVITY SHEET FOR DEDUCING COMPOUND WORDS FROM TWO CLUES

(Fourth-Grade Level)

Name_____ Grade_____ Teacher_____ Date_____

In each case, read the two clues and try to decide what compound word can be formed. Then write the compound word on the line. The first one has been done for you.

1. Something that a ghost might do to a child and a large black bird.

   _____scarecrow_____

2. Something that a person spreads on a piece of bread and something that a child might drink.

   _____

3. An animal that a child might ride and a part of a cat's body.

   _____

4. A kind of tree and a type of fruit.

   _____

5. A type of reptile and something to sit on.

   _____

6. Something a person can use with peanut butter on a sandwich and something that a person can catch.

   _____

7. A type of metal and part of a person's body.

   _____

8. Somewhere to live and a type of insect.

   _____

9. A part of a person's body and a piece of jewelry to wear on a finger.

   _____

10. The opposite of work and a part of a house.

    _____

11. A color and a part of a car.

    _____

12. Something it may do on a cloudy day and an item of clothing.

    _____

ACTIVITY SHEET FOR DETERMINING THE MEANING OF DERIVATIVES

(Approximately Sixth-Grade Level)

Name_____ Grade_____ Teacher_____ Date_____

Read each of the derivatives in the column on the left. Then write the approximate meaning of each of these derivatives in the column on the right. Try to use the root word to help you determine the meanings. You may use a dictionary if you want to.

1. reappear _____

2. uncomfortable _____

3. underground _____

4. tricycle _____

5. monorail _____

6. quadrangle _____

7. decade _____

8. antebellum _____

9. postpone _____

10. exhaust _____

11. midsummer _____

12. proceed _____

13. telegram _____

14. transatlantic _____

15. submarine _____

16. multicolored _____

17. superhuman _____

18. underweight _____

19. beneficial _____

20. antiwar _____

ACTIVITY SHEET FOR USING WORDS CONTAINING A GREEK OR LATIN WORD ROOT IN SENTENCE CONTEXT

(Approximately Sixth- or Seventh-Grade Level)

Name_____ Grade_____ Teacher_____ Date_____

A. The Latin word root <u>miss</u> means <u>to send</u>. Select a word from this list containing the <u>miss</u> root, and write it in the correct sentence.

missile

dismiss

missionary

mission

remiss

1. Mr. Jackson must _____ his science class early today since

there is an important assembly at that time.

2. The _____ exploded in flames before reaching its proper

destination.

3. My father was _____ in making our house payment this

month since he recently lost his job.

4. My aunt used to be a _____ to a country in Africa.

5. Ms. Gonzalez is being sent on a very important _____ by her

employer.

B. The Latin word root <u>port</u> means <u>to carry</u>. Select a word from this list containing the <u>port</u> root, and write it in the correct sentence.

portable

portfolio

transport

deport

portage

© 1993 by The Center for Applied Research in Education

1. Every summer I see a group of Scouts trying to _____ their
   canoes in the North Woods of Wisconsin.

2. To _____ an undesirable alien is to make him or her leave
   the country.

3. Some word processors and computers are small and _____.

4. Large trucks are used to _____ different kinds of goods
   across the country.

5. My father and mother are knowledgeable about the contents of their stock
   _____.

C. The Greek word root <u>log</u> means <u>word</u>. Select a word from this list containing the
<u>log</u> root, and write it in the correct sentence.

> prologue
> eulogy
> monologue
> dialogue
> apology

1. The _____ to that author's book was written by one of her
   colleagues.

2. I believe that I owe my best friend an _____ for what I did
   yesterday.

3. Her best friend gave the _____ at my grandmother's funeral
   yesterday.

4. My mother and father had a thoughtful _____ yesterday
   about buying a new car for the family.

5. A fine _____ was given by the well-known actor who came to
   our city yesterday.

Games for Structural Analysis

Here are games for reinforcing children's ability in structural analysis skills. These games mainly would be used with children in the primary grades and lower-intermediate grades.

Contraction Clothespins. The purpose of this game is to have the child match the appropriate words to its contraction. For the game, you need twenty clip clothespins, and ten cut-out shirts of tagboard. Write each contraction on a shirt. Write the two words of which each contraction is composed on the back of the shirt. Have the child match the two appropriate clothespins to the contraction shirt and pin them on. Have the child turn each shirt over to self-check his/her work.

Plastic Egg Puzzle. Use plastic eggs or similar containers for this game. Print each word of a compound word on an egg half. Take the egg halves apart and put them into a basket. Have several children work together putting the eggs back together to form compound words. Perhaps a good reader can check the children's progress in this game.

Stacks. Print a derived word on each of a group of word cards; for example: *unhappy, thankful, remake, golden, gladly,* and *farmer.* On the reverse side of each card print the root word. Stack all of the cards in the center of a table with the derived words face up. Have the first player take a card, read the derived word, and give the root word. If he/she is correct, the child is allowed to keep the card. If he/she is unable to give the correct root word, the card is placed at the bottom of the stack. The next player takes a turn, and the game is over when all of the cards are used. The player with the most cards is the winner.

Prefix and Suffix Baseball. Print prefixes or suffixes on word cards. Each of two teams selects a pitcher who will select a word card and pitch a prefix or suffix to the batter. The batter must think of a word that contains the prefix or suffix and pronounce it. If the child can think of a word, pronounce it, and use it in a sentence, the child hits a double. A gameboard with a baseball diamond and markers for the batters adds interest and motivation.

Making Plurals. Divide the class into two teams. Say slowly and only once three nouns such as *mother, house, chair.* Then have the first player on one team say the plurals of these words in the sequence in which you said them. Teams should take turns answering until every child has had a turn. One point is given to a team for each correct plural given in the directed sequence. The team with more points is the winner. After the first round is over, begin the second round by naming three nouns whose plurals are irregularly formed such as *mouse, half, leaf.* For a more difficult game have the children spell the noun plurals accurately.

Root for the Root Word. Make 2-inch by 4-inch word cards with derived words on them such as *handful, thankless, unfriendly, humankind, teacher, unfold,* and *submarine.* Print the root word on the back of each card. Place the cards in a pile in the center of a table with the derived words facing up. Have the first player draw a card, read the derived word, and give the root word. If he/she gives it correctly, he/she keeps the card. If he/she cannot do so, the child puts the card on the bottom of the pile with the derived word facing up. Then the next player draws. The game continues until all of the cards are gone. The player with the most cards is the winner.

Word Journey. Construct fifty-two playing cards, each of which has a two-, three-, or four-syllable word printed on it. The difficulty of the game can be increased by having many polysyllabic words. Make a gameboard by gluing a mimeographed map of the United States on cardboard. Draw railway routes between major cities. Construct miniature trains of different colors for each player.

To play the game.

Place the deck of cards in the center of the table near the gameboard. Have the first player draw his/her first card from the center deck. The player who draws a word with the least number of syllables is the first to play. If he/she draws a one-syllable word, he/she may travel to the first city on the route; if he/she has a two-syllable word, he/she travels to the second town, etc. Each player in turn draws a card, pronounces the word on the card, tells how many syllables are in the word, and moves his/her train along the route. If the child cannot say the word or determine how many syllables it contains, another child can tell him/her, but he/she cannot move his/her train. The player who reaches the home station first wins the game.

Affix Relay. Divide the class into two teams. Write two words on the chalkboard to which suffixes may be added. The difficulty of the words should depend upon the abilities of the class. The first member of each team goes up to the chalkboard and writes a new word using a suffix. Each child then runs back and gives the chalk to another child who must then write another word by adding another suffix. The team that writes the most words in one minute wins the game.

Here are some words to use:

happy	play
unhappy	played
happier	playing
happiest	player
happiness	playful
happily	replay
unhappiness	plays

Contraction Tic-Tac-Toe. Construct a tic-tac-toe grid from construction paper or posterboard and print a contraction in each box. Play the game like regular tic-tac-toe, but before a player may place an *X* or an *O* in a box, he/she must read the contraction out loud, say the two words from which it was formed, and use the contraction in a sentence.

Ice Cream Syllabication Rule Scoop. Cut some ice cream cones out of posterboard. Write one of the syllabication rules *CV/C* or *VC/CV* on each scoop. Make several cones for each rule. Using different colors of construction paper, cut out circles to represent scoops of ice cream that will fit in the cones. On each circle print a word that follows one of the syllabication rules printed on the ice cream scoops (*CV/C* or *VC/CV*). Print several words for each rule. Put the ice cream scoops in a pile on a table and put the cones in two piles depending upon the rules printed on them. Each player takes turns choosing a scoop of ice cream from the pile, pronouncing the word printed on it, using it in a sentence, and matching it with the correct ice cream cone. If the player does not match the scoop with the correct cone, the ice cream scoop is placed at the bottom of the pile. If the match is correct, the player puts the cone with the scoop of ice cream on it in front of him/her. The game continues until all of the scoops of ice cream have been matched with the correct cones. Children can put up to three scoops on the same cone before they must use a new cone.

Red Apples Plurals. Make 30 red apples and four black worms out of construction paper. On each apple print the singular form of a word. On each of the four worms, print one of the plural endings: *s, es, ies,* or *ves.* Put the apples and worms in two separate piles on a table. Have the players take turns choosing an apple and matching it with the proper worm (the correct plural ending). If the word contains a *y* that should be dropped (as in *baby* to *babies*), have the player put the worm over the top of the *y* while forming the plural.

Butterflies and Root Words. Cut some large butterflies out of posterboard. Print a word that contains both a prefix and suffix on each butterfly. Print the prefix on the left wing, the root word on the body, and the suffix on the right wing. Then cut each butterfly into three pieces: prefix, root word, and suffix. Put the three sections into three different containers. Each container should be clearly labeled *Prefixes, Root Words, Suffixes*. Have the child choose a root word from the Root Word container and try to match it with the appropriate prefix and suffix wings. If the child locates the correct wings, he/she keeps the butterfly. If the child cannot find the correct wings to match the body, the child keeps the body but returns the wings to their proper containers.

What Is Semantic (Contextual) Analysis?

Semantic analysis (contextual analysis or context clues) is a word-identification technique in which the reader ascertains the meaning (and sometimes the pronunciation) of unknown words by examining the context in which they are found. That context can be the sentence, the adjacent sentences, that paragraph, or the entire passage. It also usually involves syntactic or grammatical clues.

Some reading specialists have determined that there are a number of different kinds of semantic clues. Although the categories of semantic clues differ somewhat, here is one classification that often has been used. (See Harold L. Herber's *Teaching Reading in the Content Areas*. Englewood Cliffs, New Jersey: Prentice Hall, 1967, page 16.)

- *Experience Clues*—A reader uses prior knowledge to determine the meaning of the unknown word. That is why it is imperative for a reader to have much prior knowledge to be an effective reader.

- *Association Clues*—A reader attempts to associate the unknown word with the known word. For example: The sound was so soft that it was barely *audible.*

- *Synonym Clues*—There is a synonym to the known word in the sentence to explain it. For example: I needed to consult a *foot specialist* about blisters, so I looked in the telephone directory for a *podiatrist.*

- *Summary Clues*—Several sentences can be used to summarize the meaning of the unknown word.

- *Comparison or Contrast Clues*—There is a comparison or contrast to the unknown word in the sentence or paragraph which gives its meaning.

- *Previous Contact Clues*—The reader can ascertain the meaning of the unknown word from a previous contact with a similar word.

With the current emphasis upon whole language and the emphasis upon reading as a global, language-based process that stresses comprehension of what is read from the beginning stages of reading instruction, it is clear that semantic analysis is the single most useful and important technique of word identification. Semantic analysis is most effective when used in conjunction with structural and phonic analysis and when there are not too many unknown words in the reading material. Normally there should not be more than about one in fifty unknown words in the material if semantic analysis is to be used successfully.

Semantic analysis can be presented as early as the emergent literacy level when the teacher orally gives a sentence with an omitted word. The teacher then asks the children to provide a word orally that makes sense in that sentence. This is also, in a sense, readiness for the cloze procedure. At the primary-grade reading level, the importance of semantic clues should be explained to children, and they should be encouraged to use context to deduce the meaning of unknown words they meet while reading. In addition, children at this level can be asked to read sentences silently and to underline the word that makes sense in each sentence. They also can complete simple cloze procedures.

It is very important to ensure that children in both the primary and intermediate grades be encouraged to supply *words that make sense* while reading, both silently and orally, even if the provided words are not the same words found in the reading material. Especially in the primary grades, children often are discouraged from risk taking, which in turn may hinder their reading since too much stress then is placed upon word-perfect oral reading. Keep in mind that although the student-supplied words should always make sense in the reading material, it is possible to use the practice of word substitution to excess. We sometimes tutor disabled readers who miscall up to one half of the words in the reading material and yet are able to retell the material effectively or to answer comprehension questions about the material successfully. These students should continue to have some instruction and/or reinforcement in either sight-word knowledge, structural analysis, or phonic analysis depending on their weaknesses.

All children in elementary school should be taught that semantic analysis is not merely guessing at the meaning of unknown words. Rather, it is a calculated estimate of the meaning of unknown words which demands interpretive thinking on the reader's part.

Some readers may rely too heavily on semantic clues and can, therefore, be described as *context readers*. These are the students who may need instruction and practice in the other word-identification techniques mentioned earlier. They also should be encouraged to read more carefully. A tape recorder may be helpful in their correction. However, even these children should realize the importance semantic clues play in effective reading comprehension.

To summarize, semantic (contextual) analysis is the one technique of word identification which best represents the concept of reading as a language-based process which emphasizes comprehension. It best reflects the whole-language philosophy. Thus, it probably should receive the most emphasis with children in elementary school with the possible exception of some learning-handicapped children who may need more emphasis placed on the other word-identification strategies. Even these children, however, need to understand the great importance of using semantic clues.

Strategies and Materials for Improving Semantic (Contextual) Analysis

Here are strategies and ready-to-use materials you can use to improve the semantic (context) analysis skill of your students. All of them have been used successfully by my teacher-trainees in various kinds of tutoring situations over the years. Since the strategies and materials in this word-identification technique could easily comprise a chapter by themselves, the ones chosen for inclusion here are merely illustrative.

Strategies

There are a myriad of strategies that can be used to improve ability in context clues. It is important at the outset to state that one of the first and most important techniques to teaching context clues is simply to talk with students about their usefulness. Disabled readers and learning-handicapped students often do not have any idea that a word can often by analyzed and understood by the use of its context. It is especially helpful for learning-handicapped students to have much instruction in the value and use of context clues.

Susanna Pflaum and Ernest Pascarella conducted a study which found that learning-handicapped students whose initial instructional level was at or above second grade benefited significantly from instruction in the use of context clues. Therefore, you can see how important it is to present semantic analysis to learning-handicapped students. (See Susanna Pflaum and Ernest T. Pascarella's article "Interactive Effect of Prior Reading Achievement and Training in Context on the Reading of Learning-Disabled Children" in *Reading Research Quarterly*, 20, Fall 1984, pages 138–158.)

Wide reading. Wide reading of various types of materials is undoubtedly the single most useful way of improving ability in semantic analysis. This reading can take place in predictable books and nursery rhymes in which children participate in the reading, sharing the appropriate language. It can be from experience stories, tradebooks of various types, content textbooks, newspapers of various kinds, children's magazines, and child-written materials. An excellent list of children's magazines is called *More Mailbox Magic* and can be obtained from Illinois Reading Council, 1704 East Empire, Bloomington, Illinois 61702. There is a charge for this list, so be sure to request ordering information. As stated earlier, reading is a skill that improves most with motivated practice from material children can read easily. Therefore, it follows that the more a child reads, the better a reader he/she normally will become. Unfortunately, disabled readers and learning-handicapped children often do as little reading as possible and therefore do not make good reading progress. Although it is often hard to motivate such students, it is possible with highly interesting, easy material specifically chosen for them. We have had success in tutoring such students using self-selected, interesting, easy material.

Listening for miscues. Children can be helped to become aware of disruptive miscues by having them listen to material (either teacher-read or tape-recorded), indicate when disruptions occur, and state why the miscue is inappropriate. When a student encounters an unknown word in context or is aware that a disruptive miscue has occurred, he/she should first employ the strategy of finishing reading the sentence because it may provide additional helpful information. Usually the words *after* the unknown word provide more help than the words before it. A *place-holder* (a word that makes sense and is syntactically appropriate) can be used until new information makes it necessary to try a new response. If neither strategy works, rereading the sentence containing the unknown word may help. However, before doing so, the child should examine the unknown word by using graphophonic (phonic) clues along with context clues—a powerful combination method of word attack. If none of these strategies is effective, it may be helpful to read the sentence before or after the sentence containing the unknown word.

Barbara Taylor and Linda Nosbush ("Oral Reading for Meaning: A Technique for Improving Word Identification Skills," *The Reading Teacher*, December 1983, 37, pages 234–237) recommended a four-step procedure for encouraging students to self-correct disruptive miscues. In this procedure, the following steps are followed:

1. The child on a one-to-one basis reads a 100- to 300-word passage at the instructional level to the teacher who gives very little feedback.
2. The teacher praises the child for something well done in oral reading especially his/her self-corrections.
3. One or two uncorrected disruptive miscues are shown to the child by reading his/her rendition to the child and having him/her tell what word did not make sense or sound right.
4. The child is helped to recognize the miscued words by demonstrating how graphic and context clues could have been used.

Patricia Dahl and S. Jay Samuels also have presented a strategy for using context clues. (See their article "Teaching Students to Read Using Hypothesis Test Strategies" in *The Reading Teacher*, March 1977, 30, pages 603–606.) It is as follows:

1. Use information from the passage, prior knowledge, and language clues.
2. Make a prediction as to which word is the most likely to occur.
3. Compare the printed and predicted words for goodness of fit.
4. Accept or reject the prediction.

Computer software. There are some programs that may be of use in improving ability in semantic analysis. However, this word-identification technique can be better improved by actual reading. Appendix I of this *Handbook* contains a list of computer software manufacturers and distributors.

Magazine pictures. An example of a readiness activity for contextual analysis is to give the child pictures from magazines or catalogs. Then read some sentences aloud or record them on tape, omitting one word in each sentence that can be completed by the use of one of the pictures. Have the child show the picture from the group of pictures which takes the place of the omitted word.

Rebuses. Another readiness activity is to have the child dictate (or the teacher formulate) a chart that uses rebuses (pictures) in place of some of the difficult but interesting vocabulary words. One of the most effective ways to use rebuses is by providing them in recipes for cooking or baking activities. The recipe is written on chart paper. Baking gingerbread figures, bread, or cookies; frosting cupcakes; making peanut brittle, butter, or anything else is appropriate to this kind of activity.

Word cards. Print some structure or function words such as *a, an, and,* or *the* on individual word cards. Cut pictures from old magazines or catalogs that can be used along with the word cards to form phrases. Have the child choose pictures and word cards to form phrases as shown in the illustration.

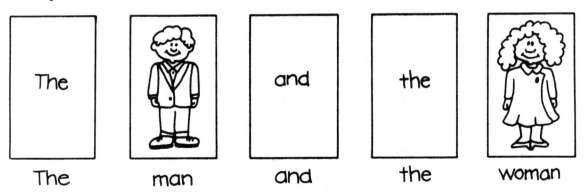

Fill in the blanks. Print a number of sentences on the chalkboard or on a transparency. Each sentence should have an omitted word that could reasonably be replaced by a number of different alternatives. Have a child read a sentence aloud, completing it with one possible option. Other children in the group can suggest alternatives. Read each sentence orally if your pupils cannot do so. In this instance, the pupils only suggest possible words for the omitted word. Here are some examples:

I would like to receive a _____ for my birthday.

My favorite food is _____.

My mother's favorite color is _____.

I would like to play _____ after school today.

Variation:

Divide a large piece of 12-inch by 18-inch manila paper or newsprint into fourths. Print four sentences on the chalkboard. In each sentence one word is omitted that can be illustrated by a primary-grade child. Have the child read each sentence silently and draw the illustration of the omitted word in the proper place on the sheet of paper. Each sentence should allow for a creative response. Here are several sentences that can be used in this activity:

The zoo animal I like best is the _____.

I want a _____ for my birthday.

Jack walked as slowly as a _____.

Maria's favorite toy is _____.

Crossword puzzle. A simple crossword puzzle can be useful in helping a pupil improve ability in semantic analysis. The crossword puzzle in this instance should contain sentences with an omitted word and a list of the words that can be used to complete the puzzle.

Extraneous words. Print a number of sentences on the chalkboard, a transparency, or a ditto master. Each sentence should contain one irrelevant word. Have the child cross out the irrelevant word and then read the sentence with that word. Here are two sentences to illustrate this strategy:

When a dog meets a porcupine in the woods lake, it can lead to real trouble.

A clear, purple lake can be beautiful.

Linked cards. Attach three word cards together with a ring in the upper left corner. Write a sentence with one word missing on the first card. Have the student predict the missing word. After he/she makes the first prediction, have the child flip to the second card, which has the first letter of the missing word written on it. Have the child then confirm the prediction or make another one. Finally, have the child flip to the third card that shows the correct word.

Charting goals. Richard Allington has suggested the following for improving ability in context. His suggestions reflect the whole-language philosophy very well. (See his article "If They Don't Read Much, How They Ever Gonna Get Good?" in *Journal of Reading*, 21, October 1977, pages 57–61.)

1. Assess the amount of reading in context that occurs in a group's reading class.
2. Set a goal of 500 words in context for each lesson.
3. Avoid having a mini-lesson in word analysis during the context reading.
4. Chart the number of words a student reads in context during a lesson.

Writing descriptions. Hold up two pictures. The first picture could be of a playground ball, while the second could be of a group of people dancing at a ball. Ask the children what the two pictures have in common. Have them make up sentences about what is taking place in each picture. Write the sentences about the two pictures on the chalkboard. Try to have them use the word *ball* when describing both pictures.

Self-monitoring. It is important for children to learn to monitor their silent and oral reading. Although the concept of metacognition or self-monitoring is explained in detail in the next chapter, very briefly, it is a mind-set in which a child consistently thinks about what he/she is reading. If he/she is not comprehending the material effectively, the child learns how to apply *fix-up strategies*, also explained in detail in the next chapter. Good readers monitor their comprehension much more effectively than do poor readers.

Newspaper puzzles. An interesting strategy for older students involves cutting a number of short clippings from the newspaper. Then tear each clipping in two uneven pieces so that most of the printed material is kept intact. Then have the student try to read the message aloud using context clues to fill in the missing parts of each article.

The cloze procedure. With all of its variations, this is one of the most useful ways of improving ability in semantic analysis, since it involves using both semantic and syntactic clues. The cloze procedure is described and illustrated in detail in Chapters 2 and 4 of this *Handbook*. These chapters contain a number of ready-to-use versions of cloze that can be used equally well to improve contextual analysis ability, and comprehension ability as well as to diagnose competency in those two skills.

Very briefly, the child must have a number of readiness activities before being exposed to actual cloze procedures, and this chapter discusses several of them. Select sentences from experience stories and print each sentence on a strip of tagboard omitting one word. Then print each omitted word on a word card. Have the child place the proper word card in each sentence strip. You can make slits in each sentence strip if you want. Then have the child read each sentence aloud.

As another example, print a short passage on the appropriate reading level on a transparency and place masking tape over the words to be omitted. Do not omit more than one out of every ten words. Have a child or several children guess each omitted word. After the guess is made, remove the masking tape and have the children compare the actual word with their guesses.

A variation of the last activity, *zipper cloze* involves printing some sentences on an overhead projector with one word covered by a small piece of tagboard. Place a piece of tape across the tagboard to fasten it to the transparency so that the tape serves as a hinge. Then when you want to show the word to the children after having them guess what it might be, lift the tagboard flap. In the upper primary grades children should be able to discuss why various answers may or may not be possible in terms of semantic and syntactic clues.

The cloze procedure can take many forms—traditional cloze, the deleted words placed at the bottom of the sheet, random cloze, deletions of more than one word at a time, cloze combining graphophonic (phonic) and contextual clues, word length as a clue, and deletions of a specific class of words (part of speech).

It is important to remember that when any variation of the cloze procedure is used to improve ability in semantic analysis, a synonym of any deleted word must be accepted as correct. To do otherwise simply penalizes the child for making good use of context clues.

One variation of the cloze procedure which was not discussed earlier can be called *treasure cloze*. In this version, give the child directions to locate a long-list treasure. Smudge some of the words in the directions so they cannot be seen. Have the children try to fill in all the missing words so that they can locate the hidden treasure. Here is a brief example:

Mark hid a bag of gold and s_____ coins in a secret hiding pl_____. If you want to be able to f_____ them, you have to follow these directions. First go to the old gr_____ road by the cemetery. Then walk down that road for exactly three m_____. On the right you will see a very large tr_____. The treasure is b_____ in front of the tree. Dig a h_____ about three feet deep, and you will find a b_____ with an old lock on it. Break the l_____ with a h_____ and take all the gold and silver coins. If you f_____ them, you can keep them!

Analogies. Another way of improving ability in context clues especially in the intermediate grades is using analogies. Put incomplete analogies on the chalkboard, a transparency, or a duplicating master. Here are two formats for presenting analogies:

- pride:lion gaggle:_____(geese)_____
- Men are to women as boys are to_____(girls)_____.

Mystery words. Another activity appropriate for the upper-primary-level or lower-intermediate-level is to provide nonsense words that the student is able to pronounce but that are not familiar in meaning. This activity can utilize the chalkboard, a transparency, or a duplicating master. Give a sentence that builds meaning for the word. Have the child then suggest a word or several words that might fit in that position in each sentence. Here are some examples:

rxopr   My father is very *rxopr* when he first wakes up in the morning.
proqft   My mother would like to receive a *proqft* for her fortieth birthday on Tuesday.

Riddles. A variation of riddles can be used to improve ability in semantic analysis and phonic analysis. Write each riddle on a card, laminate it, and put in only the initial letter of each answer. Here are several examples:

I am found in a kitchen and messages often are put on me. I am a r_____. (refrigerator)

I am a useful kitchen appliance that can heat food up very quickly. I am a

    m_____. (microwave)

I am one of a child's favorite foods. I am p_____.

(pizza)

Activity Sheets for Reinforcing Semantic Analysis

Here are several ready-to-use activity sheets that you can duplicate and use in their present form or you can modify in any way you wish. More important, they can serve as models for your own activity sheets. The answers are given at the end of this chapter.

DEDUCING A MYSTERY WORD FROM STORY CONTEXT

(Third-Grade Level)

Name_____ Grade_____ Teacher_____ Date_____

Read this story to yourself. It contains one mystery word. This same word makes sense in all of the blanks in the story. As you read the story, try to use context clues to determine the mystery word. You may have to read most of the story before discovering what the word is. After you have decided what it is, write the mystery word in all of the blanks in the story.

WHAT IS THE MYSTERY WORD?

Cindy sometimes felt as if she were the only child in the world who did not have her own _____. Most of her friends had a _____ in their bedroom, and she wanted one very badly.

If she had a _____ in her bedroom, Cindy felt she could really enjoy some of her spare time. Cindy's fourteen-year-old brother Dave had his own _____ and spent lots of his time learning from it—at least he *said* that he learned many things from it.

Of course, the Gardner family had one _____ in their living room and another one in their family room downstairs. However, the family always was arguing about _____. Cindy's dad wanted to watch the national news on one _____, while her mother wanted to watch the local news on the other _____. Dave

usually was upstairs in his bedroom at that time watching a

rerun of an old comedy on his _____, and Cindy

didn't have anything to do but sit and wait for dinner.

After dinner things were no better for Cindy. No one in

the Gardner family wanted to watch what she did on

_____, and she felt really left out most of the

time. If only she had enough money to buy her own

_____, she would be really happy. However, she

did not.

Cindy had asked her grandparents to buy her a

_____ for her birthday next month, and maybe,

just maybe, they really would. Oh, how much Cindy hoped

that they would. Then she would really be happy!

LOCATING AND CORRECTING INCORRECT WORDS IN STORY CONTEXT

(Fourth-Grade Level)

Name_____ Grade_____ Teacher_____ Date_____

Read this short story to yourself. It contains ten words that do not make sense. Cross out each incorrect word and write the correct word above it. When you have finished, reread the entire story to be sure that it is completely correct.

PARROTS

Parrots are very popular with people since they is fascinating creatures. Most parrots are every beautiful since they are covered with brilliantly colored feathers of red, blue, gold, white, and green, among other colors. Very few other birds in the world can move the beauty of parrots.

People also are impressed with the ability of parrots to "talk." For example, the African Grey parrot can be taught to talk so that it sounds like a man, a woman, or a child. There have been parrots who could train many jokes or recite a whole speech. Of course, parrots cannot really "talk," but merely imitate the sounds they hear. Interestingly enough, only parrots that have said hatched and raised by people can learn how to talk, and even they cannot talk all of the time.

Parrots also are like people in that they usually are very loyal to them mates. Many times parrots who are "husband" and "wife" stay together for life. They also are good parents to their young.

It is easy to tell a male and female apart in most cartons. Males are often more colorful than are females although this is not always the case. Some parrots such as cockatoos live a very long time such us more than 70 miles, and some people think that they can live even longer than that.

USING SEMANTIC ANALYSIS IN SENTENCE CONTEXT
(Fifth-Grade Level)

Name_____ Grade_____ Teacher_____ Date_____

Read each group of sentences silently. Then put an X in the box after the statement that helps you understand the first sentence.

1. I heard that Mr. Gomez was forced to go into bankruptcy yesterday.
   In this sentence, Mr. Gomez's finances are important. □
   In this sentence, Mr. Gomez's travel plans are important. □
   In this sentence, Mr. Gomez's physical health is important. □

2. My older brother is a member of a fraternity.
   In this sentence, the brother's religion is important. □
   In this sentence, the brother's friends are important. □
   In this sentence, the brother's appearance is important. □

3. The summit of that mountain certainly is beautiful.
   In this sentence, a certain part of the mountain is important. □
   In this sentence, the appearance of the mountain is important. □
   In this sentence, the type of mountain is important. □

4. Jenny's aqua dress is lovely and appropriate.
   In this sentence, the style of the dress is important. □
   In this sentence, the age of the dress is important. □
   In this sentence, the color of the dress is important. □

5. That aggressive man doesn't appear to be a pleasant person.
   In this sentence, the personality of the man is important. □
   In this sentence, the appearance of the man is important. □
   In this sentence, the age of the man is important. □

6. I think Mrs. Evans is a very <u>maternal</u> woman.

    In this sentence, the woman's <u>behavior</u> is important. ☐

    In this sentence, the woman's <u>appearance</u> is important. ☐

    In this sentence, the woman's <u>age</u> is important. ☐

7. The <u>ancient</u> mummy apparently was very well preserved.

    In this sentence, the <u>type</u> of mummy is important. ☐

    In this sentence, the <u>age</u> of the mummy is important. ☐

    In this sentence, the <u>location</u> of the mummy is important. ☐

8. That dog seems to be <u>belligerent</u>.

    In this sentence, the <u>behavior</u> of the dog is important. ☐

    In this sentence, the <u>age</u> of the dog is important. ☐

    In this sentence, the <u>breed</u> of the dog is important. ☐

9. I am usually an <u>optimistic</u> person.

    In this sentence, the person's <u>appearance</u> is important. ☐

    In this sentence, the person's <u>behavior</u> is important. ☐

    In this sentence, the person's <u>financial status</u> is important. ☐

10. When Elsa received an *A* in science on her report card, she jumped up and down <u>jubilantly</u>.

    In this sentence, the girl's <u>intelligence</u> is important. ☐

    In this sentence, the girl's <u>age</u> is important. ☐

    In this sentence, the girl's <u>way of reacting</u> is important. ☐

Strategies for Teaching Spelling Skills to Learning-Handicapped Students _____

Here are several suggestions for teaching spelling skills to learning-handicapped students. Many of these ideas are equally applicable to any children who have difficulty with mastering spelling.

At the beginning it is important to understand that spelling success is mainly dependent upon visual memory and auditory discrimination ability. Therefore, a learning-handicapped child who is weak in either of these perceptual channels will likely have difficulty with spelling skills. Most learning-handicapped children who have difficulty in reading also have difficulty in spelling, while the child who is competent in reading well may be a good speller also.

It is important to teach learning-handicapped students a good method for studying spelling words as well as some special strategies that may be especially helpful for them. Here is a general method for teaching children how to spell a word:

1. Present the spelling word using it in sentence context.
2. Have the child close his/her eyes and try to visualize the word.
3. Have the child check his/her visual image with the spelling word as found on the chalkboard or in a book.
4. Have the child again shut his/her eyes to see it and say it softly.
5. Have the child check it by writing it and then comparing it to the model.
6. When the child can reproduce the word correctly, he/she goes on to study the next word.

For the learning-handicapped child who has great difficulty in learning spelling words, this plan may not be sufficient in itself to ensure success. If the child has a good visual memory, this can be stressed in learning spelling words. If the child has an adequate auditory channel but poor auditory discrimination, activities such as those described earlier in this chapter may be helpful. Although *invented spelling* in a whole-language setting may well be effective for many students, it might not be for learning-handicapped children who may need spelling skills presented in isolation much of the time.

The Fernald Tracing Method

Described earlier in this chapter, this method may work well for teaching spelling skills as well as reading skills. The same may be the case with the Gillingham-Stillman Method which also was described earlier. Gillingham and Stillman define spelling as ". . . the translation of sounds into letter names (oral spelling) or into letter forms (written spelling)." Gillingham and Stillman suggest that a few days after blending is started, the analysis of words into their component sounds should begin, as in the following examples.

> Teacher: "Listen, I am going to say a word very slowly—/map/, /m/-/a/-/p/ , /m/-/a/-/p/ , /m/-/a/-/p/. What sound did you hear first? . . . Yes, /m/ . . . What letter says /m/? Find the *m* card and lay it on the table. What is the second sound? Listen. /m/-/a/-/p/." The lesson continues until the child has heard and recognized all three phonemes in the word <u>map</u> and can see the word laid out before him with the letter cards. The child is then told to write the word *map*.

For more detail on this approach, consult: Anna Gillingham and Bessie Stillman, *Remedial Training for Children with Specific Disability in Reading, Spelling, and Penmanship* (Cambridge, Massachusetts: Educators Publishing Service, 1968, page 52).

Graphs and Games

Learning-handicapped children may benefit very much from seeing their spelling progress in a concrete way such as in *graphs of progress*. *Spelling games* also may be of benefit to them in learning spelling words. Here are a few simple spelling games:

Spelling Houses. Construct three small houses from a cardboard box. Label each with a sign such as: *Maria's Playhouse, Jay's Ranch House,* and *The Gingerbread House.* Cut out large pieces of gray paper to represent stones. Print words from a spelling lesson on these stones, and place them a few feet apart leading to each house. Place the children in three groups. Have one child start at the opposite end of the room and walk to the house by stepping lightly on each stone and naming and spelling the word as he/she does so. If the child cannot recognize a word, another child continues. Keep a record of the child's progress to the house in an envelope. After all students reach their goal, substitute new stones.

Round-Robin Spelling Words. Have one child say a word he/she remembers and spell it; have the next child repeat that word and add one of his/her own; have the third child repeat both and add another, etc. Continue until one child misses a word and then begin again. Write the missed words on the chalkboard.

Find the Words. Write a long word on the chalkboard. Have the children try to make a list of as many different words as they can find in the long word.
Here is an example: *extraordinary*

extra	ordinary
din	or

Other Spelling Activities

Scrambled spelling words. You can have learning-handicapped children try to unscramble spelling words. However, before they attempt to do this, they should be familiar with the words. Otherwise, it may be very difficult for them.

Word completion. You can also have them supply missing letters in words contained in their spelling list. For example:

c _ me   but _ er   wom _ n

Color coding. You can use color coding as an aid in learning spelling words. For example, have children write spelling words using blue for consonants and red for vowels. They can use marking pens or colored pencils.

Tracing. Have the children trace spelling words that have been printed dot-to-dot. In addition, all of the tracing activities mentioned earlier in this chapter in the section on sight-word recognition can be helpful in remembering difficult spelling words.

Magnetic letters. As mentioned earlier in Reading Recovery, magnetic letters in spelling practice can be useful.

Writing spelling words with resistance. Have children roll out a large flat square of clay and then write spelling words into the clay using a stylus or pencil.

Proofreading. Scrutinizing material with spelling errors can be helpful for older learning-handicapped students.

Crossword puzzles and word searches. These activities can also be useful in helping children learn spelling words.

However, perhaps more important, is the necessity of teaching learning-handicapped children to be aware of the importance of spelling words correctly and of making the effort to do so.

ANSWERS TO "SIGHT-WORD SEARCH"

```
w   r   p   o   t   f   t   y   s   u   l   m   i   p   q
z   p   p   q   l   r   i   v   e   r   m   o   y   s   v
r   m   o   u   v   p   y   z   z   i   f   f   t   c   a
t   r   e   a   l   s   m   i   j   k   f   c   o   r   y
c   c   b   d   r   y   x   x   l   p   g   n   u   o   y
b   c   e   r   y   o   e   q   g   r   s   u   m   n   p
b   o   d   y   h   q   w   x   i   p   r   t   u   v   z
a   c   r   y   f   g   c   r   a   g   n   o   s   q   t
l   i   p   q   v   w   x   z   y   m   p   u   y   s   m
e   c   o   l   o   r   m   y   f   g   p   l   s   t   f
r   e   f   m   i   g   h   t   q   c   b   l   e   f   v
c   x   f   l   j   k   r   s   i   j   l   p   e   x   r
e   i   x   r   j   p   u   z   p   u   r   o   y   b   c
m   n   r   d   o   z   b   e   o   u   c   y   e   g   j
r   z   l   w   v   x   b   p   g   q   h   o   y   r   e
j   y   a   j   w   l   b   o   c   f   w   r   g   i   m
```

ANSWERS TO "CROSSWORD PUZZLE"

Across
1. book
7. hard
21. young
41. earth
62. left
67. ride

Down
1. boy
10. don't
27. river
39. herd
60. he

ANSWERS TO "DOUBLE CONSONANT SUBSTITUTION"

1. lend, sake
2. mouse, hen
3. kill, wind
4. bid, dig
5. sick, pat
6. cat, far
7. ramp, can
8. pain, mail
9. hand, bat
10. day, plate

11. had, mat
12. hail, ball
13. ran, tail
14. wail, sag
15. tame, cake
16. hate, ray
17. car, take
18. rank, bang
19. day, sad
20. back, take

ANSWERS TO "INITIAL CONSONANTS"

1. girl   cat, bat
   deer   horse
   bird   pig
   dog, hog   boy
   bear   goat
   lion   fox
   mouse, louse   fish
   man   cow
2. teacher   paper
   desk   toys, boys
   book, hook   gym
   pencil   rooms
   door   light
   window   table
   girls   fish, dish
   paste   bathroom
3. puppy   kitten
   bicycle   ball
   puppet   kite
   bat, cat   girl
   toy   book
   father   mother
   wagon   sister
   pet   dog

ANSWERS TO "INITIAL CONSONANTS AND VOWELS"

1. pie   4. bicycle
   apple   toy
   cookie   ball
   hamburger   game
   raisins   puppy
2. lion   5. mittens
   bear   socks
   tiger   coat
   seal   jacket
   monkey   pants
3. fork, pork
   sink
   refrigerator
   dish, fish
   pan

ANSWERS TO "DIPHTHONGS"

proud, round, flowers, mountains
Mystery word: perfume

ANSWERS TO "CONSTRUCTING COMPOUND WORDS"

1. bathroom
2. dishcloth
3. bluebird
4. housefly
5. workbook
6. newspaper
7. birdhouse
8. snowman
9. sandman
10. butterfly
11. homework
12. sailfish

ANSWERS TO "DEDUCING COMPOUND WORDS FROM CLUES"

1. scarecrow
2. buttermilk
3. ponytail
4. pineapple
5. toadstool
6. jellyfish
7. copperhead
8. housefly
9. earring
10. playroom
11. greenhorn
12. raincoat

ANSWERS TO "DETERMINING THE MEANING OF DERIVATIVES"

1. appear again
2. not comfortable
3. below the ground
4. a vehicle with three wheels
5. a track with one rail
6. a figure with four sides
7. ten years
8. before the (Civil) War
9. wait until after (later)
10. what comes out (of a vehicle such as a car or bus)
11. in the middle of summer
12. go forward
13. a message sent to a distant place
14. across the Atlantic Ocean
15. a vessel for going under the water
16. made up of many colors
17. more than human
18. less than normal weight
19. good, helpful
20. against war

ANSWERS TO "WORDS WITH GREEK OR LATIN ROOTS"

A. 1. dismiss
2. missile
3. remiss
4. missionary
5. mission

B. 1. portage
2. deport
3. portable
4. transport
5. portfolio

C. 1. prologue
2. apology
3. eulogy
4. dialogue
5. monologue

ANSWER TO "THE MYSTERY WORD"

television

ANSWERS TO "LOCATING AND CORRECTING INCORRECT WORDS IN STORY CONTEXT"

Incorrect Word	*Correct Word*
is	are
every	very

move	match
on	or
train	tell
said	been
them	their
cartons	cases
us	as
miles	years

Answers to "Semantic Analysis"

1. In this sentence, Mr. Gomez's finances are important.
2. In this sentence, the brother's friends are important.
3. In this sentence, a certain part of the mountain is important.
4. In this sentence, the color of the dress is important.
5. In this sentence, the personality of the man is important.
6. In this sentence, the woman's behavior is important.
7. In this sentence, the age of the mummy is important.
8. In this sentence, the behavior of the dog is important.
9. In this sentence, the person's behavior is important.
10. In this sentence, the girl's way of reacting is important.

Ready-to-Use Strategies and Activities for Correcting Disabilities in Comprehension and Basic Study Skills

There are a number of languages such as Spanish and Finnish that are phonetically regular. It is a very simple process to learn how to pronounce such a language effectively. In the past some educators equated such word pronunciation with reading even though there was no comprehension involved in this process.

Obviously, this type of word pronunciation cannot be called reading. It is merely word calling or "barking at the words." To be termed reading, comprehension or understanding must occur. This, of course, is much more difficult to master in a foreign language than is simple word pronunciation.

This chapter is designed to help you effectively present comprehension skills and basic study skills to your students whether they are in the primary or intermediate grades. It contains many classroom-tested teaching strategies and *ready-to-use materials* you will find time-saving and extremely effective for such teaching.

I have written an entire inservice aid devoted to the teaching of comprehension and study skills entitled *Reading Comprehension Activities Kit* (West Nyack, New York: The Center for Applied Research in Education, 1990), and I recommend consulting this resource if you want even more detail about how to teach these skills effectively. Nevertheless, this chapter should certainly give you a good start in presenting these most important aspects of reading.

What Is Reading Comprehension?

Reading comprehension is a very complex process, and is difficult to define in simple terms. Briefly, comprehension is constructing and reconstructing meaning from the printed material. It is an *interactive process* that requires the use of prior knowledge in combination with the present printed material. When this definition is used, it is important to consider the characteristics of both the reader and the printed material. In the case of the reader, his/her prior knowledge about the material, interest in reading the material, purpose for reading the material, and ability to pronounce the words found in the material should be considered. In the case of the printed material, the number of difficult words, the syntax or sentence structure in the material, the length of the sentences in the material, and the format of the material should be taken into account.

Although both prior knowledge and features of the printed material are important, in most cases the reader's prior knowledge is of the primary importance. In addition, the more prior knowledge a reader has, the less use that he/she needs to make of the printed material. This is why a specialist in a specific area (history, biochemistry, etc.) usually reads material in that area much more rapidly than a person with less prior knowledge.

Contemporary research in comprehension also focuses on *schema theory*. Schema theory attempts to explain how a person stores information or knowledge in his/her mind, how the knowledge currently possessed is used, and how new knowledge is acquired. Another recent focus of comprehension is *metacognition*, which is concerned with the child's awareness of his/her own thinking as he/she is attempting to understand the printed material. It is important for a child to learn how to monitor his/her own comprehension ability. Research has found that good readers are much better at monitoring their comprehension than are poor readers. This chapter contains some materials devoted to metacognition.

The Various Levels of Reading Comprehension

In the past, comprehension skills usually have been divided into four major categories: literal, interpretive, critical, and creative. However, today comprehension is considered by most researchers to be a *language-based process* that cannot accurately be divided into levels such as these. Instead, reading specialists posit two major categories of comprehension: vocabulary knowledge (word meaning) and the understanding of the reading material.

Some contemporary researchers in comprehension have stated that since comprehension cannot accurately be divided into subskills in research, the various levels of comprehension should not be taught to children. However, it is important to try to teach the most important elements of comprehension separately, at least sometimes, to all students, but perhaps especially to disabled readers and learning-handicapped children. For example, how can the reading teacher be certain that a child can answer interpretive ("Think and Search") questions effectively if the teacher does not make a concerted effort to ask this type of question?

Here are the various levels of comprehension and the more important subskills that comprise them.

Textually Explicit (Literal or Factual) Comprehension

- responding to "Right There" questions (found in the reading material)
- locating the directly stated main idea
- locating significant and irrelevant details
- placing a number of items in correct sequence or order
- reading and following directions

Textually Implicit (Interpretive or Inferential) Comprehension

- responding to "Think and Search" questions (the reader has to deduce the answers from reading the material)
- answering questions that call for interpretation
- drawing conclusions and generalizations
- predicting the outcome
- summarizing what is read
- sensing the author's mood and purpose
- locating the implied main idea

Critical (Textually Implicit or Evaluative) Reading

- responding to "Think and Search" questions (the reader has to evaluate the reading material)
- discriminating between real and make-believe (fact and fiction)
- evaluating the accuracy or truthfulness of the reading material
- comparing information from several printed sources
- sensing an author's biases
- recognizing propaganda techniques such as the bandwagon technique, testimonials, emotionally-loaded words, and card-stacking

Scriptally Implicit (Script Implicit, Schema Implicit, Creative, or Applied) Comprehension

- responding to questions "On My Own" (the reader has to combine prior knowledge with the printed material to arrive at new knowledge or actions)
- applying knowledge gained from reading to one's own problem-solving
- bibliotherapy (solving a problem through reading about a similar problem)
- cooking and baking activities after reading recipes
- art activities as a follow-up to reading
- creative writing of prose and poetry (including the use of invented spelling if necessary)
- construction activities as a follow-up to reading
- rhythm activities as a follow-up to reading
- creative dramatics and socio-drama
- puppetry
- scientific experiments
- creative book reports
- any reading that appeals to the emotions (affective aspect of reading)

The Basic Study Skills

The reading study skills are the strategies that enable a student to comprehend and remember content material effectively.

The reading study skills may be organized in categories such as the following:

- Selecting Information
- Organizing Information
- Locating Information
- Using Graphic Aids
- Following Directions
- Improving Reading Rate and Flexibility

The strategies and ready-to-use materials described and illustrated in the next part of this chapter will provide instruction and/or reinforcement in the majority of these important basic reading study skills. They should be presented using content (expository) material such as literature, social studies, and science.

Strategies and Ready-to-Use Materials to Improve Comprehension Skills and the Basic Study Skills

Here are numerous strategies and ready-to-duplicate activity sheets that can be used to improve comprehension and basic study skills. Many of the strategies can be adapted for use with either children reading at the primary-grade or intermediate-grade level. Although each activity sheet has been designed for a certain grade level, many of the activity sheets can also be adapted for use at various grade levels.

The Language-Experience Approach, Predictable Books, and Big Books

The language-experience approach is a very effective way to improve the comprehension ability of children at the emergent literacy level. When a child dictates a language-experience story, it is obvious that he/she uses his/her own prior knowledge and language patterns. Therefore, comprehension of the story at a later time will pose no problem. The same can be said of stories that are written by children using invented spelling. Details on how to implement the language-experience approach with disabled readers and learning-handicapped children of various ages is found in Chapter 5.

Predictable books are another excellent way to improve comprehension skills at the emergent literacy level. As stated in Chapter 5, since predictable books use patterned language, the child can quickly and effectively learn to read them. Since their content is interesting and predictable, comprehension of such books is extremely easy and enjoyable. A list of predictable books is found in Chapter 5 of this *Handbook*.

Big Books are another fine way to improve comprehension ability at the emergent literacy level. Big Books are large-sized books with predictable language patterns. They originated in New Zealand and are used extensively there. They are becoming quite common in kindergartens and first grades in North America especially when whole language is used. The teacher reads the Big Book to the children, having the children join in the reading when they can. The Big Books often are read many times. Often the Big Book can be purchased with small copies of the same book that a child can read independently later. Sometimes they also are accompanied by a tape recording of the Big Book that the child can listen to using a headset while following along in a small copy of the book. Here are two good sources for purchasing Big Books:

Rigby
P.O. Box 797
Crystal Lake, IL 60014

DLM Teaching Resources
One DLM Park
Allen, TX 75002

Wide Reading of Easy, Interesting Materials

Wide reading of relevant, interesting narrative and expository (content) materials at the independent and low instructional reading level is the *single most effective way of improving reading comprehension in both the primary and intermediate grades.* The more a student reads with the purpose of understanding what is read, the more effective his/her comprehension skills will become since reading is a skill that improves the best with motivated practice. In that respect it is like many other skills, such as playing a sport. The better athlete is often the one who participates the most in motivated practice. This also is why good readers who enjoy reading for pleasure and information usually become better readers who enjoy reading even more. Such students understand what they read and find reading to be interesting, motivating, and fulfilling. They usually read for meaning, making extensive use of context clues, making good use of their prior knowledge, and using effective fix-up strategies when needed.

Unfortunately, most disabled readers, reluctant readers, and learning-handicapped students do not find reading gratifying and, therefore, avoid reading if they can. They usually do not make use of prior knowledge, do not set purposes or make predictions before reading, do not make good use of context, and do not monitor their reading comprehension. Therefore, their comprehension skills do not improve as much as they should.

In tutoring hundreds of children, we have found it very difficult to motivate such children to do wide reading for either pleasure or information. They simply are unwilling to make the effort to read unless unique strategies are presented to them that sustain their interest or unless materials are chosen that specifically appeal to their interests and needs. Even then their reading is neither consistent nor motivated in many cases. That is why the following statement made by one of my colleagues does not always apply to such children although it is applicable with many children: "Children learn to comprehend best by simply reading." It is very important to provide students with all types of reading problems with strategies and materials that are really relevant and applicable to them.

Prediction Strategies

Prediction strategies are one of the most effective, yet simple, ways of improving reading comprehension that any teacher can easily employ. Teaching children to activate prior knowledge and use prediction strategies often requires no special materials or expense, yet it can increase their comprehension skills significantly. My teacher-trainees consistently use prediction strategies during tutoring and have found them highly successful. We have used prediction strategies with children in the primary grades, intermediate grades, and in junior high school equally effectively. However, it is important for a student to be exposed to prediction strategies on a regular basis if his/her comprehension skills are to improve significantly.

Before the child reads a story, you can motivate prediction by asking questions such as these:

- What is the title (name) of this story?
- What do you think this story might be about?
- Look at this picture on the cover of the book. What do you think the book might be about?

During the reading of a story, prediction strategies can greatly enhance a child's comprehension and can also enable him/her to be a more active comprehender. Here are examples of questions my teacher-trainees have used with the children during reading to motivate active comprehension. They often are best used with a story that has clearly delineated story divisions:

- What do you think will happen next in this story?
- What do you think (story character) will (should) do now?
- What would you like (story character) to do next in the story?

A prediction strategy may consist of approximately these parts: activation of prior knowledge, prediction, reading the material, and confirming or disconfirming the predictions.

The activation of prior knowledge is very much related to the formulation of predictions as you might imagine. As stated before, it is imperative that a child's prior knowledge be activated (used) before reading to ensure the child's maximum comprehension ability.

Either the teacher or the child can try to activate a child's prior knowledge. Of course, the child must have considerable instruction and practice before he/she can do this independently. You can activate prior knowledge by trying to relate what the child is going to read to what he/she already knows by asking such questions as these, for example, about the book *Sarah, Plain and Tall* by Patricia Maclachlan:

- Have you read any other books or stories about a child whose mother or father has died when he or she was young?
- Have you read any other book or story about a child who had a housekeeper but not a mother?
- How do you suppose a child feels when his or her father and his or her father's housekeeper are going to get married?
- Why do you think that?

You also can activate prior knowledge by using semantic mapping (webbing), computer simulations, television programs, demonstrations, experiments, guest speakers, pictures, videotapes, films, and other techniques. Such activities should help children to either support or reject the schema (prior knowledge) they currently have about the reading selection. As explained later in this chapter, you may also pose questions both to activate prior knowledge and to set purposes for a child's reading.

The Anticipation Guide

An Anticipation Guide helps children to activate their prior knowledge before reading and also uses statements instead of questions before reading as a beginning way to involve children in their reading. Statements require children only to recognize and respond, while questions require children to provide an answer. The end result of this process should be the production of the children's own statements and questions. A start can be made in this process in the primary grades and it can be refined and extended in the intermediate grades. We have used the Anticipation Guide very effectively with all types of disabled readers and learning-handicapped children, especially in the intermediate grades and in junior high school.

Here is a brief description of an Anticipation Guide, adapted from *Content Area Reading* by J.E. Readence, T.W. Bean, and R.S. Baldwin (Dubuque, Iowa: Kendall/Hunt Publishing, 1981):

1. *Identify the major concepts.* The teacher first reads the material and identifies the most important concepts.
2. *Determine children's knowledge of these concepts.* The teacher determines how the major concepts in the material support or refute the children's prior knowledge in the area.

3. *Create statements.* The teacher creates three to five statements about the material. The statements are those in which the children have enough knowledge to understand the statements, but not enough to make any of them completely known.

4. *Decide statement order and presentation style.* The order of the statements should follow the order of the statements presented in the material. The teacher writes the guide on the chalkboard, a transparency, or a ditto.

5. *Present guide.* The teacher reads the directions and statements orally or has the children read them silently depending upon their reading ability. Tell the children that they will share their thoughts and opinions and that they must defend them. The guide can be done individually or with a partner. Often it is more effective if a child works with a partner.

6. *Discuss each statement briefly.* The teacher asks for a show of hands from children to indicate their agreement or disagreement with each statement.

7. *Have children read the material.* The teacher tells the children to read the material with the purpose of deciding what the author may say about each statement.

8. *Conduct follow-up discussions.* After they have read the material, have the children again respond to the statements. The Anticipation Guide can serve as the basis for a post-reading discussion in which the children can share what they have learned and how their prior knowledge has been influenced by the reading.

A Sample Anticipation Guide

Here is an anticipation guide at about the fifth-grade reading level. You can duplicate and use it in its present form if it seems applicable for your students. More important, it can serve as a model as you construct your own Anticipation Guide from either narrative or content material at the appropriate reading level.

The answers are given at the end of the chapter.

SAMPLE ANTICIPATION GUIDE

(Approximately Fifth-Grade Level)

Name_____ Grade_____ Teacher_____ Date_____

Here are some statements about *chimpanzees*. Read each statement to yourself and put an X next to each statement that you agree with. Be sure to be able to defend your ideas later when we talk about the statements.

☐ 1. Like humans, chimpanzees can use a precision grip to hold objects between their thumb and fingers.

☐ 2. Chimpanzees can make simple tools to help them solve their problems in the wild.

☐ 3. A chimpanzee's legs are longer than their arms, similar to a human being.

☐ 4. Although chimpanzees eat mainly fruit, leaves, seeds, and flowers, they may also eat ants, honey, eggs, caterpillars, and even other small animals, but never other chimps.

☐ 5. Chimpanzees are a well-protected animal species and are expected to survive for many more years in the wild.

Now read the following story to yourself. Remember what you should look for as you read the story so we can discuss later what you learned from reading this story.

CHIMPANZEES

It seems amazing to us that chimpanzees are so much like humans. In fact, they are more nearly like humans than any other type of animal.

Chimpanzees are similar to human beings in many surprising ways. For example, they love chimpanzee babies, and every chimp in the community is excited when a new baby is born. Like human children, chimpanzees take a long time to grow up. They must learn how to get around on their own, how to find safe food to eat, how to fight, how to display (show off their strength), how to avoid danger, and how to make nests. Like humans, chimpanzees use the precision grip for holding small objects between their thumb and fingers and the power grip to hold large objects. Chimpanzees can also make simple tools to help them solve problems they meet. For example, a chimp may sometimes make a sponge from a leaf by chewing it and then dipping it into water. A chimp also may strip the leaves from a twig and then use the stripped twig to probe inside a termite mound. The termites then lock their jaws around the twig, and the chimpanzee draws the twig out and licks off the termites.

Of course, chimpanzees are different from human beings in many important ways. For example, chimps have big

© 1993 by The Center for Applied Research in Education

expandable mouths for carrying fruit and other objects. This leaves their hands free for moving in trees or holding a baby chimp. A chimpanzee's arms are longer than its legs, and they have very flexible arm joints. For example, they can hang by one hand and turn their bodies completely around. Although chimpanzees eat mostly fruit, leaves, seeds, and flowers, they sometimes also eat ants, honey, termites, caterpillars, birds, and small mammals; however, they never eat other chimps.

Chimpanzees have mainly been studied by the famous scientist, Dr. Jane Goodall. She has observed chimps in Africa for more than thirty years and has contributed a great deal of the knowledge we now have about chimpanzees. Perhaps, most important, she has learned that chimpanzees are now dying out at an alarming pace. For example, much of their habitat is being taken over by farming, logging, and mining. Then, too, hunters sell chimps for pets, to act in animal shows, and to serve as laboratory animals. Hunters may kill several adult chimps just to capture one wild infant chimp, and nine out of ten baby chimps die before they reach their destination. Do you think chimpanzees should be trained to entertain people or should be allowed to live free in the wild?

The Directed Reading Activity (DRA)

The *directed reading activity* (DRA) is the most common way of improving comprehension skills in both the primary and intermediate grades. It can be used with both narrative and content materials. It is best illustrated in the basal reader teacher's manuals when directions are given to the teacher about how to conduct the lesson. Very briefly, here are the basic steps that comprise the directed reading activity:

1. *Develop prior knowledge for reading the story.* The teacher helps the children relate the story to their own prior knowledge. The children also are encouraged to formulate their own purposes for reading the story.

2. *Presenting new vocabulary.* Especially in the primary grades, the teacher presents several of the most important new words found in the material. This vocabulary presentation should be in context and always should encourage children to apply their own word-identification strategies.

3. *Guided silent reading.* The children then read a significant portion of the material or the entire material while focusing on their purpose and predictions. The teacher encourages them to make predictions before reading and to confirm or refute their predictions.

4. *Purposeful oral reading.* The children read aloud to answer a specific question or to satisfy a particular purpose.

5. *Extending skill development.* The teacher focuses on the word-identification and comprehension skills recommended in the manual. These skills can later be reinforced independently with workbook pages, computer software, other commercial materials, or teacher-made materials.

6. *Enrichment activities.* This last step of the lesson gives ideas for follow-up activities that add to each child's understanding of the concepts and ideas presented in the story. Some suggested activities are relevant independent reading, dramatic play, creative writing of prose or poetry, art activities, or cooking and baking activities.

The Directed Reading-Thinking Activity (DR-TA)

The directed reading-thinking activity (DR-TA) was developed many years ago by Russell G. Stauffer, professor emeritus of the University of Delaware. However, it remains an excellent strategy to use both with good readers, disabled readers, and learning-handicapped students. We have used it successfully many, many times in tutoring sessions both in the primary and intermediate grades with all types of students.

DR-TA works equally well with both narrative and content material. It is so successful because it encourages active involvement with the reading material by having children formulate hypotheses about the material and later confirming or disconfirming (proper term used in whole language) them. It can be used on a group or individual basis.

Here are the steps of DR-TA:

1. Tell the children the title of the story (chapter), have them read it for themselves, or show them an illustration from the material. On the basis of this information, have them formulate predictions about the material. If an informational book is being used, help them to activate their prior knowledge. The predictions can be written by either the child or the teacher so that they can be referred to during the reading.

2. Tell the children they should read to find out if the material confirms the predictions made. Then have them silently read a portion of the material or the entire selection.

3. Have the children then discuss each of their predictions, indicating which ones were confirmed and which ones were not. The written predictions can be corrected if you wish. Help the children determine what criteria should be used in determining whether or not the predictions were confirmed.

4. If the material was not read at one time, alternate periods of silent reading and discussion until the entire material has been read. In each case, emphasize the validity of the reasoning the children are using rather than the correctness of the original predictions.

To summarize, you can see that DR-TA requires students to be active participants in their reading, encourages reading for specific purposes, and stresses higher-level comprehension.

Semantic Mapping (Semantic Webbing)

Semantic maps can be used in both the primary and intermediate grades as an aid to reading comprehension as well as a motivator for writing. Semantic maps are also called semantic webs, story maps, story webs, advance organizers, and think-links. In any case, they are graphic configurations or representations that illustrate the relationships among an event's components and the important ideas and details from a topic that may have been read. They are designed to organize schema (prior knowledge) and specialized vocabulary. They can be used with both narrative and content material. There are as many variations of a semantic map as there are researchers in the area, and you are encouraged to experiment with your own version of a semantic map.

In formulating a semantic map, it is useful to first display a completed map on the chalkboard or a transparency and tell the children how it can help them to improve their comprehension of what they read. At the primary-grade reading level, the map obviously has to be a simple one. Tell the children how the map illustrates the relationships between the main ideas and important details. Then put a partially completed semantic map on the chalkboard or a transparency after the children have read a basal reader story or a content selection.

Only after they have had considerable experience with completing semantic maps should the children be asked to construct one independently. At first, a partially completed map can be put on a ditto master for them to complete. It often is helpful for a child to work with a partner in completing a map or in constructing their own map. If this technique is not presented carefully with much preparation, a child can experience frustration and never wish to use it again. *It also is important that semantic mapping be used as a strategy fairly often instead of just once or twice if it is to be eventually used independently.*

A story map can be modified slightly when it is designed to teach *story grammar*. A story grammar or story structure can involve helping students to recognize the setting, the plot, and the resolution of a story. The more formal story map can be illustrated to include the following elements, from Robert J. Tierney, John E. Readence, and Ernest K. Dishner's *Reading Strategies and Practice: A Compendium* (Boston: Allyn and Bacon, 1985, pages 155–156):

STORY MAP

THE SETTING
    Characters
    Place
THE PROBLEM
THE GOAL
    Event 1
    Event 2
    Event 3
    Event 4
    Event 5
THE RESOLUTION
A SERIES OF QUESTIONS WHICH ARE RELATED TO THE STORY

Adapted from *Reading Comprehension: New Directions for Classroom Practice*, 2d ed. by John D. McNeil. Copyright © 1987, 1984 by Scott, Foresman and Company. Reprinted by permission of HarperCollins Publishers.

To summarize, semantic maps can be used as a pre-reading device, as a way of eliciting from students the prior knowledge that they have about a topic. Rather than writing randomly all of the concepts and vocabulary terms before reading, the teacher tries to organize them under the appropriate headings as the discussion continues. Semantic maps also can be used as guides during reading, as students add to their own personal maps while they read a selection silently. Finally, they can be used as post-reading guides for review. Also important, semantic maps can be used as a motivator for writing following reading. This use of semantic maps is well illustrated in K-W-L Plus, which is described later in this chapter.

Sample Semantic Map

The following example presents a partially completed semantic map about camels at about the fourth- or fifth-grade reading level. Several children may work together to complete it. You may duplicate this map and use it in its present form or use it as a model. There are many variations of this technique. You are encouraged to help children to develop their own versions of semantic maps.

SAMPLE STORY MAP

(Approximately Fourth- or Fifth-Grade Level)

Name_____ Grade_____ Teacher_____ Date_____

Read this story about camels to yourself. Then finish the story map found after the story. You can look back at the story if you wish.

HOW IS A CAMEL'S BODY WELL SUITED TO LIVING IN THE DESERT?

The body of a dromedary camel, a common one-humped camel, may look peculiar to you with its long curved neck, skinny legs, tiny ears, and huge feet. However, every part of the camel's strange-looking body is well suited to living in a hot, dry, and sandy desert.

For example, desert winds often blow sand into the air. To protect their eyes, camels have long eyelashes that catch the sand. However, if some sand gets into an eye, the camel has a special eyelid to get it out. Like a windshield wiper on a car, this extra eyelid moves from side to side and wipes the sand away. Since the eyelid is very thin, a camel can see through it and keep on walking through a sandstorm with its eyes closed.

A camel's head has built-in sun visors to keep the bright sunlight out of its eyes. There are broad ridges of bone above each eye that stick out far enough to shield the eyes when the sun is overhead. The ears of the camel are very small to make it harder for sand to get into them.

To keep sand from blowing into their noses, camels can shut their nostrils. When there is no sand blowing in the wind, a camel opens up its nostrils and breathes through its nose. When the wind begins to whip up the sand, the camel just closes its nose.

Long legs and long necks are great advantages for dromedaries in the desert. Camels can raise their heads more than 12 feet in the air and can often see for many miles in the desert. This makes it easier for them to find food and water. The huge feet of camels help them to walk on sand without sinking into it. A camel's foot may be as big as a large plate.

Although someone once said that a camel looks as if it was made of spare parts from five or six other animals, its peculiar-looking body enables it to survive in places where few other animals could live.

© 1993 by The Center for Applied Research in Education

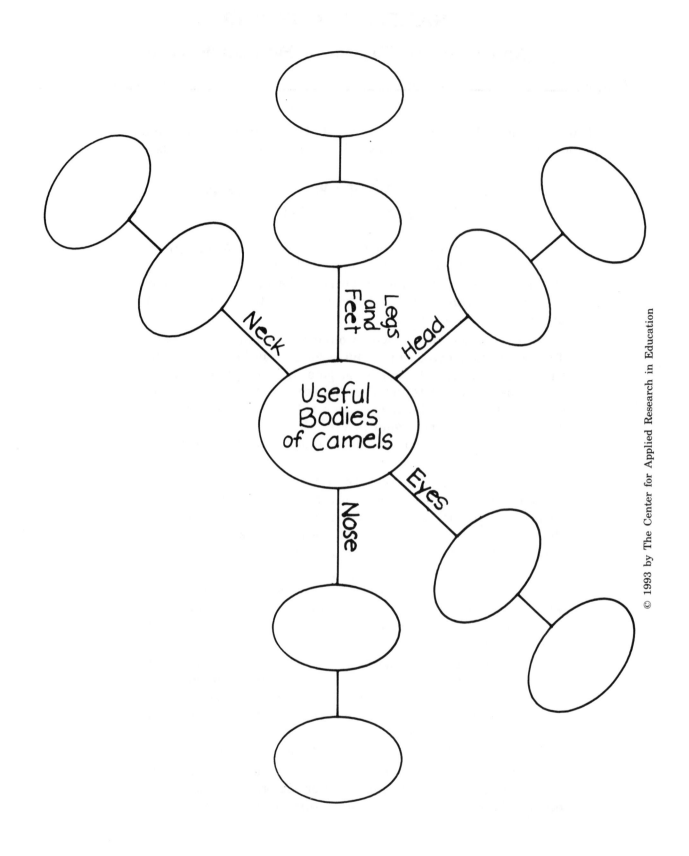

Useful
Bodies
of Camels

Neck

Legs
and
Feet

Head

Eyes

Nose

Story Impressions

Story impressions is a strategy for improving comprehension ability that can be used before, during, and after reading text. It is designed to develop children's understanding of story knowledge (story schema) and help children set a purpose for reading the material. This instructional strategy integrates both prior knowledge and purpose setting. In story impressions, significant story clues derived from the important points of setting, character, and plot are chosen to guide children's thinking about a particular selection. Based on these clues, the children compose a hypothetical story summary before they begin to read the story.

To briefly illustrate this strategy, I have chosen the book *Chrysanthemum* by Kevin Henkes (New York: Greenwillow Books, 1991). It describes a mouse named Chrysanthemum who loves her name until she goes to school where the other children tease her for being named after a flower. She is very unhappy until the music teacher, Mrs. Delphinium Twinkle, tells the class what a lovely name Chrysanthemum is and that she is going to name her baby Chrysanthemum when it is born.

If story impressions were going to be used before a group of children or one child reading on about the second- or third-grade level, you could write the following clues on the chalkboard to help the children formulate a predictive summary of the book. Using these story clues in the order they are presented, have the children predict the story plot by composing a *hypothetical summary*. This summary can be written by the children or dictated to you. After the children complete the summary, they read the text and compare their plot predictions to that of the author.

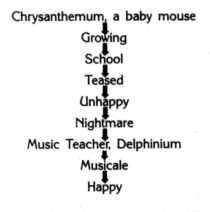

Chrysanthemum, a baby mouse
↓
Growing
↓
School
↓
Teased
↓
Unhappy
↓
Nightmare
↓
Music Teacher, Delphinium
↓
Musicale
↓
Happy

As the children read the story, they compare their Predictive Summary with the actual story and revise it as they read. They write a correct statement on the Story Summary side of the activity sheet (see the Story Impressions Activity Sheet). It is helpful if each predictive summary statement is numbered as it is given so that the same number can be given to any statement that needs to be corrected. After the children have finished reading the story, they will have reconstructed that predictive summary so that it conforms to the actual story.

The focus of post-reading instruction should be on developing questions that stimulate critical and creative thinking about the story theme. During the discussion, encourage children to share their views and ideas and to discuss. Your role is to be a moderator who facilitates discussion and promotes participation by all of the group members.

Sample Story Impressions Sheet

Here is a blank story impressions activity sheet that can be completed for any story. You can duplicate as many of these sheets as you need for your children.

STORY IMPRESSIONS ACTIVITY SHEET

Name_____ Grade_____ Teacher_____ Date_____

Predictive Summary	*Story Summary*

K-W-L

K-W-L is an acronym for *What Do I Know—What Do I Want to Know—What Have I Learned?* Developed by Donna Ogle, a Professor at National-Louis University in Evanston, Illinois, K-W-L stresses a child's prior knowledge, encourages him/her to develop questions to read to answer, and directs him/her to look for answers to their questions. This strategy is very effective in helping children comprehend content material because it helps them use their prior knowledge the entire time they are reading. My teacher-trainees have used K-W-L successfully with junior high school students in helping them comprehend both their social studies and science texts.

To begin K-W-L with "What Do I Know?" identify the most important concept in the text and ask children to tell what they know about this concept. As the children provide the information, ask questions so that they can link their knowledge to that of the author. At this point your role should be to focus and guide children's thinking so that they better understand what they already know. As children identify the information they already know, have them write it on the K-W-L Worksheet (see the sample sheet) under the column labeled "What I Know."

In the second step "What Do I Want to Know?" provide motivation by focusing on what the children want to learn. Encourage them to formulate their own questions about the topic they are studying and give them time to write their questions under the column labeled "What I Want to Find Out." Once the children have written their questions, have them read the material looking for answers.

In the last part of K-W-L, have the children report what they have learned from reading the material. Have the children write down what they have learned in the column of the worksheet "What I Have Learned." Have them do this without referring to the text. However, if there is disagreement, have the children reread the passage to check their statements for accuracy.

Note: If a child cannot write his/her own questions and responses on the K-W-L Worksheet, you may have the child dictate them to you. In addition, a child can work with a partner on the worksheet if you wish.

K-W-L Plus

Ellen Carr and Donna Ogle have added a writing component to K-W-L that we also have found effective. It is called *K-W-L Plus.* (See their article "A Strategy for Comprehension and Summarization" in *Journal of Reading*, 30, April 1987, pages 626–631.) K-W-L Plus helps children to organize information they have learned from using the K-W-L sheet to write a summary or a report. When children have finished reporting what they learned and the "L" section of the worksheet is finished, the children organize their learning by using a mapping or webbing technique. (See the description presented earlier in this chapter.) The material in the "L" section of the worksheet can help children identify appropriate categories and the specific information learned can be attached to the appropriate categories. The webbing technique used in K-W-L Plus can replace the traditional outline that is commonly used in writing a report. Children can often construct a semantic map (web) more easily than a traditional outline, and we have found it very effective in helping them write a summary or a report.

Sample K-W-L Worksheet

Here is a blank sample K-W-L Worksheet you can duplicate and use with your students. It probably is more effective in the intermediate grades and above, although it undoubtedly could be used as early as third grade. It should be used with content (expository) material.

K-W-L WORKSHEET

Name_____ Grade_____ Teacher_____ Date_____

K	W	L
What I Know	What I Want to Find Out	What I Have Learned

QARs (Questioning Strategies)

Effective questioning is undoubtedly the single most effective and simple way of improving a child's comprehension if used wisely. (Since *questioning strategies* were explained and illustrated in detail in Chapter 4, they are mentioned only briefly in this chapter. You should consult Chapter 4 if you need more detail about them.)

As stated earlier, *pre-questioning* can help the child set purposes for reading and make predictions about the content. Often a child will comprehend most effectively if the pre-questioning involves extensive use of student-formulated questions of various kinds that he/she will then read to answer.

Effective questioning *during reading* also can greatly add to the child's comprehension of the material. Questioning during reading can mainly involve predictions of what is going to happen later during the reading. However, it also can consist of the child's responding to questions at various levels, with the focus being upon the higher-type questions.

Obviously, questioning *after reading* has been the most common for many years. After reading, it is important for you to ask as many implicit comprehension questions as possible, with less emphasis on explicit questions. It also is important to ask mainly important or relevant questions after reading.

As explained in Chapter 4, it is important to refrain from asking *diversionary questions* after children have read material. A diversionary question may detract from the comprehension of the story by encouraging the child to go off on a tangent while relating his/her own personal experiences that may not be relevant at that time.

QARs are an excellent strategy for you to use in thinking about how to ask comprehension questions. This is really a way of looking at comprehension questions to determine what type they are. As explained earlier in this chapter, comprehension questions can be categorized in the following way:

- "Right There"—textually explicit questions in which the answer is found directly in the material. This is also called *reading the lines*.
- "Think and Search"—textually implicit questions in which the child must interpret the material to locate the answer. This is also called *reading between the lines*.
- "On My Own"—textually implicit questions in which the child must interact with the material by combining his/her prior knowledge with the printed material. This is also called *reading beyond the lines*.

The Concept Question Chain

The *Concept Question Chain* is a set of questions used for discussing narrative or expository text that is based on R. M. Gagne's premise that details are linked together to form concepts and concepts to form generalizations. (See his book *The Conditions of Knowledge*, New York: Holt, Rinehart and Winston, 1970.) The Concept Question Chain consists of three levels of questions that can easily be related to QAR: literal, interpretive, and applied. We have used the Concept Question Chain effectively with students in the intermediate grades and junior high school.

To develop a Concept Question Chain, read a text selection and identify one theme or concept that students can very easily develop from it. Use the theme or text-based concept as a framework for writing literal, interpretive, and applied questions. You should begin by formulating the questions for the *interpretive level*, since this level provides direction for developing the literal and applied questions. Literal questions should follow from the interpretive questions. They should be designed to locate the essential facts or details children should remember from the material and should not dwell on unimportant information. The applied questions should encourage children to apply the theme or concept beyond the text selection and to create and expand the concept that was learned from the material.

In using the Concept Question Chain to stimulate discussion after the children have read the material, the literal questions should be asked first, followed by the interpretive and applied questions.

It may be helpful to examine a Concept Question Chain constructed from the book *Mirandy and Brother Wind* by Patricia C. McKissack and illustrated by Jerry Pinkney (New York: Alfred A. Knopf, 1988). This is the delightful story about Mirandy, an African-American girl who lived near the beginning of the twentieth century, and her desire to win the junior cakewalk. The cakewalk was first introduced in America by slaves and was performed by couples who strutted and pranced around a large square keeping time with fiddle and banjo music. As the dancers paraded by, older people judged them on appearance, grace, precision, and originality of dance steps. The winning couple won a beautifully decorated cake. The book describes how Mirandy tried to capture Brother Wind as it was said that anyone who captured the wind could get it to do his or her bidding. In the end Mirandy won the cakewalk with Ezel, a normally clumsy boy who became very graceful when he had the chance to dance with Mirandy, a girl whom he apparently liked very much.

Concept. If a person wishes and tries hard enough to make something good happen, it might really happen.

Literal Questions:

1. What season (time) of the year was it when Brother Wind came back?
2. What did Mirandy put on Brother Wind's footprints to try to catch him?
3. Who did Mirandy get the quilt from to try to catch Brother Wind?
4. Who had stuffed the cracks in the barn so that Brother Wind couldn't get out?
5. Who won the cake at the junior cakewalk?

Interpretive Questions:

1. Why do you think some people in the past believed that anyone who catches the wind could do whatever they wanted to do?
2. Why do you think Grandmama Bealey told Mirandy that nobody could ever catch Brother Wind?
3. Why was Brother Wind able to escape from the quilt that Mirandy threw over him?
4. Why did Mirandy think she had been able to capture Brother Wind in the barn?
5. Why do you think clumsy Ezel was able to dance so well in the junior cakewalk?

Applied Questions:

1. When a child wishes he or she could get something that he or she really wants—like a bicycle—how could the child make that dream come true?
2. What kinds of things could you do to win the cake in a real cakewalk?
3. Would you like to dance in a cakewalk? Why or why not?

Reciprocal Questioning (ReQuest Procedure)

Since reciprocal questioning was mentioned in Chapter 4, it will be described only briefly in this chapter. *Reciprocal questioning (the ReQuest Procedure)* is an extremely successful strategy in helping children become active questioners at the higher levels of comprehension. The original ReQuest Procedure was developed by Anthony Manzo (see his article "The ReQuest Procedure" in *Journal of Reading*, November 1969, pages 123–126), and since then has been used and revised by many different reading specialists. Briefly, here are the steps in this procedure:

1. The teacher first tells the children to ask the type of questions about each sentence in a selection that they think the teacher might ask.
2. The teacher then answers each question as fairly and fully as possible and tells the children that they subsequently must do the same.
3. Then the teacher and the children both silently read the first sentence.
4. The teacher closes the book, and a child asks questions about that sentence that the teacher is to answer.
5. Next, the child closes the book and the teacher asks questions about the material. The teacher should provide an excellent model for the child's questions. The questions should be mainly of the higher type such as textually implicit (interpretive and critical) and scriptally implicit (creative or applied) questions.
6. After a number of additional sentences, the procedure can be modified to use an entire paragraph instead of individual sentences. Questioning should continue until the child can answer the question: "What do you think will happen next in this selection?"

The ReQuest Procedure is also sometimes called *reciprocal questioning* and is very valuable because it clearly shows children how to formulate and answer implicit comprehension questions instead of just explicit questions. We used reciprocal questioning in tutoring a fourth-grade boy named Matt several years ago. Matt's main reading problem was interpretive comprehension. Although we had tutored him during the fall semester using mainly activity sheets to improve his interpretive comprehension, we had been largely unsuccessful because he just marked any answer that he saw and did not even bother to read the material. The following semester I suggested reciprocal questioning as the major strategy to improve Matt's interpretive comprehension skills, and it proved highly successful. Matt truly enjoyed reading the material so carefully that he could ask his tutor questions about it that she truly could not answer! He found "tricking her" to be highly motivating, and she really could not answer all of the detailed questions he asked her, especially of somewhat longer selections. Therefore, reciprocal questioning can be very helpful in improving higher-level comprehension skills.

Self-Monitoring (Metacognition) of the Reading Material

As has been stated before in this *Handbook* it is very important that children monitor or evaluate their own comprehension ability. They should be aware of when they are not understanding what they are reading. Good readers normally are competent at self-monitoring, while poor readers usually are not. Students also should be able to locate the sources of their comprehension difficulty when they do not understand what they are reading. In addition, they should know how to correct the comprehension difficulties they are experiencing by applying the appropriate fix-up strategies.

One technique that can be used to demonstrate competency in metacognition is a self-monitoring checklist of reading comprehension. This may help a child become aware of his/her reading strategies and fix-up strategies.

Self-Monitoring Checklist of Reading Comprehension

Here is a self-monitoring checklist of reading comprehension. You can duplicate and use it in its present form or modify it in any way you wish. You also can use it as a model for constructing your own checklist of this type.

SELF-MONITORING CHECKLIST
OF READING COMPREHENSION SKILLS

(Upper primary-grade or intermediate-grade level)

Name_____ Grade_____ Teacher_____ Date_____

	Yes	No
1. Do I already know something about what this material is going to be about?	☐	☐
2. Do I need to ask myself some questions about what the material might be about even before I begin to read it?	☐	☐
3. Do I need to predict what the material will be about even before I begin to read it?	☐	☐
4. Do I understand why I am going to read this material?	☐	☐
5. Do I know how fast I should read this material?	☐	☐
6. Do I need to read every word of this material carefully?	☐	☐
7. Do I need to read all of the material more than once to understand it?	☐	☐
8. Do I need to read the first sentence of each paragraph more than once?	☐	☐
9. Do I know what I should do if I meet a word in the material that I do not understand?	☐	☐
10. Do I usually look up the meaning of unknown words in the dictionary as I am reading?	☐	☐
11. Can I answer most of my teacher's questions after I have finished reading the material?	☐	☐
12. Am I able to remember what I have read well enough to retell it after I have finished reading?	☐	☐
13. Am I able to remember what I have read well enough to answer most of the questions on a test about the material?	☐	☐
14. Can I decide what information in the material is important and what information is not important?	☐	☐
15. Can I state the main idea of the material after I have finished reading it?	☐	☐

Visual Imagery

Visual imagery, also called *mental imagery*, has been taught in schools as a way of appreciating literature, though not usually taught as a strategy for improving comprehension. However, it can be very effective for this latter purpose if the reading material lends itself to making images of what is read. Nonetheless, many children do not use this technique unless they have instruction and practice in doing so.

Although the use of visual imagery can be extended in the intermediate grades, it usually begins in the primary grades. As an example, G. M. Pressley taught eight-year-old children to construct mental images for the sentences and paragraphs they read. When he compared these children with a control group whose members just read the story, the imagery group remembered more of the story's events. (See Pressley's article "Mental Imagery Helps Eight-Year-Olds Remember What They Read" in *Journal of Educational Psychology*, 68, January 1976, pages 355–359.)

John D. McNeil described in his book *Reading Comprehension: New Directions for Classroom Practice* (Glenview, Illinois: Scott, Foresman and Company, 1984) one interesting procedure for helping children find out what is important in reading material and to change this material into mental images. This procedure is called *Mind's Eye* and consists of the following elements:

1. *Key Words*—Children should be taught to recognize important words in sentences and passages. Have children first underline *key words*, then form mental images only from these key words. Later have children pick out key words on their own and immediately create mental images for them.

2. *Discussion of Images*—After silent reading of key words, ask children questions that help them make clear mental images such as: What kind of pictures do you see about these words? This discussion can also focus on prediction: What do you think might happen next?

3. *Oral Reading*. After discussing their mental images, have children read orally to verify that their images reflect the material.

If you want to evaluate the potential value of mental imagery in improving the comprehension skills of your students, first discuss its usefulness and model how it can be helpful to your students. You may want to use an adaptation of the following strategy that is loosely based on one described by John D. McNeil:

1. Choose reading material that is unfamiliar to the students and is very good for stimulating visual imagery.

2. Divide the large group into two random groups.

3. Read the entire passage to both groups. Ask the members of one group to draw several pictures that depict what is described in the passage. Ask the members of the other group to draw several pictures of anything that interests them.

4. A few days later ask the children in both groups to write a short summary of what was found in the passage.

5. Evaluate the summaries in terms of main ideas and significant details.

6. Determine whether the group that formulated mental images seemed to remember more of the passage than the group that did not.

According to McNeil, this strategy undoubtedly can be started at about the third-grade reading level and may be effective from that level on.

Sample Activity Sheet for Using Visual Imagery
as an Aid to Reading Comprehension

Here is a sample activity sheet on using visual imagery to help improve comprehension skills at about the fourth-grade reading level. You should use it only after the child has had some instruction and modeling in the use of visual imagery. You can duplicate and use this activity sheet in its present form. You can also use it as a model for your own activity sheet.

USING VISUAL IMAGERY AS AN AID TO READING COMPREHENSION

(Approximately Fourth-Grade Reading Level)

Name_____ Grade_____ Teacher_____ Date_____

Read this short passage about <u>pileated woodpeckers</u> to yourself. Then follow the directions to complete the rest of the activity sheet.

PILEATED WOODPECKERS

Pileated (PY-lee-ayt-ehd) woodpeckers are large, fascinating birds that can be seen in many forests in North America. They are unusual birds in many ways.

Pileated woodpeckers have a black body, red crest on the top of their head, white throat and neck stripes, a black bill, and white patches on the underwings. They are sixteen to nineteen inches long and have a wing span of twenty-seven to thirty inches. These woodpeckers weigh from ten to sixteen ounces. To see a pileated woodpecker hanging on the side of a tree is a strange sight indeed.

Pileated woodpeckers are very well suited to life on the side of a tree trunk. These birds have short, strong legs and four strong toes on each foot. Their feet have two toes pointed forward and two toes pointed backward. Each toe ends in a long, sharp, curved claw that tightly grips the bark of a tree.

Chips fly as the big red-crested woodpecker hammers into the side of a tree. A long strong neck moves the bird's head back and forth rapidly as it digs a hole in a tree. A thick skull and muscles pad the bird's brain, eyes, and ears so that they are not injured by the heavy pounding. The bird may use its heavy bill to chisel out a hole in the side of a tree to make shelter and a place to raise its young. The pileated woodpecker also must do the hammering to satisfy its huge appetite for carpenter ants and beetle grubs that it finds under the bark of trees. It also eats nuts, wild berries, and other fruits. One male pileated woodpecker was found to have 469 carpenter ants in its stomach!

As with most birds, the pileated woodpecker has hollow bones, like pieces of dried macaroni, to keep its body light for flight. Because they are large birds, pileated woodpeckers have to be strong fliers. Their wings stroke like oars through the air: flap, flap, flap. They stroke a few times, fold their

© 1993 by The Center for Applied Research in Education

wings next to their bodies, and glide "downhill" through the air. As the bird travels above the treetops looking like it is riding an invisible roller coaster, it may shriek a loud cackle.

In mid-February, a pair of pileated woodpeckers make a nest in which the female will lay her eggs. A cavity is hollowed out in a tree, and a few wood chips form a cushion on the bottom. The female bird lays four white glossy eggs. After eighteen days each baby woodpecker pecks at the shell and finally out pokes a bald, pink head with two bulging lumps, one on each side, that will become two eyes. Next come two stubby limbs—the baby's wings. The squirming, naked baby has bright pink, wrinkled skin covered with small bumps. By November, each youngster goes its own way and makes its own first roost hole for winter.

Name⎯⎯⎯⎯⎯⎯⎯⎯⎯⎯

Now think about the story you have just read about pileated wood-peckers. Make several pictures in your mind about the story and then draw one of the pictures here.

The Herringbone Technique

The *Herringbone Technique* can be used effectively to improve instruction in both narrative and content (expository) material. We have used it successfully for both kinds of materials with students in the upper primary grades and the intermediate grades. A herringbone diagram can be used with either the fish outline or in its traditional form. In any case, the main idea of the material is written on the center horizontal line, while the diagonal lines contain the answers to the following questions: *Who, what, where why, when,* and *how.*

Show a herringbone form on a transparency and demonstrate its use to the students. They should not be asked to use this strategy until it has been explained and demonstrated to them. They also need some directed practice with it before they are asked to complete it independently. Even then it may be advisable for them to work with a partner in completing the form. Depending upon the material, they can complete a herringbone form as they are reading or after they have finished reading. It may work better to have them complete the form as they are reading content material and either during or after they have read narrative material.

To illustrate the herringbone diagram resembling a fish skeleton, I have chosen the book *Wheels* by Shirley Hughes (New York: Lothrop, Lee & Shepard Books, 1991). Very briefly, this book (which is intended for the upper primary grades) describes Carlos, a boy living on Trotter Street who very much wants a new bicycle for his birthday. Carlos feels especially bad when his best friend Billy receives a shiny new bicycle for his birthday. On the day of his birthday Carlos receives some presents and a beautiful birthday cake from his mother—but not the new bicycle that he wants so much since she simply cannot afford to buy him one. However, Carlos is thrilled when he receives a homemade go-cart from his older brother, Marcos. Carlos and Billy win the Non-Bicycle Race on Trotter Street with Carlos's new go-cart.

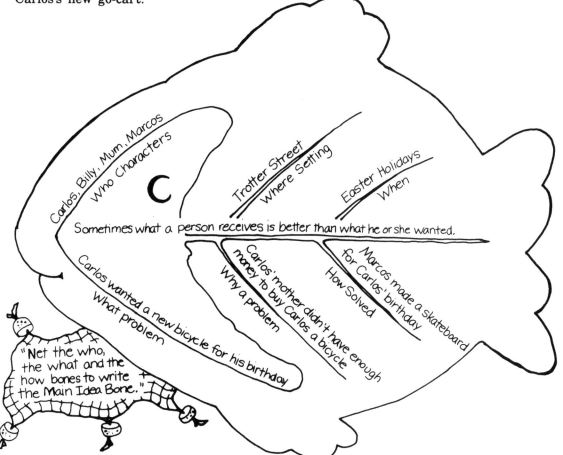

Sample Herringbone Diagram

Here is a sample herringbone diagram you can duplicate and use. You may want to modify it somewhat depending upon whether you are using it for narrative or content material. The diagram for *Wheels* may be more applicable to narrative material, while this diagram may be more applicable to content (expository) material.

SAMPLE HERRINGBONE DIAGRAM
(Approximately Third-Grade Through Twelfth-Grade Level)

Name_____ Grade_____ Teacher_____ Date_____

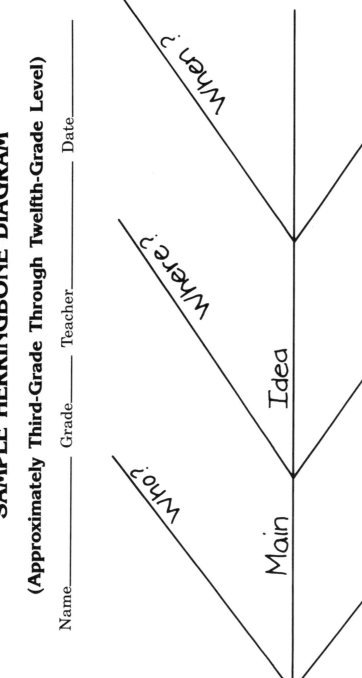

Retelling Technique

The *retelling* technique, mentioned briefly in Chapter 2, can be very helpful in improving comprehension ability. This strategy is sometimes called the *tell-back strategy* and is certainly not new. It was first used around 1920 as the major way of assessing comprehension ability on the first standardized reading tests. It was phased out after a time due to the difficulty of accurately evaluating students' responses. Such tests then used the multiple-choice format to assess comprehension ability because of the ease of evaluating that type of items. However, retelling is being used again more frequently. For example, it is used in many whole-language programs, since it is an example of process comprehension.

We have used this valuable, but simple, technique successfully many times in tutoring children at all levels from primary through junior high school. We have the child read a passage on the instructional or independent reading level and ask:

- What was this story (chapter) about?
- Can you tell me all that you remember about this story (chapter)?
- What do you remember about the story (chapter) you just read?

Text Lookbacks

Text lookbacks are another obvious but useful strategy for improving reading comprehension that can be started in the primary grades and extended to the middle and upper grades. Children with comprehension difficulties often are just not aware of the value of using lookbacks to improve reading comprehension.

To use this technique, have the child look back in the text and reread that part of it in which the answer to the question being posed is found. A number of poor comprehenders are unaware that this is an acceptable and useful process. The strategy should first be explained and modeled for a child. We have used it effectively with poor comprehenders in tutoring who simply were unaware of it, although it seems as though it should be self-evident.

Punctuation Marks

Children in the upper primary and lower intermediate grades are sometimes unaware of the different punctuation marks. In tutoring we have found that disregard of punctuation often, but not always, results in comprehension difficulties. Some disabled readers are word-by-word readers who do not pause at periods, commas, or question marks.

My teacher-trainees have stressed punctuation marks in several different ways in tutoring. One tutor made each important punctuation mark (period, comma, question mark, and exclamation point) into a "person" and put it on a card. The tutor and child first discussed each punctuation mark, and then the tutor held up the appropriate card as the child read orally. Other tutors have colored the punctuation marks on a printed page in different colors, such as red and yellow. Still other tutors have used the taped oral reading of children to help them notice their lack of attention to punctuation marks as they followed along in a copy of the printed material. Still others have provided simple sentences in which the child must put the correct punctuation marks. Awareness of punctuation usually greatly improves comprehension ability, and this awareness can be started at the primary grades and continue into the intermediate grades.

Explicit Teaching of the Implicit (Interpretive) Comprehension Skill of Discriminating Between Fact and Opinion

Explicit teaching is a strategy that can be applied to the teaching of many different elements of comprehension. I have chosen to briefly illustrate how it can be applied to teaching discrimination between fact and opinion and have included a sample activity sheet in the next section.

Introduction of Skill or Strategy. The teacher can discuss with the children newspaper advertisements that may contain biased statements. The teacher asks the children how such statements can be evaluated. The teacher asks a question such as the following to activate the children's prior knowledge: "Tell me what you know about fact and opinion. How are they alike and how are they different?" Write these possible answers on the chalkboard:

- A fact is always true.
- You can show that a fact is true.
- An opinion can be true, but it isn't always.
- Some people have opinions that are not true.
- A fact may be better than an opinion.

Labeling, Defining, Modeling, and Explaining the Skill or Strategy. The teacher then asks something like this: "Can any of you give us a statement of fact?" Write provided examples such as these on the chalkboard:

- Madison is the capital of the state of Wisconsin.
- Water freezes below a temperature of about 32°F. or 0°C.
- Automobiles have four wheels.
- A person must have a beating heart in order to live.
- My dog has two ears.

The teacher then can say something like this: "How can you tell whether all of the statements you made are statements of fact or not?" Write the following possible answers on the chalkboard:

- You can read about it in a book.
- You can ask someone who knows all about it to tell you.
- You can look it up in an encyclopedia.

In any case, it is important that children understand that some proof is required for the statement to be evaluated as true.

The teacher then can have the children give some examples of statements of opinion, such as these, which are written on the chalkboard:

- My dog is the nicest dog that has ever lived.
- This is the best school in Springfield.
- My house is prettier than your house.
- A cat is a better pet for a child than a dog.

The teacher then attempts to help the children arrive at the generalization that statements of opinion cannot be proven to be true. At this point, give the children some key words for both statements of fact and statements of opinion. Here are some key words for statements of fact: *age, location, dates, temperature,* and *actual physical characteristics.* Here are some key words for statements of opinion: *beauty, happiness, sadness, niceness, prettiness, goodness, meanness,* and *nastiness.*

Guided Practice of the Skill or Strategy. The teacher next says: "If I read that Chicago is the capital of Illinois, ask yourself if that is a statement of fact or a statement of opinion. Is it a statement of fact?" Possible answer:

- It's not a statement of fact because I know that it's not true.

The teacher responds: "How do you know that it's not a statement of fact?" Possible answer:

- I looked on a map/in an atlas/in a social studies book.

Next the teacher can say: "You can prove that the statement is wrong. Since we decided that statements of fact contain things that can be proven, even if it is proven wrong, it is still a statement of fact. For example, the following statements of fact are still false:

- New Year's Day always comes on a Monday.
- The President of the United States lives in the state of Washington.
- In winter it is warmer in New York City than it is in Miami."

The teacher then provides a review such as this: "Statements of fact can be proven. They can be proven either true or false. However, statements of opinion by definition cannot be proven."

*Activity Sheet for the Explicit Teaching
of Reading Comprehension Skill of Determining Fact and Opinion*

Here is an activity sheet at about the third-grade reading level to help children determine statements of fact and opinion. This activity sheet should only be used with a child after he/she has had some of the previously illustrated instruction. The activity sheet can be done with a partner. You can duplicate this activity sheet and use it in its present form or you can use it as a model for your own activity sheet.

The answers are given at the end of this chapter.

ACTIVITY SHEET FOR THE EXPLICIT TEACHING OF THE READING COMPREHENSION SKILL OF DETERMINING FACT AND OPINION

(Approximately Third-Grade Reading Level)

Name_____ Grade_____ Teacher_____ Date_____

Read each of these sentences. Some sentences are <u>statements of true facts</u>, some sentences are <u>statements of false facts</u>, and some sentences are <u>statements of opinion</u>. In the box before each sentence, write the letters TF if it is a statement of a true fact, write the letters FF if it is a statement of a false fact, or write the letter O if it is a statement of opinion. Then try to write a place or person that you could use to check your answer such as a science textbook, a library book about rattlesnakes, a magazine, an encyclopedia, or your teacher.

RATTLESNAKES

1. A rattlesnake probably is the meanest living creature in the world.

_____

2. Rattlesnakes get their name from the rattles on their tails.

_____

3. The body of a rattlesnake is long and rather narrow.

_____

4. Rattlesnakes have sharp teeth so that they can chew up their food.

_____

5. All rattlesnakes in the world should be killed since they are so dangerous.

_____

6. Rattlesnakes have very long and narrow stomachs.

_____

☐   7. Rattlesnakes only grow in size until they are about one year old.

_____

_____

☐   8. Rattlesnakes cannot swim at all.

_____

_____

☐   9. A person should try to kill any rattlesnake that he or she sees.

_____

_____

☐ 10. A rattlesnake can swallow a large mouse whole.

_____

_____

☐ 11. A person should wear high leather boots when walking in rattlesnake country.

_____

_____

☐ 12. Rattlesnake poison is called venom.

_____

_____

☐ 13. Rattlesnakes are the most beautiful snakes in the world.

_____

_____

☐ 14. Rattlesnakes have only one layer of skin.

_____

_____

☐ 15. A rattlesnake's tail is longer than its whole body.

_____

_____

The Cloze Procedure

As mentioned a number of times before in this *Handbook*, the variations of the cloze procedure can be used to assess comprehension ability, improve comprehension ability, and improve semantic analysis. If you want a complete description of the cloze procedure and a number of ready-to-duplicate versions of this technique, you should refer to both Chapters 2 and 4 of this *Handbook*.

The Maze Technique

The *maze technique* also has been described and illustrated in Chapter 4 of this *Handbook*. Therefore, it is just briefly mentioned here.

The maze technique is valuable both for assessing comprehension ability and for improving it. Most of the children whom we have tutored have enjoyed completing a maze technique and have been very successful with it. It probably would be more effective with learning-handicapped children than the cloze procedure, especially traditional cloze. Chapter 4 also contains a ready-to-duplicate example of the maze technique that you are encouraged to use if you find it applicable to your students.

Fix-Up Strategies

Many children, especially disabled readers and learning-handicapped children, do not know what to do when they cannot understand written material. They lack what are called *fix-up strategies*. There are several fix-up strategies in which children should receive instruction and reinforcement.

Sound-and-Sense Strategy

The *sound-and-sense strategy* is a fix-up strategy designed to help children know what to do when they cannot identify a word. This strategy can be a beginning step in helping young children identify unknown words and self-monitor their reading. It consists of three steps, as described in the *Houghton Mifflin Reading Series* (Boston: Houghton Mifflin, 1981):

1. Skip the unknown word and read to the end of the sentence.
2. Return to the unknown word and associate appropriate sounds for the initial and final letters of the word.
3. Return to the beginning of the sentence and reread, attempting to identify the word.

We have used the sound-and-sense strategy many times in tutoring and have found it very effective.

Rereading

Rereading is another fix-up strategy which can be very helpful. When a child rereads material, the subsequent readings should have a definite purpose—for example, to clarify a difficult but important idea. Children also should be taught to reread a particular section of text when they cannot answer a question. However, rereading is not an effective fix-up strategy if it is done without meaning or purpose.

Visual Imagery

Visual imagery is a third fix-up strategy that can improve comprehension ability. As explained and illustrated earlier in this chapter, visual imagery can be very effective in improving comprehension skills, whether the images are subsequently drawn on paper or just remain images.

Suspending Judgment

Another fix-up strategy is *suspending judgment*. Sometimes a new term is introduced in material and a clear definition is not developed within the sentence. When this occurs, the child should be encouraged to read ahead when he/she is unsure about a word meaning, a story event, or a concept. As the child reads ahead, he/she should be looking for information to develop clarity.

Asking for Help

Probably the most obvious fix-up strategy is simply *asking for help*. The help can be given by the teacher, a teacher aid, or another child. However, this strategy should not be used so extensively that it becomes a crutch that hinders the child's independence.

Survey Q3R

Survey Q3R is a study strategy that can also help comprehension both of narrative and content (expository) material. It must be modified somewhat depending on whether it is used in literature, social studies, science, or arithmetic. Survey Q3R can be presented and used at the middle-upper school levels to help in the comprehension and retention of content material. If such a study strategy is learned in the middle school, students will often apply at least the Survey part of it in secondary school and college.

Survey Q3R consists of the following steps: Survey, Question, Read, Recite, and Review. Survey Q3R was developed by Francis P. Robinson during Word War II to help military personnel in the comprehension and retention of the material they had to read. It is based on the *information-processing theory of learning*. Each part of Survey Q3R is designed to help the processing of incoming print so that the child can deal with it effectively. (See Robinson's book *Effective Study*, New York: Harper and Row, 1961.)

Although Survey Q3R must be varied somewhat to be used in the different content areas, it contains the following steps:

Survey or Preview. Have the student survey the whole textbook chapter to gain an overall impression of its content. In this survey or preview, have the student read the introduction and summary of the chapter and the first sentence in each of the paragraphs. He/she also may look at the pictures, maps, graphs, tables, diagrams, and other aids contained in the chapter. If a student would do only the survey aspect of Survey Q3R, his/her reading comprehension would improve greatly. Normally, this is the only step that a student will do later on his/her own. Only the survey aspect can be very helpful alone.

Question. Have the student pose questions that he/she wants to read to answer in this step of the study strategy. Each subheading can be turned into a question and additional questions can be formulated to read to answer. This step helps a student set purposes for reading and makes the reading more active and meaningful.

Read. Have the student read the entire chapter on a selective basis to try to answer the questions that have been posed. In this selective reading, he/she tries to fill in the gaps in the reading by capitalizing on prior knowledge.

Recite. This step applies to only one section of the material at a time. After the student has read a section purposefully, he/she can recite the important information in either an oral or written form depending on which is more efficient.

Review. This step is taken after the student has read the entire chapter. He/she tries to review the important concepts, generalizations, and facts gained from the chapter. He/she may use the written notes that were made in the fourth step (Recite).

The following are variations of the Survey Q3R technique:

- Survey Q4R—Survey, Read, Recite, Record, and Review
- PQRST—Preview, Question, Read, State, and Test
- PQ5R—Preview, Question, Read, Record, Recite, Review, and Reflect
- OARWET—Overview, Achieve, Read, Write, Evaluate, and Test
- Triple S Technique—Scan, Search, and Summarize

If you want detailed information on how to modify Survey Q3R for use in literature, social studies, science, or mathematics, consult the following source: Wilma H. Miller, *Reading Teacher's Complete Diagnosis & Correction Manual* (West Nyack, New York: The Center for Applied Research in Education, 1988, pages 289–290).

ANSWERS TO "CHIMPANZEES"

Checked statements should be 1, 2, and 4.

ANSWERS TO "RATTLESNAKES"

1. O	6. TF	11. TF
2. TF	7. FF	12. TF
3. TF	8. FF	13. O
4. FF	9. O	14. FF
5. O	10. TF	15. FF

The material for this activity sheet was taken from the following source, which would also be a good reference for the child to use in completing it: "Rattlesnakes," *Zoo Books*, Volume 6, August 1989, pages 1–15.

Special Strategies and Delivery Systems for Teaching Reading Skills to Disabled Readers and Learning-Handicapped Students

How can we best enable disabled readers and learning-handicapped students to achieve the greatest amount of success in reading? That question is the main focus of this chapter. Although unique strategies and materials for teaching severely disabled readers and learning-handicapped students have been discussed in several other chapters of the *Handbook*, this entire chapter is devoted to this topic.

Visual Perception Programs to Use with Learning-Handicapped Children

The main visual perception programs that can be used with learning-handicapped children are described in some detail in Chapter 5 and they are mentioned only briefly here.

As covered in Chapter 5, visual perception programs like the *Frostig Program* and the *Getman-Kephart Program* are sometimes used to improve the visual perception abilities of learning-handicapped children who are weak in the visual channel. In general, these programs consist of some physical activities and some paper-and-pencil activities. The physical activities normally consist of such exercises as use of a balance beam, sighting exercises, and chalkboard exercises. The paper-and-pencil activities usually use worksheets designed to improve visual perception ability in eye-motor coordination, figure-ground relationships, constancy of shape, position in space, and spatial relationships.

Phonic Programs to Use with Learning-Handicapped Students _____

Chapter 5 also describes in detail several formal phonic programs that can be used with learning-handicapped students who have a good auditory channel. Several of them will be mentioned briefly here. The *Orton-Gillingham Phonic Method* is a multisensory approach to reading, writing, and spelling that teaches units of sounds or letters of the alphabet. It was developed for teaching these skills to students who are language-disordered. The method is referred to as an alphabetic method since the sounds represented by the letters are learned one at a time using a multisensory approach. The learner sees the letter, hears the sound it represents, traces it according to certain specified hand movements, and writes it. In this way, the visual, auditory, and kinesthetic modalities are used simultaneously. If you want a detailed description of how to use this method, you can consult the following source: Anna Gillingham and Bessie Stillman, *Remedial Teaching for Children with Specific Disability in Reading, Spelling, and Penmanship* (Cambridge, Massachusetts: Educator's Publishing Service, 1968).

Another phonic approach that might be of some value with a few learning handicapped students who have a good auditory channel is the *Hegge-Kirk-Kirk Remedial Reading Drills*. In the beginning stage it is primarily a phonics method that differs from the ordinary phonics systems in its completeness and in its emphasis on certain principles of learning and retention. This method is mainly applicable to children who have failed to learn to read after a number of years in school.

This phonic approach should be used only in the following instances:

1. It is applicable only to children whose reading is on the first-, second-, or third-grade level.
2. The child must be severely disabled in reading; that is, have a reading level two or more years below grade level.
3. Any extreme visual or auditory deficiencies must have been corrected.
4. The child must be trainable in auditory blending.
5. The child must be willing to learn and be cooperative.
6. The child must lack the perceptual-motor abilities developed by the drills and must need to develop skills in recognizing details.
7. Teachers of children who use this approach must transfer the ability to sound words to a natural reading situation.

The details of the *Hegge-Kirk-Kirk Remedial Reading Drills* are not included in this *Handbook* due to their complexity and space restraints. However, if you want to learn more about this phonic approach, you can consult the following resource: Samuel A. Kirk, Sr. Joanne Marie Kliegban, and Janet W. Lerner, *Teaching Reading to Slow and Disabled Readers* (Prospect Heights, Illinois: Waveland Press, 1978, pages 141–144).

Other Strategies to Use with Disabled Readers and Learning-Handicapped Children _____

There are several other strategies that can be used with severely or moderately disabled readers and learning-handicapped children. One of the more useful probably is the *neurological impress method*. This approach was designed for students with severe reading disabilities. It is a system of unison reading in which the child and the teacher read together, the voice of the teacher being directed into the ear of the student at a fairly close range. The child or teacher uses a finger as a locater as each word is read. The finger should be at the location of the word. At times, the teacher may be louder and faster than the child and at other times the teacher may be softer and slower than the child. No preliminary preparation is made for the material before the child sees it. The theory behind the method is that the auditory feedback from the reader's own voice and the teacher's voice reading the material establishes a new learning process.

Echo reading is a strategy that can be used with older disabled readers to develop efficiency in sight-word recognition. In this technique the teacher reads first, and then the child repeats or echoes what the teacher has read. Material can be read in phrases or sentences, and fingerpointing is also used in this strategy. A common variation uses recorded reading material that the child first hears while following the material and then reads along with the recording. Although there are many read-along tapes available, my teacher-trainees usually make their own read-along tapes, choosing material that really interests the child. In addition, many tutors must slow down their oral reading in making the tape if the child is to be able to read along with it.

A child can *read material to fluency* if he/she is disabled or learning handicapped. This is similar to *repeated readings* in which a child is given reading selections that consist of from 50 to 200 words. Have the child practice the selection and time him/her, after which you record the reading rate and number of errors on a chart. The rereading is done again and again until the child achieves a rate of 85 words per minute. Evaluate the child's comprehension consistently during this technique. One danger of its use is that if overused, it will become boring for the child.

Psychological Counseling Approaches to Use with Disabled Readers and Learning-Handicapped Children

There are several psychological counseling approaches that can be used with disabled readers and learning-handicapped children. One of these is *relieving stress*. The following stress-reducing strategies can be taught to children:

1. Students can be taught to set reasonable and attainable short-term goals.
2. Students can be taught to establish incentives to work toward and to provide themselves with tangible rewards when their goals are met.
3. Students can be encouraged to monitor the behavior they seek to change.

Hypnosis has been recommended to improve study habits and concentration and to reduce test anxiety. Self-hypnosis can be taught to very susceptible children. However, not all people can be hypnotized, and its value in reading improvement has not yet been clearly established.

Reality therapy is a nonpunitive approach designed to help disabled readers and learning-handicapped children acquire strategies that will help them deal with their social and emotional difficulties and rejections. For a description of Fuller and Fuller's ten-step program, see the following source: Gerald B. Fuller and Diane L. Fuller, "Reality Therapy: Helping LD Children Make Better Choices" (*Academic Therapy*, 17, January 1982, pages 269–277).

Suggestopedia and suggestology are alternate names for a system of instruction that states that potential for improved learning can be achieved by a combination of positive suggestion and relaxation. The key components of suggestopedia are:

1. Suggestions that emphasize the worthiness of the individual
2. Relaxation and imagery
3. Exciting presentation of learning and active learning
4. Music and environmental sounds

For more information on suggestopedia, consult the following source: Georgi Lozanov, "The Suggestological Theory of Communication and Instruction" (*Suggestology & Suggestopedia*, 1975, I, 1–14).

Relaxation training tries to help people relax, usually by employing self-suggestion. Biofeedback-induced relaxation training can decrease impulsivity and increase attention to task in learning-handicapped children. Such therapy does not improve reading skills directly, but rather may allow children to attend more effectively to learning tasks and/or to demonstrate their reading ability.

Behavior modification tries to change behaviors by systematically rewarding desirable behaviors and either disregarding or punishing undesirable behavior. Such techniques are mainly based on operant conditioning, the learning model from which B. F. Skinner developed teaching machines and programmed instruction.

A brief description of the steps included in behavior modification are:

1. Specify carefully the behavior to be modified and the desired outcomes with behavioral objectives.
2. Collect data on the occurrence of this behavior under present conditions (establish a baseline).
3. Change the environmental setting using stimulus change and reinforcement to induce behavior change in the desired direction.
4. Continue to collect data to show degree and direction of change until the objective is achieved.
5. If the change is not enough, modify the program.

Positive reinforcement probably is most effective with some children. Among the effective tokens we have given in tutoring situations are pennies that could be exchanged for such small items as erasers shaped like animals, candies (if allowed by school), and stickers (very popular). Privileges can also be used as positive motivation. The reinforcement schedule is changed as progress toward the desired behavior occurs.

Some teachers prefer giving only social reinforcers such as praise or making graphs of progress. They believe that deviant behavior should be ignored unless someone is being hurt or kept from learning, in which case the offender is removed temporarily. It is important to find something the child does that can be rewarded even if in the beginning this is nothing more than staying seated.

For more detail on how to implement behavior modification, you can consult the following source: S. Axelrod, *Behavior Modification for the Classroom Teacher* (New York: McGraw-Hill, 1977).

Remedial Reading Delivery Systems

There are a number of different ways in which corrective or remedial reading instruction can be given both to disabled readers and learning-handicapped children. This part of the chapter briefly describes several of them.

Of course, remediation in reading can be provided within the regular education or special education classroom. It may be provided by the teacher, with or without backup services from a reading specialist, or by a tutor or reading specialist in the classroom. This remediation has the advantage of being well integrated with the child's regular reading program. It is part of the *Regular Education Initiative*, which is described later in this chapter.

If remediation is done outside of the classroom, it can be delivered in several different ways. Such delivery systems are called *pull-out programs*. One such out-of-classroom resource are *reading rooms*. These can be Chapter I reading centers in which the school population median income must fall below a specified level. They are mainly federally financed. The students in such rooms usually come from regular-education classrooms, although they may also come from special education classes.

Another delivery system is the use of *resource rooms*. As a result of Public Law 94-142, a number of children are receiving their reading instruction outside of special education classes, either in a regular classroom, a reading room, or a resource room. This is called *mainstreaming*. In some schools special education students receive instruction in one or more subjects in a resource room from a teacher who has been trained to provide for their needs. According to some research, learning-handicapped children achieve better in regular education classrooms in which reading instruction is individualized or supplemented by well-designed resource programs. (See Nancy A. Madden and Robert E. Slavin's article "Mainstreaming Students with Mild Handicaps: Academic and Social Outcomes" in *Review of Educational Research*, 53, Winter 1983, pages 519–569.)

Some schools combine remedial reading and enrichment in *reading labs*. Sometimes writing, language, and spelling instruction are provided in *language labs*. This is most typically done in the middle grades and junior high school.

Sometimes children with severe reading disabilities and those who do not respond to remedial instruction in their schools are referred to a reading clinic or center for more intensive and complete diagnosis. Many of these centers are affiliated with universities or colleges and combine the training of graduate students with reading instruction for children. Others are private or part of hospital outpatient services. Most of them have on their staffs professionals from clinical psychology, psychiatry, neurology, pediatrics, social work, ophthalmology, and speech or audiology.

There are a few *remedial schools* for children with severe reading disabilities. They may be very good or they may be quite ineffective. There also are *summer programs* designed to help children either make gains in reading or at least not lose some of the reading achievement they have made during the past year.

To evaluate pull-out programs, it could be said that there must be good integration with the child's regular reading teacher and reading program for it to be effective. Otherwise, there may be no real reading achievement gains made by such a program.

The Regular Education Initiative or Inclusion

A number of reading specialists feel that programs which require the categorization and labeling of children, especially those who are mildly handicapped, should be replaced with a unified educational program. The emphasis on mainstreaming many special education students is referred to as the *Regular Education Initiative* (REI) or *Inclusion*. This results in many former special education children being placed in regular education classes with their educational programs being planned and delivered cooperatively by regular and special education teachers as well as by the appropriate support personnel. Of course, improving learning for all children can be delivered in regular education classrooms only if instruction is adjusted to meet their individual needs.

The REI (Inclusion) movement probably has resulted from the following dissatisfactions with categorizing children:

1. Labeling children can be harmful to them.
2. Presenting learning-handicapped children with the same instruction that has already failed for them is not effective.
3. Regular classroom instruction and the special reading instruction in a center or resource room are often poorly coordinated.

4. Children who are removed from the regular classroom may lack individualized instruction.

5. Results produced by pull-out programs are often unsatisfactory.

6. Many children prefer to receive extra help from their own classroom teacher.

Individual Education Plans

After a learning-handicapped child has been assessed, the multidisciplinary team (the child's teacher, principal, and all of the specialists who have evaluated the child) meets with the parents to share the information gathered. If a parent wishes the services, an Individual Education Plan (IEP) is developed.

One of the most critical decisions to be made is where the child's needs would best be met—a regular classroom, a pull-out program, or a special class. The law states that the student's needs should be met in the least restrictive environment able to meet his/her needs. These are as follows: regular class, regular class with resource specialist support up to one-half of the school day, and special day class.

Once the educational setting has been decided, the educational goals should be determined and each subject area considered. It often is standard policy to give a child differential standards. Here are several examples of differential standards:

• Oral tests may be given to the child instead of written tests.
• More time may be given to complete assignments.
• The child may respond in social studies and in science orally instead of in writing.
• Tests may be given on an individual basis.
• A different grading standard may be used with different standards for promotion.

After the differential standards are considered, the goals included in the IEP are written. They should be extensive enough to ensure that the child will show growth toward his/her optimum potential.

APPENDICES

Appendix I
Computer Software

There is a wealth of excellent software available to help children learn reading, vocabulary, comprehension, study skills, spelling, and writing. New programs are being created every day. The software companies listed below can send you catalogs and other information about what they have available.

When looking for software, it's important that you understand what hardware is being used in your school. *Hardware* refers to computer equipment, not only the central processing unit (CPU) or actual computer, but the monitor, keyboard, mouse, sound card, and other equipment used to run the programs. Not all software will run on all computers.

If your school is able to purchase new computers, be sure the computers are capable of running the software you'd like to use. If you are a complete novice with computers, you will need the guidance of someone with expertise.

Accolade
550 W. Winchester Boulevard
San Jose, CA 95128

Beagle Brothers, Inc.
3990 Old Town Avenue
San Diego, CA 92110

Brøderbund, Inc.
17 Paul Drive
San Rafael, CA 94904

Central Point Software
9700 SW Capital Highway
#100
Portland, OR 97219

DLM
One DLM Plaza, Box 4000
Allen, TX 75002

Davidson & Associates
3135 Kashiwa Street
Torrance, CA 90505

Golem Computers
P.O. Box 6698
Westland Village, CA 91360

Grolier
Department 336
Sherman Turnpike
Danbury, CT 06816

Hartley Courseware
133 Bridge Street, Box 419
Dimondale, MN 48821

Hayden Software
600 Suffolk Street
Lowell, MA 01854

K-12 Media
6 Arrow Road
Department A
Ramsey, NJ 07446

Laureate Learning Systems
1 Mill Street
Burlington, VT 05041 .

Mindscape, Inc.
344 Dundee Road
Northbrook, IL 60062

Scholastics, Inc.
730 Broadway
New York, NY 10003

Sierra-on-Line
P.O. Box 485
Coursegold, CA 93614

Springboard Software
7808 Creekridge Circle
Minneapolis, MN 55435

Spinnaker Software
215 W. First Street
Cambridge, MA 02142

StyleWare, Inc.
5250 Gulfton, Suite 2E
Houston, TX 77081

Sublogic Corporation
713 Edgebrook Drive
Champaign, IL 61820

Sunburst Communications
39 Washington Avenue
Pleasantville, NY 10570

SVE
1345 Diversay Parkway
Chicago, IL 60614

Appendix II
List of Materials for Use in a Reading Improvement Program with Disabled Readers or Learning-Handicapped Students*

American Guidance Services, Inc.
Publishers Building
Circle Pines, MN 55014

Program: *Goldman-Lynch Sounds and Symbols Development Kit*

Reading Skills: phonic analysis

Grade Levels: primary, intermediate

Barnell Loft, Ltd.
958 Church Street
Baldwin, NY 11510

Program: *Multiple Skills Series*

Reading Skills: all

Grade Levels: 1–9

---

*These materials are only representative of the many materials that can be used in any reading improvement program with disabled readers and learning-handicapped children. You are encouraged to write to any of the publishers listed in Appendix IV for a complete catalog of their products.

This program teaches all of the basic reading skills such as sight words, phonic analysis, structural analysis, context clues, and comprehension. There are four booklets on each level, a teacher's manual, ditto masters, and a class record sheet. The program is also available in Spanish.

Program: *Specific Skills Series*

Reading Skills: all

Grade Levels: 1–12

These are specific and concentrated exercises for different purposes. Each booklet is devoted to one reading skill on one reading level: Following Directions, Working with Sounds, Locating the Answer, Getting the Facts, Detecting the Sequence, Getting the Main Idea, Drawing Conclusions, Identifying Inferences, and Using the Context.

Program: *Supportive Reading Skills*

Reading Skills: all

Grade Levels: 1–9

This program supplements the *Specific Skills Series*.

Benefit Press
1250 Sixth Avenue
San Diego, CA 92101

Program: *Comprehension—Critical Reading Kit*

Reading Skills: comprehension

Grade Levels: 1–9

This kit contains high-interest reading selections from language arts, social studies, and science.

Program: *Comprehension and Critical Reading Workbooks*

Reading Skills: comprehension

Grade Levels: 3–8

These workbooks develop comprehension skills in such areas as locating main ideas, identifying details, noting relationships, and critical reading.

Bowmar/Noble Publishers
4563 Colorado Boulevard
Los Angeles, CA 90039

Program: *Letter Sounds All Around*

Reading Skills: alphabet, beginning sounds

Grade Levels: 1–3

This is a multimedia program containing filmstrip/cassette lessons to motivate children. It includes artwork, music, and interesting dialogue.

Program: *Primary Reading Series*

Reading Skills: comprehension

Grade Levels: 1.3–2.5 (reading), 4–8 (interest)

This contains six kits including high-interest story cards at the interest level of older children. On the back of each card are questions to teach and evaluate the basic comprehension skills. It contains a teacher's guide.

Program: *Best*

Reading Skills: word attack

Grade Levels: 1–adult

Basic phonic skills are taught and practiced through this tutorial kit. Word attack skills are developed through pictures, letter cards, orientation tape, and a record pad.

Program: *Sports Reading Series*

Reading Skills: comprehension

Grade Levels: 2–4.3 (reading), 4–8 (interest)

This consists of three reading kits with high-interest, low-readability story cards about professional sports. On the back of each card are questions to evaluate comprehension.

Program: *Quicksilver Books*

Reading Skills: comprehension, writing

Grade Levels: 3–4.5 (reading), 4–8 (interest)

This consists of six sets of books in display boxes. Five copies of each book and a teaching guide are included.

Charles E. Marrill Publishing Company
1300 Alum Creek Drive
P.O. Box 508
Columbus, OH 43216

Program: *New Diagnostic Reading Skilltext Series*

Reading Skills: comprehension

Grade Levels: K–6

This is a workbook series that combines simple-to-use format with short stories and skill development. It stresses main idea, following directions, vocabulary, and critical reading.

Program: Merrill Phonics Skilltext Series

Reading Skills: phonic analysis

Grade Levels: 1–4 (reading), 1–8 (interest)

This consists of seven workbooks that put phonic analysis into immediate context. Each book stresses new skills while reviewing already-learned skills. The teacher's guide reviews all of the basic phonic generalizations.

Program: Reading Reinforcement Skilltext Series

Reading Skills: structural analysis, vocabulary, comprehension, dictionary

Grade Levels: 1–5 (reading), 1–8 (interest)

This program is designed for a child who reads below grade level and needs interesting stories with low-readability levels. Ten workbooks introduce and review reading skills while developing self-esteem.

Continental Press
520 East Bainbridge Street
Elizabethtown, PA 17022

Program: Continental Press Materials

Reading Skills: all

Grade Levels: 1–adult

These materials are used very commonly in reading improvement programs. This company publishes ditto masters and workbooks of all types to reinforce the various reading skills. You should request their catalog for an exact listing of all their current materials.

Curriculum Associates
5 Esquire Drive
North Billerica, MA 01862

Program: Sound Start

Reading Skills: sight, phonics

Grade Levels: K–1

This consists of a flip-chart easel, ditto masters, and a binder with a teacher's manual. It consists of a forty-lesson step-by-step program to help beginning readers make the transition from speech to printed material.

Program: Clues for Better Reading

Reading Skills: comprehension

Grade Levels: 1–9

This consists of three kits and a primary workbook that contain stories, activity and answer cards, ditto masters, and entry tests for each skill area.

Program: *Context Phonetic Clues*

Reading Skills: phonic analysis

Grade Levels: 3–6 and remedial

This is an intensive phonic program for disabled readers and learning-handicapped children. Clue cards have words on one side and context clues on the other. The teacher reads the clues and the child gives an answer.

DLM Teaching Resources
P.O. Box 4000
One DLM Park
Allen, TX 75002

Program: *Cove School Reading Program*

Reading Skills: sight words, phonic analysis

Grade Levels: K–2

This consists of a simple format with large letters and provides sequenced instruction for children having difficulty learning to read. Six workbooks emphasize consonants, short vowels, consonant blends and digraphs, vowel digraphs, and long vowels.

Program: *Swain Beginning Reading Program*

Reading Skills: phonic analysis, comprehension

Grade Levels: 1–3

This program is for the beginning reader who is having difficulty. It contains two lesson books, blackline masters, and five child readers.

Program: *Essential Sight Word Program*

Reading Skills: sight words

Grade Levels: 1–4

This is a slow-paced sight-word program for disabled readers and learning-handicapped children. It gives much exposure to difficult words through over 200 different activities.

Program: *Survival Words Program*

Reading Skills: survival words

Grade Levels: 1–4 (reading), junior high (interest)

This program teaches survival words through worksheets and storybooks.

Program: *Reading Comprehension Series*

Reading Skills: comprehension

Grade Levels: 2–7

This program stresses comprehension for disabled readers and learning-handicapped children. It consists of eight workbooks which teach context, main idea, details, sequence, spatial relationships, comparison, cause and effect, and study skills.

DLM also publishes Big Books and many games that teach and practice all the reading skill areas.

Economy Publishing Company
P.O. Box 25308
1901 North Walnut
Oklahoma City, OK 73125

Program: *Guidebook to Better Reading Series*

Reading Skills: comprehension

Grade Levels: 5–adult

This program contains diagnostic exercises, review exercises, and reading for pleasure with high-interest, low-vocabulary materials.

Educators Publishing Service
75 Moulten Street
Cambridge, MA 02238

Program: *Primary Phonics*; *More Primary Phonics*

Reading Skills: phonic analysis

Grade Levels: K–4

This is a two-part series of supplementary phonic analysis. Individual readers and accompanying workbooks increase in difficulty in a sequential, structured phonic approach.

Program: *Starting Comprehension: Stories to Advance Thinking and Reading*

Reading Skills: comprehension

Grade Levels: PP–2

This program consists of twelve workbooks that reinforce important comprehension skills.

Program: *Explore the Code*

Reading Skills: phonic analysis, structural analysis

Grade Levels: 1–6

These are twelve illustrated workbooks that are a supplementary phonic program. The program contains basic phonic presentations and vocabulary.

Globe Book Company
50 West 23rd Street
New York, NY 10010

Program: The "Reading for Survival" Series

Reading Skills: word analysis, comprehension

Grade Levels: 1–8

This program consists of seven soft-cover textbooks for the older disabled reader or learning-handicapped child as well as the nonreader. Students progress from the alphabet to third-grade reading level, although it can be used with older students who are severely disabled in reading. The lessons are organized around up-to-date life skills.

Program: The "Real Stories" Series

Reading Skills: comprehension

Grade Levels: 3–6

This program consists of four soft-cover texts that build comprehension skills. Nonfiction stories emphasize writing lessons and open-ended discussion questions.

Program: Reading Power Through Cloze

Reading Skills: comprehension, vocabulary

Grade Levels: 4–7

This program consists of four workbooks that teach and test with the cloze procedure. The program stresses main idea, details, and predicting outcomes.

Good Apple
P.O. Box 299
Carthage, IL 62321

Program: Shortcuts for Teaching Phonics

Reading Skills: phonic analysis

Grade Levels: K–4

This is a collection of easy-to-use activities designed to teach all of the phonic skills. It contains large letter activities, large picture activities, bingo-style cards, and 530 mini cards.

Program: Shortcuts for Teaching Comprehension

Reading Skills: comprehension

Grade Levels: K–4

This program consists of Part I and Part II. They present and reinforce the subskills that are necessary to effective comprehension.

Jamestown Publishers
P.O. Box 6743
Providence, RI 02940

Program: *Comprehension Skill Series*

Reading Skills: comprehension

Grade Levels: 4–12 (reading), 6–adult (interest)

Each booklet in this series develops a specific comprehension skill. Description of the skill, a lesson, and exercises to evaluate students' progress are included. A read-along cassette is available.

Program: *Skills Drills*

Reading Skills: comprehension

Grade Levels: 4.5–6.5 (reading), 6–12 (interest)

Disabled readers progress through three levels with these reproducible worksheets. Five comprehension skills are stressed in these high-interest, low-level activities.

Macmillan Publishing Company
866 Third Avenue
New York, NY 10022

Program: *Macmillan Reading Spectrum*

Reading Skills: all

Grade Levels: 2–8

This comprehensive reading program emphasizes all of the various reading skills. It consists of eighteen booklets that are self-directing and self-correcting. Set A is designed for grades 2–6, while Set B is designed for grades 3–8.

Modern Curriculum Press
13900 Prospect Road
Cleveland, OH 44136

Program: *Starting Off with Phonics Workbooks*

Reading Skills: phonic analysis

Grade Levels: K–1

This is a complete emergent literacy program that contains six workbooks. It has lessons with games, songs, and tactile exercises.

Program: *Thinking About Reading*

Reading Skills: comprehension

Grade Levels: 2–6

This program attempts to develop critical reading skills. It uses the Directed Reading-Thinking Activity (DR-TA) and prediction. It has a student workbook with a teacher's guide.

Raintree Publishers
205 West Highland Avenue
Milwaukee, WI 53203

Program: *Fairy Tale Clippers*

Reading Skills: vocabulary, comprehension

Grade Levels: 2–3

This program consists of books, read-along cassette tapes, and skill cards that stress vocabulary.

Program: *Life Cycle Clippers*

Reading Skills: comprehension

Grade Levels: 1–2

These books present information about animal life. The program consists of eight books, read-along cassette tapes, book jackets, student skill cards, and a teacher's manual.

Reader's Digest
Random House School Division
400 Hahn Road
Westminster, MD 21157

Program: *Reading Skill Builders*

Reading Skills: vocabulary, comprehension

Grade Levels: 1–9

The exercises stress the various comprehension skills. Less-able readers read from lower-level selections. The program also contains ditto masters for each level.

Program: *Triple Takes*

Reading Skills: comprehension

Grade Levels: 3–8

This program uses real-life topics. Each unit contains three types of exercises.

Riverside Publishing Company
8420 Bryn Mawr Avenue
Chicago, IL 60631

Program: *Discovering Phonics We Use*

Reading Skills: phonic analysis

Grade Levels: 1–6

This is a supplementary phonic series with puzzles, riddles, word games, and letter substitutions.

Program: *Comprehension We Use*

Reading Skills: comprehension

Grade Levels: 1–6

This program consists of six workbooks that stress comprehension.

Scholastic Inc.
2931 E. McCarthy Street
P.O. Box 7501
Jefferson City, MO 65102

Program: *Phonics*

Reading Skills: phonic analysis

Grade Levels: 1–3

This consists of six workbooks that stress various elements of phonic analysis.

Program: *Word Mastery with Puzzles*

Reading Skills: phonic analysis, vocabulary

Grade Levels: 1–6

These game-like workbooks stress important reading skills. Each workbook covers two grade levels.

Program: *Vocabulary Skills*

Reading Skills: structural analysis, vocabulary

Grade Levels: 1–6

This consists of six workbooks that can be used to teach and reinforce vocabulary skills.

Program: *Reading Comprehension*

Reading Skills: comprehension

Grade Levels: 3–6

While reading good literature, students practice the various comprehension skills.

Science Research Associates, Inc.
155 N. Wacker Drive
Chicago, IL 60606

Program: Reading for Understanding (1, 2, 3)

Reading Skills: comprehension

Grade Levels: 1–3 (kit 1), 3–7 (kit 2), 7–12 (kit 3)

Each kit teaches implicit (interpretive) comprehension. Students are encouraged to work at their own pace while analyzing ideas and making judgments.

Program: SRA Skills Series

Reading Skills: phonic analysis, structural analysis, comprehension

Grade Levels: 1–3 (phonic analysis), 3–7 (structural analysis), 4–8 (comprehension)

The child focuses on one reading skill at a time. Each kit has forty-eight teaching units and contains skill cards, cassette lessons, activity sheets, tests, and student progress folders.

Program: Cracking the Code

Reading Skills: word attack

Grade Levels: 4–9

The reader and workbook give the older less-able student basic work attack skills. The selections have themes that appeal to the older student.

Sunburst Communications
39 Washington Avenue, Room WJ6
Pleasantville, NY 10570

Program: Strange Strange World Hi/Lo Series

Reading Skills: comprehension, vocabulary

Grade Levels: 2–3 (reading), 5–12 (interest)

This consists of three programs that combine filmstrips and magazines. Worksheets are designed to improve reading skills.

Program: Stories of the Unusual

Reading Skills: comprehension, study skills

Grade Levels: 2–6 (reading), 4–10 (interest)

This is a high-interest multisensory program that gives the disabled reader or learning-handicapped child reading at a comfortable level. The child finishes the story by reading a short selection. Content-area materials and study skill lessons accompany each unit.

Program: *You Can Be a Better Reader*

Reading Skills: comprehension, vocabulary

Grade Levels: 5–10

This is in a filmstrip and cassette interview format that involves the child in looking for main ideas and inferences. Interesting stories provide new vocabulary and figures of speech. Worksheets and a teacher's guide are included.

Steck-Vaughn Company
P.O. Box 2028
Austin, TX 78768

Program: *Building Sight Vocabulary*

Reading Skills: sight words

Grade Levels: K–3

This three-book series uses game formats and stories to introduce and practice the basic sight words.

Program: *Reading Comprehension Series*

Reading Skills: comprehension

Grade Levels: 1–6

This consists of short selections with controlled vocabulary. Seven workbooks are included in this program.

Xerox Education Publications
1250 Fairwood Avenue
Columbus, OH 43216

Program: *Read-Study-Think*

Reading Skills: comprehension

Grade Levels: 3–9

This is a series of books that are designed to improve both explicit and implicit comprehension.

Here are some publishers of games that can be included in a reading improvement program:

Barnell Loft, Ltd.
958 Church Street
Baldwin, NY 11510

Creative Publications
5005 W. 110th Street
Oak Lawn, IL 60453

DLM Teaching Resources
One DLM Park
P.O. Box 4000
Allen, TX 75002

Garrard Publishing Company
1607 North Market Street
Champaign, IL 61820

Kenworthy Educational Service
138 Allen Street
Ellicott Station
P.O. Box 60
Buffalo, NY 14205

Milton Bradley
Springfield, MA 01101

Science Research Associates
155 N. Wacker Drive
Chicago, IL 60606

Trend Enterprises
P.O. Box 64073
St. Paul, MN 55164

Appendix III
List of Test Publishers*

Academic Therapy Publications
20 Commercial Boulevard
Novato, CA 94947

Allyn and Bacon
470 Atlantic Avenue
Boston, MA 02210

American Guidance Service
Publishers Building
Circle Pines, MN 55014

Bobbs-Merrill Educational Publishing
4300 West 62nd Street
P.O. Box 7080
Indianapolis, IN 46206

Bomar/Noble Publishers
P.O. Box 25308
Oklahoma City, OK 75308

William C Brown Company
2460 Kerper Boulevard
Dubuque, IA 52001

Chapman, Brook & Kent
P.O. Box 21008
Santa Barbara, CA 93121

Consulting Psychologists Press
577 College Avenue
Palo Alto, CA 94306

CTB/McGraw Hill
Del Monte Research Park
Monterey, CA 93940

Developmental Learning Materials
One DLM Park
P.O. Box 4000
Allen, TX 75002

Economy Publishing Company
1901 West Walnut Street
P.O. Box 25308
Oklahoma City, OK 73125

Educational Testing Service
Box 999
Princeton, NJ 08540

Educators Publishing Company
75 Moulten Street
Cambridge, MA 02138

Essay Press
P.O. Box 2323
La Jolla, CA 92037

Franklin Watts
730 Fifth Avenue
New York, NY 10019

Garrard Publishing Company
1607 North Market Street
Champaign, IL 61820

Gorsuch Scarisbrick Publishers
576 Central
Dubuque, IA 52001

*These publishers are representative in the area. Other test addresses are found in the *Handbook* itself.

Houghton Mifflin Company
1 Beacon Street
Boston, MA 02107

Kendell/Hunt Publishing Company
2460 Kerper Boulevard
Dubuque, IA 52001

Language Research Associates
P.O. Drawer 2085
Palm Springs, CA 92262

Charles E. Merrill Publishing Company
1300 Alum Creek Drive
Columbus, OH 43216

NCS Interpretive Scoring Systems
4401 West 76th Street
Minneapolis, MN 55435

Richard C. Owen Publishers
P.O. Box 585
Katonah, NY 10536

Prentice-Hall
113 Sylvan Avenue
Englewood Cliffs, NJ 07632

Pro-Ed
5341 Industrial Oaks Boulevard
Austin, TX 78735

Psychological Corporation
555 Academic Court
San Antonio, TX 78204

Rand McNally Company
P.O. Box 7600
Chicago, IL 60680

Riverside Publishing Company
P.O. Box 1970
Iowa City, IA 52244

Scholastic Testing Service
480 Meyer Road
P.O. Box 1056
Bensenville, IL 60106

Science Research Associates
155 North Wacker Drive
Chicago, IL 60606

Stoelting Company
1350 South Kostner Avenue
Chicago, IL 60623

Teachers College Press
Columbia University
1234 Amsterdam Avenue
New York, NY 10027

Richard L. Zweig Associates
20800 Beach Boulevard
Huntington Beach, CA 92648

Appendix IV
List of Publishers of Reading Materials and Reading Software

Academic Press
111 Fifth Avenue
New York, NY 10003

Academic Therapy Publications
20 Commercial Boulevard
Novato, CA 94947

Addison-Wesley Publishing Company
2725 San Hill Road
Menlo Park, CA 94025

Allied Educational Press
P.O. Box 337
Niles, MI 49120

American Library Association
50 East Huron Street
Chicago, IL 60611

Apple Computer
20525 Mirana Avenue
Cupertino, CA 94015

Association for Childhood Education
    International
3615 Wisconsin Avenue, NW
Washington, D.C. 20016

Avon Books
1790 Broadway
New York, NY 10019

Bantam Books, Inc.
School and College Marketing Division
666 Fifth Avenue
New York, NY 10019

Barnell Loft, Ltd.
958 Church Street
Baldwin, NY 11510

Basic Skills Program
Office of Basic Skills Improvement
400 Maryland Avenue, SW
Room 1167, Donohoe Building
Washington, D.C. 20202

Benefit Press
1250 Sixth Avenue
San Diego, CA 92101

Bowmar Noble Publishers
4563 Colorado Boulevard
Los Angeles, CA 90039

Center for Applied Research in Education
110 Brookhill Drive
West Nyack, NY 10995

The Children's Book Council
67 Irving Place
New York, NY 10003

Cobblestone Publishing, Inc.
20 Grove Street
Peterborough, NH 03458

Contemporary Books Inc.
180 North Michigan Avenue
Chicago, IL 60601

Continental Press
520 East Bainbridge Street
Elizabethtown, PA 17022

Council for Exceptional Children
1920 Association Avenue
Reston, VA 22091

Creative Classroom
Macmillan Book Clubs
866 Third Avenue
New York, NY 10022

Curriculum Associates
6620 Robin Willow Court
Dallas, TX 75248

Dell Publishing Company
Education Department
245 East 47th Street
New York, NY 10017

Developmental Learning Materials (DLM)
One DLM Park
Allen, TX 75002

Drier Educational Systems
25 S. Fifth Avenue
P.O. Box 1291
Highland Park, NJ 08904

Early Years/K–8
P.O. Box 3330
Westport, CT 06880

The Economy Company
1901 North Walnut Street
Box 25308
Oklahoma City, OK 73125

Educational Activities
1937 Grand Avenue
Baldwin, NY 11510

Educational Teaching Aids
159 West Kinzie Street
Chicago, IL 60610

Garrard Publishing Company
1607 North Market Street
Champaign, IL 61820

Good Apple, Inc.
Box 299
Carthage, IL 62321

E. M. Hale and Company
Harvey House Publishers
128 West River Street
Chippewa Falls, WI 54729

Harcourt Brace Jovanovich
School Division
6277 Sea Harbor Drive
Orlando, FL 43887

Harper & Row, Inc.
10 East 53rd Street
New York, NY 10022

Hartley Courseware
133 Bridge Street
Dimondale, MI 48821

Hayes School Publishing Company
321 Pennwood Avenue
Lexington, MA 02173

Heinemann
70 Court Street
Portsmouth, NH 03801

Highlights for Children
2300 West Fifth Avenue
P.O. Box 269
Columbus, OH 43216

Ideal School Supply Company
11000 S. Lavergne Avenue
Oak Lawn, IL 60453

Instructor Publications
545 Fifth Avenue
New York, NY 10017

International Reading Association
800 Barksdale Road
Newark, DE 19711

Jamestown Publishers
P.O. Box 6743
Providence, RI 02940

Kenworthy Educational Services
Box 60
138 Allen Street
Buffalo, NY 14205

Laidlaw Educational Publishers
Thatcher and Madison
River Forest, IL 60305

Learning Associates
P.O. Box 561167
Miami, FL 33156

Learning Tree Publishing
7108 South Alton Way
Englewood, CO 80112

Library of Congress
National Library Service
    for the Blind and
    Physically Handicapped
1291 Taylor Street, NW
Washington, D.C. 20542

Litton Educational Publishing
7625 Empire Drive
Florence, KY 41042

Macmillan Children's Book Group
115 Fifth Avenue
New York, NY 10003

McCormick-Mathers Publishing Company
A division of Litton Educational
    Publishing
7625 Empire Drive
Florence, KY 41042

McGraw-Hill Book Company
8171 Redwood Highway
Novato, CA 94947

Media Materials
Department MDR
2936 Remington Avenue
Baltimore, MD 21211

Microcomputer Workshops Courseware
225 Westchester Avenue
Port Chester, NY 10573

Milliken Publishing Company
1100 Research Boulevard
P.O. Box 21579
St. Louis, MO 63132

Milton Bradley
Springfield, MA 01101

Minnesota Educational Computer
    Consortium (MEEC)
3490 Lexington Avenue, North
St. Paul, MN 55126

Modern Curriculum Press
13900 Prospect Road
Cleveland, OH 44136

National Council of Teachers of English
1111 Kenyon Road
Urbana, IL 61801

NCS/Educational Systems Division
4402 West 76th Street
Minneapolis, MN 55435

Open Court Publishing Company
Cricket Magazine
315 Fifth Street
Peru, IL 61354

Richard C. Owen Publisher
P.O. Box 585
Katonah, NY 10536

Paperback Sales, Inc.
425 Michigan Avenue
Chicago, IL 60611

Pitman Learning, Inc.
Fearon/James/Quercus
500 Harbor Boulevard
Belmont, CA 94002

Prentice-Hall
113 Sylvan Avenue
Englewood Cliffs, NJ 07632

Prentice Hall
Educational Book Division
113 Sylvan Avenue
Englewood Cliffs, NJ 07632

Putnam Publishing Group
51 Madison Avenue
New York, NY 10010

Radio Shack
Publicity Department
300 One Tandy Center
Fort Worth, TX 76102

Raintree Publishers
310 W. Wisconsin Avenue
Milwaukee, WI 53203

Random House/Knopf/Pantheon/
    Villard/Times Books
201 East 50th Street
New York, NY 10022

Reader's Digest Services, Inc.
Educational Division
Pleasantville, NY 10570

Remedia Publications
P.O. Box 1174
Scottsdale, AZ 85252

Riverside Publishing Company
8420 Bryn Mawr Avenue
Chicago, IL 60631

Scarecrow Press, Inc.
52 Liberty Street
Box 656
Metuchen, NJ 08840

Frank Schaffer Publications
1028 Via Mirabel, Department 34
Palos Verdes Estates, CA 90274

Scholastic, Inc.
730 Broadway
New York, NY 10003

Scholastic Book Service
904 Sylvan Avenue
Englewood Cliffs, NJ 07632

Schoolhouse Press
191 Spring Street
Lexington, MA 02173

Science Research Associates, Inc.
155 North Wacker Drive
Chicago, IL 60606

Scott, Foresman and Company
1900 East Lake Avenue
Glenview, IL 60025

Silver Burdett & Ginn
191 Spring Street
Lexington, MA 02173

Simon & Schuster
1230 Avenue of the Americas
New York, NY 10020

Slosson Educational Publications
P.O. Box 280
East Aurora, NY 14052

Special Learning Corporation
42 Boston Post Road
P.O. Box 306
Guilford, CT 06437

Steck-Vaughn Company
Box 202
Austin, TX 78767

Story House Corporation
Bindery Lane
Charlotteville, NY 12036

Sunburst Communications
Room D57
39 Washington Avenue
Pleasantville, NY 10570

Teaching and Computers
Scholastic, Inc.
P.O. Box 645
Lyndhurst, NJ 07071

Teaching Resources Corporation
50 Pond Park Road
Hingham, MA 02043

Treetop Publishing
220 Virginia Street
Racine, WI 53405

Troll Associates
100 Corporate Drive
Mahwah, NJ 07430

The Viking Press
Viking Penguin
625 Madison Avenue
New York, NY 10022

The White Rabbit Children's Books
7777 Girard Avenue
La Jolla, CA 92037

Albert Whitman Company
5747 West Howard Street
Niles, IL 60648

World Book—Childcraft International, Inc.
Merchandise Mart Plaza
Chicago, IL 60654